The Georgia-Florida Contest in the American Revolution, 1776–1778

The Georgia-Florida Contest in the American Revolution, 1776–1778

Martha Condray Searcy

THE UNIVERSITY OF ALABAMA PRESS

Publication of this book was made possible, in part,
by financial assistance from the Andrew W. Mellon Foundation and the
American Council of Learned Societies.

Library of Congress Cataloging in Publication Data

Searcy, Martha Condray, 1932–
   The Georgia-Florida contest in the American Revolution, 1776–1778.

   Bibliography: p.
   Includes index.
   1. Saint Augustine (Fla.)—History—Revolution, 1775–1783. 2. Florida—History—
Revolution, 1775–1783—Campaigns. 3. Georgia—History—Revolution, 1775–1783
—Campaigns. 4. Castillo de San Marcos (Saint Augustine, Fla.) 5. Saint Augustine
(Fla.)—Fortifications, military installations, etc. I. Title.
F319.S2S44   1985   973.3'3   84-187
ISBN 0-8173-0225-5

For Hugh F. Rankin

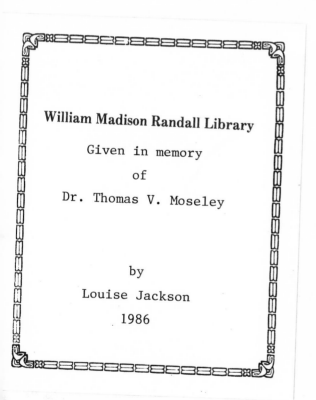

Contents

Preface   ix

    I. Introduction   1

   II. 1776: Raids and Counter-Raids   24

  III. 1776: Invasion and Retreat to the Altamaha   52

  IV. 1777: More Invasions and Retreats   79

   V. 1777: Internal Problems, External Stalemates   98

  VI. 1778: The Last Georgia Campaign—and Retreat   126

 VII. 1778: British Initiative   148

VIII. Conclusions   169

Notes   183

Bibliography of Sources Cited   265

Index   275

Preface

Georgians and Carolinians had failed in earlier attempts to conquer the Spanish Castillo San Marcos, in St. Augustine; and during the American Revolution, in 1776, 1777, and 1778, the rebels tried and failed again to take the fortification, then a British stronghold. Each of these three expeditions was more unsuccessful than its predecessor. Between these formal campaigns, vicious partisan warfare devastated much of the area between the Altamaha and St. Johns rivers.

The Georgia-Florida campaigns of 1776, 1777, and 1778 have not been a popular subject with either professional or amateur historians. Indecisive and lacking the glamour of contemporary campaigns in the North and later campaigns in the South, they appeared to be isolated from the mainstream of the revolutionary struggle. Military students, acutely aware of modern technology, would not believe that such old-fashioned and amateurish warfare could teach any valuable lessons. Certainly none of the participants in these campaigns covered themselves with glory; ancestor hunters were apt to find that deeds of valor were sullied by atrocities.

A scarcity of rebel documents has encouraged myth-mongering. Sociopolitical disorganization and the mundane matter of a paper shortage kept written orders and reports to a minimum. Savannah was fought over three times during the American Revolution, and the first evacuation was disorderly. Some records were destroyed, either deliberately or accidentally; others disappeared during the confusion caused by different military occupations. Natural disasters and subsequent warfare in the area took a heavy toll on all material remains of the culture. Many of the surviving records, both public and private, were lost through the carelessness that accompanies poverty.

Recent trends in modern society have made such "dirty little wars" more interesting to a variety of students. Military historians now find guerrilla warfare to be quite relevant. Improvements in the collection, organization, and accessibility of documents make the importance of the 1776–78 Georgia-Florida campaigns in the overall Revolutionary military struggle more apparent. Cultural historians have noted that wars frequently accelerate sociopolitical changes; for the Southeastern Indians, as well as the whites, this was a "critical period."

This study was undertaken because available secondary sources do not provide a sufficiently detailed account of events in this place during this time. Therefore, the resulting work is primarily a narrative of who did what to whom and secondarily a consideration of the causes and consequences of those actions.

A thorough investigation answers some of the questions about these campaigns, particularly why they failed. Did the rebels lose or the British win? A close examination of the leaders, troops, auxiliaries, and conditions involved substantiates the rebels' handicaps of divided command, personal quarrels, difficult terrain, and miserable weather. Although this work emphasizes military aspects, this topic exemplifies a struggle between a well-organized minority and a disorganized majority, conflict between civil and military authorities, effects of war on the civilian populace, and the interaction of economic matters with military affairs. This study clarifies the importance of these military activities in the subsequent British strategy during the occupation of Georgia and the Carolinas.

The assistance of many individuals and institutions is gratefully acknowledged. Virginia Rugheimer, of the Charleston Library Society, treated me so kindly when I first inquired for a manuscript about Colonel Thomas Brown, that I was encouraged to extend my studies in history. Eleanor Merritt, of the Howard-Tilton Memorial Library, at Tulane University, is the best "finding aid" yet invented; the staff of that institution has been very helpful. I especially appreciate the assistance of Light T. Cummins and James P. Pate in guiding me through unfamiliar source material. The expertise of Connie Stephenson, of the Georgia Historical Society, in Savannah, and Eugenia Arana and Jacquelin Bearden, of the St. Augustine Historical Society, made my research at those institutions a particular pleasure. Personnel at the William L. Clements Library, University of Michigan, and the Georgia Department of Archives and History, in Atlanta, have provided encouragement and advice as well as documents. Special thanks are extended to Vivian Child and Heather Lancaster for graciously allowing me access to their private manuscript collections.

I am indebted to Professor Hugh F. Rankin for his patience, encouragement, and guidance in the preparation of this work. Professors Kenneth Coleman and Melvin Herndon read portions of the manuscript, the final version of which benefited from their comments.

The Georgia-Florida Contest in the American Revolution, 1776–1778

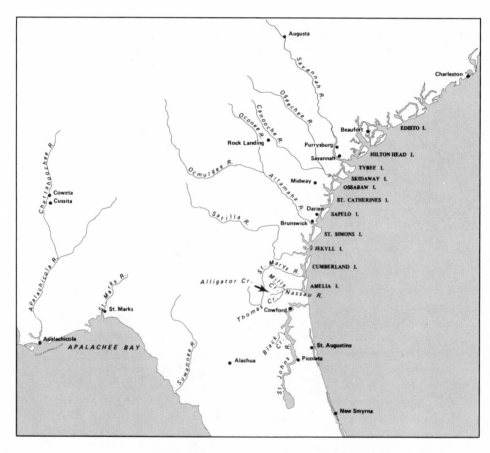

Georgia and East Florida, 1776

I

Introduction

POSSESSION OF Georgia and Florida had been a "debatable" issue long before the American Revolution. The Spanish, French, and English contended with the Indians and each other for territorial rights. Strategic considerations were of primary importance to the Europeans, but the profit motive was not negligible. Most of Georgia and part of Florida were ideally suitable for plantation agriculture, and a network of navigable rivers extending far into the interior offered access to markets for both staple and extractive products. Potential for trade enhanced the value of the area. Early settlers from Europe, struggling in swampy forests or sandy pine barrens and coping with "varmints" that ranged from mosquitoes to alligators, must have cursed the acquisitiveness of their masters and the tall tales of propagandists.

The English complicated the boundary disputes when they carved Georgia from land that had been granted to South Carolina. Georgia's eastern and northern boundaries, the Atlantic Ocean and the Savannah River, remain the same to this day, but in 1763 the western boundary was relocated from the Pacific Ocean to the Mississippi River, and the southern boundary moved down from the Altamaha River to the St. Marys. When the British acquired Florida south of the St. Marys as part of the 1763 settlement of the French and Indian War, they divided it into two provinces, separated by the Apalachicola River. Because East Florida was the southernmost continental colony, her eastern and southwestern boundaries, the Atlantic Ocean and the Gulf of Mexico, were unchanged by her new masters, though some controversy existed over ownership of the Keys. In 1764 Britain increased the size of West Florida at Georgia's expense by moving West Florida's northern boundary from the thirty-first parallel to thirty-two degrees twenty-eight minutes along a line drawn eastward from the junction of the Yazoo and Mississippi rivers to the Chattahoochee.[1]

European settlement was confined to a small portion of these broad provinces. By various treaties, the Indians had ceded small pieces of land, and until about 1770 these areas were ample for the needs of the Europeans. After the Treaty of Augusta (1763), the Georgians held undisputed rights to a strip of land from the Atlantic coast inland to a few miles above where tidal action ceases and all the land between the Savannah and Ogeechee rivers as far upstream as the Little River above Augusta. By the Treaty of Picolata (1765), the British agreed to limit white settlement in East Florida to the northeastern corner—bounded on the north and east by the St. Marys and the Atlantic, on the south by the St. Johns at its source, and on the west by intersecting lines drawn westward from the Atlantic to the mouth of the Oklawaha River and southward from "the Pine Stump upon St. Marys"—plus the coast as far inland "as the tide flows."[2]

As in Britain's other colonies, the economic base of Georgia and East Florida was agricultural. A plantation economy developed rapidly only as far south as the Altamaha River. Until the Peace of Paris (1763), both Spain and Britain claimed the region between the Altamaha and St. Johns, but, because neither Georgia nor Florida was strong enough to enforce the claims, the area was tacitly regarded as neutral ground. This section remained virtually uninhabited except for a group of renegade Englishmen who lived between the Satilla and St. Marys and a few scattered garrisons.[3] When the 1763 settlement gave Florida to Britain, agricultural investment moved southward from the Altamaha toward the St. Johns.

One aspect of the agricultural development in Georgia and the Floridas, as in Britain's other mainland colonies, changed radically during the last half of the eighteenth century. Although the traditional headright system of granting lands continued in operation, the usual grant being not more than a few hundred acres, some of the new ones were for enormous tracts, consisting of thousands of acres.[4] Georgia's Trustees had based their land policy on the military policy of having a male capable of bearing arms on every fifty acres of settled land. They also were probably aware that, during the first century and a half of British colonization, speculation in land by proprietors had been spectacularly unprofitable. About the middle of the eighteenth century, however, such proprietorships became very profitable indeed, and people of wealth rushed to revive old claims and to acquire new lands.[5] Georgia and East Florida, possessing rich soil and few settlers, offered attractive investment possibilities for both Englishmen and wealthy colonials, especially those from neighboring South Carolina. The Carolinians, like the Englishmen, were usually absentee proprietors. Many of the large tracts remained undeveloped.[6]

The soil and climate of Georgia and East Florida were suitable for a wide variety of subtropical products. By 1772 Georgia's export trade in rice, indigo, timber, naval stores, and provisions was thriving. Cowpens were numerous. A few settlements produced silk on a small (and unprofitable) scale. East Florida was still importing provisions, but many planters carried on agricultural experiments, especially for staple production, and the results were encouraging. In 1771 St. Augustine exported more indigo than did Savannah. Both colonies were producing cotton.[7]

In the 1770s Georgia and the Floridas were the newest and weakest of all Britain's continental colonies—and the least rebellious. The majority of the population were not native-born; indeed, most were recent immigrants. Although the population was more heterogeneous than that of the northern provinces, the cultural basis of both Georgia and East Florida was English; the Spanish had departed en masse from the Floridas after their cession to England. Scotch Highlanders had arrived in Georgia in the 1730s, and other Scots and Scotch-Irish followed in waves of immigration that varied from a trickle to, more usually, a flood. In addition to significant minorities of French and German Protestants, approximately a thousand Catholic laborers from northern Mediterranean countries settled at New Smyrna, about seventy-five miles south of St. Augustine. During the early 1770s, the population of Georgia was about thirty-one thousand; that of East Florida, nearly three thousand.[8]

Rice and indigo plantations in Georgia were worked almost exclusively by Negro slaves who were brought directly from Africa.[9] Most East Florida planters also followed the example of the older southern colonies. The few who experimented with white indentured labor met resounding failure. As Patrick Tonyn, wartime governor of East Florida, analyzed the labor problem, the expenses of maintaining white servants equaled the value of their labor when the produce was not to be for their own profit.[10] Small planters, possessing few or no slaves, settled wherever they could find room, usually on the frontier.

The Europeans located their settlements according to their needs for defense, water transportation, and agricultural potential. Population density naturally was greatest near the capitals, on the coast. St. Augustine, the capital of East Florida, was by far the oldest town, and its fortifications were superior. Between one and two thousand people, most of them unfree laborers, lived on a cluster of plantations near Mosquito (now Ponce de Leon) Inlet, about seventy-five miles south of St. Augustine.

Georgia's capital, Savannah, had grown and prospered after the middle of the eighteenth century. At its height before the Revolution, it may have consisted of four hundred houses. Augusta, at the fall line of the Savannah River, was the center of Indian trade in the Southeast; perhaps a thousand people lived in about a hundred houses.[11] Approximately six hundred Quakers inhabited Wrightsborough township, near the Little River about thirty miles from Augusta. Queensborough, on the Ogeechee River, with about seventy families in town and two hundred families in the vicinity, was the center of Irish settlement after 1768.[12] New Ebenezer, upriver from Savannah, was the center of German settlement in Georgia and contained about five hundred residents in 1774. Midway community, thirty miles south of Savannah, may have had more than three hundred whites and fifteen hundred African slaves. Sunbury, nine miles east on the Midway River, had been Georgia's second port of entry since 1763, and its population consisted of between eight hundred and a thousand.[13] Hardwick, on the Ogeechee River, had been proposed at one time as the capital of Georgia, but its inhabitants had never numbered more than about a hundred.[14] Darien, on the north bank of the Altamaha River, was the center of Scotch Highlander settlement. Other population centers were mere hamlets.

Land transportation between population centers was possible, but the network of navigable rivers and the protected inland waterway along the coast made water transportation easier, faster, cheaper, and safer. St. Augustine, Savannah, and the smaller ports conducted little direct trade with Britain. British cargo, mail, and passengers were forwarded from Charleston by coaster as the opportunity offered.

The scattered frontiersmen in Georgia and East Florida were acutely aware they were surrounded by Indians who had ceased to feel hospitable toward white settlers who wanted Indian land. The warriors of the Creek Confederacy alone outnumbered the entire Georgia militia.[15] Even the smaller tribes posed a threat.

Southern colonists rarely could forget the Indians. The Europeans were living on land "given" or "sold" to them by the Cherokee, Creek, Choctaw, Chickasaw, and several smaller tribes. The Cherokees claimed land from the Ohio River almost as far south as present Atlanta, and the Creeks inhabited Georgia as well as part of Alabama and Florida. Both the Chickasaws and Choctaws lived between the Alabama and Mississippi rivers. None of these boundaries were firmly fixed, and the tribes frequently shared hunting grounds.

By 1775 the Creek Confederacy was the strongest and most numerous Indian group in the Southeast. The Upper Creeks lived in Alabama, east of the Alabama River and north of present Phenix City, and the Lower Creeks inhabited central and south Georgia as well as part of Florida. At the time of the American Revolution, the Creeks considered the Florida Seminoles to be part of their confederacy, but separatist tendencies had appeared among the latter tribe.[16]

With the advent of European manufactured goods, the Indians had acquired a new and higher standard of living. They needed to retain their land, however, in order to maintain their trade. The Southern Indians welcomed the Europeans as traders if not as settlers. From the Europeans the Indians wanted metal and textile goods and arms and ammunition. In return, they bartered deerskins and, in the seventeenth and early eighteenth centuries, slaves. Imported metal and textile goods led to the decline of traditional handicrafts. European armaments were an asset in both hunting and war, but they made the Indians dependent upon their European suppliers. Guns had turned hunting into big business and increased intertribal wars, both for slave-captives and in competition for hunting grounds.[17]

Because hunting, whether for skins or meat, necessitated vast uninhabited lands, from the time of the arrival of the first European settlers, the Indians' greatest complaint was the expansion of white settlement in violation of treaties. The Indians and the English both respected custom and precedent in law, but held utterly different concepts of property rights and land tenure—and this caused friction. Southern Indians practiced a form of economic communism, a whole tribe holding its land in common. Tribal ownership permitted private, as well as communal, utilization, but custom with the force of law forbade the private alienation of any land without the consent of the entire tribe.[18]

Following their resounding defeat by the Carolinians in the Yamassee War (1715–16), the Creeks adopted a tribal policy of neutrality toward all Europeans that they steadfastly pursued until the American Revolution was well underway. The Indian trade had become an important factor in all colonial economies. "Emperor" Brim had recognized the value of Indian friendship and trade to the competing colonies, and he had hoped that his Creek Confederacy could hold the balance of power among the French, English, and Spanish. The advantage to the Creeks of European competition for Indian favors was obvious.[19]

The Treaty of Paris (1763) brought tremendous changes to the Southeastern Indians. When the French withdrew from Alabama and the Spanish from Florida, the Creeks found themselves virtually surrounded by sparse, but expansive, English settlements. Still, the British proclamation of a boundary line for settlers—inspired more by the desire to reduce military expenditures than to foster native welfare—favored the Indians.[20] The British established Northern and Southern departments to supervise Indian affairs, and in 1762 the Crown appointed John Stuart, a Scot with considerable experience in the colony of South Carolina, as superintendent of the Southern Indian Department. The British were preoccupied with the centralization of colonial administration for the sake of efficiency, and Stuart attempted to carry over this policy to the various Indian tribes by establishing "medal" chiefs in each major group, through whom he planned to deal with the tribes. Although the practice did not effect centralization of Indian organization, it did increase the influence of the individual chiefs who attained such honors. Those who were the most successful in transacting tribal dealings with the Europeans achieved supremacy within their tribes. The British generally continued their policy of stimulating strife among the tribes in fear that, if the Indians ever united, they would demolish the settlements.[21]

Because of their increasing dependence on the trade in deerskins, the Indians needed more, not less, hunting grounds, and colonists settling beyond the boundary line were a constant problem. The Indians began to make a distinction between the British officials and the American settlers and regarded the former as their defense against the latter.[22] Both the southern whites and the southern reds feared they could not live together in harmony, and neither could afford to ignore the other. When civil war broke out among the British settlers, both sides immediately considered the military potential of their Indian neighbors. The use of warriors and Indian policy in general would play a crucial part in the military plans of both British and American leaders.

The governments of Georgia and East Florida followed the typical pattern for royal colonies: a governor and council appointed by the Crown and an assembly of representatives elected by qualified residents. The two colonies, however, differed from the others in three ways. Georgia's governor, Sir James Wright, was an extraordinarily able colonial official who deserved the respect with which he was regarded. East Florida's population was so small that no popularly elected assembly met until 1781. Both provinces were on the British establishment; their governmental apparatus, including salaries of officials, was largely paid for by grants from Parliament.

Like the West Indian colonies, both Georgia and East Florida recognized the need for British protection and support. Georgians protested against the Sugar Act (1764)[23] and much more vigorously against the Stamp Act (1765), but neither colony sent delegates to the Stamp Act Congress. The Georgia assembly and its constituents were informed of activities to the northward, however, and the *Georgia Gazette* for the first time mentioned a group called the "Sons of Liberty." Although Governor Wright was greatly upset about the disturbances, after the Stamp Act had been repealed, he and the assembly could congratulate each other on how well they had handled the problem. No violence or property destruction had occurred in Georgia.[24]

The Mutiny Act was the next parliamentary measure to cause turmoil. After repeal of the Stamp Act, and in spite of publication of the Declaratory Act,[25] 1766 had been a quiet year. Although Parliament had passed this Mutiny Act in 1765, not until January 1767 did Governor Wright receive a request from the commanding officer of British troops in Georgia for barracks necessities (light and heat, beds and bedding, barracks furniture and cooking utensils, rum or beer, salt and vinegar, wood, and axes). Georgia's Commons House of Assembly promptly refused.

Two months later, the assembly requested that General Thomas Gage, British commander in chief in North America, send more troops to Georgia for the forts at Augusta, Cockspur, and Frederica and resolved to provide a money payment as a substitute for barracks necessities. A quarrel between commons and council prevented passage of the measure. Under pressure from Governor Wright, General Gage, Parliament, and King George III, the two houses passed a tax bill in April 1768 providing £200 for barracks necessities.

Meantime, Britain had adopted a new policy of consolidating regular troops in large, strategically located garrisons, rather than scattering small groups along the frontier. Four months after Georgia had settled the barracks necessities controversy, the twenty-eight soldiers in that colony, one officer and twenty-seven enlisted men, were transferred out of the province. Both the governor and the assembly protested the removal and requested more troops, but to no avail.[26]

East Floridians wanted all the troops they could get. Civilians in this new frontier colony appreciated both the security that regulars provided and also the money spent on the army's account. Because St. Augustine was one of the strategic sites selected for a major garrison, adequate barracks were built for the troops. Directly and indirectly, the garrison stimulated the provincial economy.[27]

On 14 October 1767, in the midst of the turmoil over the Mutiny Act, the *Georgia Gazette* published the import duties imposed by the

Townshend Acts. A new assembly was elected the next spring, but Governor Wright, fearing dissension, did not call it into session until November. When it met, he informed it that he had royal instructions to dissolve the lower house if it considered a circular letter from the Massachusetts house of representatives objecting to parliamentary taxation of the colonies. For more than a month, the Georgia assembly proceeded with routine business. But when it went on to consider the circular letters received from the Massachusetts and Virginia lower houses, Wright dissolved it on 24 December 1768.[28]

Not until the following September, after three meetings in Savannah that month, did a group of Georgians resolve on a nonimportation agreement. However, the merchant community in Savannah and the planters were far from unanimous, and few were enthusiastic, about the measure. Despite threats by other colonies, the nonimportation association was virtually ignored in Georgia. The Townshend Acts, except for the duty on tea, had been repealed by the time the assembly met again in October 1770.[29]

Although Georgians were not eager to rebel and their economic interests frequently did not coincide with those of the other continental colonies, they did take their political principles seriously. Claiming the rights of Englishmen, they had proclaimed their loyalty, dutifully petitioned the Crown, and instructed the colony's agent in London to work for the repeal of parliamentary measures that they regarded as unconstitutional.

During the winter of 1769–70, after several years of listening to ringing declarations about "no taxation without representation," the Georgia Assembly suddenly declined to tax inhabitants in the area between the Altamaha and the St. Marys because they were not represented in the lower house. Although the four parishes there (St. David, St. Patrick, St. Thomas, and St. Mary) were being settled rapidly, they were still relatively sparsely inhabited; not until the treaty in 1763 had the Spanish threat been removed and lands there been granted. Governor Wright concurred that the lower parishes should be represented, and late in 1768 he had made such a request to the secretary of state, though only the king could grant representation. On 21 February 1771 Wright received royal permission to allow representation for the four southern parishes. Subsequently, the settlers between the Altamaha and the St. Marys were represented in the Georgia assembly and taxed by it.[30]

Forewarned by this controversy, Wright took steps to avoid a repetition when the political division of Indian lands acquired in 1773

was considered. The governor advised William Legge, Earl of Dartmouth and the secretary of state, that representation should be
allowed any new parish as soon as it contained one hundred voters or
families. Dartmouth immediately informed Wright that his suggestion had been approved.[31] Although the territory acquired in 1773
was not sufficiently settled to warrant representation before revolutionary activity began, the whole affair had demographic significance.
The population figures used by Wright as criteria for eligibility for
representation suggest that the four parishes south of the Altamaha
had at least one hundred heads of families in each of those parishes
before 1770. The "sparseness" of population between the Altamaha
and the St. Marys rivers was merely comparative; the area was not
nearly so "unsettled" as some historians have intimated.

As the focus narrowed on political principles and constitutional
interpretations, rather than on the several issues of economic expedi-
ency, the contest intensified in Georgia. The governor and his council
exercised what was left of the royal prerogative; the assembly claimed
more power in the province than the House of Commons did in
Britain. The closer each side adhered to its principles, the less room it
had to maneuver. A compulsion to obstruct "dangerous" precedents
by the opposing side brought the colony's government to an impasse.

In 1771 Wright dissolved the assembly in February and again in
April. The following year, while the governor was on leave in England, James Habersham, secretary of the colony and president of the
council, allowed the assembly to sit for less than a month before he
dissolved it. Although relations between the executive and legislative
branches improved after Wright returned in February 1773 and no
more assemblies were dissolved in colonial Georgia, the power struggle had forced the opposition in the assembly into closer association
with opposition parties in other colonies. In the spring of 1773, the
Georgia assembly appointed its first Committee of Correspondence to
keep in touch with other colonies about matters concerning them all.[32]

While people around Savannah played politics, the other inhabitants of Georgia pursued their normal preoccupations: food and
shelter, land and Indians. By 1771 both the Cherokees and the
Creeks had fallen deeply into debt to the traders among them, and
the traders suggested that the Indians liquidate their debts with land
cessions. Consequently, John Stuart, British superintendent of Indian
affairs in the Southern Department, was directed to arrange a joint
cession of the land, from the subsequent proceeds of which the
traders were to be compensated for the two tribes' debts. One faction

of the Creeks opposed any further land cessions, but it was overruled. Perhaps the determinant in that tribe's compliance was that Escochabey, a headman of the important Creek town of Coweta, on the Chattahoochee River, favored the settlement. He was a friend of George Galphin, a Georgia trader to whom Coweta owed large debts.[33]

At Augusta, Georgia, on 1 June 1773 the Creeks and Cherokees executed a treaty ceding a large amount of land: 2,100,000 acres. The land was in two tracts: the smaller one, claimed by the Creeks only, was a long and narrow strip between the Altamaha and Ogeechee rivers and not far inland from the Atlantic coast; the larger one, claimed by both tribes, was far inland between the Savannah and Ogeechee rivers, bounded on the south by the Little River, twenty-two miles above Augusta, and extending northwestward beyond the Broad (or Dart) River. For many years to come, these areas would be called the "Ceded Lands."[34]

Georgians were too preoccupied with Indian problems to pay as much attention to the various "tea parties" in December 1773 as they might have otherwise. Some Creeks refused to become reconciled to the 1773 land cession, and they killed fifteen whites and two blacks on the northwestern frontier during the winter of 1773–74. Whites retaliated, sometimes attacking the innocent, and a full-scale Indian war seemed imminent. Wright requested British regulars to defend his province, but no troops could be spared from the north. The British government did comply with Wright's, Tonyn's, and Stuart's urgings that all trade be stopped with the Creeks, and in the fall (20 October 1774) at a conference in Savannah, both Indians and whites reaffirmed their previous agreements and promised to keep the peace.[35]

At the Savannah Congress, on 14 October, Wright discovered that Jonathan Bryan, a prominent Georgian, had persuaded a group of Lower Creeks to "lease" him some land in north Florida. The Lower Creeks and Seminoles jointly claimed the land in question, the fertile Apalachee-Alachua area in the vicinity of present Gainesville. Neither the Seminoles nor Superintendent Stuart agreed to the cession. The Creeks who had signed Bryan's deed, when it was interpreted for them, tore their seals and marks from the paper. Bryan's development schemes came to naught.[36] Now that the Indians were quiet, Georgians could turn their attention to politics again.

Although their need for British defense against the Indian threat made many Georgians hesitant about antagonizing the royal government,[37] a group in and near Savannah reacted to news of the Intolerable Acts by holding public meetings in Savannah during the summer of 1774.[38] The most radical element came from the Congregationalist community in St. John's Parish, and its members fully intended to persuade their fellow citizens to choose delegates to the First Continental Congress that was soon to meet at Philadelphia. Their attempts were defeated.[39]

Some Georgians objected not only to the Continental Congress but also to the Savannah meetings. The loyal party circulated petitions claiming that the protesters did not represent the true sentiments of the province. Supporters of the meeting issued objections to the petitions. Both sides charged fraud in gaining signatures.[40]

The St. John's delegates decided to send their own representatives to the Congress and held meetings later in August at Midway. With three other southern parishes, they elected Dr. Lyman Hall, a local resident, as their delegate to the First Continental Congress. However, he declined to serve.[41]

Georgia, the Floridas, Newfoundland, and Nova Scotia did not send delegates to the First Continental Congress. Although they received information about the actions of that body, the southern colonies remained quiet while it was in session. Governor Wright feared, however, that, when the South Carolina delegates returned home, they would influence the opposition party in Georgia's assembly to carry out the Congress's resolutions. He had adjourned the Georgia commons until 15 November; now he prorogued it until 17 January 1775.[42]

Georgians resorted to more extralegal meetings.[43] The Georgia assembly met in Savannah on 17 January 1775; the provincial congress, representing only five of Georgia's twelve parishes, convened on 18 January. Some prominent citizens were members of both bodies. The congress proceeded to elect Archibald Bulloch as its president. Next, it elected three delegates to the Second Continental Congress, which was to meet in May in Philadelphia: Archibald Bulloch, Noble Wimberly Jones, and John Houstoun. Then, it adopted a milder version of the Continental Association. Finally, it adjourned on 25 January. To prevent the assembly from officially approving the actions of the provincial congress, Wright prorogued it on 10 February.[44]

Georgia's trade quickly became disorganized. The night of 15 February 1775 a Savannah mob attacked a customs officer and two sailors from HM Armed Schooner *St. John,* which happened to be at Savannah for a few days, acting as guards. They tarred and feathered the tide waiter and drowned one sailor.[45] The parishes of St. John's

and St. Andrew's had adopted the Continental Association indepen-
dently, but Wright had prorogued the assembly before representatives of the other parishes could take action. Where local committees
were operating, the association was enforced; elsewhere in the province, business went on as usual, or as nearly so as possible. St. John's
Parish tried to secede from Georgia and join South Carolina, but the
offer was rejected by South Carolina.[46] South Carolina and several
other provinces cut off trade with Georgia; and, when the Second
Continental Congress met in May, it placed an embargo on trade with
Georgia (except St. John's Parish) as well as with East Florida.[47]

It was obvious that Georgians were not unanimously committed to
the revolutionary cause. The three delegates elected by the provincial
congress to attend the Second Continental Congress declined to serve
because they could not claim to represent a majority of the province.[48]
On 21 March, St. John's Parish again elected Dr. Lyman Hall to
represent it; although he refused to go to Philadelphia previously,
this time he went. On 13 May the Continental Congress unanimously
admitted him, but he refrained from voting because he represented
only one parish.[49]

In the spring, the frustrated patriots of Georgia sent both rice and
specie to aid the Bostonians. St. John's Parish was especially gener-
ous.[50]

Tempers grew shorter as the weather got hotter. In May members
of Georgia's Commons House refused to meet, and Governor Wright
prorogued the assembly until 7 November.[51] Revolutionary incidents
increased after news of Lexington and Concord reached Savannah on
10 May. The very next night, rebels raided the public powder magazine in Savannah. They divided the powder between Georgia and
South Carolina Whigs; and, according to tradition, American soldiers
used part of it at the Battle of Bunker Hill.[52]

The occasion of the king's birthday on 4 June precipitated another
incident in Savannah. Part of the usual ceremony of celebrating this
event was the firing of the battery's twenty-one guns. On the night of
2 June, they were spiked and thrown down the bluff. Some of them
were recovered and drilled out in time for the customary festivities on
4 and 5 June. Whigs held their own convivial meeting at Tondee's
Tavern on the night of 5 June. The Sons of Liberty proceeded to
warn several presumably loyal men in Savannah, both permanent and
temporary residents, to leave the province within seven days or suffer
the consequences.[53]

As Georgia Whigs continued to hold meetings in Savannah
throughout the month of June, two factions became discernible. The

moderate group, though proclaiming American rights, still hoped that a workable compromise could be effected between Britain and the colonies. Radical Whigs, drawing their main strength from Christ Church and St. John's parishes, were determined to take Georgia along the path chosen by most of the other continental colonies. On 22 June the latter group selected a Council of Safety and elected Savannah's delegates to Georgia's second provincial congress.[54]

The 102 delegates to that congress met in Tondee's long room at Savannah from 4 July through 17 July 1775. Only two parishes, St. Patrick and St. James, were unrepresented. Christ Church and St. John's, the two parishes that most strongly supported the radical Whigs, lacked only two votes of having a majority and dominated the congress. The delegates reelected Archibald Bulloch as their president. They first took care of revolutionary business by adopting the Continental Association; electing five delegates to the Second Continental Congress (John Houstoun, Archibald Bulloch, the Reverend John J. Zubly, Noble W. Jones, and Lyman Hall); appointing committees; approving a petition to the king; and adopting many resolutions, including one which stated that disobedience to the provincial and Continental Congresses was illegal.

They then proceeded with the customary business, including a tax measure, of any colony's assembly. The congress extended an assembly's ordinary powers, however, by providing for its own succession and changing suffrage rules. The most significant immediate change resulting from the congress was that, when that body adopted the Continental Association, the Continental Congress and South Carolina removed their bans on trade with Georgia.[55] In Savannah, bread and flour had become scarce, and rum and sugar were very expensive.[56]

Enforcement of the association in that province proved to be less than easy. Article Eleven of the association had stipulated only that local committes should be formed to handle enforcement and that violators of the association should have their names and details of the violation published in the gazette, so that they would be publicly known and dealings with them would be avoided.[57] Local committees frequently went far beyond such verbal sanctions in obtaining signatures and punishing violators.

Opposition to rebel authority took various forms. Some importers and exporters simply resorted to the many waterways in thinly settled areas.[58] Other citizens resisted mightily, and they were mightily abused.[59] The rebels would rue the day (1 August 1775) they tarred and feathered Thomas Alexander Brown.[60] This young man, from a prominent Yorkshire family, had arrived at Savannah in the autumn of 1774 with his seventy-four indentured servants on a ship he had chartered, the *Marlborough*. He acquired large tracts in the Ceded Lands and invested heavily in their development. His appointment as magistrate in the backcountry clearly indicated he had become a prominent citizen on the Georgia frontier.[61]

Brown took time off from his plantation duties to attend the rebels' meetings and voice opposition to their measures. His stand made him increasingly unpopular with the backcountry's malcontents. They referred to him as a "Scotchman" and an "Indian trader," names that have stuck for two centuries. Even worse, the rumor was spread that he was an emissary of the British administration—specifically the son of Lord North—who had been sent to poison the minds of the people. When someone warned him of retribution, he went to his house at New Richmond, in South Carolina.[62]

The rebels had been circulating their Articles of Association and urging sympathizers to sign them, and Brown had been apprehensive that a test oath would be attached to the articles. It was, and formidable "committees" terrified many local residents into signing both the articles and the oath. From 100 to 140 armed "Sons of Liberty" of St. Paul's Parish, in Georgia, visited Brown in New Richmond, across the river in South Carolina, and invited him to sign both the articles and the oath. He tried in vain to reason with his callers. About fifty of the group declined to participate in the impending violence and rode away.

As the mob advanced, Brown shot the leader, Chesley Bostick. Then, six or eight men rushed Brown. With his sword, "which understanding the use of pretty well," he defended himself, in spite of receiving six or seven wounds, until someone struck him from behind with a rifle barrel. That blow ended the unequal struggle. It fractured Brown's skull, and he claimed it left him senseless for two days.[63]

Because Brown was no longer in condition to resist anything, the "committee" hauled him off to Augusta. There they tarred and feathered him, then drew him in a cart as a public exhibition "from the head of Augusta to Mr. Weatherford's."[64] Then they tied him to a tree and placed burning lightwood sticks under the soles of his feet. Somewhere along the way, they beat him.[65] The next morning Brown "voluntarily" swore repentance for his past conduct and vowed that in the future he would behave differently, that he would "protect and support the rights and liberties of America."

A physician in the neighborhood who knew Brown attended him; and his guard, "having relented at the cruel sufferings he had endured," allowed him to escape. Another sympathizer furnished him with a horse, and he rode off to the up-country of South Carolina. Despite his new vows to support the patriot cause, he was published as a person "inimical to the rights and liberties of America."

The Sons of Liberty feared that Brown would collect sympathizers and seek retribution. St. Paul's Parochial Committee applied for protection to the commander of the Augusta militia, James Grierson, but he refused to call out his troops without orders from Governor Wright. Meantime, Brown and his loyalist friends had become immersed in thwarting rebels in the South Carolina up-country. Georgia could wait for Brown.[66]

Throughout that summer, as the tempo of politics accelerated in Georgia, incidents of violence increased. On 27 June a mob in Sunbury forced a customs officer to leave town while it "liberated" a vessel that had been seized for carrying illegal cargo.[67] Raiders in late June and early July repeatedly removed military supplies from the public storehouse in Savannah.[68] On 10 July a group of Georgia and South Carolina Whigs stopped a British ship at the mouth of the Savannah River and removed its cargo of about six tons of gunpowder that was intended for the Indian trade before allowing the vessel to proceed to Savannah.[69] A South Carolina privateer seized another cargo of guns and ammunition, intended for the East Florida garrison and the Indians, in a British ship off the St. Augustine bar in August.[70] On 17 September Georgia Whigs captured yet another vessel on its way to Savannah that was loaded with powder for the Indian trade.[71] Such incidents caused the British government to order the Royal Navy to convoy ships carrying cargo for Indian trade and diplomacy as well as munitions for troops.[72]

Governor Wright and his council had continued to meet, but the royal government in Georgia was powerless. Wright and the loyalists could not even communicate with London or with royal officials in colonies to the northward. Georgia mail continued to pass through Charleston, where the local committee intercepted it. Wright begged for troops and naval support; the Charleston committee substituted letters reporting that "all's well" in Georgia. By the end of June, royal government in Georgia and its loyal supporters were being effectively isolated from those of similar sentiments in other colonies.[73] In June and July, Governor Wright was so discouraged that he wrote home, described the situation as hopeless and uncontrollable, and requested permission to return to England.[74]

From the time the second provincial congress met in July, the Whig leaders provided the only effective government in Georgia. The congress, the Council of Safety in Savannah, and the Parochial

Committees assumed whatever powers in whatever areas they deemed to be expedient. The only restraint on their members was the possibility of being removed from office. The provincial congress was the only body elected by the voters; three congresses were elected in 1775. The congress selected the Council of Safety and Parochial Committees. When the congress was not in session, the council had executive, legislative, and judicial duties. It controlled the province's military activities, diplomatic negotiations, financial affairs, and press censorship. Parochial Committees ruled their areas. The courts virtually ceased to function except for issuing routine legal papers. Some royal officials received threats when they attempted to carry out their duties; generally they were merely ignored. The British government finally included Georgia on the list of colonies that could be abandoned by royal officials whenever they believed it necessary for their safety.[75]

The system of local committees and the provincial delegation to the Continental Congress linked Georgia to the other colonies in rebellion. Three of Georgia's delegates, Bulloch, Houstoun, and Zubly, had reached Philadelphia when Congress reconvened on 13 September. As a staple-exporting colony, Georgia's first item of continental business concerned her trade. She sought some modification in the Continental Association. Georgia was still in the stage of development where it had to import most necessities except food and timber; the only way to pay for imports was by exporting extractive and agricultural products. Although the other continental colonies could neither provide a market for Georgia's lumber, rice, and indigo nor supply essential items for the vitally important Indian trade, Congress did not approve any changes in the association. Zubly ardently supported the colonials' rights within the British Empire, but he opposed both independence and the establishment of a republican form of government. As radical sentiment increased in Congress, his situation became intolerable and he returned home early in November. Bulloch left Philadelphia later in the month, but Houstoun remained until at least 22 December.[76]

East Florida was indisputably loyal to Britain, and a steady trickle of refugees from Georgia and Carolina began seeking asylum over the border during the last six months of 1775. On 2 November Governor Patrick Tonyn, of East Florida, issued a proclamation inviting Tories in other colonies to relocate in his haven. Some refugees brought their families and movable property with them; others arrived in pitiful condition. The economy of East Florida was severely dislocated by the hostilities and the sudden increase in population. The continental embargo disrupted normal trade with other colonies; and rebel privateers, following a pattern that dated back to the Spanish wars, raided British shipping off St. Augustine's bar. These activities created acute shortages of some supplies. Real estate values and food prices soared. Rich refugees stimulated trade within the colony; poor refugees became public charges.[77]

Governor Tonyn was much alarmed when he discovered that secret correspondence was being carried on from his province to the rebel committees of Georgia and the Carolinas. By October he had spent considerable money trying in vain to discover who the participants were.[78] Georgia's gross overestimations of East Florida's strength indicate that the East Florida correspondents were none too accurate.

The administration of each colony nervously eyed the other across the St. Marys River while it contemplated military action. East Florida was exposed to attack and her defenses in terms of arms, fortifications, and soldiers were weak. In midsummer, Governor Tonyn had only eight hundredweight of gunpowder on hand.[79] The old Spanish fort at St. Augustine had withstood every attack against it so far, but other military installations had fallen into ruins. The governor repaired some fortifications and dismantled others he could not garrison.[80]

East Florida's posts, including St. Augustine, Smyrna, Fort Matanzas, Cowford (present Jacksonville), and the Lookout House, on North Anastasia Island, had been garrisoned by Britain's Fourteenth Regiment, consisting of about three hundred men, and a detachment of the Royal Regiment of Artillery, numbering one officer and nine enlisted men. During 1775 about 160 men had been transferred to other colonies where royal authority was endangered, and by October only thirty-five or forty effectives of the Fourteenth remained in St. Augustine. Reinforcements arrived in early December from Pensacola: three companies of the Sixteenth Regiment, including five officers and eighty-two enlisted men, commanded by Captain Colin Graham. Unfortunately, only fifty-eight privates were fit for duty.[81] The schooner *St. Lawrence,* carrying a crew of thirty men and commanded by Lieutenant John Graves, had reached her new station at St. Augustine in October.[82]

The colony's small population made its potential militia force far from formidable, and the poor record of colonial militias during the past two centuries was a favorite topic for regular army men. The military potential of loyalist refugees was problematical; based on their past performances in other colonies, not much could be expected from them. Governor Tonyn begged continually for more help.[83]

Meanwhile, the new leaders of Georgia envisioned innumerable

British regulars swarming over the border. By summer, Governor Wright believed that two ships and five hundred soldiers would be the minimum force required for him to regain control of his province. No such force was available.[84]

The Georgia militia was reorganized after the Second Provincial Congress met in July because many of the officers refused to sign the Continental Association. The strong personal relationship between each leader and his followers could be a liability as well as an asset. Whenever a leader withdrew, for whatever reason, his followers tended to show more allegiance to him than to an impersonal cause. Some Whig militiamen elected new officers, and on 8 August the Council of Safety requested Governor Wright to commission these men; he refused. By November the council itself was issuing commissions as it saw fit.[85] That same month, the Continental Congress authorized one battalion of Continental troops for Georgia and appropriated $5,000 for that purpose.[86]

Early in 1775 Superintendent Stuart had estimated that not more than two thousand effective men were available in Georgia.[87] Certainly some frontiersmen had fled from the province during the Indian troubles, but subsequent immigration into the Ceded Lands probably brought the militia strength back to normal by the end of 1775.

The Indians were a vital and unpredictable component in the Southeast's military picture. Superintendent Stuart, although he had his critics, had been an able administrator, and both sides recognized his enormous influence over the tribes. At the beginning of the colonial troubles, British Indian policy had been flexible, and his aim had been to assure the traditional neutrality of the southern Indians, especially the Creeks. Nevertheless, frontier settlers feared that an indiscriminate Indian war of British instigation was imminent. The attempts of Whigs in South Carolina, much more precipitate than those in Georgia, to control Stuart had forced him to flee from Charleston in May. When his tormentors caught up with him at Savannah in June, he failed to convince them of his good intentions. He moved on to St. Augustine, arriving there on 21 June.[88]

During the summer, the rebels organized their own Indian departments. The South Carolina committee had appointed three men to transact all that colony's affairs with the Creeks: George Galphin, who had been a prominent trader for some thirty years; David Zubly, brother of Georgia's delegate to the Second Continental Congress; and LeRoy Hammond.[89] These arrangements were superseded when the Continental Congress divided their united provinces into three geographical districts for the purpose of handling Indian affairs. The Northern and Middle departments were to have three commissioners each; the Southern Department, including the Cherokees and all tribes south of them, five. Congress appointed two men for the Southern Department: John Walker, of Virginia, and Willie Jones, of North Carolina. The South Carolina Council of Safety was to nominate three: George Galphin, Robert Rae, and Edward Wilkinson, all longtime traders. Galphin had traded with the Lower Towns, and Rae had traded with the Upper Towns; these two men would conduct most of the rebels' dealings with the Creeks until 1779.[90]

Some of the traders joined the American cause, and the patriots made every effort to lure the Indians to their side. The warriors might even be persuaded to fight against the king's troops, though the southern commissioners realized that their best immediate hope was for the Indians to maintain strict neutrality.[91] The southern tribes' new standard of living depended on trade, which had been disrupted. Both sides realized that supplies for trading would be the key to dealing with the Indians.[92]

By the fall of 1775, Stuart was trying to obey his superior's orders to organize all the southern Indians as a fighting force to assist the British but to restrain them from an indiscriminate attack on the frontier.[93] The southern Indians were not firmly united and allied to the British side. Disunity among the tribes, consistently stimulated by the British in the past, had turned from an asset into a liability. The Cherokees and Creeks had a long tradition of less than cordial relations between them, and the British had encouraged the Creek-Choctaw War long after the participants yearned for peace.[94]

The extremely loose internal organization of the tribes presented enormous obstacles to organizing them for discriminating attacks on the rebels. The governments of all the Southeastern tribes were similar. They lived in towns, one hundred houses being a large town; and each town selected, by various methods, its own chiefs, who were assisted by a council of elders. The town chiefs composed a national council, which met only once or twice a year. Although the chiefs separately and in council had great influence and prestige, they did not have coercive power. The strength of custom was the strongest power regulating individual and group behavior.[95]

The Creeks, the largest tribe, were also the most faction-ridden. The individual's first loyalty was to his clan.[96] Different headmen favored different traders and even different European colonies. Opinion on the Ceded Lands had not been unanimous, and ill feeling about that matter persisted. The Creeks were caught unaware by the advent of the American Revolution. Interruption of trade and acute shortage of ammunition, combined with troop movements and militia rallying, led them to believe they were to be the target of hostilities.[97]

The Southeastern Indians had adopted many elements of white culture, including the whites themselves, for as many as three hundred Scots and Englishmen lived within the Creek domain.[98] When those whites chose different sides in the quarrel between king and colony, the Indians' confusion increased. Although dissident factions existed in both the Upper and Lower towns, generally the Upper Creeks, led by the medal chief Emistiseguo, of Little Tallassee, were pro-British; and the Lower Creeks, led by Escochabey, of Coweta, were neutral or pro-American. Nevertheless, in spite of friendly relations with their American traders, the Lower Creeks had felt most annoyingly the pressure of the westward-moving frontier. The Seminoles appeared to favor the British. Disagreement within the Creek tribe led to inaction.[99]

In August a Creek headman, the Cussita King's brother, visited St. Augustine, where friendly "talks" ensued. As he and a trader were returning to the Creek Nation with some ammunition, Georgia rebels waylaid them and seized the ammunition. The Creeks bitterly resented this robbery.[100]

Tonyn reported that he had urged the Cussita King's brother to keep the Creeks neutral, if armed conflict between the whites occurred, until they had consulted with himself or with Superintendent Stuart. Already, however, the governor was considering the use of Indians to aid in the defense of East Florida if the Georgians and Carolinians attacked his province.[101]

Rival agents confronted each other in September at the Usichee town. David Taitt, the British deputy, met Robert Rae, a rebel commissioner, and David Holmes, acting deputy of another rebel commissioner (George Galphin). On this occasion, the Creeks sent a "talk" to Governor Wright promising to maintain neutrality in the whites' quarrel and to listen to no talks except those from British officials. The assembled headmen urged the immediate resumption of trade, and they were especially insistent about ammunition supplies.[102]

In the middle of September, Jonathan Bryan sent Thomas Gray, a trader whom he favored, with four Indians to the Cowkeeper's town, at Latchoway. Their purpose was to persuade the Seminole headmen to sign Bryan's lease again and to cooperate with the Georgians if they invaded East Florida. Tonyn immediately sent a constable and two soldiers with a warrant for Gray's arrest and an invitation for the

Seminole headmen and the four Indians from Georgia to come talk to him in St. Augustine. If this plan failed, Tonyn anticipated capturing Gray before he could recross the St. Marys into Georgia.[103]

Gray was apprehended at Latchoway, however, and brought to St. Augustine. The Indians accepted Tonyn's invitation to visit him at the same time. Gray's interrogation was less than severe inasmuch as the governor learned that, through his Indian mother, he was related to all the headmen and in their favor. He insisted that he had refused to sign the rebel association in Georgia and feared for his safety in that province. Tonyn offered him East Florida land, granted in family right, and Gray proposed to bring his family to settle in East Florida.[104]

Although Gray maintained that his recent visit to Latchoway was merely to look for some horses and denied that he was serving as Bryan's messenger, he recounted in detail Bryan's other attempts to persuade the Seminoles to acquiesce in the "lease" of their land. Bryan's efforts had been unsuccessful, but his persistence irritated the Indians.[105]

Early in December, Superintendent Stuart and Governor Tonyn persuaded some Lower Creeks—Cowetas, Hitchitas, Cussitas, Chihaws, and Uschitas—to meet them for a conference at Cowford, on the St. Johns River. Tonyn had not heard from the British secretary of state for the colonies since the July dispatches, nor had he been informed of Gage's intention to utilize the Indians in military activities. Both the superintendent and the governor emphasized the problems the rebels would face in supplying the Indian trade and the dishonest land practices of some prominent Whig leaders in Georgia. Tonyn had already begun negotiations with William Panton, a prominent trader in Georgia, to move his headquarters to St. Augustine and take over the Indian trade in East Florida. The economic arguments impressed both the Pumpkin King, of Osichess, and the Long Warrior, of Chiaha, but they pointed out that tribal policy must be determined in a full Creek council.[106]

Immediately after the Cowford conference, Stuart issued direct and specific orders to David Taitt and Alexander Cameron, his deputies, to lead the Creeks and Cherokees in cooperating with loyalist military efforts against the rebels. Perhaps he did not realize that no loyalists in Georgia or South Carolina were operating then, at least not in a military manner.[107]

Late in 1775 the Georgia rebels began raiding loyalist plantations on the East Florida side of the St. Marys boundary line. At a special meeting on Sunday, 24 December, the Council of Safety in Savannah considered a letter from John Wereat, who declared that several vessels were loading timber "up Sapelo and other rivers to the southward." Their obvious intent was to pursue the traditional and profitable, but now forbidden, West Indian and Florida trade. The council decided to order the committees "to take effectual measures to prevent such wicked and daring attempts." The men employed and attendant expenses would be paid from public funds.[108]

Jermyn Wright was a brother of the governor of Georgia and a major landholder in that province and in East Florida; his three plantations on the St. Marys were worked by one hundred or more slaves. Two of his plantations were on the south side of the river. A four-hundred-acre tract about twelve miles from the river's mouth was a productive rice plantation. The larger tract of five hundred acres, about eighty miles upstream, produced provisions and timber. When Captain John Mowbray visited Wright at his lower plantation at Christmas, he found it to be in a flourishing condition. By the end of the year, both plantations had been devastated by raiders from Georgia who burned the buildings and cut the rice dams. Wright abandoned those two plantations and collected all his Negroes at his principal plantation on the Georgia side of the St. Marys.[109]

This plantation was also about twelve miles from the river's mouth and as accessible by water as by land, but during the Indian scare of 1773–74 Wright had fortified it. "Wright's Fort" consisted merely of a simple wooden stockade around some plantation buildings, but it was the strongest refuge for loyalists in St. Mary's Parish.[110]

By 18 January 1776 four British men-of-war and other ships had arrived at the mouth of the Savannah River with orders to procure provisions for British forces to the northward. The Georgia Council of Safety, forewarned from Charleston, had ordered militia to Savannah and had taken all feasible precautionary measures. When the ships appeared, Governor Wright summoned two leading Whigs, Noble W. Jones and Joseph Clay, and informed them that, though one of the vessels would be stationed at the mouth of the Savannah, the others were there merely to purchase supplies. The governor warned that, if the naval commanders were not allowed to proceed peaceably on their mission, they would undoubtedly seize what they needed and destroy much property in the process.[111]

Instead of heeding Wright's advice, the Council of Safety arrested the governor, his council, and other royal officials. Two days later, they were paroled on their promise not to leave Savannah or to try to communicate with the British ships. The same promise was demanded of all nonassociators. The council ordered more militia to the city and requested that South Carolina return the powder "borrowed" after its capture at Savannah.[112]

Early in February, more British ships arrived. The mission of these vessels, carrying two hundred troops, was to purchase provisions for the British garrison at Boston. On the night of 11/12 February, Wright and some of his council broke their paroles and escaped to Cockspur Island, at the mouth of the Savannah River; the next morning, they boarded HMS *Scarborough*.[113]

Wright made one final effort to save royal government in his province. Again he warned Georgians of the retribution their folly would bring. At the same time, he requested Sir Henry Clinton, commander of British troops for southern operations, to send five hundred to one thousand troops. The governor claimed that most Georgians had been coerced into disloyalty and would return to their natural allegiance if they could be assured of protection from the radicals. Captain Andrew Barkley, commander of the British naval force at the mouth of the river, agreed that armed support could save Georgia, but Clinton was too occupied farther north to send help, and Barkley himself was under orders to take his troops, ships, and supplies back to Boston immediately.[114]

The British target was several vessels loaded with rice that were anchored above Savannah. Early in March, in the "battle of the riceboats," the British acquired fourteen or fifteen ships and a cargo of 1,600 barrels of rice. Four British sailors, two Americans, and one Indian were wounded.[115] British officials in Georgia estimated that between two and three hundred slaves reached the British ships at Cockspur and left the colony on board the transports and merchant ships. Colonel Stephen Bull, commander of the South Carolina forces serving in Savannah, reported that about two hundred Negroes had deserted to the British by 13 March.[116]

Both sides released their prisoners, and the Whigs allowed royal officials and Tories to leave Georgia if they wished to do so. Many did. When Governor Wright and the British troops sailed away at the end of March, they left the loyalists in Georgia in a desperate predicament. There was no longer any official opposition to control of that province by the rebels.[117]

II

1776: Raids
and Counter-Raids

ON 27 FEBRUARY 1776 the Continental Congress created a Southern Military Department, consisting of Virginia, the Carolinas, and Georgia, under the leadership of Major General Charles Lee. Brigadier General John Armstrong commanded South Carolina and Georgia.[1] On 4 November 1775 the Congress had authorized three battalions of Continental troops for South Carolina and one battalion for Georgia. Officers were to be designated by the respective state governments, and recruiting would be allowed in Virginia and North Carolina. The troops were to be enlisted only until 31 December 1776 and could be discharged sooner if Congress thought proper.[2]

Georgia's provincial congress proceeded to organize its Continental battalion and on 29 and 30 January 1776 elected its officers: Lachlan McIntosh, colonel; Samuel Elbert, lieutenant colonel; and James Habersham, major. The election results disappointed Button Gwinnett, a leading radical, who had hoped for the command.[3]

Congress had specified that each regiment would consist of 728 men, including officers, and be divided into eight companies, each of which would consist of 76 privates, 2 drummers or fifers, 4 corporals, 4 sergeants, 1 ensign, 2 lieutenants, and 1 captain. Rations for each man would consist of: one pound of beef or three-fourths pound of pork or one pound of salt fish per day, one pound of bread or flour per day, three pints of peas or beans per week (or equivalent vegetables), one pint of milk per day, one-half pint of rice or one pint of Indian meal per week, and one quart of spruce beer or cider per man per day or nine gallons of molasses per company of 100 men per week. Each company of that size was to receive three pounds of candles and either twenty-four pounds of soft soap or eight pounds of hard soap per week.[4]

During the spring of 1776, about six hundred militia men were on duty in Georgia. The state was also raising two troops of horsemen (sixty horses each), commanded by Captains William McIntosh and

24

Leonard Marbury, to guard the southern and western frontiers against raids by British and Indians.[5] Recruiting for Georgia's Continental battalion, however, was unsatisfactory. Georgians still had not been informed of the time specified for enlistments; consequently, McIntosh accepted enlistments for six, twelve, or eighteen months—whatever he could get. By early May only about four hundred men had enlisted. One reason for the recruiting problem was the state's limited financial resources. Money promised from Congress had not yet arrived; Georgia currency was not acceptable outside the state; and neighboring South Carolina paid larger bounties. Georgia's defenses were obviously inadequate for a buffer zone. In March and May, Congressional committees recommended, with the concurrence of state authorities and military commanders, that additional troops be raised for both South Carolina and Georgia.[6]

At the same time, Georgia was desperately trying to augment her meager armaments. Congress had modified the nonexportation association to allow colonial produce to be exported to pay for arms and ammunition, and the Georgia Council of Safety appointed Samuel Elbert, Edward Telfair, and Joseph Habersham to arrange for this trade. The council also ordered the cannon and military stores at Fort Frederica and Cockspur Island to be secured.[7]

In the best colonial tradition, some traders worked for both sides. Georgia appointed Thomas Young to supply the state's Continental battalion with clothing; Governor Tonyn, of East Florida, appointed him to supply the West Indies with provisions from Georgia. When Young's duplicity was discovered, he lost the clothing he had imported into Georgia, and he was among those listed in Georgia's 1778 Act of Confiscation and Banishment. Because other traders who worked for both the British and the rebels were luckier or more skillful in evading detection, they remain unknown.[8]

On 1 January 1776, while Governor Wright was still in Georgia but before the British naval forces had appeared in the Savannah, Congress had recommended that Georgia, South Carolina, and North Carolina undertake a joint expedition at Continental expense against St. Augustine.[9] News of the proposed invasion was no surprise to Governor Tonyn; St. Augustine had been full of rumors all winter. By spring he was far better prepared than he had been when Congress precipitately planned the conquest of East Florida.[10]

East Florida's military situation had improved in terms of both men and material. In the face of a rebel invasion from the continent, HM Schooner *St. John* and a sloop, whose master was William Chambers, removed 162 barrels of gunpowder from New Providence, in the

Bahamas, and reached St. Augustine with the prized cargo on 7 March.[11] On 22 and 28 February, 222 regulars of the Sixtieth Regiment reinforced St. Augustine from Britain.[12]

Britain's Sixtieth Regiment, the "Royal American," had been established in 1756 expressly as a fighting force trained to combat the French and Indians in colonial warfare with their own unorthodox methods. The regiment was to be recruited primarily from British colonials of foreign descent, secondarily from foreign protestants, and not more than fifty foreign officers could be commissioned. The parliamentary act which permitted the creation of this unique corps in the British military machine specified that the foreign soldiers should not serve outside of "America" and that no foreign officer should hold a rank higher than lieutenant colonel. In 1765 another parliamentary act removed the limitation on rank of foreign officers by allowing any protestant who had served in the regiment for three years the privilege of engaging in any employment, civil or military, in any part of the British dominions except Great Britain and Ireland; at the same time, the term "America" was expanded to include the West Indies. The regiment subsequently served in whatever part of the world it was needed.[13] In theory, it was the ideal military force to send to a frontier colony that was threatened by rebels and Indians.

East Florida still lacked any formally organized militia, but the government proposed to rectify that deficiency immediately. On 30 March the council reported on the number of white male inhabitants in the province between sixteen and fifty years of age who were capable of bearing arms: 42 on the St. Marys and Nassau Rivers, 53 on the St. Johns, 200 at Smyrna.[14]

Also, British negotiations with the southern Indians were progressing satisfactorily. Some loyalist traders moved from Augusta to Pensacola, and Superintendent Stuart intended to supply the Creeks with both trade and presents through West Florida.[15] The Seminoles of Latchoway (Alachua) could be reached easily from St. Augustine. The Creeks flatly refused the Georgia Whigs' order to turn over to them David Taitt, Stuart's deputy.[16] Tonyn confidently called on the Indians for aid to repel the expected invasion. He asked the Seminoles to station warriors between St. Augustine and the St. Johns and between the St. Johns and the St. Marys.[17]

Acutely aware of the importance of the inland waterways and of their vulnerability, the governor asked General Clinton for small vessels to be used in naval patrol. The river systems that had functioned as roads to markets would be equally useful as military highways. Besides reassuring planters settled along the river banks, the patrols might be an effective deterrent to the invasion itself.[18]

The British ministers themselves had been considering a southern campaign for some time.[19] Southern loyalists had repeatedly assured officials that the majority in that section would welcome and support British regulars against the rebels.[20] Superintendent Stuart's reports about Indian allies were nearly as encouraging.[21] Consequently, Major General Henry Clinton was shocked and disappointed when he arrived with a large British invasion force at Cape Fear in March 1776 to learn that loyalists in North Carolina had risen prematurely in February and had been decisively defeated at Moore's Creek Bridge. Plagued with indecision, Clinton summoned the "locals" to a conference at Cape Fear.[22]

While the British hesitated, Georgians took steps in March and April to improve their governmental organization. On 15 April the third provincial congress issued a temporary state constitution, the Rules and Regulations of 1776.[23] When the new government went into effect on 1 May, Archibald Bulloch was elected by the one-house legislature as president and commander in chief.[24] On 20 May, when Button Gwinnett and Lyman Hall took their seats, Georgia again was represented in the Continental Congress.[25]

During the spring, both the British and Americans increased their efforts in Indian diplomacy without obtaining any concrete results. Late in January, Congress had authorized the exportation of colonial produce to pay for the importation of £40,000 worth of goods for the Indian trade. The Northern and Middle departments were each to receive goods to the value of £13,333: 6: 8, and the remainder would be assigned to the Southern Department. The Secret Committee was to handle the transactions; the departmental commissioners would be responsible for establishing trading posts, licensing traders, and distributing the goods to them. Congress authorized the purchase of more goods to be used for presents in treaty negotiations with the Indians. In late April, Congress chose a five-man standing committee for Indian Affairs.[26]

A month earlier Congress had resolved: "That Indians be not employed as soldiers in the armies of the United Colonies, before the tribes to which they belong shall, in a National Council, held in the customary manner, have consented thereunto, nor then, without the express approbation of Congress."[27] At least one member of Congress regarded this restriction as "very absurd and impolitic."[28] On 25 May his colleagues agreed that it was "highly expedient to engage the

Indians in the Service of the United Colonies." A few weeks later, the Congress resolved to permit General Washington to employ Indians wherever they would be useful and to pay them $100 for every commissioned officer and $30 for every private they captured from the British army.[29]

George Galphin, the new Whig commissioner for the Creeks, had been especially active, and he had capitalized on his prewar influence with the Lower Creeks. This part of the nation, except the Yuchis and Hitchitas, held a council at Cussita on 23 March, and perhaps it was his influence that was responsible for the headmen's suggestion that the whites compose their differences so that the Indian trade could be resumed on a normal basis. More likely, the Creeks were simply reiterating their traditional policy of neutrality while they tried to peer into the future.[30]

Conflicting reports reached East Florida from the Indian country. On 18 April a man named Buchanan arrived in St. Augustine from Pensacola and reported that both the Creeks and the Cherokees were ready to support the king and were merely waiting for instructions.[31] Certainly, however, both the Seminoles and the Lower Creeks were becoming increasingly unenthusiastic about giving military aid. The Seminoles, even including the devoted Cowkeeper, refused to give armed assistance to the British until they knew the sentiments of the entire Creek Nation. Taitt's influence was far stronger among the Upper Creeks where he resided.[32]

Although Georgians had little hope of obtaining adequate supplies of Indian trade goods in the immediate future,[33] they were worried enough about possible attacks on the frontier to put Marbury Bryan (Jonathan Bryan's son) and some seventy men loaded with presents on the trail to the Lower Creeks in April. They intended to leave some presents at the Indian border on the Altamaha as payment for the land "leased" by Jonathan Bryan. Thomas Gray, the half-breed interpreter favored by Bryan, and six other men were commissioned by Georgia to go to the Creeks, spread Whig propaganda, and seize Taitt. Hearing of this, Tonyn rushed a warning to the British agent and urged him to capture the Georgians and to encourage Creek loyalty to the British.[34]

In April, Thomas Brown, of late a refugee from South Carolina and Georgia, led a pack-horse train of gunpowder intended for the South Carolina loyalists through the Indian country from St. Augustine. As he diligently propagandized the towns along the trail, he sent reports back to Tonyn. The major Seminole groups, including the Cowkeeper, of Latchoway, the King of Oconee, and the King of

Mikasukie, were firmly attached to the British; the Lower Creeks, however, were not inclined to render the military aid they had promised to East Florida.[35]

The Chiaha warriors obviously coveted the powder Brown was transporting, and he surmised that he certainly would not get safely past the Cowetas with his pack-train intact. He sent an express to Taitt, who responded promptly. Assembling the Lower Creek chiefs and headmen at Chiaha on 1 May, Taitt extracted a promise from all except the Cowetas, Hitchitas, and Cussitas not to listen to the Whig "talks." The Lower Creek headmen requested the Oconee King to lead a large group of Seminole warriors to St. Augustine immediately; the Cowkeeper and a party from Alachua had already been in that city for approximately a month.[36]

Still puzzled about the whites' civil war and starved for trade goods, Creek delegates from both the Lower (mainly Coweta and Cussita) and Upper Towns (mainly Okfuskee) met the Whig Indian commissioners at Augusta on 1 May. The Americans tried to stimulate the Creeks' bent toward neutrality. The former blamed the king's ships for stopping the flow of trade goods and boasted that they themselves could make adequate cloth and ammunition to supply the Indians. Bragging about rebel victories over the king's troops (probably referring to the evacuation of Boston), they accused Stuart of instigating Indian attacks on the frontier with the ulterior motive of destroying the tribes. Because the Whigs had virtually nothing to offer the Indians in the way of the traditional presents, they were unusually liberal with liquor; they gave the Cowetas alone between ninety and one hundred kegs of rum. And, once again, the Americans asked the Creeks to expel Taitt, the British agent within their nation. Again, the Creeks refused.[37]

Although Taitt prevailed upon the Lower Creeks to refrain from seizing Brown's gunpowder and even to provide an escort for the pack-train through Indian territory, the vengeful loyalist had to change his plans. Friends in St. Augustine sent a warning that a party of rebels was waiting to intercept him on the way to the South Carolina backcountry. Taitt received even worse news. Superintendent Stuart had written from Cape Fear to his deputies that General Clinton wanted all military operations by the Indians suspended until further orders; the warriors were merely to be held in readiness for the present. Certainly there were no imminent Creek attacks for Taitt to restrain.[38]

During the summer, the center of southern Indian trade and diplomacy shifted to Pensacola. Superintendent Stuart sailed from St.

Augustine in the *Hinchinbrook* on 8 June and arrived in Pensacola on 24 July. That place was to be his home for the rest of his life. Although the new location facilitated his contact with the major southern tribes, it seriously hampered communication with other civil and military officials. Govenor Tonyn had succeeded in forging strong bonds of friendship with various Seminole tribes, especially that of Cowkeeper, of Alachua; and, because the Seminoles lived so much nearer St. Augustine than Pensacola, they continued to orient themselves toward the East Florida governor's residence.[39]

The Creeks made their decision that summer. Ill-considered action by the Georgians reinforced encouragement and persuasion by the British. The important Lower Towns of Coweta and Cussita had especially friendly relations with the trader George Galphin, one of the new Indian commissioners appointed by the patriots; Escochabey, of Coweta, was definitely propatriot. Then Thomas Few (or Fee), a habitual Indian-baiter who had murdered a prominent Creek a few years earlier, murdered a Lower Creek warrior on the Ogeechee River.[40]

At the Congress of Augusta in May, the Chevulky Warrior had announced that this atrocity would prevent good relations between the Georgians and the Creeks so long as it remained unpunished. Because according to all arrangements between the Indians and the whites, the Indians were entitled to see justice done, the Georgians invited two Creeks to remain in the settlements to witness the punishment of the murderer. Nevertheless, the whites tried to trick them by hanging a man who actually had murdered his wife, not the Indian.[41]

The unavenged warrior had clansmen in the Upper Towns, and at this point, the Creeks were probably as firmly united as they had been at any time since the Yamassee War. Most of them were pro-British and anti-American. A Coweta took the mandatory compensation in blood by killing a white at Okmulgee.[42] In September a rebel killed a Cussita warrior; as a result, the last major town with strong prorebel sympathies developed a blood feud with Georgia.[43]

A more mundane reason for Indian disenchantment with the Whigs was the effectiveness of the British blockade. Georgians had to face the fact that they did not have and could not expect to obtain the traditional Indian presents and trade goods: arms and ammunition, cloth and clothing. Early in the summer, Georgians had promised the Lower Creeks that they were going to stop planting indigo so they could devote their time and energy to manufacturing cloth and ammunition for the Indian trade, but by July they were preparing to offer cattle to the Indians as a substitute.[44]

Late in July a party of rebels under Captain John Pulliam had a skirmish with Indians on Beaverdam Creek. When two warriors were killed, the others fled.[45]

By the end of the summer, it was clear that there were actually two different Indian policies for Georgia. The rebel leaders, horrified by the potential devastation inherent in their position between the British forces and the Indian tribes, were striving to mollify their red neighbors and at least keep them neutral. Frontiersmen, on the other hand, were exuberantly self-confident after their defeat of the Cherokees and wanted nothing less than a full-scale Indian war so that they could conquer more good land. They not only considered it highly desirable that trade with the Indians cease, but they also wanted General Lee and his Continentals to help them exterminate the "savages" or at least drive them from their homes. Such Georgians were as much a worry as any external enemy for the Council of Safety and the Indian commissioners.[46]

More action had occurred in the eastern waters than in the western woods. At ten-thirty on the morning of 1 April in St. Augustine, Governor Tonyn received a message from St. Marys that rebels from Savannah had arrived there to seize a schooner laden for the West Indies. Within half an hour, he requested Lieutenant William Grant, of HM Schooner *St. John,* to disrupt the raid. At five o'clock that afternoon, as she was ready to sail, one captain, one lieutenant, and fifty soldiers of the Fourteenth and Sixteenth regiments boarded— and one hogshead of rum was loaded.[47] The vessel sailed out of St. Augustine's harbor at seven-thirty the next morning. Grant found it necessary to punish Samuel O'Kiff (Keefe?) with twelve lashes for drunkenness and disobedience. Presumably the schooner's rum supply had diminished during the night.[48]

Reaching the St. Marys River on Wednesday morning, 3 April, Lieutenant Grant and his men spent the next four days collecting rice and rebels on land and sea. By Friday they had captured from the Georgia rebels the sloop *Betsy,* which was loaded with forty-three barrels of rice. The next day, Grant received a message that the rebel snow *Christy* had been taken in the St. Simons River. Loyalists in the area voluntarily sent hogsheads of rice to the *St. John;* more was confiscated from a man named Miller, "a Notorious Rebel." On Sunday the *St. John* received on board a prisoner.[49]

Lingering inside the St. Marys bar for another week, Grant sent out expeditions. His patience was rewarded. On 12 April, the prize snow *Christy* returned with a captured sloop, the *Neptune.* The *St. John* loaded 451 weight of fresh beef the next day. On 14 April, she crossed the St. Marys bar and sailed for St. Augustine with three prizes and large cargoes of provisions.[50]

HMS *Hind*, twenty guns, 160 men,[51] under Captain Henry Bryne, arrived at St. Augustine from St. Vincent on 11 April with three companies, Second Battalion, of the Sixtieth Regiment. In the harbor, Bryne found HM Armed Schooner *Hinchinbrook*, six guns, 30 men, commanded by Lieutenant Alexander Ellis.[52] The lieutenant informed the captain that the rebels were fitting out armed vessels in Georgia rivers. Ordering the *Hinchinbrook* to accompany the *Hind*, Bryne sailed out of St. Augustine's harbor on 16 April, ostensibly bound for St. Vincent. Once under sail, both vessels changed course to the northward.[53]

They anchored near the Midway River on 21 April. The *Hind* was too large to cross the bar, but the next morning her tender and boats and the *Hinchinbrook*, all manned and armed, moved upriver toward the town of Sunbury. There, they found a brig loading lumber and a twenty-gun ship, intended to be a privateer, on the stocks. Lieutenant Ellis burned both rebel vessels.[54]

As the schooner, tender, and boats moved downriver and through the inland waterway to rejoin the *Hind*, about "650" Georgia "Crackers" fired upon the flotilla from St. Catherine's Island. After a brisk half-hour engagement, the rebels retreated to the shelter of the woods. The tender's hull and sails were damaged, but the British suffered no casualties. On 25 April the *Hinchinbrook* and the other vessels reached the *Hind*'s anchorage.[55]

When the *Hind* sailed southward for Antigua the next day,[56] the *Hinchinbrook* moved northward to join Clinton's force at Cape Fear. Ellis's sudden departure from St. Augustine on 16 April had frustrated Tonyn's plan to continue patrolling the St. Marys River and adjacent waters. The governor contended that the *Hinchinbrook* had relieved the *St. Lawrence*, which had been stationed to serve in East Florida and that, therefore, the *Hinchinbrook* had inherited the same duty. Tonyn had intended to station her and another vessel with fifty soldiers in the St. Marys. Lieutenant Ellis, however, claimed that his orders gave him ample discretion regarding his service in East Florida and that he was not supposed to serve that province only; he intended to sail to Cape Fear to clarify his orders. When he left St. Augustine's harbor with the *Hind*, he did not notify Tonyn of his plans until after he had crossed the bar; he sent a message back to the governor by the pilot boat. Tonyn was outraged.[57]

Lieutenant Ellis's orders were both clarified and expanded when he reached Cape Fear on 4 May. After taking provisions to the *Raven* and *Cherokee*, which were stationed at the mouth of the Savannah

River, he was to transport Indian Superintendent Stuart to Pensacola and then resume his station at St. Augustine.[58]

The three companies of the Second Battalion of the Sixtieth Regiment transported from St. Vincent to St. Augustine by the *Hind* included eighty-two veterans, Lieutenants Benjamin Wickham and John K. Muller, and Major James Mark Prevost. All three captains were absent. The veterans were to assist in the speedy training of the raw recruits from Europe. More officers, all formerly of the First Battalion, arrived from Jamaica between 16 and 22 April. Captain George McIntosh was assigned to the Third Battalion, and Lieutenant Colonel Lewis V. Fuser and Captain Patrick Murray to the Fourth Battalion. Colonel Augustine Prevost, Fourth Battalion, commanded all the regular troops in East Florida.[59]

As welcome as these reinforcements were, their arrival created a problem. Colonel Prevost expected a manpower increase to a total strength of twelve hundred, but the barracks in St. Augustine were totally inadequate for even the existing garrison. On 24 April he reported that the barracks were in ruins and needed both furniture and utensils as well as structural repairs. Ordinarily the repairs would have been the responsibility of the engineering officer, but there was none in St. Augustine at that time. Consequently, the problem was turned over to Barracksmaster C. Shirreff.[60]

By 14 May Shirreff had completed a detailed survey of the barracks problem and prepared estimates on renovation of the barracks for Tonyn. This well-designed building, large and well ventilated, had a ground story of brick and an upper story and verandas of wood. Tonyn pointed out that it would have been cheaper in the long run to have built the structure from local stone, *cocina* from Anastasia Island, at St. Augustine, and that he had been trying for two years to get the repairs made.[61] Delay was no longer possible. The extensive structural work would cost an estimated £1,519:10:1. Repair of usable furniture and utensils and purchase of new items would cost an additional £1,448:15.[62]

Materials were available locally, but money was a problem. Shirreff could not pay local merchants and workmen with bills drawn on the barracksmaster general at headquarters in Halifax as he had been ordered to do; because communication no longer existed with the northern colonies, local people would not accept such bills. As a temporary expedient, so that work on the barracks could continue, Tonyn signed a draft for £500 on the Treasury in England. He wrote home requesting immediate instructions on a new procedure for meeting such expenses.[63]

Tonyn informed Lord George Germain, secretary of state for the colonies, that the fort at St. Augustine could be used occasionally to quarter a battalion along with six-months provisions and "firing" if some of the officers were quartered in town and if an upper floor were constructed in some of the casemates. The fort was so small that the governor could not recommend using it for regular quarters. Although the engineer had reported to him that five of the casemates were bombproof, he doubted this. He mentioned that the fort's outworks had never been finished.

The governor, irritated by the attitude of both Shirreff and Prevost, complained to Germain that they would have completely ignored him if they had not needed his help in financial matters. Tonyn expected the secretary to make clear to these erring servants of the Crown the important place of the civil governor in military affairs.[64]

Georgia finally took the offensive. In May, after noting that some loyalists—particularly the Wrights and Martin Jollie—were building "forts and fortifications," the Council of Safety decided to clean up the "debatable land." On 14 May it ordered Captain William McIntosh and his "Troop of Horse" to reduce Wright's Fort and capture the Wrights, Jollie, and any other disaffected men—black or white—as well as their provisions and armament. McIntosh was further ordered to take such shipping as lay in the St. Marys River if at all possible and to bring into Georgia livestock from East Florida, especially that belonging to (David) Anderson. He was also directed to choose the sites for and build log forts on the Altamaha and on the St. Marys.[65]

The Georgians obviously had four items in mind: men, armament, livestock, and slaves. In the newly settled border lands, men naturally followed local leaders, who were inevitably large landholders. If these loyalist leaders could be removed, the Whigs could deal more easily with their scattered opponents.

It was these leaders who had fortified their plantations and accumulated weapons. Neither Georgia nor East Florida possessed a plentiful supply of ammunition. Georgia had not yet succeeded in finding a reliable new source of supply; thus, she was dependent on what could be captured from ships coming in to supply St. Augustine. East Florida's small stock had to be shared with the friendly Indians. Gunpowder was a very desirable item indeed.

Food supplies were also increasing in value. Population shifts and disruption of routine adversely affected the economy of these agricultural provinces. Food production declined at the time when expansion was desirable. Troops and refugees entering East Florida put pressure on food supplies there, and troops maneuvering in south Georgia interfered with the production of that which they themselves needed. The livestock in question was not the typical scrawny herds of cattle for the family use of subsistence farmers. Between the Altamaha and St. Johns and in the interior of Georgia were large and ideal tracts of pastureland that were used for cattle ranges. Many herds were enormous; roaming almost wild, they were managed by cowboys, locally called "cattle hunters."[66] Thomas Nixon, a London merchant who had multiple interests in East Florida, claimed that he could supply British forces with 12,000 head of cattle per year, delivering 1,000 each month at the mouth of the St. Marys. Thomas Brown had suggested in February that the large herds in the interior, especially those belonging to the Whig Indian commissioners, should be driven into territory under British control.[67]

Slaves were a still more worrisome form of property. Each side feared raids by the other; stealing slaves was almost like stealing cash besides destroying a plantation's labor supply and, therefore, its ability to produce. The Georgians, informed that British forces to the northward had armed slaves against their masters, dreaded the possibility of British agents from East Florida organizing a slave insurrection. Remembering their experiences when Spain held the Floridas, the Georgians did not doubt that such an event was possible.[68]

News traveled quickly between the two southernmost provinces. On 19 May Governor Tonyn noted the arrival in East Florida of a large group of refugees from North Carolina and Georgia, including some prominent citizens from the latter colony.[69] The next day, he informed his council of the Georgia plan to remove the cattle of East Florida residents into Georgia and to destroy plantations between the St. Marys and the St. Johns. Some livestock had already been driven into Georgia by East Florida traitors.[70]

The governor immediately took defensive measures. He requested Colonel Prevost to send a captain and a detachment to guard the St. Marys crossing, arm the settlers in that area, and instruct them to move their cattle south of the St. Johns River. The herd belonging to a man named McKenzie, who was imprisoned by the rebels, should be driven out of Georgia and across the rivers into East Florida; civilians, led by one Sanchez, McKenzie's partner, would undertake that task. HM Schooner *St. John* was to transport the troops to the St. Marys, command any additional vessels seized there, keep communication open with St. Augustine, and be ready to evacuate the troops if necessary. The *St. John* was to be relieved by the *Hinchinbrook* if and when she returned to the St. Augustine station. On the same day, the governor issued letters of marque to George Osborne, a mariner, who claimed he had sustained many injuries from the Georgia rebels.[71]

Not even Governor Tonyn, however, could control the weather. On 21 May the *St. John* and the sloop *Pompey*, the St. Augustine pilot boat, embarked seventy men of the Fourteenth and Sixteenth Regiments who were commanded by Captain Colin Graham of the Sixteenth; the vessels could not leave St. Augustine's harbor until two o'clock in the morning of 27 May. After fighting contrary winds and eastward currents all day, they anchored northeast of Cumberland Island at seven o'clock that night.[72]

Two days later, the British force finally reached its destination. On the afternoon of 29 May, the two vessels anchored in the St. Marys River, where the troops transferred from the *St. John* to the smaller *Pompey*. That sloop and the schooner's cutter then proceeded upriver in the hope of intercepting the Americans.[73]

Early in the morning of 31 May, the *St. John* captured a Georgia sloop inside the St. Marys bar. The crew claimed they had been forced to carry ammunition for the rebels, and they divulged valuable information. Having crossed the river on the previous day, the Georgia force would be coming down the south side of the St. Marys, in East Florida territory. The rebels had already raided the Jollie, Bethune, Kennedy, and Clark plantations and captured the owners.[74] On the night of 22 May, the raiders had forced William Taylor, resident agent on William Chapman's rice plantation, to flee to Amelia Island. They had burned the plantation buildings and the cutter *Florida Packet,* destroyed a tar kiln and a crop of rice, driven off the cattle, and either stolen or dispersed about forty slaves from Chapman's plantation.[75]

Lieutenant Grant, of the *St. John,* immediately sent an express to Captain Graham suggesting that the troops intercept the Georgians when they returned to the ferry. The British did catch up with the rebels at that ferry, but not until after the latter had recrossed into Georgia. Both sides fired at each other across the river; three Georgians were wounded, and one man from the Fourteenth Regiment was killed. In the confusion, three of the captured loyalist planters escaped, and that night the British sent a small boat across the St. Marys to rescue Bethune, Kennedy, and Clark.[76]

It is entirely possible that these raids across the border were by unauthorized parties bent on plunder, while McIntosh and Prevost both intended to keep their land forces strictly inside the limits of their respective colonies and use them only for defensive purposes. Captain Graham's troops did not cross the St. Marys in pursuit of the

Georgia raiders on 21 May. Following Colonel McIntosh's advice, the Georgia Council of Safety on 2 July resolved that "militia" forces should not invade East Florida to make reprisals without specific orders from the president of the council. On 11 July Lieutenant Grant ordered the *St. John*'s cutter not to touch the Georgia bank of the St. Marys under any circumstances. That same day, however, the Georgia Council of Safety commissioned a man named Kelly to make reprisals inside East Florida "for depradations they have made on this colony."[77] It is most likely that the rebel raids on plantations along the St. Marys in late May were carried out by William McIntosh's troop of horse with some aid from local militia as the result of orders from the Council of Safety and that they were personally directed by Colonel Lachlan McIntosh, who at that time was on Georgia's southern border "on some Important Business."[78]

As raids and counter-raids continued along the border, settlers in the area scrambled to remove themselves and their property to safer locations.[79] Both sides tried to control strategic points along the rivers and the shipping in them. The British were able to maintain a fairly effective naval patrol at least as far north as the St. Marys;[80] the Georgians had one armed vessel in the area, usually stationed at "Gaskins."[81]

Both sides built new fortifications. It may have been about this time that the East Florida governor ordered the construction of Fort Tonyn, twenty-five miles upstream on the St. Marys near the King's Road ferry and the cow-ford. Mounting swivel guns, this square wooden fort became the main British strong point on the northern frontier.[82]

The Georgians repaired some forts that Governor Wright had described as ruinous in 1773 and hurried to fortify key points, such as the port town of Sunbury.[83] By July the front of that town was protected by earthworks about five feet high, fronted by a ditch that was ten feet wide. A fort in the center of town was equipped with one twelve-pounder cannon and two or three three-pounder field pieces. About twenty soldiers of the Georgia Battalion were constantly on guard, and forty inhabitants functioned as "minute men."[84] By 20 June a detachment of the same battalion was stationed on the Alta-maha River.[85]

For a man trained in the ways of the regular British army, Tonyn adapted with startling ease to the type of warfare he was required to wage. Two troops of Rangers in Georgia had been disbanded in 1767, in accord with the British government's theory that Georgia was no longer a frontier colony after the establishment of the Floridas, but the Rangers had certainly proved their worth.[86] James Grant, first governor of East Florida, had stressed the utility of Rangers under his own command in his province—"a Troop of Rangers would be of more real Service than half a Regiment"—but he could not obtain authorization for such an expense. During the Indian scare of 1774, a troop of Rangers that was organized under the command of Angus Clark was paid for out of East Florida's Indian fund.[87] In March 1776 General Henry Clinton directed East Florida's governor to raise a regiment of mounted infantry for service in that province and promised to confirm Tonyn's commissions; thus, the officers would take rank from the date of the governor's commissions. On 1 June Governor Tonyn authorized Thomas Brown to raise a regiment of mounted Rangers and appointed him as lieutenant colonel of the regiment.[88]

Brown did most of his recruiting that summer among loyalists in the backcountry, but Tonyn was soon able to send the most suitable type of reinforcements to the small British force on the border. In mid-June twenty "cattle hunters," armed with rifles, reached the St. Marys. They may have been "Samuel Williams and five men employed as Rangers with His Majesty's Troops at St. Marys," "Angus Clark and his Party employed with His Majesty's troops at St. Marys," and "John Bethune . . . and two men employed with Captain Graham's Detachment at St. Mary's."[89]

Brown later stated "that the King's Rangers were principally raised in South Carolina" and that they were:

> Indian traders and countrymen who have a perfect knowledge of the language, customs, manners, and disposition of the different tribes of Creeks and Cherokees . . . expert woodsmen capable of swimming any river in the province . . . and are the best guides in the southern district.

It is not clear, however, whether the recruits of 1776 possessed all the characteristics of the experienced Rangers of 1780. And certainly many of Brown's men in the East Florida Rangers were refugee Georgians. General Augustine Prevost declared that the East Florida Rangers were "mostly people of some property."[90]

In June, St. Augustine had an increase in more conventional force. Although Tonyn and Prevost were disappointed that the entire Sixtieth Regiment would not be stationed at St. Augustine as they had expected,[91] the military situation in East Florida had improved substantially within six months. On 8 June a transport reached St. Augustine containing two hundred recruits for the Sixtieth Regiment, presents for the Indians, carriages for the guns at Fort St. Marks and ordnance stores. Two brigs carrying provisions were also off the bar. The St. Augustine garrison now consisted of the remnant of the Fourteenth Regiment, three small companies of the Sixteenth Regiment, and three old and twelve new companies of the Sixtieth Regiment.[92]

Germain believed that this new strength would deter any invasion attempt by Georgia and further encourage both the loyalists and the Indians.[93] Tonyn was even more confident; he wanted to take the offensive. His new forces, he believed, made him strong enough at least to stage a diversion in Georgia that would aid Clinton in the Carolinas. Although the governor charged the Indian superintendent with being dilatory and begged for more money to handle his own Indian expenses, he included in his advantages the force being raised by Brown, in whom he had complete confidence.[94]

The Georgians agreed with Tonyn's analysis of the situation, and they had an abiding terror of a large-scale Indian attack on their province. As Tonyn said, "The Americans [were] a thousand times more in dread of the Savages than of any European Troops."[95] Late in June, news reached Savannah and was forwarded to General Lee at Charleston that five or six hundred regulars and Indians from St. Augustine had reached the St. Marys River. If any Indians were there, they were merely the Cowkeeper's party of warriors who had joined Captain Graham; as usual, however, the Georgians grossly exaggerated the number of their enemies. Fearing that this enormous British force intended to invade Georgia in conjunction with an attack by sea, Archibald Bulloch, president of the Council of Safety, ordered Colonel Samuel Elbert to march all the out-detachments of the Georgia Battalion immediately to headquarters at Savannah for the town's defense. The various parish militias were to replace the detachments. The council ordered Colonel McIntosh to hold the line at the Satilla River if he could and to retire to the Altamaha if he must.[96] These fears were groundless.

Georgia Whigs found themselves virtually deserted in their feeble state. All spring and summer, Georgia asked for aid from the neighboring colony of South Carolina and from the Continental Congress. She was answered with good wishes.

Lachlan McIntosh, Jr., commanding a company of the Georgia Battalion that was stationed at Darien on the Altamaha about 13 July, was driven to complain to his father, the colonel. The company consisted of twenty-four men, two corporals, and a sergeant. Two of the men, "By name Gray and Martin," deserted on the road to

Darien. The company did heavy guard duty, being particularly worried about a possible attack from the privateer Osborne. They expected to be relieved in a month, or two at the most. McIntosh had only five or six rounds of cartridges per man. Because all the troops lacked cartridge boxes, they were forced to carry their ammunition in their pockets—"verry unhandy," as McIntosh said. The soldiers were so ragged that they were almost naked. By 24 August six or seven were ill with a violent fever; one had died on the twenty-third.[97]

In spite of the company guarding the Altamaha, loyalist sympathizers continued to escape to East Florida. Early in August, George Aaron, Henry Laurens's overseer at New Hope plantation, defected with five of Laurens's slaves and one Negro belonging to William McIntosh, five or six good horses, and all of James Baillie's clothes. Accompanied by eight or ten militiamen, Baillie pursued Aaron, but he escaped.[98] Far less frequently a loyalist "deserter" from East Florida crossed the border into Georgia.[99]

The Georgia Council of Safety took stronger measures against loyalists who remained. On 28 May the council ordered parish committees to be diligent in collecting fines assessed against nonassociators. In his speech to the provincial congress on 5 June, President and Commander in Chief Bulloch urged that body to make "some further laws respecting these non-associates."[100] Less than a month later, the council published a long list of names of persons whose "going at large" would not be in the best interest of the province—or its new rulers. William Panton's name was on the list. He had moved to St. Augustine, and from the Floridas he began a career that dominated the southern Indian trade for the rest of his long life.[101] On 26 July, following directions by Georgia's provincial congress, the Council of Safety ordered all male inhabitants of Savannah to take the test oath; any who refused would be incarcerated.[102]

The increasing stream of refugees seeking asylum in the British Floridas created numerous problems. On 20 June, Tonyn forwarded to Whitehall a petition from twenty-one Georgia and South Carolina loyalists who had grievances against the British navy. Finding land routes under control of the rebels, the refugees had escaped in small boats—only to have their property seized by Royal Navy officers.[103] In December 1775 a parliamentary statute had named those colonies in rebellion, virtually declared their citizens outlaws, and made their shipping subject to confiscation.[104] In retaliation the Continental Congress on 23 March 1776 had authorized privateers and empowered them as well as the Continental navy to seize as prizes all British shipping. On 6 April the Congress defied the British navigation acts and opened ports under its control to any and all foreign trade.[105] Now the British naval officers were interpreting their orders as though *all* Americans were in rebellion; thus, they were seizing the vessels and property of any inhabitants of those colonies they could capture. Tonyn protested vigorously.[106]

Settlers from England, as well as refugees from other provinces, continued to come into East Florida. Tonyn required all immigrants to take the oath of allegiance; he made no exception for Thomas Nixon, the merchant, a man named Weemes, and three others who arrived in Captain Lofthouse's *Betsy*, even though they and their effects had been inspected by naval officers at Portsmouth. Weemes and three others brought orders for a ten-thousand-acre land grant, and they intended to settle on the St. Johns River. They wanted to bring provisions and their other property from rebellious colonies into East Florida, and they requested from the governor protection for vessels used for that purpose. He referred them to the royal naval officers.[107]

East Florida also faced a problem with dissidents. Tonyn called them the "inflamed faction." Four men were his personal political enemies, and he suspected their loyalty to Great Britain. William Drayton, chief justice of East Florida, was a double first cousin of William Henry Drayton, a prominent South Carolina rebel. James Penman, a planter and storekeeper, was Drayton's "particular friend and companion." Spencer Man, another storekeeper, was a notary public and clerk of court. Dr. Andrew Turnbull, secretary of the province and clerk of the East Florida council, was proprietor of the large settlement at New Smyrna. The labor force on his plantation was mainly white indentured servants, who were devoutly Catholic. These four men were the leading advocates of summoning a provincial assembly, which the governor viewed as a sure source of sedition and rebellion.[108]

Both Drayton and Turnbull were implicated in Jonathan Bryan's Indian scheme. Also, the governor and council blamed the judge for the grand jury's presentment in June 1775, which represented the lack of a provincial assembly in East Florida as a grievance and ordered the publication of the presentment in Georgia and South Carolina newspapers. Tonyn privately accused Drayton of managing packed juries and had him suspended from office on 15 February 1776, but the chief justice was determined to vindicate himself.[109]

On 27 February Andrew Turnbull presided over a meeting at Wood's Tavern, in St. Augustine, where a large group signed an address of loyalty to the king. The majority elected Turnbull to carry it to England. Tonyn was insulted because he was given merely a copy instead of the original document, and he was outraged because of the irregular procedure, which bypassed the governor in transmitting the address. The whole affair savored to him of other "spontaneous" meetings and other "addresses" and "petitions" to the king in colonies farther north.[110]

Eighty-five of Tonyn's adherents signed their own address of loyalty to the king on 11 March and, of course, transmitted it through regular channels. The governor had tried to discredit Turnbull's faction by saying that the signers of the first address included no men of property; in fact, both large and small property owners were included in each group. Possibly, the largest property owners were more heavily represented in Turnbull's group; with numerous dependents, such as freed white servants who still gravitated toward the largest landholder in their areas, these large landowners would have increased their power with the institution of representative government.

As members of government, Turnbull and Drayton should not have left the colony without leave of absence being granted by the governor. They had good reason to suspect that such leave would not be granted, so they sailed for England without requesting it. Tonyn promptly summoned the council and suspended Turnbull, too.

In September, Drayton returned to East Florida—fully vindicated by Whitehall. Germain ordered Tonyn to reinstate him in his office of chief justice without loss of salary. The secretary had not yet received Tonyn's report of the suspension of Turnbull, and he warmly recommended that Tonyn give special encouragement to the valuable settlement of New Smyrna and to its proprietor. Germain also implied that the governor had been remiss in pursuing political disputes and petty personal quarrels when unity was needed in such perilous time.[111] Tonyn hotly denied the implied accusation, and, though he had no choice but to obey a direct order, he wrote to Germain that the decision to reinstate Drayton would not have been made if the relevant East Florida council minutes had not been lost at sea. Therefore, he was sending duplicates. For a while, East Florida's internal problems and factional struggles were pushed into the background by much more urgent problems.[112]

Meanwhile, Clinton had finally decided to attack Charleston instead of Savannah. If South Carolina came under British control again, surely Georgia would fall into line; with these two provinces, both Floridas, and the Indian territory reunited to the Crown, much real estate and a strategic advantage would be regained.

But the Carolinians defeated the invasion. On 28 June they frustrated an assault on Sullivan's Island, in Charleston harbor. Thoroughly battered and chagrined, General Clinton and Admiral Sir Peter Parker withdrew to the northward to join General William Howe in the invasion of New York.

When they departed, they left some Indians as well as white loyalists in dire straits. The Cherokees had not waited to learn the outcome of the British assault on South Carolina. In July, enraged by continued white settlement beyond treaty lines, they attacked the frontiers of Georgia, the Carolinas, and Virginia. The retaliatory campaign against the Cherokees, in which some loyalists cooperated with rebels, so devastated their villages and resources that the tribe played only a small role in the war until the British secured Augusta in 1780.[113]

Raiders from Georgia became bolder and penetrated farther into East Florida; in some instances they were aided by local people. On 1 July an American lieutenant and twelve men crossed the St. Marys River near its source. They raided the plantation of John Wilkinson, a London merchant, located west of the St. Johns River. When they left, they took with them more than thirty of Wilkinson's slaves and a family from an adjoining plantation.[114]

When three armed men appeared at "Russell's plantation" on 1 July, a Mr. Ross recognized as East Florida residents George Mills and Bryan Docherty. Suspecting this to be an American party, he sent a warning to St. Augustine. A group of volunteer riflemen rushed to the threatened area, and Governor Tonyn sent a message to the Cowkeeper, who was leading a party of Indians between the St. Marys and St. Augustine, urging him to hurry his warriors to the St. Marys.[115]

The riflemen were supposed to track the rebels, and the Indians and British troops at the St. Marys were to cut off the Americans' retreat if they reached the border. A plantation agent, however, ordered the Indians to position themselves at Black Creek to guard the plantations west of the St. Johns and sent the riflemen to join the troops at St. Marys. Tonyn believed this muddle in orders permitted the raiders to escape with their booty.[116]

On 6 July the governor received another report of the raid from a man named Gray, who petitioned for a troop detachment to be stationed where it could protect the plantations under his care on the west side of the St. Johns River.[117] The East Florida council offered a £100 reward for apprehension within four months and conviction of Mills and Docherty for their part in the raid on Wilkinson's plantation, but the Georgians were far from being intimidated.[118]

The war was definitely coming home to residents near the border. After their arrival on 29 May, the British troops had established their camp on the south side of the St. Marys opposite Wright's Fort and a hospital on the north bank near the stockade. HM Schooner *St. John* was anchored in the river downstream.[119]

On 2 July, while Mills was away raiding the Wilkinson plantation, the *St. John* sent a party upriver to seize his sloop, which was rigged, manned, and armed to serve as a tender. It was brought down the next day and sent to Cumberland Island. Supplies of wood, water, and fresh beef reached the ship's company from that island.[120]

Some gentlemen from England had recently settled on Jekyll Island, and they found their situation nerve-racking. Both reports and rumors of raids circulated swiftly along the border. On 4 July the gentlemen sent a canoe to the *St. John,* and the following day Lieutenant Grant dispatched the pilot boat, manned and armed, to Jekyll.[121]

The Georgia rebels renewed their attacks on Wright's Fort.[122] The morning of 11 July was rainy and windy. When a sloop was sighted off the St. Marys bar, the *St. John* sent the pilot boat to give chase. Then the company settled down to routine. At four in the afternoon, the *St. John* heard two guns fired from Wright's Fort, the signal of an American attack. Half an hour later, the schooner sent upstream in the cutter Master Peter Bachop, Lieutenant Bucher of the Sixteenth Regiment, and six seamen armed with five muskets, two poleaxes, and two cutlasses; shortly afterward, a corporal and four privates followed in a canoe. Both parties were merely to reconnoiter; they were to gain information and, if necessary, evacuate the sick from the hospital. By the time they reached Wright's Fort, the loyalists in the stockade had repulsed the rebels.[123]

At six o'clock that evening, Wright's Fort repeated the emergency signal; about 120 Georgia horsemen and infantry were attacking the hospital. A rebel party was hidden in the marshes below Wright's landing, and, as the cutter neared the fort, opened fire. The canoe pulled away in time, but in the cutter Seaman John Snodden fell dead and Seaman Alexander Gray was wounded. The Americans captured Master Peter Bachop, Lieutenant Bucher of the Sixteenth Regiment, and Seamen John Wisdall, Christopher Howard, and William Harland. After setting the cutter on fire, the rebels stripped the dead, wounded, and captured of their personal property and confiscated everything they could carry from the hospital, including bedding and provisions. When the Georgians retreated toward Savannah, they took twenty of Wright's slaves with them.[124]

The *St. John*'s company remained under arms all night. At nine o'clock, several local residents came on board. An hour later, the corporal arrived with news of the attack on the cutter. When drums were heard at two o'clock in the morning, Grant surmised that troops were moving; he could only guess whose troops. The surgeon came on board and reported that all the hospital's sick were safe in the stockade. From him, Grant obtained a full account of the fighting.[125]

Although tension was increasing, the border area seemed calm again. On the morning of 13 July, the *St. John* sent the surgeon back to the fort to evacuate the sick and wounded. Lieutenant Grant borrowed a boat from Wright and sent it to Cumberland Island for wood and water. Two residents of Cumberland, Messrs. Martin and McCredie, reached the *St. John* in a canoe on 15 July. That afternoon, the surgeon arrived with some of the sick from the hospital. The following afternoon, the evacuation of the hospital to the *St. John* was completed. At three o'clock, the St. Augustine pilot boat arrived bringing provisions for the troops and two barrels of rum for the *St. John*. The British force settled down again to waiting and watching.[126]

When the British fleet off Sullivan's Island, at Charleston, dispersed on 10 July, HM Frigate *Sphynx*, twenty guns and 160 men, the Sloop *Raven*, fourteen guns and 125 men, and the Armed Vessel *Cherokee* were stationed off Cockspur Island, at the mouth of the Savannah River.[127] Governor Tonyn knew from experience that this force could not control the inland waterway. Vessels could traverse it from Charleston to Savannah and there transfer cargo to fast sailing ships, which could reach the sea through St. Augustine Creek. Between the middle of June and the first of August, one ship carrying a cargo of indigo worth £8,000 and three rice ships used that route; in August the rebels expected six vessels from the West Indies to slip in the same way.[128]

The East Florida governor was not entirely happy either with the land forces for defending his colony. The recent additions to the garrison were mainly foreign recruits, and by the middle of July they were in a mutinous mood. Tonyn commented that this was not unusual for new levies, but obviously East Florida did not live up to their expectations. Because of the unreliable disposition of the new contingent, two hundred fit-for-duty veterans had to be employed building the necessary works and training the recruits. Tonyn recognized the impossibility of defending his three-hundred-mile frontier without cavalry, especially against Georgia's mounted troops, and there was no cavalry in his garrison.[129] When passengers bound for London from St. Augustine on the brigantine *Perkins* were captured at sea by the American schooners *Franklin* and *Hancock*, they told the Boston Committee of Correspondence, Inspection, and Safety on 15

August that the garrison at St. Augustine consisted of 700 troops, including 150 of the Fourteenth Regiment. Although the figures were not far from accurate, if the East Florida Rangers were included, certainly not all that number were effective soldiers.[130]

In the summer of 1776, the British regular force in St. Augustine seems to have consisted of the following: the Fourteenth Regiment, two or three companies, Major Jonathan Furlong, Captain Ross, 3 lieutenants, 13 sergeants, 21 corporals, 8 drummers, and 98 privates; the Sixteenth Regiment, three companies, Captain Colin Graham, 4 other officers, and 82 men; the Sixtieth Regiment, Second Battalion, three companies, Major James Mark Prevost, Lieutenants Benjamin Wicker and John K. Muller, and 82 men; the Third Battalion, six companies, Major Van Braam, Captain George McIntosh, 1 other officer, and 112 men; the Fourth Battalion, six companies, including 12 officers (Colonel Augustine Prevost, Lieutenant Colonel Lewis V. Fuser, Major Beamsley Glazier, Captain Patrick Murray, and a Captain Wulff) and 187 men.[131]

Sometime during the summer, a troop of Georgia horsemen was stationed between the Satilla and the St. Marys to protect the large cattle herds in that region. The East Floridians' "Two Troops of Horse" drove two thousand head of cattle out of south Georgia and across the St. Marys. This herd probably was the same twelve hundred head of cattle that Tonyn claimed had been driven out of East Florida by Georgians and then recovered by his riflemen and driven back into East Florida. Thirty men from St. Augustine, probably on this same cattle-rustling expedition, actually entered the camp of the Georgia horsemen and captured six of the soldiers; thereupon, the troop of horsemen moved its camp forty miles north of the Satilla. A man named Rogers, who was caretaker of the herds belonging to a Mr. Williamson of Charleston, reported that the East Floridians had driven out of Georgia nearly four thousand head of cattle, and he charged the Scots living in south Georgia with complicity in the raids.[132]

On or about 16 July Captain Osborne's privateer *Governor Tonyn* raided the South Carolina plantation of John Berwick and stole eight slaves.[133] The Georgians, in return, maintaining that the best defense was a good offense, renewed their drive to push the Floridians below the St. Johns.

By 26 July all the British troops on the St. Marys were sick; their camp was on swampy ground. The *St. John*'s boat and the East Florida governor's sloop *Florida* went upstream to evacuate the troops, apparently to Amelia Island. About this time, the Wrights and their slaves left Wright's Fort and camped on Cumberland Island.[134]

Not even the tension caused by anticipating a sudden attack could entirely relieve the tedium for the seamen doing guard duty on the St. Marys. On 27 July the *St. John*'s crew members were following their usual routine, exercise in small arms and making musket and pistol cartridges and wads for the guns, when Captain Graham came on board to consult with Lieutenant Grant. At two o'clock in the afternoon, an American deserter named Jamieson reached the *St. John* in a canoe from "St. Julies."[135]

J. Kitching, British collector of customs at Sunbury, learned on 1 August that the Georgians were preparing an expedition in his town to attack the *St. John*, to reduce Wright's Fort on the St. Marys, and to plunder Amelia Island and the adjacent plantations. The expedition would consist of a large flatboat armed with one twelve-pounder cannon and six swivel guns; two small schooners, one with two field pieces; and about 180 men.[136]

Kitching hurried to Cockspur Island and the next day contacted Captain John Stanhope, of HM Sloop *Raven,* and told him the news. Stanhope refused to take any action. The *Raven*'s provisions were depleted; and, if HM Frigate *Sphynx* did not arrive within a few days, he would need to go in search of relief. The captain also maintained that, in any event, his orders did not include his taking action on a matter of this kind. On 4 August the disgusted Kitching boarded a schooner bound for St. Augustine; he could only hope that he would reach there in time and that Governor Tonyn would order a force to assist at St. Marys.[137]

The East Florida governor was already uneasy because of other news he had received. On 5 August he wrote to the commanding officer of the ships at Cockspur that an expedition against East Florida was being prepared in South Carolina and Georgia and that it would come via the inland waterway. The Americans were building vessels for the expedition, including rowboats designed to carry an eighteen-pounder on the bow. Four vessels were being built in Beaufort, South Carolina, two in Savannah, and several others elsewhere. The rebels were also fitting out a privateer at Sunbury and other armed vessels in various Georgia creeks. The Pensacola and Jamaica packet, Lieutenant Arthur Clarke commanding, was then at St. Augustine and had sighted American cruisers in the Florida Keys.[138]

The warnings came too late. Very early in the morning of 5 August, John Martin of Jekyll Island sighted an American schooner that was commanded by Captain Woodruff and was transporting forty men. Captain Miller's flatboat, armed with a four-pounder and six swivel guns, and another vessel carrying 220 men were coming from Sunbury. The Americans were definitely en route to capture the *St. John*, attack Wright's Fort, and seize every slave on Amelia Island. Martin wrote a hasty note to a man named Anderson, his brother-in-law, and told him to take the boat at Walsist's camp, probably on the south end of Jekyll Island; cross to the north end of Cumberland Island; walk to a plantation there; and ride a horse to the south end of the island. From there, a warning could be sent to the Wrights, Lieutenant Grant, and Mr. Egan on Amelia. Martin cautioned Anderson to stay on Cumberland and to keep out of sight.[139]

By seven o'clock that morning, Lieutenant Grant had received the warning. He promptly sent the bad news to Egan and Captain Graham, sailed the *St. John* from the St. Marys mouth down to the north point of Amelia, and cleared his ship for action. At two in the afternoon, he moved two miles farther southeast, anchoring a quarter mile from shore, and sent two sailing boats to assist Graham, who had the *Florida* and the *Pompey*, which were serving as transports. Sometime during the day, the Wrights and their slaves fled from Cumberland to Amelia Island.[140]

Stephen Egan, Lady Egmont's agent on her Amelia Island plantation and collector of customs at St. Marys, was determined to defend the estate. He had received Anderson's warning before Grant's and had sent a message to Graham. Irate because of Grant's crossing the bar, he believed the new position indicated that the lieutenant intended to abandon the planters, the troops, and the provincial vessels to capture and destruction.[141]

The Americans were expected to reach Amelia at ebb tide that evening; at eight o'clock, Grant sent a boat to watch for their approach. The enemy did not appear.[142]

On the morning of 6 August, the *St. John* anchored at a point where the north tip of Amelia was two miles west-northwest. Lieutenant Grant wrote to Graham suggesting that the *Florida* and the *Pompey* join the *St. John* and that Graham detail twenty of his soldiers to prevent boarding by the rebels; Wright's slaves could join those of Egan and camp on the north end of Amelia. Graham promised to consult the Wrights and Egan and to reply that evening. Grant also wrote for guidance to Captain Thomas Bishop, of HM Frigate *Lively*, 20 guns and 130 men, which had reached St. Augustine from New York transporting cash and supplies for the troops. At four o'clock, the pilot boat and the small sloop *Rook* returned to the *St. John* from assisting the troops in the *Pompey*. When the enemy still did not appear at ebb tide, Grant sent the pilot boat to Graham for his answer to Grant's earlier suggestions. Graham replied that he would write on the following morning.[143]

That same day, Tonyn reported to his council in St. Augustine that he had received news from St. Marys that an expedition of between 240 and 300 rebels and three vessels was at the border. The council advised him to request aid from Captain Bishop and to place the private sloop of war *Governor Tonyn*, ten guns and forty men, commanded by Captain Osborne, under Bishop's command. The armed schooner *Lady William* (Captain Gickie) was also in port. At eleven o'clock that night, the governor wrote to Bishop that he was directing both the *Governor Tonyn* and the *Lady William* to report to Bishop the following morning; he requested that all three vessels hurry to the St. Marys.[144]

At four-thirty in the morning of 7 August, the *St. John* saw off the south end of Cumberland Island several small boats towing a large, one-masted flatboat, which flew the liberty flag and carried three guns and many men. The *St. John*'s guns were loaded with round and grape shot, small arms were loaded, and hand grenades were readied. By five-thirty the boats towing the flatboat were gaining on the *St. John*. At six o'clock the flat fired three shots past the schooner; the *St. John* fired one shot in retaliation. Then the *St. John* saw a rebel schooner, a small vessel, and several boats round Cumberland. In a calm, the *St. John*'s boats towed her; she hoisted the British colors and fired one gun. At eight o'clock, she crossed the bar.

The rebel schooner, the small vessel, and the boats proceeded unopposed southward into Amelia's North River toward Egan's landing. At nine-thirty an explosion and smoke indicated that Graham had blown up the governor's sloop *Florida*. The Americans captured the schooner *Pompey*.[145]

The *St. John* remained anchored off the bar, and, when Graham's troops appeared on Amelia beach at four-thirty that afternoon, Grant sent boats to evacuate them. Instead of leaving the island, Graham chose to stay. Because he was out of provisions, the *St. John* sent him one cask of flour, one of pork, and one of rum in the sloop *Rook*. Then, at five-thirty, the *St. John* sailed for St. Augustine; she did not reach port until 16 August.[146]

On 9 August at two o'clock in the morning, Egan reached St. Augustine with his slaves and dispatches from Grant. He brought news of the withdrawal of the *St. John* and the British troops from the St. Marys. After conferring with his council, Tonyn requested Captain Bishop to keep the *Lively* in East Florida to await events and more dispatches. At the same time, the governor wrote to Colonel Augustine Prevost requesting that a force of one hundred men be stationed at the St. Johns River.[147]

On the same day, Captain Bishop wrote to the governor that Captain Osborne in the *Governor Tonyn* had met a boat from the *St. John* that morning and been informed of the British withdrawal. The *Lady William* had not been able to sail from St. Augustine. Under the circumstances, Bishop could do nothing for East Florida. He had sent Osborne to Cockspur with Tonyn's letters; he himself would sail for New York.[148]

Kitching arrived in St. Augustine on the ninth. He suggested that Tonyn send an armed vessel to Sapelo or St. Catherines Sound to cut off the rebels on their return to Savannah; no such ship was available. Although his warning had not been in time, Kitching did bring some valuable information. He described Sunbury's fortifications in detail. A loaded Bermuda brig, carrying a ten-man crew and equipped with a few swivel guns, was ready to sail. A schooner, commanded by a man named Batton (Ratoon?), had been taken into Continental service to sail for supplies, gunpowder, and ammunition, but she was not yet manned and armed. Miller's ship, a privateer, had not yet been launched; she was being guarded by fifteen or twenty men.[149]

The small British force on the border had not been able to stop the rebel invasion from Georgia. After burning Wright's Fort, the Georgians broke up most if not all the plantations between the St. Marys and the St. Johns. Egan and the Wrights took their slaves to the St. Johns. Charles Wright, who was "upwards of sixty years of age," and twenty-four of the Wright's slaves died of exposure and malnutrition.[150]

Now the St. Johns became East Florida's line of defense. Captain Graham and his troops reached that river via Sisters' Creek and Hester's Bluff on 15 August, but most of the soldiers were sick. Border defense was taken over by Captain Alexander Ross, who took post at Cowford with one hundred men from the Fourteenth and Sixteenth Regiments and the Second Battalion of the Sixtieth Regiment. On 15 August the East Florida council forbade any person to cross the St. Johns without written permission from the governor. It also ordered publication of a proclamation prohibiting all persons from keeping boats or canoes on the west side of the river and Sebastian Creek after sunset.[151]

Tonyn was unhappy; he believed that, if the British force at St. Marys had acted in concert, it might well have thwarted the rebel attack. The British contingent on the border had consisted of seventy regulars, twenty-three irregular riflemen, Egan's twelve armed slaves, Wright's fifty slaves, and three vessels and their crews. With Captain Graham's approval, the riflemen had been away from camp on an operation planned by themselves. Wright had evacuated his blacks to prevent their capture. Tonyn blamed Grant, of the *St. John,* for the loss of the *Florida* and the *Pompey.* By the middle of August, the British were virtually confined to the narrow limits between the St. Johns and the Atlantic.[152]

III

1776: Invasion and
Retreat to the Altamaha

A s CONTINENTAL COMMANDER of the Southern Department, General Charles Lee was seriously concerned about the situation on the Georgia-Florida border. President Bulloch informed the Georgia Council of Safety on 18 June 1776 that Lee wanted two of its members to confer with him in Charleston about Georgia's defense. The council decided to send Colonel Lachlan McIntosh as well as Jonathan Bryan and John Houstoun.[1]

This committee, which reported to the council on 5 July, had emphasized to Lee Georgia's value and vulnerability and had made concrete suggestions for solving her problems. It enumerated the citizens' zeal for liberty as an asset along with excellent harbors and waterways as well as ample provisions of timber, livestock, and rice and stressed the province's function as a protective barrier for South Carolina. The main concerns were raids in search of provisions and slaves by the British fleet and the East Florida garrison, possible war with "at least 15,000 Gunmen" in the Indian tribes, and a possible slave insurrection that would be instigated by the British in East Florida. The committee stated that Georgia's primary objectives were "Men, Fortifications and a good understanding with the Indians."

After pointing out that Georgia was unable to bear the expense for such operations, the committee proposed that six Continental battalions, raised elsewhere, be stationed in Georgia and that the existing four troops of horse be augmented to a regiment and put on the Continental establishment. The committee wanted Congress to appropriate funds for fortifications and guard boats that would halt communication among Georgia's enemies. Because the traditional Indian presents were not available, the committee proposed that Congress arrange for the purchase of five thousand cattle, which would be distributed instead. These would be an acceptable substitute for ammunition and clothing, and the committee pointed out that "fixing the Idea of Property" would not only be a step toward civilizing the Indians, but also would keep them peaceful for fear of reprisals.[2]

General Lee was convinced of the importance of defending Georgia, and he urged the Congress to augment the Continental establishment for that province. He considered the conquest of East Florida to be desirable; he sought permission along with a sufficient force to attempt it. Like Governor Tonyn of East Florida, the general particularly appreciated the necessity for cavalry—he wanted one thousand—in the southern district. Lee proposed that the cavalry force be established on the same basis as the Georgia troopers: privates, fifty shillings sterling per month; quartermaster, four pounds; lieutenant, six pounds; captain, ten pounds. The men would be furnished rations, but would supply their own arms, horses, and forage.[3]

Lee intended to reinforce Georgia with the equivalent of a battalion as soon as he was certain that the British fleet no longer menaced Charleston. He assured the Georgians that, if the British appeared to threaten that coast when they left Charleston, he would march to their assistance with all the force at his command.[4]

Particularly discouraging to the Georgia Whigs had been South Carolina's refusal to send any aid to her weaker neighbor when a British fleet was falsely reported to be off the Georgia coast.[5] Lee had urged the South Carolinians to move one of their provincial regiments to the southern colony; the South Carolina council demurred.[6] The general promptly ordered all the North Carolina force and Colonel Huger's Second South Carolina Regiment to march to Purrysburg, on the South Carolina side of the Savannah River, under Brigadier General Robert Howe's command.[7]

Lee also proposed that the South Carolina council send commissaries to south Georgia to purchase cattle. His purpose was twofold: to stock a magazine of supplies for Charleston at little cost and to deprive the British to the southward of a means of subsistence. He pointed out that the troops necessary to protect the commissaries could also dislodge the British from their post on the St. Marys.[8]

Then the outlook brightened for Georgia Whigs. Congress augmented the Continental establishment for Georgia.[9] Two more battalions, one of which was to consist of riflemen, were to be raised; recruiting would be permitted in Virginia and the Carolinas. Four row galleys for Georgia's defense were to be built at the expense of the United States. Two artillery companies, fifty men each including officers, would be raised to garrison the forts at Savannah and Sunbury.

A regiment of Rangers, "liable to act on horseback, or foot, as the occasion may require," was to be raised in Georgia and put on the Continental establishment. Like South Carolina's regiment of Rangers, it would consist of a lieutenant colonel commandant, a major, ten captains, twenty lieutenants, a surgeon, a paymaster, twenty sergeants, and five hundred privates. The pay would differ from that of Georgia horse troops already organized. Congress resolved:

> That the pay of the lieutenant colonel commandant of rangers, be the same as colonel of foot; the major, that of a lieutenant colonel; a captain, that of a major; and the lieutenants that of captains; and sergeants that of ensigns of foot of the continental forces: That the surgeon be allowed 33⅓ dollars per month; the pay master 26⅔ds; and the privates 12½ dollars per month, to provide themselves with horses, guns, and provisions, for themselves and horses.

Another battalion, whose enlistments were to run for the duration of the war, was authorized for Georgia on 16 September. A chaplain was to be appointed in each Continental regiment and was to receive the same pay as a surgeon. Congress appropriated $60,000 for the use of the Continental battalions in Georgia.[10]

Flagging enthusiasm was stimulated on 8 August by arrival of the news at Savannah that the United Colonies had declared their independence from Great Britain. Georgia's George Walton, Lyman Hall, and Button Gwinnett had signed the Declaration. Two days later, President Bulloch led the official celebration.[11] When the news reached St. Augustine, probably about 11 August, the citizens there enthusiastically burned effigies of John Hancock and Samuel Adams in the public square.[12]

The best news of all for the Georgians was that General Lee planned to attack East Florida. He knew he lacked sufficient strength to besiege St. Augustine; he had no artillery at all. He believed, though, that the Georgia force, plus one thousand more men, could demolish the plantations between the St. Marys and the St. Johns and thus intimidate the Creeks. Because South Carolina's First, Second, Fourth, and Fifth Regiments finally had been put on the Continental establishment as of 18 June, Lee could order a third of them to march outside the province without awaiting the approval of the South Carolina council. The Third Regiment (Rangers) was put on the Continental establishment on 24 July.[13] By 5 August Governor Tonyn had been informed that his province was to be invaded.[14]

Generals Lee and Howe and their troops started marching from Charleston toward Savannah between 31 July and 7 August. One observer in Charleston estimated that Lee had 1,500 men with him.[15]

In addition to the Virginia and North Carolina Continentals, the detachments consisted of 1 captain, 3 subalterns, 4 sergeants, and 70 rank and file from each of the First and Second South Carolina Battalions; 130 men plus their officers from the Third (Ranger) Battalion of South Carolina; and 30 men and their officers from the South Carolina Artillery. Lee reached Purrysburg by 15 August.[16]

The previous day, Captain Osborne, in the privateer *Governor Tonyn,* had sailed into Daufuskie Creek to dislodge an American party, probably a detachment from Colonel Stephen Bull's militia regiment, on Bloody Point, South Carolina, opposite Cockspur Island. Osborne fired several rounds, killing some rebels, and burned the camp and guardhouses. American musket fire wounded Osborne in both thighs.[17]

When Lee reached Savannah, he found two prisoners there: Peter Bachop, who had been captured in the attack on Wright's Fort on 11 July, and James Loftin, a lieutenant in the East Florida Rangers. Lee ordered that they be sent to Charleston and kept in irons en route, at least at night, to prevent their escape.[18]

On 19 August General Lee conferred with the Council of Safety at Savannah. Considering that the British post on the St. Marys had been destroyed and the plantations between the St. Marys and the St. Johns had been broken up, as well as his inability to besiege St. Augustine, Lee wanted to know whether or not the council still believed an invasion of East Florida was worthwhile. If so, how did it intend to transport and supply the troops?

The council ordered Jonathan Bryan and Nathan Brownson to deliver its reply to Lee. It believed that, if the rural population of East Florida were forced to seek refuge in St. Augustine, shortage of provisions would force its capitulation. The farther the Americans could drive the enemy from the border, the less chance the British would have to tamper with either slaves or Indians. One troop of horse could then adequately patrol the St. Johns. If the East Floridians were fully occupied with defense, they could not send forth privateers to raid Georgia.

The council did not believe any problems concerning supplies would be encountered north of the Altamaha, and it proposed transporting the troops and supplies beyond that river primarily by water. Boats could be procured at Savannah and Sunbury. Wagons would be useless beyond fifty miles from Savannah, but horses were readily available. It all sounded very simple.[19]

All the troops had arrived in Savannah by 18 August. Every corps, including the Georgia Battalion, paraded on 19 August. Two days later, at five-thirty in the afternoon, Colonel Peter Muhlenberg's Eighth Virginia Regiment and Captain Hardin's Company paraded in the rear of the Garden Battery. On 22 August these two corps marched to Sunbury. A captain and sixty men proceeded to Skidaway Island on 25 August.[20]

General Lee hesitated to put Colonel William Moultrie, of South Carolina, hero of the Battle of Sullivan's Island, in command of the expedition because his brother was John Moultrie, lieutenant governor of East Florida. William declared that his biggest obstacle was not his brother's position but his own lack of men and supplies. He agreed to accept the command only if he had eight hundred [more ?] men and more supplies. Lee promptly sent to Augusta for the items Moultrie demanded.[21]

The expedition was grossly underequipped. One of the worst deficiencies for marching men was shoes. The only solution available was "negro shoes" and deerskin "Monkeshins" and leggings. Moultrie claimed that the expedition even lacked a medicine chest. Wagons did become a necessity, and considerable difficulty was experienced in procuring them. Boats were more easily obtained in Savannah.[22]

Dissension plagued the expedition from its outset. By the end of August, the officers of the Georgia and South Carolina Continentals were arguing about precedence.[23] Although General Lee had learned to respect the fighting qualities of southern troops, the touchy pride and delicate sense of honor of some gentlemen exasperated him beyond bearing. In Charleston he argued with the South Carolina council about the advisability of sending military assistance to Georgia and about who would have what duty. He wanted the problem of command solved by putting all troops on the Continental establishment; there should not be any provincial troops except the local militia. In Savannah he quarreled with the civil authorities. If some Georgia gentlemen had known what he really thought about them, Lee would have been too busy with duels to bother much about the British. The Georgians had an irritating habit of proposing projects far beyond their resources. Lee said he would not be surprised "if they were to propose mounting a body of Mermaids on Alligators."[24]

Under the circumstances, Lee must have welcomed Congress's orders of 8 August recalling him, in mid-campaign, to the northern theater of operations. Exactly when the message reached him is unknown, but by 6 September he was in Charleston. From there, he proceeded to Philadelphia. Robert Howe, of North Carolina, was left in command of the various Continental troops then in Georgia.[25]

In the face of such an imminent threat, the East Floridians bestirred themselves to organize a militia force. Governor Tonyn summoned the residents to the statehouse on 20 August and appointed their officers: Lieutenant Governor John Moultrie, colonel; Robert Bisset, lieutenant colonel; and Benjamin Dodd, major. The St. Johns district would have two companies, St. Augustine four, and the Smyrna plantations one. Each of these companies would consist of a captain, one lieutenant, two sergeants, two corporals, and twenty-five privates. In addition, four companies would be composed of black enlisted men with two or three times as many white officers as the other companies. The total militia force would consist of eleven companies, including 319 [?] enlisted men.[26]

The three highest-ranking officers of the militia represented the three geographical concentrations of population in East Florida. Each was a wealthy planter. Moultrie's lands were in the vicinity of St. Augustine. Bisset's Palmarina plantation was at Mosquito Inlet. Benjamin Dodd had arrived in East Florida just recently, in the spring of 1776, and had purchased two plantations, one on the St. Marys and the other on Trout Creek, a tributary of the St. Johns. By the end of the summer, rebel raiders had destroyed all the buildings on Dodd's plantation at the St. Marys.[27]

Tonyn had assembled a large number of Seminole warriors on the west side of the St. Johns to help repel the expected invasion. When a group from Mikasuki arrived bringing word that the Creek national council did not sanction the proposed attack on the rebel whites, but instead intended to maintain the peace, all but one party of Seminoles refused to participate in the governor's plan. He immediately wrote to Stuart and Taitt to send Creek warriors to his assistance. The Seminoles would fulfill their promises to the British only if assured of the approval and support of the Creek Nation.[28]

The governor complained bitterly about his lack of naval support. Captain Bishop had made no effort to attack the Georgia vessels or to assist the British troops who were floundering southward from the St. Marys; instead, he had taken the *Lively* on to New York. He had even ordered Captain Osborne, of the privateer sloop *Governor Tonyn*, to leave the border area and carry dispatches to Cockspur. Under the circumstances, the governor felt justified in taking into provincial service on 6 September Captain John Mowbray and his sloop *Rebecca*, armed with ten guns, which he stationed on the St. Johns, as well as a scout boat with swivels. Captain Mowbray's *Rebecca* cost £200 per month for three months; she was constructed to mount fourteen guns.[29]

On 29 August an American brig, sixteen guns and one hundred men, commanded by a man named Turpin, seized a refugee ship from Cockspur, the *Clarissa*, outside the St. Augustine bar. The master and passengers had already gone ashore, but the cargo of lumber, household furniture, and slaves was still on board. Tonyn immediately asked the *St. John* and the *Rebecca* to pursue the raider. Mowbray could get only ten hands for the *Rebecca,* and the *St. John* was ten miles away in the North River having barnacles scraped from her bottom, "which was become a perfect Oyster bank."[30]

By eleven o'clock that night, the *St. John* was at St. Augustine ready to sail, but three accidents prevented her departure the next morning. At daylight, three vessels appeared outside the bar. A Virginia sloop and a schooner got among the breakers on the bar at nine o'clock, and the *St. John* sent her boat to assist them. An hour later, a sloop from St. Christopher, laden with rum, ran aground, and the *St. John* again sent help. Then Lieutenant Grant signaled the harbor launch to aid the vessels, but by that time the American raider was beyond pursuit.[31]

Governor Tonyn tried to coordinate East Florida's military and naval resources. On 5 September he laid before his council Mr. Egan's information about American intentions toward East Florida and his petition for protection of the plantations, including Lady Egmont's, on the St. Marys. Tonyn wrote that day to Colonel Prevost that establishment of a naval force on the St. Johns was absolutely essential to protect the planters there. He had added six seamen to Mowbray's nine-man crew, but fifteen men were insufficient to turn the *Rebecca* into a fighting vessel. The governor wanted the colonel to furnish one officer and thirty-five privates for the *Rebecca*. Tonyn ordered the *St. John* to proceed to the St. Johns River, and he believed, based on Lieutenant Grant's request, that she needed a force of one sergeant and twelve privates. At the same time, the governor also requested that the military force at Smyrna be increased to eighteen or twenty men.[32]

On 7 September the commanding officer of the British troops stationed at Cowford, on the St. Johns, sent an express to St. Augustine: a large American force had been seen on the north side of that river. Understandably, planters in that area were alarmed.[33] At least one party was reported to have crossed the St. Johns and destroyed some plantations to its south. The rebels robbed one "Courvozie" and his family of their possessions, including thirty slaves, and then drove them from their habitation into the woods.[34]

On 8 September Colonel Augustine Prevost, commanding officer of His Majesty's troops in East Florida, summarized the strength of the garrison in that colony. The total numbered 27 officers and 974 enlisted men; the garrison had finally reached the strength the rebels had long and prematurely attributed to it. Five companies of the Fourteenth Regiment included 8 officers, 3 staff officers, and 149 enlisted men; 21 were sick and 28 were on duty away from St. Augustine. Three companies of the Sixteenth Regiment consisted of 2 officers and 108 men; 13 were sick and 81 were on duty away from St. Augustine. Parts of the Second, Third, and Fourth Battalions of the Sixtieth Regiment were stationed in St. Augustine. Three companies of the Second Battalion numbered 2 officers, 1 surgeon's mate, and 87 men; 13 were sick and 20 away on duty. Six companies of the Third Battalion included 2 officers and 306 men; 39 were sick and 34 were away on duty. Six companies of the Fourth Battalion consisted of 7 officers and 315 men; 20 were sick and 30 away on duty. The Royal Artillery contingent included 1 officer and 9 men; 1 was sick and 2 were assigned elsewhere. One captain, one lieutenant, and three ensigns were not included because they were on duty away from East Florida.[35]

The effective strength of the force was not so impressive as it first appeared. Those incapacitated by illness numbered 112. One hundred men in each of the Third and Fourth Battalions of the Sixtieth Regiment were Germans, who were not available for immediate duty because they did not understand English. Some of the veteran troops had to be employed in repairing fortifications instead of in training these new recruits. And the rebels had captured 1 sergeant and 5 privates of the 100-man force that was stationed on the St. Johns.[36]

A band of Indian warriors had forced the marauders from Georgia back from Cowford and pursued them until they crossed the St. Marys. The Indians desisted from a surprise night attack only because they saw men dressed in conspicuous British regimentals seated at the camp fires; the rebels had confiscated their prisoners' coats.[37]

Colonel Prevost and Lieutenant Colonel Fuser, influenced by the "inflamed faction," suggested to Tonyn that East Florida join Georgia in a treaty of neutrality. The governor rejected their proposal.[38]

In the midst of his difficulties, Governor Tonyn was beset with unexpected problems on East Florida's southern frontier. On 8 July he had informed his council of a letter from Captain Robert Bisset, of Palmerina plantation, that reported excesses committed by an Indian party at Mosquito Inlet. When the rebel privateer had made her daring raid just off the St. Augustine bar, Tonyn had written to the planters in that region to warn them and to inquire about their plans for defense if Turpin sailed there.[39]

The answers the governor received on 1 September were not encouraging. Both Robert Bisset, at Palmerina, and Andrew Turnbull, the doctor's nephew and manager in his absence,[40] believed the slaves could be safely hidden by sending them down the Indian River or into the woods. Bisset did not believe a serious danger existed of the American vessel attacking the settlements at Mosquito because the bar there was so shallow. He pointed out, however, that, if a sea attack occurred, the plantation hands could not obstruct it because they were unarmed. Both Bisset and Turnbull agreed that discontented whites at New Smyrna would probably join any rebel force and plunder the plantations. Thus, the unruly colonists at Smyrna plantation required a military guard when troops were needed elsewhere.[41]

Another of Tonyn's problems arrived from a totally unexpected direction: Virginia. When Captain Bishop, in the *Lively*, had arrived in New York with Tonyn's dispatches on 22 August, he had been ordered to sail to the southward again immediately. He was to call at the Virginia capes to deliver instructions to HM Sloop *Otter;* go to Cape Fear, North Carolina, to order the ships there to New York; then to sail on to St. Augustine with stores and provisions. When the British fleet at the Virginia capes dispersed on 5 August, HM Sloop *Otter*, fourteen guns and 125 men under Captain Matthew Squire, convoyed about thirty merchant vessels, fifteen bound for Bermuda and the West Indies and fifteen for St. Augustine. The escort and the merchantmen separated during passage. On 10 September the *Otter*, her tender (the sloop *Fincastle*), and two merchantmen belonging to an individual named Mitchell arrived at St. Augustine. The merchantmen ran aground on the bar; although one was unscathed, the other suffered heavy damage to both ship and cargo. The *Otter* carried 28 prisoners who were being sent to St. Augustine by John Murray, Lord Dunmore, royal governor of Virginia.[42]

The day after the *Otter* arrived, Tonyn requested Captain Squire to take that ship and her tender, commanded by Lieutenant John Wright, to join the *St. John* and the *Rebecca* in defending the St. Johns River. Captain Squire refused. On 18 September Tonyn requested him to send one of the king's ships to ascertain that no rebel troops were between the St. Johns and the St. Marys. That would allow the *St. John* and the *Rebecca* to leave their stations and proceed to the St. Marys, while armed boats patrolled between the two rivers.[43]

Captain Squire proposed a compromise. He agreed to keep the *Otter* off the St. Augustine bar until another king's ship arrived, and he would order the tender, *Fincastle*, to the St. Johns—if the governor would make other arrangements for his prisoners while his ship was in port. East Florida's council immediately agreed to put some of them in Fort St. Marks. Colonel Prevost transferred twelve of his men to the *Fincastle*.[44]

As the Georgians had foreseen, St. Augustine was becoming seriously overcrowded with poeple who needed food and lacked weapons. The council ordered spies to be sent out and directed that all provisions and arms in the vicinity be secured in St. Augustine.[45]

The British ships stationed at Cockspur were also having difficulties feeding themselves and their charges. On 11 September a letter reached Tonyn from Captain Stanhope, of HM Sloop *Raven*, off the St. Augustine bar, requesting provisions for those vessels. The council agreed to supply the captain with rum, rice, and flour.[46]

By the end of the month, the ships at Cockspur were in a desperate predicament; they were nearly out of provisions. At the Savannah River on 29 September, following orders from Captain James Reid, of HM Frigate *Sphynx*, the pilot's schooner embarked forty blacks with one week's provisions and sailed for St. Augustine. Two days later at ten o'clock in the morning, after destroying nearly everything of value on Tybee Island, the *Sphynx* and the Armed Vessel *Cherokee*, under Lieutenant John Ferguson, set sail. At three-thirty that afternoon, they met HM Frigate *Lively*, commanded by Captain Bishop; they joined the *Lively*, which was bound for St. Augustine.[47]

Tonyn was also having serious problems maintaining communications. The *Duke of Cumberland* packet arrived at St. Augustine with the mail from England early in the morning of 3 September, and she sailed for New York on 9 September. Three weeks later, badly storm-damaged, she returned to St. Augustine and sank in the bay. The mail was saved and sent by the *Lively*. The crew and her guns were transferred to the *Betsy*, under Captain Lofthouse, which commuted regularly to England carrying East Florida produce and passengers.[48]

By the middle of September, the rebel invasion of East Florida had collapsed. When General Lee left Savannah, he ordered some of the Virginia and North Carolina Continentals to follow him northward. The men who remained encamped along Georgia's southern rivers sickened quickly; at Sunbury, fourteen or fifteen deaths occurred every day. Medical supplies were nonexistent. Because Georgia was unable to supply either men to replace the departed Continentals or more food and medicine, South Carolina recalled her troops. There was nothing left for the Georgians to do but to hurry home before the Floridians discovered their weakness. The main body of the American force had advanced only as far as Sunbury; the rebel's advance guard had reached the St. Johns River, but had not even threatened St. Augustine.[49]

Battle casualties of the campaign were few indeed, if any, inasmuch as the main bodies of the opposing forces remained about 150 miles apart, but property damage was enormous. One report claimed that every settlement in East Florida north of the St. Johns was demolished. The rebels destroyed both buildings and provisions, and the British accused them of killing women and children.[50] Troops were not particular about whose property they utilized, and it was probably at this time that American soldiers destroyed the fences on Lachlan McIntosh's plantation and consumed his crops. Sunbury itself suffered considerable damage. Tonyn reported that the East Florida planters were in great distress, which he could do little to alleviate, but some of them did remain on their plantations.[51] Undoubtedly the settlements close to the Georgia border suffered more than those on the St. Johns.

General Lee reached Philadelphia and reported to Congress concerning his southern campaign on 7 October. He attributed the failure of the East Florida expedition to the necessity of diverting troops to the Cherokee frontier and to sickness among the Americans. Tonyn concurred. Lee also gave some credit to the St. Augustine garrison, grossly overestimating its strength.[52]

Congress's orders for Lee to join the northern army necessitated changes in command of the Southern Department. A month after Lee's departure, General John Armstrong, also of Virginia, was on his way northward too. Brigadier General James Moore, of North Carolina, was appointed to head the Southern Department, and Brigadier General Robert Howe, another North Carolinian, commanded South Carolina and Georgia. Howe made his headquarters in Charleston.[53]

During his brief stay in the south, General Lee had formed an accurate view of Georgia's importance to the Continental cause and of her special weaknesses. He also had formulated some sound plans to make her less vulnerable. One of his strongest suggestions was that the citizens restrain the loyalists who were living between the Altamaha and the St. Marys; they most certainly had carried information about Georgia's plans, strengths, and weaknesses to the British in East Florida. At least one parish, St. Andrew's, complied.[54]

In August 1776 Georgia's military strength consisted of Colonel McIntosh's battalion, one company of independent artillery (23 privates and 3 officers), and about 2,500 militia. The militia, many of whom held loyalist sympathies, was unreliable. Lee, who respected

McIntosh's abilities, considered his battalion to be one of the finest on the continent; nevertheless, he doubted the zeal of these men to act harshly against their own friends and relations who had chosen the other side. Therefore, Lee proposed to send the Georgia Battalion into one of the Carolinas and to replace it with troops from South Carolina. Moving the battalion out of Georgia would provide the additional benefit of giving it an opportunity to fill its ranks; there simply were not enough men in Georgia to do so. Lee believed that armed galleys were essential for controlling the waterways and maintaining communication among the strategically sited forts he wanted established on the southern rivers. If Georgians refused to abandon their settlements south of the Altamaha, and Lee was virtually certain they would refuse, horse patrols would be essential in that area.[55]

Both Lee and General Robert Howe urged Georgia and South Carolina to evacuate their sea islands, all of which were indefensible. Simply removing the livestock would dissuade the British from occupying or even raiding them. The Georgia Council of Safety ordered the owners of cattle on the islands to remove them to the mainland by 1 November; any cattle still on the islands after that date would be destroyed without compensation to the owners.[56]

The Georgians tried to strengthen their military situation. On 16 September the Continental Congress elected Lachlan McIntosh as brigadier general of the Georgia Brigade. Once again, Button Gwinnett was disappointed in his hopes for command.[57] To compete with recruiters in Virginia and North Carolina, which were offering bounties of $70 and 100 acres of land to men who would enlist for the duration of the war, Georgia since 12 July had offered a bounty of 100 acres to those who enlisted for three years or the duration. The regular U.S. bounty for men enlisting for the duration of the war, unless released sooner by Congress, was as follows: for noncommissioned officers and privates, twenty dollars; colonels, 500 acres of land; lieutenant colonels, 450; majors, 400; captains, 300; lieutenants, 200; ensigns, 150; and noncommissioned officers and privates, 100. On 21 November the Continental Congress directed that enlistments should be either for three years or for the duration of the war, preferably the latter.[58]

North Carolina and Virginia did not object to Georgia's recruiting within their borders so long as no attempt was made to enlist soldiers or marines already in state or Continental service or indentured servants and apprentices without the approval of their masters. When Lee authorized Georgia to recruit among Virginia and North Carolina Continental troops serving in South Carolina and Georgia, however, North Carolina became so incensed that she recalled all her Continental troops.[59]

The out-of-state recruiters were not as successful as they had hoped, but Georgia's critical problem was shortage of supplies, especially munitions. In November the Continental Congress recommended to the states that they establish magazines of provisions and munitions for the use of both militia and regulars. Georgia experienced no particular difficulty in establishing food magazines on the Ogeechee and Altamaha rivers, at Augusta, and between Savannah and Augusta about forty miles above Savannah. Rice and salt meat were still easily available.[60]

Munitions and medicine, on the other hand, were in very short supply. Georgia had leased and bought vessels and sent them out with local produce to exchange for arms and ammunition. In midsummer Archibald Bulloch, Jonathan Cochrane, and John Giradeau were named as a secret committee to procure military supplies. Like other rebellious colonies, Georgia tried to obtain munitions from the Caribbean islands. Captains Oliver Bowen and Job Pray not only carried on the munitions trade, but also attempted to recruit seamen in the French and Danish West Indies. While he was still in Georgia, General Lee had written on behalf of the struggling colonies to the French governor of Cape Francois requesting small arms, powder, field pieces, woolen and linen textiles, and drugs, especially "bark." Malaria and typhus were taking a heavy toll among the southern troops. On 20 September Congress ordered the Medical Committee to forward three hundred pounds of Peruvian bark to the Southern Department. Congress agreed on 1 November to supply Georgia with $3,000 and some military stores.[61]

By the end of 1776, General McIntosh could report 538 men, including deserters, in the First Georgia Battalion of Foot, who were scattered about the state on guard duty. The Second and Third Battalions still existed only on paper. All their officers except Colonels Samuel Elbert and James Screven were in Virginia and North Carolina. To compete with South Carolina recruiters, Georgia had increased the bounty by ten dollars (and two dollars to the officers for each man), but no recruits had been gained from Virginia and North Carolina. Three hundred undisciplined men were in the four corps that composed the horse regiment; they were patrolling the frontiers. The two companies of artillery had about forty men.[62]

Tonyn believed that the military force in Georgia consisted of only 274 infantrymen, 100 South Carolina Rangers, and 50 Georgia Rangers. The First Battalion was stationed at Savannah, and the Rangers garrisoned Fort Barrington, from which a fifty-man detachment, relieved at two-week intervals, manned an unfortified camp thirty miles south of the Altamaha on the Satilla River.[63]

Georgia possessed virtually no ordnance or military stores. No barracks existed nor plans for building any. Clothes, blankets, and tents were not provided for the troops. There was no stock of medicines nor public hospitals. Stocks of wood, salt, and forage did not exist. There were no entrenching tools available; the quartermaster could not supply a single ax. What truly horrified General Howe was that no apparent steps were being taken to remedy Georgia's obvious military deficiencies.[64]

At the end of 1776, Tonyn reported that Georgia and South Carolina were being well supplied by vessels arriving from France and its islands and even from the British West Indies.[65] For once, the governor was misinformed.

As early as 2 May, the Georgia Council of Safety had appointed Daniel Roberts and William Le Conte to determine what dry goods were actually in Savannah. On the same day, Archibald Bulloch issued a proclamation that made it illegal to charge exorbitant prices for scarce items; outlawry would be the fate of those who depreciated the currency. Some Savannah merchants were selling goods at exorbitant prices, and the names of those who persisted would be published.[66] The prices of necessities were so high that Bulloch considered them to be extortionate. By July a sheet of paper was a "very scarce article." On 25 July the Council of Safety ordered that all goods "secreted on Savannah River, or in any stores whatever" be taken into the possession of the state. A week later, the council ordered all merchants who were still storing any goods to sell them to the public. One merchant, Thomas Reid, was specifically ordered to bring his goods to Savannah to sell them to the inhabitants.[67]

The council finally appointed a committee to consider ways to supply the province with dry goods; the only possibility seemed to be trade with the French West Indies.[68] One merchant declared that the small cargoes brought into Savannah sold so profitably that the lucky importers could buy up large quantities of Georgia products for export. He feared to acquire a large stock for export, however, until he had some assurance of the availability of shipping—and vessels, equipment, and masters were unobtainable.[69] The state was so poor it could not supply the men of the Georgia Battalion with even minimum clothes and equipment; their condition was pathetic.

Civilian property, even in noncombat areas, had suffered severely.

The house of James Hume, attorney general of Georgia and Governor Wright's nephew, had been occupied by troops during the "battle of the rice boats" or the "first siege of Savannah" (January–March 1776). The soldiers had ripped down all the wallpaper and burned the chimney piece in the best room.[70]

Georgians had good reason to fear a retaliatory attack upon their province, now termed a "state," and by late September the East Florida Rangers and their Indian auxiliaries were well enough organized to begin recovering control for the British of the border area as far north as the Satilla River. The first reports to reach General McIntosh indicated that Langley Bryan and a person named Proctor were leading "200 Indians" and McGirth, M[oore?], Sampson, and Williams were leading parties of horsemen into south Georgia. The general ordered Captain William McIntosh and his troop of horse to cross the Altamaha and give chase. He also ordered "Capt Colson" [of the Eighth (Rifle) Company of Georgia's First Battalion?] and eighteen men as well as Cornet Valentine Beard and eleven of the North Carolina Light Horse to march immediately to Fort Barrington, on the Altamaha. Both the militia and the Continentals in the area were too sick to be of much use.[71]

Then came reports that British vessels were in the area again. The *Rebecca* and the *St. John* guarded the St. Johns River. Captain Osborne's privateer captured a rebel brig in the St. Marys River.[72]

On 6 October the Council of Safety received information that the East Floridians planned to attack Georgia by land and by sea. McIntosh hurriedly recalled the detachment of the Georgia Battalion on duty at Beaufort, South Carolina, and disposed his feeble force to meet the emergency. The troops on St. Catherines Island were dispersed. A corporal and six men were stationed at St. Catherines and Sapelo islands; between thirty and fifty men at Sutherland's Bluff, "near Mr. Gwinnetts Plan[ta]tion, up Sapelo River"; and the rest moved to Sunbury. One or two armed boats were stationed between Broughton Island and Frederica. Only two hundred men in the Georgia Battalion were well enough to be considered fit for duty.[73]

The British naval force effectively guarded East Florida's waterways. When Lieutenant John Ferguson, of HM Armed Vessel *Cherokee*, anchored at St. Augustine on the morning of 5 October, he found a surprising number of British naval vessels: HM Frigate *Lively;* two sloops, *Raven* and *Otter;* two schooners, *St. Lawrence* and *St. John;* the snow *Elizabeth*—and Master Figtree's transport.[74]

From St. Augustine, the ships sailed northward up the Atlantic coast. At six o'clock in the evening of 11 October, the frigate *Sphynx* resumed her station at the mouth of the Savannah River. She had obtained enough provisions at St. Augustine to last for three weeks at full allowance.[75] That same day, HM Schooner *Hinchinbrook,* under Lieutenant Alexander Ellis, left St. Augustine to patrol the coast up to the St. Marys.[76] The next day, HM Frigate *Lively* departed St. Augustine so hurriedly—to escape being caught on a lee shore in a gale—that she left Captain Bishop and his boat's crew behind. On 15 October the *Lively* joined the *Sphynx* on the Savannah station. Both these vessels, with the *Raven* and *Cherokee,* were to join Admiral Howe's fleet at New York (the *Sphynx* reached New York on 26 October, and the *Lively* was there by 5 November), but the *Otter,* the *Hinchinbrook,* and the *St. John* were stationed at St. Augustine for the defense of East Florida. Both the *Otter* and the *St. John* were unfit for sea service,[77] but on 15 October, off St. Augustine's bar, the *Raven,* commanded by Captain Stanhope, captured the rebel brig *Friendship,* whose master was Ephraim Townshend, that had set out from Savannah laden with four hundred barrels of rice. It was soon discovered, however, that this cargo belonged to Roger Kelsal, a refugee from Georgia, whom Governor Tonyn had licensed to bring provisions for the use of the garrison.[78]

The South Carolina navy came to Georgia's assistance. Early in November, the South Carolina Navy Board ordered the Brigantine of War *Defence,* under Captain Thomas Pickering, to cruise southward and make a special effort to take the privateer *Governor Tonyn.* Then the board sent the *Defence* and the *Comet,* commanded by Captain Edward Allen, with a lieutenant, sergeant, two corporals, and twenty-eight privates of the Second South Carolina Regiment to attempt to capture the *Otter,* the *Hinchinbrook,* and two ships loading in the St. Marys under their protection. Off St. Augustine on 14 November, the *Cherokee* captured the *Esperance,* bound from Philadelphia to Charleston laden with flour and lumber—and flying French colors. On 1 December the *Hinchinbrook* captured another *Friendship* bound from Boston to Charleston with a cargo of "Onions, Cranberries, Tobacco, Apples, Cabbages and other Articles." Captain Allen's *Comet* returned to Charleston on 5 December with two prizes: a Jamaican sloop, the *George;* and a schooner, the *Maria,* owned in Liverpool and bound from St. Vincent.[79]

The Georgians' alarm had increased late in October when the Rangers and Indians appeared on the Satilla River. William McIntosh, now a lieutenant colonel, attacked one party; killed an Indian; took two prisoners, named Williams and Bell; and reported that Williams had expected assistance from John Proctor and fifty Indians.

General McIntosh suddenly decided that the Altamaha River, not the St. Johns, was Georgia's "natural" frontier.[80]

McIntosh intended to adopt the traditional defense system of galleys stationed at the rivers' mouths and patrolling the adjacent waterways and of forts at strategic sites with horse patrols between them. A strong garrison should be at the first landing on the Altamaha. The headquarters of the Horse would be Fort Barrington, on the Altamaha, which was to be rehabilitated immediately, and a subaltern's command should scout southward from there to the Satilla. A stockade was to be built at Beard's Bluff, on the Altamaha and one troop stationed there to patrol the area to the head of Canoochee River. A stockade should be built on the Canoochee, and that troop of horsemen could patrol to Marbury's fort, on the Ogeechee River. From the stockade to be built there, another troop could patrol to Hovendon's Fort, on the Broad River. The men at that fort could scout to the Savannah River. Each troop was to move to a different post every month. Thus, all the settlements would be secure, communications maintained, and each post could aid the others if the need arose. No person was to leave the state without a pass from the president, and anyone who entered it was to be sent under guard to headquarters.[81]

Before McIntosh's plans could be carried out, he received news that on 27 October the Floridians and their Indian allies had destroyed "Old Williams" (William Williams) plantation, just south of the Altamaha, then crossed that river and attacked newly occupied Fort Barrington, which was defended by only eighteen men. The same express brought an unconfirmed report that a plantation just ten miles from St. John's meetinghouse, at Midway, had been robbed on 28 October. Another party burned several small settlements near Beard's Bluff. At about the same time, Captain Oldis and sixty men, all former Georgians, in an armed schooner attacked "Frederica Island" (St. Simons?), burned the settlement of one Whittier and killed several people there, then sent boats upriver to raid the settlement of a man named Carney on the Turtle River. St. Andrew's and St. John's parishes panicked. The militia could not be of service; all its members were occupied with moving their families out of the area.[82]

The only Indian party operating with or for the British at that time that can be positively identified is the one that appeared at Fort Barrington. A Chiaha chief and eighteen or nineteen kinsmen, ostensibly on a hunting trip, attacked forty Georgia Rangers and killed four and wounded two.[83]

The raiders retired safely into East Florida. The South Carolina Horse that came to Georgia's assistance arrived too late for action. Major Marbury, ordered to bring his troop of Light Horse southward from Ogeechee, did not arrive at all.[84] Insubordination in the Georgia Light Horse seriously hampered its effectiveness. On 13 December McIntosh ordered the arrest for disobedience of Captains McFarland, Benjamin Few, and Cade as well as Lieutenant William Bugg.[85]

McIntosh was convinced that Georgia would be the target of a major British offensive in the winter of 1776–77.[86] Tonyn agreed that it should be. Although the governor knew he lacked sufficient strength to garrison any territory he might conquer, by early October he believed the East Florida forces could stage a major assault on the southern and western frontiers of Georgia if the British attacked the coast.[87] By the end of November, Tonyn's reports had convinced Sir William Howe of the possibility of a major British success in the south. The general recommended to Whitehall that the British attack Georgia and South Carolina in the *next* campaign during the winter of 1777–78.[88]

Governor Tonyn spent Christmas Day writing dispatches. One of his most serious difficulties was lack of money. Parliament had made no financial provisions for military and naval operations in East Florida, and the governor's contingent fund was grossly inadequate for wartime needs. Naval patrols were essential to protect the plantations and provision supplies; because insufficient king's ships were available, the governor had no choice but to employ private vessels in the provincial service. He also had to pay the charges for transporting regular troops by water; for the Rangers; for rice and presents for Indians; and for subsistence for prisoners, refugees, and slaves.

As instructed by William Knox, secretary of the Lords Commissioners of the Treasury, on 11 November Tonyn had drawn on Treasury Agent Anthony Wheelock and applied the amount to the contingent fund debts. On 25 December the governor informed Admiral Richard Lord Howe that he was drawing on him for £1,200 to continue adequate naval service. Tonyn informed General William Howe on the same day that he was drawing on him for £1,500 for military expenditures. The governor himself had paid the bills up to that point; he wanted to be reimbursed.[89]

Repairs of the fortifications and defense lines at St. Augustine were completed by winter. Most of the labor had been provided by the king's troops. The north curtain, (Spanish *Cubo* line) running west from Fort St. Marks to Sebastian Creek, had been completed before

11 April. Then Colonel Prevost wanted a guardhouse at the gate of the northern barrier (Spanish *Hornabeque* line). This work was supervised by Lieutenant Colonel Lewis V. Fuser. The repairs were relatively inexpensive, and the improved fortifications assured both the security and the morale of East Floridians.[90]

Organization of the militia improved morale, too. Not only was an additional force now available to help repel invasion, but also the militia would overawe the blacks.[91]

Tonyn was worried about the low inventory of his province's ordnance stores. He had requisitioned forty-five gun carriages in both 1774 and 1775, but by 31 October 1776, when he submitted still another requisition, he had received only seven for twelve pounders. A letter from General Amherst had led him to believe that Captain Figtree's transport would bring the carriages, but it brought only goods for Messrs. Drayton and Penman. Tonyn considered the possibility that Figtree might have broken a contract. The governor faced another problem: what to do with unserviceable stores on hand. Should they be turned to the Tower of London or disposed of locally?[92]

Increasing numbers of Georgians were becoming refugees, northward or southward according to their political persuasions. The Council of Safety's order to evacuate the sea islands immediately hurried them on. Tonyn's orders to the Rangers and Indians to attack American parties and drive cattle into East Florida were a further spur to those near the border.[93]

The fleeing loyalists brought some problems to Tonyn. He complained repeatedly about royal naval officers seizing loyalist refugee vessels for condemnation in admiralty court. The governor stated that many refugees left their slaves and other property behind for fear of having it confiscated. He believed that more loyalists would come into East Florida if it were not for their fear of the risk of losing their property to the British navy as well as to the Americans.[94]

On 1 November forty-nine refugees in East Florida petitioned the king. They had expected to receive grants of land when they arrived in this British haven, but they found all the east coast land already granted. The petitioners sought a new Indian cession, approximately the lands involved in Bryan's scheme, to settle on. In support of the petition, Tonyn enclosed a list of 112 persons who had been granted 1,438,000 acres. Sixteen grantees had established settlements on 222,000 acres; all the other grantees were absentee landowners who had not developed their property.[95]

Refugees and prisoners increased the governor's financial problems. Some of the loyalists needed financial assistance. Black run-
aways from Georgia, who had fled to the Royal Navy for protection,
had been dumped in St. Augustine. And some of Lord Dunmore's
twenty-eight prisoners were still in St. Augustine.[96] Twelve of the
prisoners who had arrived in the *Otter* had been transferred to Fort
St. Marks; Tonyn reported that Captain Squire had released the
others at the St. Marys. The governor paroled Lieutenant Colonel
Anthony Lawson in the hope that the Americans would release
Captain John Batut, of the Fourteenth Regiment, or a British lieutenant colonel. Tonyn believed that William Westcott, master of a brigantine, had been mistaken for an American, and he released him after
obtaining a written promise that he would not sue Lord Dunmore for
false imprisonment. The governor reported that the other prisoners
had applied to Chief Justice William Drayton for writs of habeas
corpus, but the cases would not be decided until 6 January 1777.[97]

Fortunately for the British, the East Florida economy was flourishing. The small naval force in the province had secured the inland
waterway and the plantations. Unmolested planters had raised
enough provisions for the following year and were exporting lumber
and naval stores to the West Indies. Indigo production had declined,
but some Floridians, including Governor Tonyn, regarded the production of lumber and naval stores as more profitable and more
dependable. Shipping was extensive; as many as forty or fifty vessels
sometimes crowded St. Augustine's harbor. Tonyn deprecated the
dangers of the bar; he claimed that wrecks had been caused mainly by
the negligence or malice of the pilots. In December he retained the
Rebecca for another month because the warships had gone to convoy
the vessel taking East Florida's produce to England. The only problem about provisions pertained to those imported from England; by
Christmas Day a supply ship was three months overdue. When less
than a month's supply of salt beef remained, Tonyn suggested the use
of fresh beef for both the soldiers and the seamen. He sent a sloop to
New York with rice and oranges for the troops there and hoped that
General Howe would send him salt provisions in return.[98]

One of Governor Tonyn's heaviest expenses was for the East
Florida Rangers. The regular troops were unqualified for scouting,
foraging for cattle, or repelling raiders unless they were accompanied
by Rangers and Indians. Expenses for these special forces were not
included in the contingent and Indian fund accounts. One of the
most important of their duties was to provide fresh beef for the

garrison, a chore they performed well by confiscating cattle in south Georgia and driving the herds across the St. Johns. Tonyn believed that regular troops could not do this work; they would obtain more than was necessary, and storage was impossible. Raids on the frontier plantations kept the rebels in constant state of alarm and thus deterred another thrust toward St. Augustine. Tonyn pointed out that use of such marauders effectively employed some daring men, who otherwise would join the rebels in Georgia.[99] As both the governor and the rebels had long since realized, to maintain the British post at St. Augustine was not sufficient. Unless the hinterland and its plantations were protected, lack of provisions could force the garrison to capitulate.[100] Securing the border was the primary function of the East Florida Rangers and their Indian auxiliaries.

The British had spent large sums of money to keep the southern Indians friendly and willing to assist them. These expenses included supplying presents and trade goods as well as maintaining frequent communication with the major tribes, especially the Creeks. Superintendent Stuart's deputy was supposed to draw on Stuart in Pensacola, who could draw on the commander in chief in North America. Because regular communication was lacking between the Floridas and the commander in chief, this financial procedure simply did not work. During most of 1776 no system existed for anyone in the Southern Department to be reimbursed. Tonyn had instructed his private agent to pay for some items; he could only hope that the Treasury would reimburse him. In August, Stuart had requested permission to draw directly on the Lords Commissioners of the Treasury. Permission was granted as far as the ordinary expenses of the Southern Indian Department were concerned, but, for extraordinary expenses, Stuart was required to send detailed justification with his bills and, if merchandise was involved, to send an estimate to London and then await the Treasury's decision.[101]

Governor Tonyn gave the Cherokee attacks and the threat of Creek attacks much credit for forcing the Georgians to abandon their invasion of East Florida.[102] The fact remained that, though small parties of warriors (almost entirely Seminoles) did aid the British or carry on feuds with the Georgians, the Creeks had not swept out along the frontiers to devasta.e the rebels. David Taitt was correct in saying that the Creeks would prefer "to enjoy the advantages of a neutrality by being paid from both parties." Stuart was equally correct in stating that the Indians were determined to defend Pensacola and St. Augustine because those were the only centers left for British trade goods.[103]

On the other hand, the Creek-Choctaw War dragged on, and the Creeks had no intention of fighting a full-scale war with the Georgians on their eastern front until they had attained peace on the western. Also, reports and refugees from the devastated Cherokee country reached the Creeks in late summer. The rebels threatened similar vengeance on the Creeks if they stirred. Some staunch loyalists, believing that the British had instigated the Cherokee assault on the frontier, joined the rebels. The Indians were disillusioned about British promises of support and success.[104]

The Creeks did not launch an attack against the rebels because the Indian superintendent did not tell them to do so. They had been receiving conflicting reports and advice from the whites for more than a year; convinced that Stuart was the king's true representative to the Indians, most of them decided to be guided by him in critical matters regarding relations with the whites. Stuart had not countermanded his orders from Cape Fear; he definitely had not given orders for a large-scale Creek offensive. Samuel Thomas, the Lower Creek interpreter, wrote to the superintendent that he and Taitt were having great difficulty in keeping the Creeks "off the Settlements"; in spite of their efforts, two unauthorized parties were out in September. When Governor Tonyn requested warriors to aid East Florida, Creek headmen observed that the superintendent's and the governor's "talks" conflicted. They decided to defer a decision until after they had conferred with Stuart in Pensacola.[105]

The British achieved three significant successes in Indian diplomacy during the autumn. The first came when they gained a prominent defector from the rebels. David Holmes was George Galphin's nephew and had handled his business affairs in the Creek Nation since the older man had been preoccupied with political matters; in September Holmes joined the British Southern Indian Department. Galphin wrote to the Creeks that Holmes would supply their needs from Pensacola until trade goods were available again at Augusta; the implication was that Holmes was still working for him. The rebel commissioner may have been trying to mislead the Creeks, or Holmes may have been trying to play a double game at that time. Most likely, Holmes tried to convince the rebels that he was still working in their interest until he was secure with the British. Whatever the case, he performed valuable service for the latter and his subsequent actions proved his loyalty. Before the end of September, he was delivering "talks" from Stuart to the Lower Creeks.[106] Some Georgians suspected that Galphin was being employed by the British government. Holmes's defection may have been the cause of this rumor.[107]

The British made one of their wisest diplomatic moves when they appointed Alexander McGillivray as assistant commissary to the Creeks. Although he was only about nineteen years old and was no warrior, he possessed important family connections and extraordinary administrative ability.[108]

By far the most spectacular British diplomatic success was the conclusion of a peace treaty between the Choctaws and Upper Creeks. The two tribes themselves had been suggesting a peace for quite some time, but the British had refused to countenance such a treaty for fear that the Indians, if not diverted, would become more troublesome to British settlements on the frontier. After war between the whites broke out, peace and unity between the tribes were essential so that the Indians could concentrate their forces against the rebels. Accordingly, the headmen from the Choctaw and Upper Creek tribes met Stuart at Pensacola from 16 to 26 October and concluded their treaty with much pageantry, which obviously pleased observers. Now that their western front was secure, the Upper Creek chiefs immediately agreed to send assistance to the hard-pressed Cherokees.[109]

At the end of October, about five hundred Lower Creeks also reached Pensacola to confer with the superintendent. He reported that he intended to try to persuade them to go to Governor Tonyn's assistance but that Galphin's energetic efforts made his success doubtful. However, Stuart did succeed, and the Lower Creek warriors were preparing to travel to St. Augustine when a false report arrived that a large body of armed rebels was marching against the Creek towns. They immediately looked to their own defense. On this occasion, the Creeks put in motion nearly three thousand warriors.[110]

At this time, Stuart flatly stated that he had always been averse to an indiscriminate attack by the Indians. He realized, however, that now he must employ them to assist the Cherokees and the East Floridians or lose their allegiance altogether.[111]

Late in August, the Georgians had sent Thomas Gray, who was working for the American side again, and three other men to propagandize among the Lower Creeks (specifically, to deliver "talks" from General Lee and Jonathan Bryan) and to bring five or six headmen to Savannah or Charleston for a conference. As soon as news reached the Lower Creeks that the rebel emissaries were on the way, parties from Chiaha and Cussita set out to apprehend them.[112] By 22 October, Gray had fled for his life from the Creeks.[113]

Nevertheless, a dissident faction was still active among the Creeks, particularly at Cussita. In October, while most of the tribe were focusing their attention on Pensacola, twelve emissaries of that faction from Cussita went to Silver Bluff, South Carolina, to confer with George Galphin. The Whigs had received Indian presents and trade goods from the French West Indies. They distributed them liberally among their few callers, promised steady trade in the future, and declared that the British would have no trade goods because all their shipping had been intercepted by the rebels. When Brown and Taitt proposed to lead two hundred Upper Creeks to relieve the Cherokees by attacking the Ceded Lands, the dissidents, led by Handsome Fellow, of the Okfuskees, threatened retribution against Pensacola.[114]

Some Cussitas further hampered Brown by stealing all his pack-horses and two saddle horses, worth 120 guineas each, and taking the animals into the Cherokee lands. Persuaded by the messages from Lee and Bryan, the Cussita dissidents had intended to visit Savannah; they desisted only when the Creeks received the false report that the "Virginians" were on the way to devastate their nation.[115]

Again the Creeks hesitated, their councils divided. It was at this time that a Chiaha party attacked Georgia Rangers at Fort Barrington; bragging about this exploit encouraged others. The rebel attack failed to materialize. Trade goods from Georgia Whigs were equally ephemeral. But so were the redcoats in the backcountry that the British had promised would march with the Indians.[116]

By 8 November Brown and William McIntosh, Stuart's deputy to the Lower Creeks, had persuaded thirty Hitchitas, under Hycut, to travel to St. Augustine to assist the British. The warriors planned to set out in about twenty days, and Brown hoped to follow with others when they returned from Pensacola. Brown warned Tonyn that the Indians should be employed soon because they were at fighting pitch.[117]

William Panton had ordered Indian supplies from England, but they had not arrived by 27 November. Governor Tonyn wanted Panton to send a vessel directly; the brig *Appalachicola* was ready to sail. The governor requested Lord George Germain to allow Davis, Strahan, and Company, Panton's suppliers in England, to export ammunition to East Florida for the Indian trade. The trading houses had no stock left, and Tonyn had lent them ammunition from the king's magazine.[118] As Panton had observed earlier in the year, it was foolish to send trade goods into the Indian country unless adequate ammunition was sent also; only by obtaining deerskins, for which ammunition was necessary, could the Indians pay their debts to the traders. When goods for the Indian trade reached Pensacola in British transports, the Creeks had a clearer view of their national interest.[119]

The Creeks became more active in December. One party presented Georgia scalps and prisoners to Stuart at Pensacola.[120] Tallachie, a principal chief of the Lower Creeks, assured Tonyn that all the Indians would support the British.[121] By 12 December General McIntosh had been informed that a large party of horsemen and Indians were either at or near the St. Marys preparatory to raiding south Georgia. Having conferred with General Howe, he ordered William McIntosh to take post at Fort Barrington, rechristened Fort Howe, and to direct the building of stockades at Beard's Bluff, the Satilla, and the St. Marys. The Georgia and South Carolina Light Horse "at the Southward" were to remain there until further notice, and all troops on the southern frontier were to be kept ready for action at a moment's notice.[122]

Even before McIntosh could send these orders, he learned from the commanding officer at Fort Howe that Indians had murdered one Hover of the Light Horse "upon or near the Road within Six Miles of ———." The general immediately sent his brother William and Major Leonard Marbury to Fort Howe with a good supply of ammunition and orders to hunt the killers "for ever." Then, McIntosh himself went to the Altamaha to direct operations. About seventy recruits, newly arrived from Virginia, were welcome indeed.[123]

By 19 December Lieutenant Colonel William McIntosh had captured three Indians who were accused by another of murdering Hover. The general had the prisoners put in irons in Savannah and immediately sent the accuser and Tom Gray back into the Creek country with yet another "talk."[124]

Stung by charges from one Wells that the Light Horse was negligent, McIntosh urged his subordinates to hurry the establishment of their posts and patrols. No more than one or two men in a company were to be on furlough at the same time—and then not for more than one or two weeks. Civilians-turned-Rangers did not readily take to discipline.[125]

Those Georgians who were still civilians found it easier to criticize than to support their army. The Georgia convention voted only £50 for rebuilding Fort Howe (Barrington) and nothing at all for the fort General McIntosh wanted at the first landing along the Altamaha. He was irate at such penury; he judged these to be the two most important posts in Georgia. He hoped to do something about these fortifications with fatigue duty, but so few men were available that little could be accomplished that way. The general ordered a detachment of infantry to the first landing on the north side of the Altamaha; a sergeant and twelve men of this party were to be stationed on the Sapelo River. The others were to keep a constant guard at the landing as well as the mouth of Cathead Creek and to build barracks for themselves at the "old Fort" [site of Fort King George below Darien?].[126]

Poor discipline could defeat McIntosh's careful plans and explicit orders. About Christmas a guard boat left her station so that the men could refresh themselves—"pleasuring and idling their Time," the general called it—on Sapelo Island. A St. Augustine schooner commanded by a man named Kebly (Kelly?) and pretending to be a trading vessel from Cape Francois—the men including a Sergeant Montgomery who had deserted from Captain Woodruff's company—arrived in time not only to plunder the island of slaves from "Mrs. Mackay's Plantation" and other property but also to capture Captain Woodruff and three of his men. The row galley's crew captured seven of the plunderers. The British immediately offered to exchange Woodruff for Lieutenant Beecher [of the Sixteenth Regiment, who had been captured 11 July at Wright's Fort?]. Although appreciating that the British had paroled Colonel Lawson, McIntosh questioned the prudence of releasing Beecher, who had been in captivity long enough to have acquired considerable knowledge of the rebels' plans and weaknesses. Also, the general was not certain whether prisoner exchange was the responsibility of the military or civil sphere in Georgia's new government. So he left the decision to General Howe.[127]

A party from East Florida, perhaps led by Lieutenant (or Captain) York of the Rangers, raided a cattle herd in Georgia; and a detachment of the Georgia Horse, commanded by Captain Charles S. Middleton, crossed the St. Marys in pursuit. Not finding their quarry, the rebels relieved Cornelius Rains of two Negroes and three horses and one McGuire of a Negro boy, a mare, a saddle and saddlebags, his rifle, and "some of his cloth." The Georgians returned to camp at the Satilla River, where some of the plunder was sold, then marched to a new site at a bluff on that river to begin building a stockade fort.[128]

At the very end of 1776, Indians threatened the interior posts. Lieutenant Jeremiah Bugg commanded twenty-seven men of a company of Light Horse that was stationed at Beard's Bluff, about forty miles above Fort Howe on the Altamaha. Late in the evening of 27 December, Indians wounded a man outside the "fort or Loghouse." Early the next morning, the lieutenant led twelve men to reconnoiter. When they were about four hundred yards from the fort, the Indians fired, killing four men and Bugg's horse. The white survivors fled to the fort without firing a shot and left their officer to help himself as best he could. The Indians scalped the dead and stuck an arrow into each. When the lieutenant returned to the fort, he found his men so panic-stricken that they refused to venture forth again or even to try to maintain their post. As soon as they had buried their dead, they all deserted. Lieutenant Bugg could prevail on only one man to go with him to Fort Howe to report the attack.[129]

IV

1777: *More Invasions and Retreats*

THE INVASION of her "natural" frontier and the assault on the garrison at Beard's Bluff created shock waves in Georgia. Not knowing that Beard's Bluff was abandoned and believing that Lieutenant Colonel McIntosh and Major Marbury with most of the Light Horse were ranging south of the St. Marys, General McIntosh ordered Lieutenant Ignatius Few with eleven horsemen and a detachment of the First Battalion, consisting of a captain, two subalterns, and forty men, to march to the fort's relief. Captains McFarling (McFarland?) and Cade were still under arrest for disobedience, but they volunteered to accompany the relief expedition; their offer was accepted. Captain (Chesley?) Bostick and forty men would follow the first party.[1]

When General McIntosh learned that his brother and Marbury had merely chased a few East Floridians back across the border and recaptured some cattle and that they were back at the Georgia Rangers' headquarters at Fort Howe, he changed his orders. The detachment of the First Battalion was to return to Savannah; Captain Bostick and his forty men were to reoccupy Beard's Bluff; William McIntosh, who complained of poor health, would be relieved at Fort Howe by Colonel Samuel Elbert, and that garrison would be strengthened by the addition of twelve men from the First Battalion.[2] Georgia's Council of Safety wanted a third of the militia mobilized to scout by rotation on the frontier.[3]

The general soon learned that the men who had abandoned the fort at Beard's Bluff had received no pay during the entire seven months they had been enlisted. All the Georgia Light Horse suffered similarly. Money with which to pay them was simply not available. McIntosh did succeed in obtaining £150 to pacify the men in Captain Jeremiah Bugg's company so they would return to duty. Major Marbury, however, promised his men at Fort Howe that he would go to headquarters and not return until he had obtained some money for them; his stay in Savannah was prolonged. Marbury was so indignant that he resigned his commission on 24 January. Captains Myddleton and Bugg resigned on 15 February.[4]

Officers for the Light Horse were so scarce that McIntosh had no alternative but to release Captains McFarland, Cade, and Few and permit them to resume their commands. Upon receiving their promise to behave better in the future, the general ordered them to duty at Fort Howe under Colonel Elbert.[5]

Georgia's Light Horse numbered between three and four hundred men who were detached at frontier outposts. The inflation rate in Georgia had made their pay (twelve dollars a month) inadequate for buying good horses and provisions.[6] Not surprisingly, under the circumstances, the regiment remained deplorably undisciplined. McIntosh finally suggested an exchange, the South Carolina Horse to serve in Georgia and the Georgia Horse in South Carolina, until discipline improved. McIntosh told Howe, "I would have no objection to such an Exchange somewhere myself for a while, if it could be done with [pro]priety."[7]

The Continental troops in Georgia were so poorly supplied that they were often driven to steal civilian property. General McIntosh fumed,[8] but he could do nothing to alleviate the situation.

Beard's Bluff Fort remained unoccupied for more than a week, and several Indian parties reportedly entered the province through the gap left between the Altamaha and the Ogeechee. McIntosh was indignant. He hoped the Rangers could catch the raiders; instead, they could not prevent more entering. In retaliation, the Georgians seized six innocent Creeks who were in the settlements and put them in irons.[9] Captain Richard Winn's company of Carolina Horse was at or near Fort Howe, on the Altamaha, by 10 January 1777.[10] When there had been no further alarms by 24 January, McIntosh ordered the company to return home. He countermanded his order the following day, however, when he received a report of a new threat.[11]

Mowbray's privateer, from St. Augustine, was reported to be in the Sapelo River. McIntosh ordered all available forces to concentrate in that area, but the *Rebecca* succeeded in capturing a Georgia galley. After removing her arms, swivels, and a nine-pounder cannon, Mowbray destroyed the rebel vessel.[12]

Georgia's two remaining row galleys decided to attack the *Otter,* then in the St. Marys River. Captain Mowbray was warned of the plan, and the *Rebecca* joined the *Otter* the day before the galleys appeared in the St. Marys. Finding the British ships prepared for an attack, the rebel vessels withdrew to Sunbury.[13]

At the same time, Georgia faced a different kind of assault from the northward. Late in 1776 the South Carolina assembly, deciding it would be desirable to annex her southern neighbor, commissioned William Henry Drayton and John Smith to propose this matter of "common welfare" to the convention of Georgia. The two commissioners appeared before it on 23 January. Drayton discoursed at length upon the benefits Georgia would gain from the proposed merger.[14]

The Georgia convention was not impressed. The following day, it rejected the proposed merger as contrary to an article in the proposed Confederation of the United States. Button Gwinnett led the opposition to union. Drayton claimed that everyone in public office sided with Gwinnett, but that some "gentlemen of fortune" not in office, a few members of the convention, and "an officer of high military rank" agreed that his arguments were better than Gwinnett's.[15] No one who knew Drayton could have expected him to let the matter rest there.

South Carolina's commissioners had hardly reached home before Georgia's first state constitution was adopted on 5 February 1777 by the constitutional convention in Savannah. Besides being an interesting political document and a model of brevity, it throws considerable light on affairs in Georgia during the winter of 1776–77. Not surprisingly, in the 33d article, the head of the civil establishment, the governor—who was to be elected by popular representatives—was named as captain-general and commander in chief over all military (including militia) and naval forces "belonging to this state." Eight counties replaced parishes as units of government; the new counties generally followed the old parish lines, but they sometimes included more than one parish. The 35th article specified that each county containing at least 250 men liable to bear arms should form one militia battalion. When population increase warranted it, additional battalions could be formed by a legislative bill. Counties containing less than 250 males capable of bearing arms should form independent companies of militia.[16]

Apportionment of representatives based on the number of electors in each county gives demographic information. Electors were required to be white, male, at least twenty-one years old, residents of Georgia for at least six months, and either possessed of property valued at "ten pounds" and taxable in Georgia or "being of any mechanic trade." The two port towns, Savannah and Sunbury, were allowed, respectively, four and two representatives "to represent their trade." Most counties, even the new Ceded Lands of Wilkes County, were authorized ten representatives; Liberty County, which included the three parishes of St. John, St. Andrew, and St. James, fourteen. The two counties south of the Altamaha, Glynn (St. David and St. Patrick) and Camden (St. Thomas and St. Mary), were allotted only one representative each. These two and any counties subsequently formed would have their representation increased according to population growth: ten electors, one representative; one hundred electors, ten representatives. The lands south of the Altamaha had become so depopulated that the 6th article directed freeholders in Glynn and Camden counties (encompassing four parishes), "who are in a state of alarm," to choose their representatives in any other county until the two counties again possessed enough residents to qualify them for more representatives.[17]

Lyman Hall, of St. John's Parish, part of the area named Liberty County in the new constitution, corroborated the desolation between the Altamaha and the St. Marys. He estimated that Georgians had lost to the British between three thousand and six thousand head of cattle, and he flatly stated that the settlements had been demolished "in all the southern part of this State."[18]

The constitution described an extraordinarily democratic system that did not please everyone and contributed to the polarization of factions in Georgia. Lachlan McIntosh, a leader of the conservative group, complained that the new constitution contained many provisions he was "not very fond [?] of."[19] The most serious and most often repeated criticism was that increasing the representation and lowering the qualifications for both electors and representatives allowed irresponsible and avaricious individuals and groups to gain political power.[20]

Nor did harmony prevail within East Florida. Divided command and blurred lines of authority certainly were not new problems for the British Empire. In a frontier province overcrowded with conflicting personalities, however, the power struggle nearly stalemated the war effort. The main contenders were Colonel Augustine Prevost, Governor Patrick Tonyn, and Indian Superintendent John Stuart.

Despite repeated directives from Whitehall, civil and military leaders had quarreled frequently about control of troops in North America. According to the British government, the commander in chief exercised supreme authority over all the troops in all the provinces, and the brigadiers in the northern and southern districts ranked directly beneath him. In the absence of the commander in chief and brigadiers, the governor in council controlled troops within his province and was authorized to give orders to the commanding officer on the scene.[21] At the beginning of the Revolution, the secretary of state reiterated that "the orders of the Commander in Chief of His Majesty's Forces in North America, and under him of the Major Generals and Brigadier Generals, shall be supreme in all Cases relative to the operations of the said Troops, and be obeyed accordingly."[22] The squabbles continued.

Governor Tonyn quarreled bitterly with Colonel Augustine Prevost, the commander in East Florida and ranking British officer in the south. The governor had considerable military experience himself, and he took seriously that part of his commission which named him as captain-general and commander in chief (as well as civil governor) in the province. The two men differed completely on policy; Prevost wanted to stay on the defensive, and Tonyn urged offensive action.[23]

They also disagreed on the control and use of Brown's East Florida Rangers. Governor James Grant, when he had urged that a troop of Rangers for East Florida be established, had insisted that they be under the governor's command and independent of other troops.[24] The Rangers operating in East Florida during the Indian scare of 1774 seemed to have been unauthorized by Whitehall and were paid out of the Indian fund, which was directly under the governor's control.[25] Governor Tonyn had created the East Florida Rangers in June 1776, and he expected them to take orders from him. Because Brown held his commission from the governor, whose ideas of how to fight the war were in tune with his own, and his men were paid from the governor's funds, the East Florida Rangers obeyed the East Florida governor.

The Rangers had agreed to serve as East Florida provincials for three years or the duration of the war.[26] They were organized into four troops, each company supposedly having one captain, one lieutenant, two sergeants, two corporals, and twenty-five privates. The men and noncommissioned officers were uniformed in hunting shirts and breeches and armed with rifles.[27]

Germain complained that "neither Pay Bills nor Muster Rolls" of the East Florida Rangers had been received, and Brown countered that no muster master was in Florida.[28] A tentative list of officers and their ranks in January and February of 1777 has been compiled from several sources: Lieutenant Colonel Thomas Brown; Captains James Moore, John York (adjutant), Samson Williams (quartermaster), Euan McLaurin (commissary and paymaster); Lieutenants (Robert?) Philips, Hall (or Holt?), Jefferson, and Jeffres. The last two names may actually belong to just one man. Dr. John Mackie was the Rangers' surgeon.[29]

Another potential military leader was Superintendent John Stuart. The Indian superintendents were in an anomalous position. Although they reported directly to the commander in chief, they were not military officers. Early in 1769 Wills Hill, the Earl of Hillsborough, secretary of state for the colonies, had issued warrants that made the superintendents ex-officio members of the provincial councils in their district, but they were not part of the civil establishment of any colony.[30] Stuart could command several thousand warriors and backwoodsmen for the British, but his own status and exactly who his immediate superior would be were unclear. In August 1776 he had proposed embodying the four hundred "good" white men among the Indians in his district to serve with them in war. Two factors delayed what would not have been a "hasty" decision under any circumstances: Stuart's reluctance to engage the Indians in actual warfare and the extraordinary difficulty of communicating with Pensacola from other mainland colonies. Consequently, the East Florida governor managed "his" Indians as he saw fit with little interference from the superintendent in Pensacola.[31] In January, General William Howe, British commander in chief, ordered Stuart to organize and arm loyalist refugees in the Indian towns and to use them and the Indians in defending the Floridas.[32]

By early 1777, Governor Tonyn faced a severe food shortage. The East Florida economy was booming, the planters were engaging in the West Indian lumber trade, and the country people possessed adequate food supplies. Provision ships for the garrison were long overdue, however, and St. Augustine's population was swollen by distressed refugees, Indian auxiliaries, and Rangers—all of whom consumed enormous quantities of food. On 3 February the military stores contained only 221 barrels of flour, 8 barrels of good pork, and 6 tierces of rice. St. Augustine faced famine.[33]

In such dire straits, Tonyn decided that a cattle-hunting expedition must push beyond the rebel lines in Georgia; all the livestock in the lands between the American and British forces had been consumed or driven out of the area. The governor applied to Colonel Prevost for a detachment of troops to support the Rangers and Indians on the expedition. Prevost found one excuse after another to refuse to cooperate.[34]

Of all these excuses, only one was reasonable: the regular force under his command was unfit to leave the shelter of the town. The Fourteenth Regiment contained only thirty-five men who were fit for duty. Many men in the Sixtieth Regiment were too sick to be considered fit for service. The new recruits were undisciplined, partially because so many of their officers were inexperienced. Both the Sixteenth and the Sixtieth Regiments were unsuitably clothed, and all the regular soldiers were inadequately provided with shoes.[35]

Most of the colonel's problems were beyond the governor's power to alleviate. One, however, was clearly the result of lack of cooperation on the local scene. As Tonyn acidly remarked, it was unfortunate that Prevost had not informed him that the men needed shoes; a vessel in the harbor was loaded with leather for export, and local shoemakers could have made adequate shoes for the troops.[36]

Tonyn appreciated the risk involved in sending the Rangers and Indians unsupported by regulars into the Georgia lines. Chief Perryman and twenty-five of his warriors were with the Rangers at the St. Marys, and they were eager for action. The venerable Cowkeeper and a band of his warriors were between the St. Johns and St. Marys. Twenty-five Hitchita warriors were at St. Augustine and ready to join the expedition. Thus, only about two hundred men, red and white, were immediately available.[37]

The governor decided that the risk was preferable to certain starvation. After reminding Colonel Prevost that the Indian auxiliaries were under his command and that General Howe had approved sending them into enemy territory, the governor ordered the Indians and the Rangers to move northward.[38] To maintain control of any territory conquered, however, commitment of the regulars would be essential.[39]

By the end of January, the garrison was feeling the pinch of short rations, and Prevost agreed to send a small group of regulars on the cattle-hunting expedition.[40] Lieutenant Colonel Lewis Fuser would command the expedition, and both the Rangers and the Indians were strictly enjoined to obey any orders they received from the regular officers.[41]

On this expedition, there was no quarrel about command or about regular troops having to obey provincial officers' orders. In 1757, early in the French and Indian War, Whitehall had handed down a regulation that ranked provincial officers immediately below British officers of the same rank.[42] Both Fuser and Brown were lieutenant colonels; thus, according to the long-established rule, Fuser, who held a regular army commission, automatically outranked Brown, who possessed a provincial commission.

The British expeditionary force rivaled in strength the entire regular military establishment of Georgia at the time. Including officers and men, it was composed of 49 from Captain Patrick Murray's Light Company of the Fourth Battalion of the Sixtieth

Regiment; 18 grenadiers of the Second Battalion of the Sixtieth Regiment; 54 in a detachment, probably from the Third Battalion of the Sixtieth Regiment, that was commanded by Captain McIntosh; 17 Light Infantry of the Fourteenth and Sixteenth Regiments; plus Lieutenant Colonel Fuser and one Doctor Williams—a total of 162 regulars. Twenty-two Rangers from St. Augustine and two Indian interpreters, John Hambly and John Proctor, went along.[43] At the St. Marys, the British fortified a Captain Taylor's house while the Indians completed their prebattle purification rites. Captain McIntosh's detachment remained at this new "fort,"[44] probably the one later known as Fort Tonyn, but the addition of about seventy-five Indians brought the total British force up to more than two hundred men and officers. Some Rangers already at the St. Marys must also have joined the expedition. General McIntosh reported to General George Washington that Brown commanded 120 horsemen and about 60 Indians.[45]

Brown led his Rangers and Indians northward and headed for the Georgia rebels' southernmost post, the new stockade fort on the Satilla River. This fort, named for General McIntosh, was on rising ground eighty yards from the river's north bank. A hundred feet square, it had a bastion in each corner and a blockhouse in the center. Early on the morning of 17 February, twenty Rangers and fifty Indians attacked. The seventy-man garrison (most from the South Carolina Horse and the others from Georgia's First Battalion), under the command of Captain Richard Winn of the Third Regiment of South Carolina Horse, sought refuge inside the fort. A seven-hour battle followed. By nightfall one American had been killed and three wounded. The only British casualty was one Indian, who had been wounded in the neck. The headmen whom Brown praised particularly were Perryman, Philetougi, and Cowkeeper.

Winn's express requesting assistance reached Fort Howe about daylight the next day, but the forty-man garrison there could send no help. They did not inform Winn of that fact. Relief forces ordered by General McIntosh did not arrive before the fort's defenders had exhausted their ammunition and provisions. One relief force—reported by Captain Murray to be three hundred men—was within four miles of the fort but halted and encamped when fired upon by four Rangers. Colonel Fuser and 150 regulars arrived from their camp twenty miles away in time for the fort's formal surrender on 18 February.[46]

According to the terms of capitulation, the rebels would be marched to Fort Howe and remain on parole, not taking up arms again until exchanged. Lieutenants John Milton and William Caldwell would go as hostages to St. Augustine until the exchanges were made. Captain Winn refused to surrender until Fuser agreed to guarantee that he would be responsible for the conduct of the Rangers and Indians and that a company of British regulars would escort the rebel prisoners to the Altamaha opposite Fort Howe. The Americans encamped under guard that night about two miles from their surrendered post. Their guards gradually drifted away in small parties back to the British camp, and by ten o'clock the Americans, unarmed except for the officers' side arms, were left alone. Suspecting treachery, Winn led his men through woods and swamps to Fort Howe, which they reached about ten o'clock the next day.[47]

Captain Murray later stated that he and twenty of his Light Infantry escorted the fort's garrison to the relief force that was camped at a nearby swamp and the Americans, then numbering nearly four hundred men, retreated to Fort Barrington and spread exaggerated and terrifying reports of the strength of the British party on the Satilla.[48] The Whig version was widely circulated and accepted for two centuries, but no documentary evidence substantiates it. The sole reason for doubting the accuracy of Murray's account is that Georgia probably could not have assembled such a large relief force and marched it to the Satilla that quickly.

Brown reported to Tonyn that Fuser had been insufferably rude, even insulting, to the Indians, the Rangers, and the "Greens." As far as the Indians were concerned, he feared they would become disaffected by such treatment unless the governor could mollify their outrage. Brown had experienced difficulty in persuading the Rangers to proceed with the planned cattle hunt for the benefit of the regulars.[49]

The British forces burned Fort McIntosh the day after they captured it;[50] then they moved on toward their next objective, Fort Howe (formerly Barrington) on the Altamaha River, commanded now by Brown's old enemy, Captain Chesley Bostick. McIntosh concentrated all available forces, including a new galley, to reinforce Fort Howe and the next post up to the Altamaha, Beard's Bluff, and to prevent the British crossing the Altamaha. The state militia was called out to relieve the Continental troops, who were moved to the southward.[51] Because no recruits for the Second Battalion had arrived yet, McIntosh had only the remains of the First Battalion and the Light Horse with which to block the invasion. He succeeded in halting the British advance at the Altamaha line with the loss of only twelve of his own men; he himself was wounded.[52]

Faced with opposition, Colonel Fuser turned around and went back to St. Augustine. The Indians had taken all the rebels' horses from Fort McIntosh, and the Rangers collected two thousand head of cattle before they retreated. Also, the Rangers had found a store of thirty tierces of rice on the Satilla that was "liberated" by the British regulars and the boats sent from Captain Squire's *Otter*.[53]

The Georgians had been so desperate that they had again sought help from South Carolina, which responded immediately by sending 107 men of the Second Regiment, detachments of the Fifth Regiment and Fourth Artillery, and "four guns, two schooners, a sloop and storeship, with four weeks provisions for 600 men." The South Carolina forces, under the command of Colonel Isaac Motte and Lieutenant Colonel Francis Marion, left Savannah to return to Charleston on 18 or 19 March.[54]

Because of the emergency, Georgia's new constitution did not go into effect immediately. Realizing that the council might not be able to assemble and act quickly enough under the circumstances, the Council of Safety instead gave entire executive power—creating a virtual dictatorship—to President Archibald Bulloch for one month from 22 February. Shortly thereafter, Bulloch died under mysterious circumstances. Button Gwinnett, leader of Georgia's radical Whigs, was elected immediately to succeed him as president of the Council of Safety and commander in chief of the state's armed forces.[55]

General Robert Howe was alarmed by the British invasion of south Georgia and came to Savannah early in March to inspect the state's military forces. He was not favorably impressed. Not only were there still many loyalists in the state, especially in the backcountry, but also the entire Georgia regiment of Light House was in a mutinous mood. The militia was undependable at best. That left available for duty only the First Georgia Battalion, consisting of approximately four hundred men, many of whose terms of enlistments were expiring. By 16 March the First Regiment totaled merely two hundred men; therefore, General Howe kept two hundred of Colonel Thomas Sumter's Third Regiment of South Carolina Horse in Georgia.[56]

The governor of East Florida made the most detailed, and probably the most realistic, estimate of the military force within Georgia in the spring of 1777: three galleys (one of which was not yet manned), two sloops, 150 new recruits who had recently arrived from Virginia and were posted at Savannah, 200 men of the Georgia Battalion who were stationed in different parts of the state, 160 Carolinians at Fort Barrington (Howe), 15 men "at Mr. Grahams" on Tybee Island, and 10 men at Salters Island.[57]

Gwinnett described Georgia's naval force as follows:

> one fourteen Gun sloop, one Ten gun sloop, one Eight gun ditto, one Galley with an eighteen Pounder and Swivels, another with two Twelve Pounders and Swivels, and another with two eighteen Pounders, two nines and four Sixes hearing the Randolph Frigate and the Hornet Sloop were at Charlestown, I have communicated by designs to them requesting their Assistance if consistent with their duty and orders.[58]

By April, in addition to her coastal trade with Charleston and Philadelphia, Georgia had established a small commerce with the French and Dutch West Indies as well as New Providence, in the Bahamas. This trade was principally in produce and dry goods, however.[59] The situation regarding military supplies had apparently not improved since the preceding autumn.

When President Gwinnett and the Council of Safety proposed to invade East Florida and conquer St. Augustine with this slender force, General Howe was aghast. On the other hand, the Georgians expected assistance from the Continental force under his command. But the general declined to commit his troops to what he viewed as a foolhardy undertaking. He did order one battalion to Sunbury to relieve the Georgians garrisoning that post, and Colonel Sumter with his Regiment of South Carolina Horse took post at Fort Howe to patrol the southern frontier. Then the general gathered up his Continentals and went back to South Carolina. He was convinced that the Georgians lacked sufficient men, supplies, knowledge, and unity to be successful.[60]

Howe believed that a force of seven or eight thousand men was needed merely to defend the border. Instead of being augmented, the Continental forces in the south had been considerably weakened when Congress, on 5 February 1777, ordered the North Carolina Continentals under General James Moore northward to reinforce General Washington. Georgia's delegates in Congress, particularly George Walton, complained about the British invasion across the southern frontier, but Washington advised Howe that he would need to make the decision about undertaking a retaliatory expedition. Like his counterpart in East Florida, Howe decided to remain on the defensive.[61]

Undaunted, President Gwinnett proceeded to act vigorously against his enemies within and without the state. About the middle of March, he ordered the arrest of George McIntosh, General Lachlan McIntosh's brother and a member of the Council of Safety. George

McIntosh had opposed Gwinnett's election as president, but the arrest came about because the Continental Congress had recommended it after considering an intercepted letter of Governor Tonyn, which stated that George McIntosh was a British sympathizer. Because the charge was treason, Gwinnett refused to allow bail.[62]

General McIntosh did not appreciate having his brother languishing in irons in the common jail. As early as the preceding December, the general had written to George Walton that attacks had been made on the character of his brother William that were really aimed at himself. McIntosh believed it unnecessary to name to Walton "the *person* or his *Motives* [who] is at the Bottom of the whole . . . I fear it may be productive of some Injury to the state."[63] It was.

Gwinnett proceeded with his plans to invade East Florida without consulting General McIntosh. Nevertheless, the general ordered his subordinates to cooperate with the president if their assistance was requested.[64] Not until 25 March did McIntosh receive Gwinnett's request for aid from the Continentals. The general believed that the request came then only because the militia had failed to volunteer in sufficient numbers for the expedition.[65]

McIntosh dutifully prepared to march into East Florida, though he agreed with Howe that the rebels' available force was too small to accomplish much. Few of the Light Horse could be spared from their frontier guard duty. Most of the men in the First Battalion had enlisted for twelve months; when their terms expired, they were not eager to reenlist. By March the regiment numbered only about two hundred men. The Second Regiment had been recruiting in Virginia, and about 250 of these men arrived in Georgia just before the expedition set off.[66]

The rebel army had reached Sunbury by the middle of April. Here the soldiers rested, ate up supplies, and sickened, while their leaders argued until the end of the month. McIntosh and Gwinnett each insisted that he should be the supreme commander of the expedition. Finally, the Council of Safety advised both men to return to Savannah and leave the command to the ranking Continental officer, Colonel Samuel Elbert, of the Second Georgia Battalion.[67]

As usual, Governor Tonyn was well informed about what was happening in Georgia. Captain Brown, of His Majesty's Fourteenth Regiment, who had been sent to Georgia to exchange prisoners, reported that the rebels were assembling a larger army than had been expected. They also possessed a "considerable" number of large-caliber cannon, sixteen transports for military stores and provisions, and three row galleys that mounted from eight to ten guns each. Two sloops, fourteen guns each, had been purchased at Santa Crus (St. Croix) or Curacao and were expected daily. Gwinnett insisted that the number of British prisoners in Georgia was insufficient to make the exchange agreed to in the terms of the capitulation of Fort McIntosh.[68]

By this time, Prevost had received specific orders from British General William Howe, who had suffered reverses in the north and could spare no troops for a southern campaign, to remain on the defensive. These orders suited Prevost perfectly, but he and Governor Tonyn disagreed about how best to conduct the defense. Prevost was determined to protect Fort St. Marks and the walled city of St. Augustine; he was willing to sacrifice the outposts and the hinterland if necessary.[69]

The governor did not propose to abandon one inch of East Florida. He believed that if the outlying plantations were destroyed, the citadel would be forced to capitulate. Tonyn concentrated on harrying the Georgians and thwarting their invasion force. He requested the Cherokees to attack the South Carolina frontier, the Upper Creeks to raid north Georgia, and the Lower Creeks and Seminoles to annoy the advancing rebel army. Brown's Rangers and all available naval force were stationed on the St. Marys.[70]

Tonyn was not really optimistic about obtaining aid from the Indians; he reported that Superintendent Stuart was still averse to such action by warriors. The fact was that, as late as the middle of May, Taitt, in Upper Creek country, had just heard rumors of the invasion. He did not believe them because he had not received any such report from the governor. Tonyn's request for assistance did not reach Taitt until 22 May.[71] Nevertheless, by 2 April Indians had killed more than three men at (Elijah?) Clark's fort.[72] Such isolated incidents kept the Georgia frontier in a state of constant alarm.

East Florida still endured a shortage of some supplies. Late in March, a transport reached St. Augustine with about forty recruits for the two new battalions of the Sixtieth Regiment and six months' provisions for the garrison. More recruits were on the way. Musket balls were in such short supply, however, that target practice for the recruits was impossible. Rebel ships captured two vessels that were loaded with provisions for general sale in East Florida, and Tonyn begged Howe to send flour "for the public."[73]

Howe ordered Prevost to send him the detachment of the Fourteenth Regiment at St. Augustine.[74] Because of the arrival in March of the new recruits for the Sixtieth Regiment, the garrison's numerical strength declined by only about 120 men. The Fourteenth were acclimated veterans, however, and the Sixtieth's recruits were raw.

Probably about this time, Augustine Prevost wrote a letter to his French father-in-law, George Grand, complaining about the dismal conditions in St. Augustine. Grand was a merchant in Amsterdam, "a Confidential Correspondent of M. de Vergennes," and had performed at least two important services for the American rebels.[75] The records do not reveal any further questionable correspondence between the two men.

East Florida's manpower was deployed advantageously within the province. The king's troops were posted along the St. Johns. Tonyn urged the planters there to remain on their plantations and to maintain a system of express messengers to communicate intelligence to each other and to the military posts in the vicinity. Refugees performed duty in St. Augustine to relieve the regulars. In spite of the refugees' service, Colonel Prevost refused to allow them rations because he said his orders did not specify that he should do so. When the rebels crossed the St. Marys, the governor called out the militia.[76]

Captain Mowbray's *Rebecca* was now virtually the sole naval defense for East Florida. The *Hinchinbrook,* commanded by Lieutenant Ellis, had been sent express to New York during the time of provision scarcity and had not yet returned. The *Otter,* Captain Squire, had been ordered to Antigua to clean her bottom. The *Governor Tonyn* had been wrecked, and Captain Osborne was in jail. Not surprisingly, a Georgia galley seized a schooner in the St. Marys with a cargo of rice destined for St. Augustine.

Under the circumstances, the governor felt justified in taking into provincial service three transports, mounting ten guns each, that had recently arrived: the *Meredith,* under Captain Samuel Haycraft, carrying provisions from England; the *Triumvirate,* laden with provisions from New York; and the *Hawke,* under Captain John McLeod, transporting recruits for the Fourteenth and Sixteenth Regiments. Tonyn implied that he would release the transports when East Florida received assistance from naval vessels. He also employed smaller vessels, the armed schooners *Nancy* and *Polly,* to patrol the St. Johns and to act as pilots.[77]

The Georgians invaded East Florida by land and by water. The flotilla collected at Sunbury consisted of three row galleys, two armed sloops, and some transports carrying twenty cannon (twelve to twenty-four pounders) besides swivels.[78] Elbert, the new commander, embarked his four hundred Continentals, presumably all of the First and Second Georgia Battalions who were healthy enough to travel, on the morning of 1 May. They proceeded at a leisurely pace through the inland waterway. In some respects, this force was as ill equipped as its predecessor. The men were furnished raw deerskins with which to make their own moccasins. Some of the riflemen were armed with pikes. Along the way, more conventional arms were repaired, and the men were taught how to use and care for their guns.[79]

At the same time, Colonel John Baker was leading overland another force, 109 volunteers from the Georgia militia and those of his Light Horse who possessed mounts. He had expected Colonel Sumter's South Carolina Horse to participate in the expedition, but General Howe had recalled those troops. The two forces were to rendezvous at Sawpit Bluff, twelve miles from the mouth of the St. Johns River, on 12 May.[80]

The rivers were so swollen by spring floods that Colonel Baker spent two days just getting his troops across the Altamaha. At dawn on 4 May, Indians attacked his camp. Although the warriors withdrew within minutes, two soldiers were wounded, Lieutenants Robeson and Frazer, and one Indian was killed. Baker and forty men pursued the Indians as far as Finhalloway Creek, about twelve miles away from his camp, but he could not catch up with them. The Americans started marching southward the next morning, and the only difficulty they faced en route was crossing the Satilla and St. Marys rivers.[81]

On the night of 18 May, the waterborne invasion force reached the north end of Amelia Island. Colonel Elbert immediately sent a boat to bring a rebel, William Mills, on board and dispatched Lieutenant Ward, of the Second Regiment, and about twenty men to round up all the inhabitants of Amelia. One of them, William Pryce, escaped in a canoe and gave the alarm. The following day, Mills, his overseer, and his schoolmaster joined Elbert.

Because the Georgians were very short of provisions, another party, consisting of a subaltern, a sergeant, and fourteen rank and file of the First Regiment, was sent to join Ward's group on the south end of Amelia on 19 May. They were to prevent all communication between the island and the mainland, but their most important duty was to kill and salt all the beef and hogs they could procure. Ward was particularly enjoined not to mistreat any prisoners he might take, especially women and children. A group of loyalist inhabitants fired on his party, killed him, and badly wounded two of his men. As soon as he heard the news on 20 May, Elbert dispatched Lieutenant

Winfree with orders to burn every house on Amelia and to destroy all the stock. At least seven Negro slaves belonging to a man named Moore were captured.[82]

Additional bad news reached Elbert. The force under Colonel John Baker that had ridden from the Altamaha had crossed the St. Marys on 10 May and reached the rendezvous on 12 May before the flotilla reached the St. Marys.[83] A forty-man detachment under Major William Baker moved on to scout the country as far as Cowford. An East Floridian named Barefield warned Baker that a party of fifteen pro-British Indians was in the area—he himself had been captured, then released when they were convinced he was not a Georgian—and that two spies had informed him that they were on their way to St. Augustine to report on the American expedition's progress.[84]

Colonel Brown had embarked about forty Rangers and Indians aboard Captain Coates's schooner and an eight-oared boat and transported them to "the point of Sherards [Creek], and big Creek." Leaving Coates at a convenient point in the event a retreat was necessary, Brown sent two Indians and a Ranger to reconnoiter. Within three hours, they returned and announced that they had found the rebels about nine miles away. By five o'clock that afternoon (14 May), Brown's force had sighted the American camp fires and counted about 250 horses. Finding the rebel sentries too alert for a surprise attack that night, Brown left some Indians to steal as many horses as possible while he took the main body of his force back to Coates's schooner.[85]

During the night of 14–15 May, the Indians, led by the Black Creek Factor, stole about forty of Colonel John Baker's horses, even though they were sighted and fired upon by a sentinel. The next morning, Baker found the horses hobbled beside a swamp just four miles away. Suspecting an ambush and proceeding with caution, he divided his force into three parties: one was to stay in plain view to divert the Indians' attention while a smaller group cut the horses loose; when this had been accomplished, the third party was to dash between the horses and the swamp and drive the animals off. The ruse worked, but, though the Indians pursued Baker's men, who numbered about sixty horse, for a mile or more and totaled only fifteen—this was apparently the party he had been warned about—the colonel could not persuade his men to stand and fight. The Indians finally gave up the chase and moved off, setting the woods on fire so they could not be tracked. One of them, a young Chiaha, had been killed, and possibly two. Baker had two men wounded and four or five horses killed. The rebels scalped and mutilated their Indian victim(s).[86]

After his Indians had reached the schooner, Brown reembarked his whole force and moved to join the regulars at Cowford. There, to his pleasure, he found that the regulars were to cross the St. Johns at one o'clock and take a northward post.[87]

Having heard nothing from Elbert and knowing that the British were aware of the size and location of his force, Colonel Baker decided to move his camp on 16 May. Traveling northward and inland, he looked for fords upstream on the numerous creeks in the area. By that night, the British scouts had located his force. Brown and Major Prevost met to coordinate their plan of attack. The British numbered about 200; their opponents, 150 to 180 horsemen.[88]

About ten o'clock the next morning (17 May) at Thomas Creek, a tributary of the Nassau River,[89] the Americans were ambushed. Brown had left a small party in a branch of the swamp on the American flank. Then, his main body fired at the oncoming rebels at fifty yards' range. The Americans had no alternative but to retreat directly into the force of Major Mark Prevost's one hundred regulars, who were advancing rapidly with fixed bayonets in three columns. Surrounded by Rangers, Indians, and regulars, twenty or thirty of the Americans fled at the first fire.

After a five-minute skirmish, the rest of Baker's force began retreating through the swamp. The British almost captured Colonel Baker himself; one of his men stole his horse and rode away upon it. Three Americans were killed, including Lieutenants Frazer and McGowen; nine wounded, including Lieutenant Robeson; and thirty-one taken prisoner, including Captains Few and Williams. Baker and his men straggled northward in small parties. Thomas Coleman drowned crossing the Satilla. Many of Baker's wounded died in the woods, and Tonyn reported that only forty-two of the American force crossed the Satilla. The king's troops were too exhausted by the heat and too ill shod, many of them being barefoot at this battle, and the Rangers' horses were too jaded for the British to pursue the rebels.[90]

On 19 May fifteen of Baker's men reached Elbert and reported the rout of the Georgia Light Horse. On 22 May three more joined Elbert. They reported that eight men had been taken prisoner at Thomas Creek; at first, they had been well treated, but the Indians had suddenly fired on them and killed five.[91]

Tonyn had intended a concerted attack upon the Americans by land and sea, during which Captain Mowbray's *Rebecca* would lead all the British armed vessels into the St. Marys. The *Rebecca* and the *Hawke* were forced to sea prematurely by a storm, whereupon they engaged a rebel brigantine of sixteen guns on 25 May. The *Rebecca* was winning the fight until a shot from the brigantine carried away her topmast and rent the mainsail. The *Hawke* also suffered considerable damage. In this engagement. the British lost one killed and nine wounded; the American losses were undetermined. The *Rebecca* limped into port too battered to proceed on Tonyn's plan, and the rebels had time to retreat before she could be repaired.[92]

For six days, the Georgians tried to get their vessels through the narrows between Amelia Island and the mainland. All their efforts failed. They were unable to venture into the open sea; and the morass of swamps, a British battery at Hester Bluff on the St. Johns, and the force of Rangers and Indians south of the St. Marys made the land route too risky. By that time, Elbert's supplies of beef were low, and he was assured that the British knew all about his activities. On 26 May he decided to return to the Satilla. By the time he reached Cumberland Island, at least four men had deserted to the enemy. He could muster only about three hundred effective men, including the Light Horse that had joined him. The army had had nothing to eat but rice for five days. The second invasion of East Florida was finished.[93] British forces had collected ten prisoners and fourteen scalps.[94]

On 27 May Elbert ordered some of his troops to march overland from the St. Marys to the Satilla, while the remainder of the rebel force went by water. Lieutenant Colonel Harris commanded two captains, four subalterns, six sergeants, a drum and fife, and one hundred rank and file. This detachment was to land at Wright's place, on the north side of the St. Marys, march upriver to the ford, then move across country to the Satilla. Elbert said he suspected that the East Florida Rangers were hunting cattle between the St. Marys and the Satilla, and he wanted this detachment to cut off those parties. Certainly he hoped that Harris's men would find the cattle first and be able to live off the country en route. The Georgians devastated everything along the line of their march.[95]

By the time all of Elbert's men reached "the old Towne," on the Satilla, on 1 June, they were mutinous because of the lack of food. They encamped there for several days waiting for the requested salted provisions—which did not arrive. On 6 June, Elbert marched with all his men who were able to do so to Fort Howe. Reaching that post on 9 June, they marched to Darien the next day. Elbert ordered the fleet to transport the remaining troops from the Satilla back to Savannah. He himself reached Savannah on 15 June.[96]

Elbert had written from the St. Marys to McIntosh urging that the assembly should have all cattle south of the Altamaha driven away. As the colonel said, the cattle between the Altamaha and the St. Marys were "a Magazine for our Enemies."[97] At Darien, Elbert had met Colonel Screven, of the Third Regiment, with two or three hundred of his men and ordered him to proceed to the Satilla to protect cattle drivers who were starting out to round up all the stock in that area. About one thousand head of cattle were collected and driven farther into Georgia above the Altamaha. Screven returned to Fort Howe, and the Georgians did not again attempt to occupy any post south of the Altamaha.[98]

V

1777: Internal Problems, External Stalemates

THE SITUATION in the Floridas obviously required the presence of a general officer. On 1 April 1777 General William Howe appointed Augustine Prevost "to act in the Rank of Brigadier General" so long as the latter continued to serve on the North American continent.[1]

Prevost and Tonyn could not agree about East Florida's defenders any more than they had about methods of defense. The governor gave most of the credit to the Rangers, the Indians, and the tiny naval force. He was so elated about blocking the rebel invasion that he generously praised Major Mark Prevost's good judgment and conduct, especially his "humane and polite behavior" to the Rangers and Indians, which had facilitated the harmonious cooperation of the various elements in the defense of East Florida. The colonel, who credited the regulars commanded by his brother, Major Prevost, with saving East Florida, asserted that if his brother had possessed a small cavalry force, he could have captured many of the fleeing rebels at Thomas Creek. Major Prevost reported that the Rangers, who were not under his command, declined to pursue the rebels because "their horses were too much fatigued."[2]

As soon as the emergency ended, the governor and the general renewed their quarrel. Tonyn asked Prevost to pay some of the extraordinary expenses of the February expedition, such as arms for the Indians, out of his military funds. When Prevost refused, Tonyn absorbed the charges himself.[3]

Emboldened by his recent promotion, Prevost complained more vigorously about the governor's usurpation of power in military matters and demanded detailed reports on the Rangers, their numbers, and expenses incurred on their account. He threatened not to provide rations for any Rangers not on actual service. Grudgingly, he mentioned that he was convinced of the utility of such a force; he proposed that fifty Rangers be formed into one troop—the others presumably to be dismissed—which would be stationed just north of the St. Johns. These men, under his command of course, would be mounted and armed with rifles or carbines and swords. Although he mentioned that this troop could "occasionally make excursions" among the Georgia rebels and would be useful for pursuing them, such a small force stationed so close to St. Augustine obviously would be of little utility as a fighting unit. It would provide scouting service, but not much more than that. Prevost was still preoccupied with merely defensive matters.[4]

The governor politely but clearly told the general to mind his own business. Tonyn reminded Prevost that, regardless of his new rank, he had no power over a civil governor who was commissioned by the king "to levy, Arm, Muster, Command, and employ all persons residing within this Province as occasion shall serve, and them to embody and transport from one place to another." The governor's instructions did not direct him to make any "return" of the military state of East Florida to the brigadier general or to the commander in chief; this would be unprecedented. Tonyn claimed that both the Rangers and the provincial militia were entirely under his command and were to be employed for the best interests of the province in the king's service; when they were on active service with regular troops, they would be under the command of Prevost or his appointed officers.

The governor reiterated his request that Prevost order rations for the Rangers, implying that if it were not for the Rangers, there would be no rations at all. The Rangers were paid for out of provincial funds over which Prevost had no control; therefore, he was not to concern himself over their number. Tonyn said that he thought raising a troop of fifty Rangers would be a fine idea; "it would relieve the Province of a considerable Expence." The implication was that, until Prevost's fifty Rangers were raised, trained for service, and paid for by the regular military, the East Florida Rangers belonged to the governor of that province.[5]

Howe had proposed to stop the conflicts between civil and military officials by putting all the forces within each of the Floridas under the command of a single officer. Germain hesitated to give an unqualified "no" to Howe's suggestion, but he clearly indicated his disapproval. He authorized Howe to take such a step only if it were "absolutely necessary for the Promotion of His Majesty's Service." In the same paragraph, he mentioned that only two governors were then resident in the southern colonies—Tonyn and Peter Chester, of West Florida—and they were both able and experienced military officers as well as civil administrators.[6]

Admiral Richard Lord Howe did send some naval force to protect East Florida, though the first vessel to arrive, the frigate *Daphne,* did not reach there until after the invasion threat had passed. Lieutenant Ellis was ordered to take his fourteen-gun brigantine *Hinchinbrook* back to her station at St. Augustine. By 21 June three frigates, the *Perseus,* the *Galatea,* and the *Brune,* were off the St. Augustine bar. Governor Tonyn in July therefore discharged the transports *Meredith* and *Hawke,* which he had taken into provincial service. The other transport, *Triumvirate,* had required repairs before she could be considered serviceable; these were not completed before the rebels had withdrawn. Captain Mowbray's *Rebecca* remained in East Florida's service.[7]

The outcome of the second invasion of East Florida was not known before Georgia leaders began blaming each other for the expedition's difficulties. When the new state constitution went into effect in May, John Adam Treutlen was elected as governor—to Button Gwinnett's probable chagrin. The election may have been a repudiation of the provocative offensive policy of the radicals who were centered in St. John's Parish and led by Gwinnett, or it may have been a piece of political strategy by that group. Treutlen was a less controversial figure in the same political faction as Gwinnett; and the latter, as one of Georgia's delegates to the Continental Congress, was entitled to a seat in the Georgia assembly in any event.[8]

While President Gwinnett had been absent during the early stages of the expedition, the Council of Safety had met, released George McIntosh on £20,000 bail, and finally informed him of the charges against him so that he could prepare his defense.[9] Promptly setting out to clear himself before Congress, he neglected to notify the executive before his departure, a condition that had been specified in the terms of his release. The Georgia assembly decided that he should be guarded en route to Congress, so Governor Treutlen sent a guard after him, which caught up with him in North Carolina.[10]

The assembly, after considering the Florida expedition and hearing both Gwinnett and Lachlan McIntosh, approved the conduct of the president and Council of Safety. The general promptly and publicly—before the assembly—called Gwinnett "A Scoundrel and lying Rascal" to his face. Gwinnett immediately challenged McIntosh to a duel.[11] On 16 May the duel was fought in Governor Wright's meadow outside Savannah. Each man wounded the other in the thigh. McIntosh recovered; Gwinnett died three days later.[12]

No official notice was taken of the duel at the time, but, when the next assembly met, McIntosh was arrested. He was tried for murder and acquitted. Lyman Hall and Joseph Wood led the movement against McIntosh, and petitions for his removal from command were sent to Congress; however, the general had friends there. George Walton and Henry Laurens requested his transfer, and on 6 August Washington ordered him to report for reassignment.[13]

On 3 June Georgia's assembly resolved to raise two battalions, to be called "minute men," for permanent defense of the frontier. The assembly seems to have had a force like Brown's Rangers in mind. Enlistment was to be for two years, and both officers and men would receive large bounties and premiums. All the men were to be enlisted from outside Georgia, and the rank of each officer would be determined by the number of men he enlisted.[14] Also, on 14 July, the Executive Council commissioned Thomas Gray as captain of a company of Indians who were to scout along the frontier and prevent cattle raids from East Florida.[15]

The Georgia regiments were still far below strength. To encourage the officers in their recruiting efforts, General McIntosh in June ordered wholesale promotions in the First Battalion. Captain John McIntosh became major of the regiment, and Lieutenant George Walton replaced him. Other officers were advanced in turn, and the vacant commissions were left for those who could recruit the most men.[16]

Georgia had continued to recruit in North Carolina and Virginia for the Second and Third Georgia Battalions and even into Pennsylvania for the Fourth Battalion. In the spring, North Carolina had refused to allow the Fourth Battalion to recruit in that state, but did furnish supplies to troops recruited in Pennsylvania and marching through to Georgia.[17]

By the middle of summer, the new recruits were sickly. Elbert wanted to send them 140 miles into the backcountry to preserve their health. He maintained that they could return in case of emergency, and, if they were not healthy, they would be useless anyway. The seasoned First Battalion was a sufficient force for the "sickly months." General McIntosh disagreed with Elbert.[18] The First Battalion had performed hard and steady service since it had been formed. The men would surely resent preferential treatment of the new recruits.

Within a few days, General McIntosh changed his mind. The sick list was truly alarming. Colonel Elbert's Second Regiment was to move up the Savannah River. Colonel Screven's Third Regiment was to push up the Ogeechee River, after leaving a detachment of one captain, three lieutenants, and one company on guard at Sunbury. The officers were cautioned to camp at healthy sites where the water was good and to keep the men ready to march down to the coast on an hour's warning. The regiment of horse was ordered to assemble all detachments at Fort Howe. General McIntosh ordered his subordinates to report to him frequently, to question the inhabitants about the most defensible sites in their area, and to keep the men under strict discipline, especially when they had contact with civilians.[19]

Unable to obtain enough engineers and artillery officers locally, the Georgia assembly in May had sent blank Continental commissions to an agent in France and had authorized him to issue them to qualified individuals. Although the Continental Congress disapproved of this action, some of the commissions may have been issued.[20]

As usual, armaments were abysmally insufficient. Colonel Elbert complained:

> . . . the Sorry trash I have at present being such a medley of Rifles, old muskets and fowling pieces, with a few French Traders, that I have no faith in them, not above fifty of the three Hundred Stand French Arms bought the other day in South Carolina, but what are either Bursted or otherwise totally unfit for Service.[21]

Elbert ordered that all the small smoothbore guns in his regiment be fitted with the best of the bayonets and iron ramrods from the useless French guns.[22]

Motivated by the hope of luring more potential militiamen into the state and deriving some financial benefit from the state's greatest asset, Georgia opened a land office on 7 June "for the better settling and strengthening this state." The grants would be based on the old headright system; the quitrent would be two shillings per one hundred acres, but ten slaves were the maximum allowable for headright grants. Squatters on vacant land could continue to hold as much as they would be entitled to by headright. Any person who would build and operate a gristmill, a sawmill, a furnace or bloomery for working iron, or a forge for making bar iron was entitled to a large grant of land.

Each grantee was required to settle on and cultivate his land within six months—unless the enemy prevented it. Any grantee under this act must hold his land for at least five years; any transfer within that time would be invalid and would make the land subject to regranting. All absentees from the state who held lands they had not settled or cultivated were ordered to return within six months; otherwise such lands would be deemed vacant and would be subject to regranting.[23]

Georgia's financial problems had become desperate. Her currency had depreciated in value far beyond that of her neighbors or of Continental currency. Prices were soaring. The government forbade the export of certain goods and produce and took measures, including the establishment of a state insurance office to insure vessels owned by Georgians, to encourage trade with non-British areas. Neither funds nor supplies were available to maintain the troops.[24]

The Continental Congress responded to Governor Treutlen's appeal by voting $400,000 to redeem the Georgia bills of credit that had been issued to support the troops and $600,000 for other expenses of the Continental forces in that state. Henry Laurens headed the committee that recommended this measure, and upon his urging Congress appointed Joseph Clay, a Savannah merchant and friend of Laurens, as Continental paymaster for Georgia.[25] The Congress appointed James Rae as commissary general of purchases and John Bohan Giradeau as commissary general of issues for the state.[26]

Discipline among Georgia troops had never been of a high order, and the effect of the continuing power struggle among factions within the state's elite, especially the conflict between the civil and military leaders, was devastating. Morale and discipline declined steadily during the summer. Military officers and their men became involved in the McIntosh-Gwinnett quarrel. One of the general's friends reported that, when petitions for the removal of Lachlan McIntosh from his command were being circulated, Colonel John Baker forced his entire regiment to sign one.[27]

General McIntosh's order for the various detachments of the Light Horse to come southward from the western posts was ignored. Colonel John Baker directed the officers to bring their men to meet him at Augusta, from whence they would march to the south. Most of the men had lost their horses, and they flatly refused to move unless they were paid immediately. When the officers complained about their being detained in Savannah because their accounts had not been certified by Baker, he insisted that they come to his house at Midway if they wanted certification. Irate at having been criticized, Baker resigned as colonel of the Regiment of Horse on 29 August.[28]

The government in Savannah tried to supersede McIntosh's command by appointing Elbert as "commander of the Continental Troops stationed or sent to the westward," but he declined to accept the appointment. His letter of refusal to Speaker of the House Noble W. Jones was a masterpiece of composition.[29]

On 9 September Elbert reported that about half his Second Regiment was still sick at Wrightsborough, though most of the men were recovering. He had dispersed those who were fit for duty in groups under subalterns to various forts along the frontier: twenty-four men at Folsom's Fort, on the Ogeechee; forty-six at Well's Fort; twenty-seven at Captain Phillips's Fort, on the Little River; eighteen at Joel Phillips's Fort, on the Little River; and ten at Carr's Fort, on Beaver Dam Fork.[30] These "forts" probably were stockaded, lightly fortified plantation dwellings similar to Wright's Fort, on the St. Marys.

Men found it easier to desert when they were stationed on the frontier than when they were near headquarters and large population centers. Elbert reported that twenty deserted from his own Second Regiment. He blamed the light sentence, "one hundred lashes, with a great chance of having that remitted," and favored the death penalty. Colonel Baker of the Light Horse reported that three men deserted on the night of 28 August.[31]

July troop returns for the three regiments of infantry, one regiment of horse, and two companies of artillery in Georgia totaled nearly two thousand men. In October, however, only six hundred were reported to be available for duty.[32] Not more than two thousand militia could be raised under any circumstances.[33] Militia Colonel George Walton later estimated that, though some immigration had occurred to Georgia's western frontier—probably referring to the Ceded Lands—the number of loyalists leaving the state exceeded the number of newcomers; thus, the militia force had actually declined since the last official report in 1773.[34]

The continental congress considered the state of military as well as financial affairs in Georgia. After the death on 15 April 1777 of James Moore, command of the Southern Department had passed to Robert Howe, also of North Carolina. When Henry Laurens, of South Carolina, reached Philadelphia in July, he found Congress busily planning an expedition against West Florida. But, after he clarified the situation on the southern border, Congress dropped the proposed expedition against West Florida and planned another attack upon East Florida.[35]

South Carolina had not abandoned her efforts to take Georgia into protective custody. William Henry Drayton, writing letters and circulating petitions, agitated constantly in favor of the union. Governor Treutlen, upon the advice of Georgia's Executive Council, issued a proclamation on 15 July offering a £100 reward to anyone who would apprehend Drayton or any persons who were supporting his efforts.[36]

Drayton wrote a sarcastic and insulting tirade in response to Treutlen and the Georgia council. In defending the right of petition, the South Carolinian compared Georgia's leaders with the arbitrary Stuart rulers of England. Championing George McIntosh, he charged that the life and liberty of Georgia's citizens were endangered by such a tyrannous government. Charging the state's public officials with being "concealed Tories," he ridiculed them by claiming that their burlesque of government would drive Georgians to return to British rule. Drayton promised to furnish the money for a trial suit of anyone apprehended under the proclamation, but he did not venture within Georgia's boundaries.[37]

Dissension was also causing problems in East Florida. The "inflamed faction" opposed Governor Tonyn and his policy and methods. Chief Justice William Drayton questioned the governor's authority to issue commissions and letters of marque for action against the rebels in Georgia, and he made the holders personally responsible for damages they caused while acting under those commissions. Adding insult to injury, the chief justice had publicly in court referred to Brown's Rangers as "split-shirt Banditti."[38]

Late in August 1776, Captain Reid of HMS *Sphynx* had put on board Captain Osborne's private sloop of war *Governor Tonyn* two pilots, some arms, and men and ordered Osborne to procure provisions for Royal Navy ships that were stationed at the mouth of the Savannah. Consequently, James Coates, an officer on the *Governor Tonyn*, had removed twenty-three hogs as well as some beef and fowl from Little Tybee Island, in Georgia, and the stock was distributed among the ships. George Barry claimed the livestock as his property and sued Captain Osborne in East Florida's Court of Common Pleas. Chief Justice Drayton ruled against Osborne and awarded Barry damages of one hundred pounds plus costs.[39]

Captain Osborne again ran afoul of Chief Justice Drayton when he captured a rebel vessel that was loaded with corn and slaves belonging to the chief justice's brother, Stephen Drayton, of Georgia. The chief justice released one of the *Governor Tonyn*'s sailors by writ of habeas corpus and encouraged another man to run away; the latter had been placed on board by Lieutenant Grant, of the *St. John,* to be returned to Captain Squire's *Otter,* from which he had deserted. Osborne charged that Drayton had then prevailed on his financial backer, Archibald Lundie, to harass Osborne about money he owed to Lundie, though the debt was perfectly secured. As the *Governor Tonyn* was about to leave St. Augustine with the *Otter* and the *Fincastle*, Lundie came aboard the vessel with a marshal to arrest Osborne for debt. Lundie struck several of the sailors, one of whom he injured severely. Because of the loss of time (which probably meant that the *Governor Tonyn* lost the flood tide), she struck the bar, and the injured seaman drowned. Osborne sent the sloop's boat to shore to request assistance, but Lundie and his partner, Captain (William?) Taylor, seized the boat and oars, thus preventing help from going to the wreck. When Osborne reached shore, Lundie and Taylor immediately had him jailed for debt.[40]

On the other hand, the chief justice permitted Georgia rebels who were charged with treason to go at large and armed in St. Augustine and to institute civil suits against loyalist refugees.[41]

On 6 January 1777 Chief Justice Drayton ruled that Governor Dunmore's prisoners who were still in St. Augustine should be discharged "on giving Bail for their appearance at the next Sessions." Although the prisoners were so far from home that only one could find bail and thus benefit from the court's favorable ruling, the judicial proceedings cast suspicion on a provincial governor's legal authority to incarcerate prisoners of war.[42]

Governor Tonyn had caused the arrest and imprisonment of an Indian interpreter named Caine for acting in the rebel interest with the Indians. Judge Drayton freed him without requiring security for his good behavior or notifying Tonyn.[43] Captain Graham ordered one Jameson to be brought to St. Augustine to be charged with spying. Drayton refused to examine the two prosecution witnesses and discharged him.[44]

Drayton himself sued for libel and £1,000 damage and had incarcerated a Carolina refugee named Mackie, the Ranger's surgeon. Mackie was charged with having said that the South Carolinians believed that East Florida's chief justice was sympathetic to their rebellion. Drayton threatened to sue Lieutenant Colonel Brown for £3,000 on a similar charge.[45]

Lieutenant Colonel Fuser accused the governor of opening and destroying some of his mail. As a public official, Tonyn could not challenge the officer to a duel, so he took his resentment to court. The indictment was thrown out. Tonyn charged Drayton with packing the jury and pressuring its members, and he believed that Drayton had inspired Fuser's complaint in the first place.[46]

In May, when Captain Mowbray, acting under Tonyn's orders, detained the brig *Sir Basil Keith* for provincial service, James Penman promised to sue him.[47] The governor could not prevail on any of the province's legal officers to issue a warrant for impressing horses for government service.[48] Both Chief Justice Drayton and Attorney General Arthur Gordon refused to muster with the East Florida militia when the invasion threat was at its height.[49]

James Penman proposed to go in person with a flag of truce from the "Inhabitants," ignoring the government altogether, to arrange terms with the Georgians whereby East Florida would pay a stipulated sum to the rebels—ransom or tribute.[50]

Drayton frequently and publicly asserted that Tonyn would soon be replaced as governor of East Florida.[51] Governor Tonyn did not doubt that Chief Justice Drayton was the leader and instigator of opposition to the government in East Florida. He hesitated to act officially against the chief justice and his cohorts because of the recent and very marked favor shown to Drayton by Whitehall. All that Tonyn dared to do was to state the situation plainly to His Majesty's Secretary.[52]

Andrew Turnbull, nephew of Dr. Andrew Turnbull, did nothing to halt correspondence between some of his Minorcans at New Smyrna and the rebels. Tonyn was informed that those indentured servants had invited the Georgia rebels to come to the plantation and assist in an uprising. Bisset told the governor that New Smyrna's people could not be trusted with arms and that, in case East Florida was invaded, some of them should be confined in St. Augustine.[53]

In March at least three of New Smyrna's servants appeared before government officials in St. Augustine and demanded justice. They claimed that the time of their indentures had expired and that Dr. Turnbull had not fulfilled the terms of their contracts. New Smyrna's people wanted their freedom and their freedom dues. Governor Tonyn persuaded them to return to their plantation.[54]

Late in April, ninety white servants from New Smyrna deserted the plantation and walked for three days to reach St. Augustine. Governor Tonyn directed them first to Arthur Gordon, the attorney general; Gordon was one of Turnbull's attorneys. Next, the governor sent them to Chief Justice William Drayton. He passed them on to Spencer Man, a justice of the peace. Because the number of people was so large, twelve were chosen to represent the entire group and to make sworn depositions, on which legal proceedings could be based.[55] Promising that justice would be done to them, the governor persuaded most of Turnbull's servants to return to New Smyrna. The crops were in the field; another shortage of provisions was to be avoided if at all possible.[56]

The sworn statements of the servants revealed years of abuse and neglect at New Smyrna that horrified officials at St. Augustine. Henry Yonge, an attorney, doubted that the doctor knew about the cruelties committed by his overseers, though the depositions indicated that the overseers were acting under Turnbull's orders.[57]

Now the lines were clearly drawn between the governor and this other leader of the "inflamed faction," Andrew Turnbull. Tonyn proposed to see that Turnbull's servants received justice; they would be delivered from their now illegal bondage and resettled as freedmen. The survivors of New Smyrna would prove to be industrious settlers in the province. Grateful for the justice and protection given to them by the British government, they would spurn the rebels to the northward. It was time for Whitehall to choose between Tonyn and the Drayton-Turnbull faction. The governor asked for the support "of His Majesty's Ministers." He got it.[58] And it was high time.

Although Seminole and Lower Creek warriors had been active military auxiliaries of the British during the first half of 1777, Tonyn continued to insist that the Creeks should provide more aid.[59] It was not immediately forthcoming. Stuart flatly told Tonyn, "Indians are different from Regulars, we court their assistance, we do not command it." East Florida could rely on the eight hundred Seminole warriors and, possibly, on some help from the Lower Creeks. The governor should not expect substantial assistance from the Upper Creeks, however; it was 502 miles from St. Augustine to Little Tallassee, the center of Upper Creek territory where Taitt made his headquarters, and few of those Indians could be persuaded to march so far.[60]

On 20 May, in the Treaty of Dewitt's Corner (now called Due West), the Cherokees had been forced to cede all their land in South Carolina except a small strip in the northwest.[61] The Creeks were appalled at the thought of sharing the same fate as the Cherokees.[62] The Upper Creeks were threatened by an attack from whites around Seneca and Watauga, who now had nothing to fear from the Cherokees. Thus, the Upper Creek warriors refused to leave their families and villages unguarded.[63]

The president of Georgia had sent an Indian named St. Iago to the Cussitas with an effective talk. The French and Spanish had joined the rebels and not only had sent them goods but also had placed ships to blockade the harbors of St. Augustine, Pensacola, and Mobile so there would be no more English trade goods for the Indians. The whites had decided to settle their quarrels on the ocean instead of the land, so there was no longer any reason for the Indians to be offended or to take sides in the dispute.[64]

George Galphin had told the Indians that the whites were merely staging a sham dispute with the ulterior motive of involving the warriors, which would lead to their ultimate destruction. If British troops were allowed to enter Indian territory, they would turn against their red allies and exterminate them. When the warriors who had been present at the attack upon Fort McIntosh, on the Satilla, returned home, they reported that the whites had indeed fired for a long time without hurting each other, and the rebels who had surrendered were released instead of being taken captive. Thus, Galphin's talk gained credence.[65]

Tonyn was convinced that David Holmes, Galphin's nephew, was still acting in the interests of the rebels.[66] Stuart agreed that their agents were operating among every Indian tribe, but he flatly denied that Holmes was one of them.[67]

Determined to take advantage of Creek fears and of the timely arrival of Indian presents, Galphin decided to hold a conference with that tribe. On 17 June on the banks of the Ogeechee River, at Ogeechee Old Town, the Continental Indian commissioners, Galphin and Rae, and the Georgia Indian commissioners, including Jonathan Bryan, met Handsome Fellow, of Okfuskee, Opeitley Mico (frequently called the Tallassee King's son), of Tallassee, the Cussita King, and between two and five hundred warriors. Galphin demanded the return of two white prisoners and reparations for damages done by raids in Georgia, and he insisted that the Indians agree to punish future murderers. He warned that the Creeks might find themselves in the same plight as the Cherokees, and suggested that some of the chiefs might like to travel to Philadelphia to see the Continental armies. Galphin promised that he had goods ready to send to the Creeks if they would promise to protect his traders and expel Taitt and William McIntosh.[68]

Opeitley Mico and Handsome Fellow spoke for the Creeks. Both leaders insisted that presents and trade goods must be forthcoming immediately to demonstrate the Whigs' good faith. Handsome Fellow declined to visit Philadelphia, but volunteered to make the trip to Charleston. Galphin had brought little in the way of trade goods with him, but his presents of guns, ammunition, and rum were welcome, and the Indians departed well satisfied.[69]

Most of the Creeks remained quiet through June. Their councils were seriously divided. The pro-British war faction hesitated to take any action while Handsome Fellow and his neutralist followers were in rebel territory, where they could be seized for hostages or in retaliation. Such prisoners usually did not fare well, and in the Creek system anyone who instigated action that led to another's death was as guilty as the killer. In any event, Handsome Fellow's clansmen would have sought retribution against those whose actions endangered his life, and none of the Creeks desired a civil war.[70]

The tribe was experiencing other problems. Near-famine had been caused by partial failure of the 1776 corn crop; a horde of starving Cherokee refugees further strained the unusually limited food supplies. Drunkenness had become such a problem that several Upper Creek chiefs visited Taitt at Little Tallassee and asked him to prevent the British traders from selling rum.[71]

Early in the summer, Prevost complained that the Indian allies who had helped repulse the Georgians' invasion of East Florida were not reliable. He believed that Superintendent Stuart was not effectively organizing the Creeks for action.[72]

Word from headquarters had reached Prevost about British plans for action in the summer. General Howe was to strike the middle colonies while Superintendent Stuart and Lieutenant Colonel Henry Hamilton, governor of Detroit, were to lead the Indians against the western frontier. Thus, the southern colonies would be unable to send their troops to assist those in the middle. After a northern victory, Howe would lead his troops to mop up the southern region. Germain had instructed Howe to use the Indians in whatever way would be most advantageous in prosecuting the war, and Prevost believed that, if the Indians in Stuart's department would surround the southern colonies and take the offensive while the British regulars were operating in the middle region, the rebels would surrender quickly.[73]

In April, Germain had ordered Tonyn to cooperate with Stuart in the planned offensive and to "make such a Disposition of the Troops under your Command, as shall appear to you the most proper to second the Indians in their Enterprizes, and to take advantage of any favourable Opportunity which may present itself of rescuing the Province of Georgia out of the Rebels hands." Germain was quite optimistic that the southern Indians and a detachment from St. Augustine's garrison could conquer Georgia.[74]

Stuart reminded Prevost of some of the difficulties involved in waging such a war. The Lower Creek town nearest to St. Augustine was 370 miles away. Other Creek towns were nearly 600 miles from St. Augustine. The Cherokees were still farther away from a British base. No posts or magazines were located near the frontier; neither the Indians nor the British were capable of provisioning such large-scale expeditions. Stuart concluded that the Seminoles would defend East Florida, but warriors from the other southern tribes would be useful only for raids.[75]

The superintendent still maintained that Britain's best policy would be to keep the Indians loyal—and that was a difficult enough project—but not to encourage them to take the offensive. Unity for self-defense should be encouraged. Sending out small raiding parties against the rebels would not help the British cause and might be disadvantageous; if the rebels counterattacked, the Indians would have become weakened and therefore less able to defend their own lands or the Floridas against invasion. If Indians were used in war at all, they must be accompanied by white leaders. The warriors would be effective auxiliaries if and when regular British troops launched a major offensive in the southern colonies.[76]

For once, Governor Tonyn agreed with Superintendent Stuart about something: an attack on Georgia and the Carolinas from Pensacola would be impractical. Tonyn estimated that the nearest rebel settlement in Georgia was more than six hundred miles from Pensacola. All the rivers in the area flowed south and southeast instead of southwest, so transportation by water was not possible. There were no roads at all through the forests and swamps. No supplies of any sort were available within that vast territory, and there were no places where magazines could be established. Also, rebel agents had told the Indians that the British planned to march the king's troops through their country, supposedly to attack the rebels near the coast, but that, when the British army had reached the Indian towns, they would kill the warriors and enslave their women and children. Some of the Indians believed Galphin and undoubtedly would oppose a large body of regular soldiers entering their country. Tonyn thought an invasion of Georgia by combined British and Indian forces would be much more practical from East Florida.[77]

Escochabey, of Coweta, fearing an increase in neutralist sentiment, went to Little Tallassee to consult Taitt, but in July the Creeks did resume their raids into Georgia almost at will. After Handsome Fellow had led the neutralists off to meet Galphin at Ogeechee, the other Upper Creek headmen had promised Taitt that they would send war parties against Georgia later in the summer. A prominent Coweta warrior—a leader of the Tyger clan and nephew of Isen-poaphe, the Coweta headman—had been killed in a horse-stealing raid near Ogeechee; the Cowetas wanted revenge, and they had refused to meet Galphin. Isenpoaphe sent word to his kinsman of the Tyger clan, the Mad Dog of Tuckabatchee, to bring down his clansmen from the Okchais and the Alabamas to join him against the Georgians.[78]

The war faction got rid of Galphin's agent among the Okfuskees, Daniel McMurphy. They threatened his life, but Handsome Fellow's followers were able to protect him and escorted him to their kinsmen at Cussita for safety.[79]

Coweta warriors were the first to move out. While Galphin was still holding his meeting, a band from that town stole some horses from a stockade fort and lured their pursuers into an ambush. One Indian was killed and one wounded. Twenty rebels died on the spot.[80] Cowetas, possibly the same large band, also attacked another stockade fort at the forks of the Ogeechee. In this action, one Indian was killed and two wounded. Only two rebels were killed, but the fort was abandoned, and another war party burned it down.[81]

On 22 July Captain Thomas Dooley, of Georgia's Third Continental Battalion, was killed by pro-British Indians on the Oconee. After returning from recruiting service in Virginia, where he had enlisted twenty men for the Georgia Continentals, he decided to undertake a venture against the Indians before he joined his regiment. But they found him first. As his party passed through a cane swamp near Big Shoals, about seven o'clock in the morning of 22 July, the warriors attacked. Dooley was wounded early in the skirmish; a ball broke the leg bones above his ankle. His second in command, Lieutenant Cunningham, led a precipitate retreat. The Indians captured and killed Dooley and three others. A court-martial acquitted Cunningham of cowardice.[82]

One war party crossed the Ogeechee River near Morgan's Fort on the night of 31 July and killed and scalped the wife and four children of Samuel Dilkes (or Delk), who was absent. The Indians took his oldest daughter, fourteen years old, with them when they left. Lieutenants Little and Alexander led the pursuit of the raiders for forty miles, then lost the trail where they had scattered. Some of the girl's hair was found near the Oconee, and she was presumed to be dead. By the middle of August, however, she was reported to be living with the Upper Creeks.[83]

Indian leaders repeatedly stated that their warriors attacked only armed rebels, and the Dilkes massacre is the only documented exception in the South. Stuart said that the attackers had a personal quarrel with Dilkes, who had frequently abused them. Although the location of Dilkes's house cannot be pinpointed—Stuart said it was "without the settlements near the road to the Lower Creek Nation"[84]—it is highly probable he had deliberately trespassed across the Indian boundary line.

Another band routed an American scouting party on the Broad River. In resisting capture, Captain Gerard (or Gurard), of Georgia's Third Continental Battalion, was killed.[85]

By the middle of August, the Lower Creeks had sent out several raiding parties against the Georgians. Five groups of warriors from Coweta and fifty Hillabies were active.[86]

Before 26 July all the New Smyrna servants had been freed. The governor gave each family small land allotments, and he believed they would be industrious settlers. Most of them became farmers on the outskirts of St. Augustine, but some of the young men joined Brown's Rangers.[87]

With this increase in strength, the East Florida Rangers, accompanied by their Seminole allies, scouted and raided into Georgia. They operated almost freely along the Ogeechee. Tonyn reported that they penetrated to within five miles of Savannah and passed through Augusta. On 21 August the governor informed his council that Brown's Rangers had captured Fort Frederica, on St. Simons Island, and had taken several prisoners.[88]

In August twenty new Georgia recruits, commanded by Lieutenants Brown and Anderson, were ambushed en route to Fort Howe by 150 East Florida Rangers and Indians in a thick bay swamp less than two miles from the fort. Fourteen Americans were killed. Six of the men and the mounted officers escaped. When the news reached Colonel Screven the next morning, he led a party of militia and Lieutenant Colonel John McIntosh brought some regulars from Darien to bury the dead. All the bodies had been mutilated, some beyond identification. The attackers had retreated across the Altamaha at Reid's Bluff and headed for St. Augustine. The survivors were unable to tell the proportion of whites and Indians in the raiding force.[89]

On only one occasion were the operations of the Rangers checked. Late in September a party of Continental troops opposed about fifty of them north of the Altamaha, killed one or two, and captured some cattle, horses, and saddles.[90]

Alarmed settlers near the Indian line crowded into frontier forts.[91] Where Indians were concerned, Georgia frontiersmen disapproved of their leaders' conciliatory policy. The assembly might well have declared war on the Creeks if the Continental Congress had not urged the Georgians not to pursue such a dangerous course and to punish the warmongers.[92]

Rather than returning home from the Ogeechee meeting, Handsome Fellow led between twenty and one hundred warriors of Okfuskee and Cussita to Charleston. They were properly impressed by the Carolinians' military stores. After viewing a militia parade and being entertained aboard French ships, they were taken on a tour of the forts and told the story of the Battle of Sullivan's Island. Edmund Rutledge, speaking for the council of South Carolina, warned them that the British wanted to involve them in a war so that the Indians could be destroyed more easily, that the British were being defeated rapidly, and that the French and Spanish fleets would soon block the British Indian trade. Rutledge demanded that the Creeks either kill Taitt and McIntosh or at least drive them out of their nation. On 12 July Handsome Fellow and his followers agreed to maintain the peace with the rebels.[93]

To seal the new peace, when Handsome Fellow's party passed through Augusta, the Americans released to them seven Creeks who had been imprisoned in Savannah.[94] Nevertheless, four Georgia officers—Captain John Dooley and Lieutenant Bilbo, of the Light Horse, Major Pannell, of the Second Regiment, and Lieutenant Booker, of the Third Regiment—insulted and assaulted some of the neutralist delegates at Galphin's. General Robert Howe ordered the arrest of the officers, but Dooley, who was Tom Dooley's brother, refused to give himself up for trial and had to be taken by force.[95] Daniel McMurphy, one of Georgia's commissioners for the Creeks, took the entire group of neutralist Indians into protective custody to prevent their being attacked by white settlers before they could reach their country.[96]

On 13 August Handsome Fellow met Colonel Samuel Elbert, who told him that the price of peace for the Creeks was the assassination of Cameron, Taitt, and McIntosh. The headman apparently agreed to these terms, but he died on the path to Okfuskee. Leadership of the neutral faction shifted to his Cussita kinsmen, Nea Mico and Neaclucluckotico.[97]

When the Cussita neutrals reached home, they found that McIntosh had assembled there a war party of Creeks, Cherokees, and refugee loyalists for the purpose of attacking the Georgia frontier. Cameron had collected another group of 200 traders and refugees as well as 150 Cherokees at Hickory Ground, in the Upper Towns. Both expeditions were scheduled for 22 September and were to create a diversion while General Prevost moved northward along the coast.[98]

Inspired by the talks of Galphin, Rutledge, and Elbert, the neutrals determined to kill all the British traders in their nation and plunder their stores. The Cussita neutrals requested their clansmen at Okfuskee to assassinate Taitt and Cameron while they murdered McIntosh. Okfuskees of Handsome Fellow's clan attempted to kill Taitt and Cameron, who were visiting McGillivray at Little Tallassee, and Emistiseguo, the pro-British medal chief of the Upper Creeks. McGillivray possessed enough influence at this point to save the lives of his friends. Tallapoosas plundered the property of Cameron and his men at Hickory Ground, however, and all the British among the Upper Creeks fled to Pensacola.

Some Chiahas and Cowetas discovered the Cussita plot and guarded McIntosh, but the Cussitas succeeded in plundering their traders. The British among the Lower Creeks also fled to Pensacola; and Cussita and Coweta, the two major towns of the Lower Creeks, were on the verge of civil war.[99]

The neutral faction enjoyed a temporary triumph. Opeitley Mico, of Little Tallassee, sent belts to the Chickasaws and Choctaws announcing the rout of the British and urging those tribes to join the Creeks in a neutrality pact.[100]

Superintendent Stuart immediately embargoed all trade to the Creeks and insisted that they expel all rebel agents. And he had an ally among the Creeks of new importance. McGillivray was nearly unassailable because of his connection through his mother with the powerful Wind Clan. Emistiseguo virtually resigned the leadership position in favor of the younger man.[101]

McGillivray called a meeting of headmen to compose tribal differences and to restore the British position with the Creeks. At the national council, he castigated the Indians for their lack of honor and hospitality and for their economic shortsightedness.[102]

When trade goods from the Whigs were not forthcoming, it seemed clear that Galphin could not fulfill his promises, and many Creeks saw the error of their ways. Late in October or early in November, ten pro-British Upper Towns sent deputies to Stuart at Pensacola to declare their loyalty and to promise that, if trade was restored, they would fight the Americans. Stuart realized, however, that this delegation did not speak for all the Upper Creeks, and he refused their offer and did not reopen the trade. The delegation could not guarantee the safety of British agents and traders within the Creek Nation.

The superintendent also feared that loyalists would suffer if Indians without British leadership attacked the frontier and that the neutral faction would retaliate by attacking West Florida. Consequently, he advised the Upper Creeks to return home, conduct their usual winter hunt, and remain peaceful. Promising to bring the Okfuskees into line by spring, the disappointed delegation headed back to their towns.[103]

Stuart was correct in his judgment that not all the Upper Creeks were repentant. While the delegation had been at Pensacola, Handsome Fellow's successor, the White Lieutenant, of Okfuskee (Tuckanahathka), Opeitley Mico, of Tallassee, and between 100 and 350 followers visited Galphin and Rae. They asked for trade, and the Whig commissioners responded by sending eighty horse-loads of goods, rum, and ammunition.[104] This time, Colonel Elbert took the precaution of dispatching a military escort for the Indian ambassadors before trouble began.[105] In other respects, the meeting was not so successful. When the headmen protested about white settlers on Creek land, Galphin weakly claimed they were Stuart's agents.[106]

Six hundred Lower Creeks, including some Cussitas, went to visit Stuart at Pensacola, and the Lower Creeks also sent deputies to St. Augustine. These delegates were not more successful in their pleas for British trade than the Upper Creek delegates had been. After the return of those who had been to Pensacola and St. Augustine, the pro-British Lower Creeks took direct action against the neutralists. They surrounded two predominantly neutral towns, Apalachicola and Cussita, forced promises from them to renounce any pact they had made with Galphin, and took hostages to ensure that the promises were kept.[107]

Some Indian war parties were active that fall. On 19 November a detachment of Georgia Continentals killed five and captured seven Indians who had been wounded.[108]

When Lower Creek parties went out to raid the Georgia frontier and to scout for the British and when no more trade goods came from the Whigs, even the recalcitrant Okfuskees repented. In December they sent McGillivray to Pensacola to plead for them. They begged that the entire Creek Nation not be punished for their sins, and they promised they would accept anybody but Taitt as the superintendent's deputy. Stuart sent a message with McGillivray requesting that the Okfuskees come to Pensacola to see him.[109]

A report had reached Cussita in October that "a great Number of the Kings Troops embarked from St. Augustine and Landed on the

Island of Frederica."[110] This "great Number" may have been a detachment to garrison Fort Frederica, on St. Simons Island, which Brown's Rangers had taken during the summer, but British records do not confirm this. Nor do they indicate that Prevost took or had contemplated taking any offensive action against the rebels either separately or in conjunction with the proposed Indian attack.

On 10 August a British armed vessel landed part of its crew on St. Simons Island to raid the plantation of Arthur Carney, captain of the fourth company in the First Georgia Battalion. Besides Carney, the British captured five other Georgians, several Negroes, and as much household furniture as they could haul away. Carney promptly became a staunch loyalist. Americans charged that he had been aiding the British for quite some time and that he had prearranged his "capture."[111]

The Georgia assembly finally took action that had long been recommended. On 16 September it enacted legislation against all loyalists still within the state. The preamble of the "Act for the Expulsion of the Internal Enemies of This State" blamed them for transmitting intelligence to the British in East Florida. Henceforth, any male white inhabitant who was twenty-one years old or more would be compelled to appear when summoned before a special county committee; to produce at least two witnesses to vouch for his friendship to the cause of American liberty; and to subscribe to an oath acknowledging American independence and allegiance and denying any allegiance or obedience to King George.

Those who passed the test would be entitled to all privileges and protection granted to the state's free citizens. Those who failed to satisfy the requirements would be declared enemies of Georgia and the "united states" and must leave the state within forty days. Beyond that, they would forfeit a half of their estate, both real and personal, to the state, whose commissioners would administer it; the other half of the estate could be disposed of as the individual saw fit.

The act named the twelve men to compose the committee in each county (Chatham, Effingham, Burke, Richmond, Wilkes); one committee was deemed adequate for all the three lower counties of Liberty, Camden, and Glynn. The committees were to meet at least as often as the first and third Tuesday of each month; vacancies could be filled by the members' choice; at least seven members of a committee had to approve any sentence. Anyone denying the authority of the committee could be imprisoned without bail until he could be expelled; all his effects would be forfeited to the state. Any banished loyalist who returned without permission or bore arms against Georgia or any other state in rebellion would suffer the death penalty.[112]

At the same time, Georgia amended the land-office act of 7 June. Absentees were no longer required to return within six months or risk having their lands declared vacant and regranted. All former grants and allotments would remain valid; presumably, this clause applied to good Whigs and not to absentee loyalists. All surveys were to be recorded, and grants must be registered in the county where the land was located.[113]

By the middle of October, several inhabitants of Georgia had been ordered to leave the state within forty days. Because no oceangoing ships in port were scheduled to sail within the required time, their only recourse was to travel to St. Augustine through the inland waterway. When they applied to Colonel Samuel Elbert for passes, he refused to grant them on the basis that he lacked the authority to do so. Because these people obviously would proceed to St. Augustine, he questioned the wisdom of a policy that would swell the number of enemies in East Florida and give the British sources of information about conditions in Georgia. The colonel turned the problem over to General Howe.[114]

Southern commanders made a determined effort in the fall to improve the military situation in terms of both men and material. Although General McIntosh did not reach Washington's headquarters until 17 December, he "abstracted" himself from all military duties in Georgia as of 10 October. Command of all Continental forces in Georgia passed to Colonel Elbert. On 20 October Robert Howe was promoted to major general.[115]

By the fall of 1777, a fort had been built at Sunbury, on the Midway River.[116] It was named for Captain Morris, who commanded the artillery company stationed there and may have replaced an earlier fortification. The site—about 350 yards directly south of the town of Sunbury on a peninsula commanding both a bend in the Midway River, which fronted the town, and a smaller waterway that ran behind it—was well chosen. The fort was on a bluff, but swamps on three sides would deter attackers. Built by slave labor from the vicinity, this fort differed from the typical square, wood-palisade frontier defensive structure. The shape was irregular, and its walls were substantial earthworks. The enclosed court was about an acre. The eastern wall, facing the Midway, was the longest (275 feet) and had the heaviest guns. A moat surrounded the fort. The gateway, about fifteen feet wide, was near the middle of the west (land) side.[117]

On 5 December Elbert ordered Captain Defau, possibly one of the French artillery experts for whom the assembly had sent commissions to its agent in that country, to proceed to Sunbury and instruct Captain Morris' company in "the perfect use of artillery."[118]

New barracks had been constructed in Savannah by 15 October 1777. Provision magazines for the army were established at Savannah, Sunbury, and Augusta.[119] On 16 September the Georgia assembly had passed "An Act for the better Security of this State by obliging and making liable Negro Slaves to work on the several Forts Batteries or other public Works within the same."[120]

One of Elbert's first actions as commanding officer was to try to learn the number and location of the Continental troops in Georgia. They were so scattered, however, that he had not been able to obtain accurate returns by 25 October.[121]

Part of the Fourth Georgia Continental Regiment, commanded by Colonel Hovenden, had assembled in Savannah by 31 October. When he became seriously ill, command devolved upon Major Daniel Roberts.[122] News reached Savannah by 5 December that Colonel John White was marching 450 men of this regiment toward Georgia. The new recruits possessed no arms, but the supply system had improved, and Elbert was confident that adequate equipment for these men could be gotten from Charleston.[123]

Because the troops were "very bare" of clothes, Elbert ordered that complete muster rolls be given to Major (Raymond?) Demere, deputy clothier general, so that he could ascertain the quantity of clothing required.[124] When some of the officers had still not responded by 8 December, Elbert threatened to arrest them and bring them to trial.[125]

Congress had appointed Peter Taarling as army quartermaster general in Georgia and awarded him the rank of colonel. So that any deficiencies could be remedied, Elbert ordered that reports be made to Taarling of all military stores in the state and of camp equipage, including wagons and teams.[126] Governor Treutlen issued a proclamation on 21 November forbidding for three months the exportation of both salt and cordage.[127]

Elbert was determined to improve the discipline of his Continentals. Insubordination was a constant problem, partially because of lack of pay. In October the troops in Savannah were mutinous for that reason.[128]

Desertion continued and may even have increased. Men had acquired the habit of being absent without leave.[129] Galleys patrolling the inland waterway intercepted four soldiers who were posted at Sunbury and were trying to defect to St. Augustine. Probably these were the four men from the First Regiment who were court-martialed on 1 November in Savannah. Nicholas Williams was released because his corporal had told him that he was going on duty. The corporal, Thomas Wainwright, and Timothy Duffield and Andrew Watson were sentenced to death for desertion and were put in irons. On the scheduled day of execution, a council of field officers decided that only one man should be shot, as an example, and the other two would be reprieved pending the opinion of the Continental Congress. The choice was made by drawing lots, and Timothy Duffield (or Doffield) was executed immediately. The other two were not informed that they had been reprieved until after their comrade had been executed.[130]

As usual, the Light Horse was the most unruly corps. Shortly before Elbert assumed the command, the Light Horse at Fort Howe had quit that post without leave. Elbert ordered Colonel Screven, of the Third Battalion, to secure the deserters for trial. The paymaster for the Light Horse had been neglecting his duty, and the men's pay was in arrears.[131]

Four officers were involved in the Fort Howe disgrace. Lieutenant Anderson, who commanded the post when the Indian massacre near it occurred, died before trial. Lieutenant Cannon, second in command, was not held responsible for his superior's conduct and was released to rejoin his regiment. Lieutenant Robinson, who ordered the men to quit Fort Howe without authority, and Lieutenant Pope were found guilty, but they were allowed to resign their commissions.[132]

John Rice, William Wyatt, James Donaldson, David Burel, Benjamin Joyner, Christian Gamillorn, and James Barber, all of the Light Horse, suffered sixty or one hundred lashes each on 18 October for deserting their posts. Elbert commented that, according to the Articles of War, the punishment should be death and ordered that the lashes be "laid on with uncommon severity."[133]

He appointed Lieutenant Colonel Marbury, who had formerly been a member of the Light Horse, to command the regiment. The colonel hoped that the new commander could bring some order to the unit.[134]

Considerable friction existed between the military personnel and the inhabitants. On 3 December Elbert reinforced the normal guard in Savannah because he had been informed that a riot would take place in town that night. One Captain Puisang, who operated a store in another officer's house, complained that he was afraid of being assaulted by a mob; the colonel placed a sentinel at his door. On the other hand, some residents complained they had been threatened so much by soldiers that they feared for their lives. Elbert established a strict curfew for military personnel.[135]

Colonel William McIntosh, Lachlan's brother and former commander of the Light Horse, complained to Elbert in December that a party of troops stationed at Darien had plundered his plantation. This was not the first occurrence of this sort, and Elbert was irate. He ordered the perpetrators to be found and sent to headquarters for trial. Elbert said, "Those unhappy men whose conduct has held them up as enemies to the state will be dealt with as the laws direct, by persons appointed by authority of the civil power, and upon aid of the military may found necessary, on proper application it will be obtained."[136] Apparently Elbert believed that some of the troops thought the McIntoshes were Tories and had decided to take the law into their own hands. On the other hand, this incident may have been a simple case of "have nots" appropriating the property of "haves."

Elbert suggested in October that a flag of truce be sent to St. Augustine, ostensibly to arrange for a prisoner exchange but really to gain intelligence. The British had the same idea, and their emissary arrived at Sunbury about 17 November. Between then and 27 November, the Georgians and the British exchanged prisoners. John and George Aaron, both desired by the British, were deemed to be felons in Georgia, and Colonel Elbert refused to release them.[137]

By 13 October, just three days after Elbert had taken command of the Continentals, he received information that made him anticipate an immediate invasion from East Florida. Consequently, he ordered all the Continental troops to concentrate in the southern part of Georgia.[138] The invasion turned out to be another raid by the East Florida Rangers, but this was no hit-and-run affair.

A detachment of the Rangers—the Georgians called them the "Florida Scouts"—commanded by Lieutenant Sam Moore crossed the border into Georgia and moved northward. On Thursday, 16 October, they met two Georgians, Richard Eastmead and William Brunson, who had gone hunting near "Partridge Pond." The Rangers took the two men with them as far as the Little Ogeechee River, then released them after extracting a promise that they would not give information about the Rangers. Piqued because the Rangers had taken a saddle that he had borrowed from Mordecai Sheftall, a prominent rebel, Eastmead immediately reported their progress.[139]

On 19 October Elbert received this report and another indicating that the Rangers were rendezvousing in an upper fork of the Canoochee River, a tributary of the Ogeechee. This located them far north of Georgia's southern border, west of and approximately parallel to Savannah. Elbert immediately ordered Colonel Screven and a strong detachment from his Third Battalion to move down the Canoochee and Lieutenant Colonel Harris with fifty men of the First Regiment to march southward, then after dark to turn, cross the Ogeechee, and move up the Canoochee; it was hoped that the Rangers would be caught between the two forces.

Elbert enjoined strict secrecy. The men were to move only at night. Anyone they met on the way must be taken along with the troops to prevent information of the expedition leaking to the Rangers. Any man who fired a gun would be severely punished. Lest the two Continental forces meet and mistake each other for the enemy, signals were agreed upon. Each man was to wear a white cockade of paper or linen in his hat. The parole was to be "Washington." The sign was a loud "hem"; the countersign, two loud hand claps.[140]

The pincer movement did not succeed. The Rangers established a camp on the south side of the Canoochee in a canebrake one or two miles upriver from "Bowden's place" and about three miles below Ranaires'; Ranaires' and Bowdens' were about five miles apart, and both places had fords. Moore divided his forty men into small parties that raided settlements along the Ogeechee. They brought cattle, plunder, and a Mrs. Love, wife of one of the Rangers, back to their camp.[141]

Elbert again tried to trap the Rangers. On 5 December he ordered Colonel Habersham and a detachment from his regiment to cross the Ogeechee at least as far up as Fort Argyle, on the Ogeechee just above its fork with the Canoochee; and by "bribes, threats or otherwise" to get information about the Rangers. Habersham was authorized to hire or impress guides and horses as necessary. Secrecy was mandatory, and he was ordered to take along with him anyone he met whom he suspected might betray him. Again, white cockades were to be worn by the Continentals. Elbert ordered a detachment of his Second Regiment to guard the fords of the Satilla to the southward while parties scouted up the Altamaha. On 9 December he sent a subaltern and twenty-five men to reinforce Habersham.[142]

By 5 December Elbert had been informed that small groups of loyalists from the South Carolina up-country were passing through Georgia on their way to Florida. He issued orders that they should be treated as enemies.[143]

Major General Robert Howe reached Savannah by 23 December, and he was appalled by the sloppy manner in which the Georgia Continentals executed those duties that they chose to perform at all.

He and Colonel Elbert increased their efforts to obtain accurate returns on the men and matériel in the state, improve discipline, and train both officers and men. All the Continental troops in Georgia were formed into one brigade under the command of Colonel Samuel Elbert.[144]

From his post in East Florida, Tonyn warned that the need for action in the southern colonies by British forces was an urgent problem, and royal officials from Georgia and South Carolina, then in England, agreed with him. The loyalists' position was deteriorating with the passage of time. They were being forced either to swear allegiance to the new state governments or to leave. Rebel leaders were becoming even more intransigent as their hostile actions removed hope of pardon for themselves.

A large number of the colonists would still support royal government if it supported and protected them, but the downward spiral would continue unless the British took action. The sooner a major force was sent to the south, the easier restoration of royal government would be. Agricultural exports from the southern colonies were financing the rebellion. Recovery of those provinces would not only cripple the American war effort but also transfer their resources back to the British.[145] Of course, the southern Indians had long since noticed that, though the British were urging them to fight the rebels, no redcoats were doing so. The Indians had manifested their displeasure.

During the autumn of 1777, Governor Patrick Tonyn was a frustrated official. He expressed himself freely to East Florida's colonial agent in London:

> If I had been honoured with the Command of the King's Troops in this Province, Georgia would have been subdued some time ago. The impression such success would have made on the minds of his Majesty's well affected Subjects in Carolina must have had the best consequences, and I am confident Thousands would have joined at that time the King's Standard. Had this been our condition it is not improbable we might have encreased in numbers sufficient to attack Carolina.[146]

Perhaps spurred by knowledge that Germain had empowered General William Howe, commander in chief of British forces in North America, to make a colonial governor a major general,[147] Tonyn applied to Germain on 1 October for a promotion. Tonyn was a career officer in the British army; he held the rank of lieutenant colonel and had been on the half-pay list when he accepted the governorship of East Florida.[148] As a major general, he would have outranked Brigadier General Augustine Prevost. Such a simple solution to resolve conflicts in East Florida was not forthcoming.

Conflicts continued at every level. Robert Catherwood, a civilian acting as surgeon for the British military forces in East Florida, complained that he could not borrow even a shovel from the military department because the barracks master general had ordered the barracks master in St. Augustine "not to interfere" with the hospital. A flurry of high-level transoceanic correspondence was required to remedy this inconvenience.[149]

Tonyn and Prevost continued their contest for control of the East Florida Rangers. That corps had enlisted its full complement, and, when more refugees from Carolina arrived in the fall, the governor authorized the augmentation of each troop from twenty-five to forty men. He offered to halve this augmentation if Prevost wanted to enlist the new refugees in a separate corps that would be under his immediate command. By now the governor had acquired considerable practice in dealing with the Swiss officer, and he patiently explained again the principles of East Florida's constitution as a British colony and his agreement with the Rangers that made it impossible for him to relinquish command of either them or the militia. He assured Prevost that the Rangers were *virtually* under the brigadier general's command: if Prevost wanted them to perform any service or to take any station, Tonyn would be happy to issue the necessary orders immediately. When any provincial troops, including the Rangers, were on service with the king's regular troops, they would be under the orders of the commanding officer.[150]

Before the end of the year, Governor Tonyn gained a major victory over East Florida's "inflamed faction." Finally convinced that Chief Justice William Drayton's loyalty might be questionable, Germain gave Tonyn permission to suspend him from office.[151] In November 1777 the governor brought charges in the council against Chief Justice Drayton to the effect that he had generally promoted factionalism within the province and obstructed the king's service. General charges were substantiated by specific instances with supporting evidence. The council unanimously voted on 16 December to suspend Drayton from office. This time, the king confirmed the action.[152] The military managed to become involved in this purely civil matter. Colonel Fuser persuaded some of his men to sign a petition, or memorial, in Drayton's favor. He later apologized.[153]

Doctor Andrew Turnbull returned to St. Augustine on 29 November and accused Governor Tonyn of breaking up the settlements at New Smyrna.[154] The doctor had powerful friends and financial backers in England, but Germain had become convinced of his disloyalty, too.[155] Turnbull's East Florida adventure was effectively concluded. As Drayton's and Turnbull's prestige and power declined, factionalism in East Florida subsided significantly.[156]

VI

1778: The Last Georgia Campaign—and Retreat

GEORGIA'S NEW ASSEMBLY for 1778 got down to business immediately. On 10 January it elected John Houstoun as governor. Then it began to plan the annual invasion of East Florida. On 29 January the assembly promised to assist General Howe, whom it wanted to direct the expedition. After conferring with field officers, Howe recommended that the invasion not be undertaken. An estimated minimum of 1,500 troops would be necessary to capture St. Augustine, and no such numbers were available. No soldiers would be left to defend the state. Calling out the militia would disrupt essential food production. Howe recommended, instead, that all available troops be stationed in strong posts in south Georgia to protect the border. The assembly disagreed with this estimate of the situation and asked Governor Houstoun to call a council of war, consisting of himself, the general and field officers of the Continental and state troops, as well as a committee from the assembly. General Howe refused to attend in his official capacity, though he did offer to do so as a private citizen. The assembly judged his attitude to be disrespectful, even insubordinate, and requested that Governor Houstoun report him to the Continental Congress.[1]

In February that body resolved that the expedition should be undertaken. Georgia's military units should be reorganized, and any military stores there or in South Carolina could be used for an offensive operation against East Florida. About the only option given to Howe was whether he would lead the expedition or turn it over to the senior officer in Georgia, Colonel Samuel Elbert.[2] Because he lacked any alternative, Howe began to organize the offensive, but he saw no point in hurrying toward disaster.

The first step was to get the troops in shape to march. Georgia's Continentals were not responding with alacrity to the new discipline. Officers were as casual about their duties as were the men, and orders had to be repeated constantly.[3] Friction between soldiers and civilians continued. There were not enough barracks for all the troops in the towns, and soldiers frequently damaged the buildings where they were billeted as well as other civilian property. A Lieutenant McKenney was convicted of "scandalous abuse of a lady of distinction" and was discharged from the service.[4]

The soldiers were surprisingly sickly at what was considered to be the healthiest time of the year. Although military hospitals finally had been established, they left much to be desired in health care. Supplies of firewood were inadequate, and food was not always properly prepared. General Howe ordered that more attention be paid to cleanliness.[5]

Supplies and equipment for the invasion force were accumulated. Large quantities of wheat flour, Indian corn, and salted beef and pork were stocked.[6] Each battalion was furnished with an ammunition wagon and chests.[7] A mighty effort was made to obtain adequate clothing for the men.[8] Presumably, most, if not all, the Georgia Continentals possessed uniforms when they marched off to invade East Florida. What may have done as much for their morale was furnishing each Continental battalion in the state with camp colors. For the First Battalion, the field was blue, the insertions yellow; for the Second, white with blue; for the Third, green with white; for the Fourth, red with blue.[9]

On 27 November 1777 the Continental Congress had recommended to the states that they confiscate the property of inhabitants who had forfeited the "right to protection,"[10] and on 1 March 1778 the Georgia assembly passed a stronger act against loyalists. All those who had refused allegiance to the state after 19 April 1775 were subject to this act, and their entire estates were confiscated. Of the 117 Tories attainted with treason, probably most had already fled to more congenial surroundings. Anyone named in the act who returned to the state or was taken in arms against it would be tried for high treason and be subject to the death penalty if convicted. Commissioners would manage and sell the confiscated estates, and the profits would be used to redeem the state's paper money and to pay its requisitions to the Continental Congress. Many loyalists had left their families behind when they fled from the state, and in a few instances the commissioners awarded such fugitives' property to their wives or children.[11]

The government of the state of Georgia undertook on its own initiative some reorganization of the Georgia troops. Following the death of Captain Thomas Lee, the men of his artillery company, who were Continentals, were transferred to Captain George Young's company, which was on duty at the battery of the Trustees Gardens, in Savannah.[12] On 1 March the assembly voted to dissolve the Minute Battalions, which were on the state establishment, and to replace them with five independent companies under the command of a Major Wilder. The Executive Council ordered him to leave one of these new companies in the Ceded Lands and to march the other four as soon as possible to the Altamaha and wait there for orders.[13]

Georgia's Executive Council on 9 March offered a commission to any man who would raise fifteen volunteers to plunder across the border within East or West Florida. These bands were authorized to keep any booty they could take. Any Georgian who would settle for three months between the St. Marys and the St. Johns would be entitled to a five-hundred-acre land grant in that area.[14]

The records do not indicate that anyone volunteered, and the consensus among historians has been that this measure indicated the lack of realism for which the Georgia Executive Council and assembly distinguished themselves.[15] On the other hand, Georgia's records for this period are sparse. Bands of outlaws, taking advantage of the virtual anarchy outside population centers, may have raided the "good citizens" who had remained in those areas—a situation comparable to that in South Carolina which had prompted the Regulator Movement there. If so, this peculiar action by the Georgia Council may have been an effort to deflect those "banditti" toward the enemy.

Meantime, the East Floridians had taken the initiative as far as possible. As in Georgia, civil and military authorities were quarreling bitterly. Tonyn and Prevost still had not settled their disagreements over defensive-offensive policy or the command of the East Florida Rangers. The governor made good use of the resources that he could control and hoped that Prevost would be lured into cooperation. Even as the rebels prepared to invade his province, Tonyn was confident that the garrison, the Rangers, and the Indians could conquer Georgia. Surely, then, the South Carolinians could openly avow their allegiance.[16]

Tonyn was on better terms with the naval officers stationed at St. Augustine than he was with the regular army officers. British frigates, based there, cruised off that bar and as far up the coast as Charleston. They blockaded rebel shipping and brought their prizes into St. Augustine to be condemned in the admiralty court there. After the Franco-American military alliance was signed in Paris on 6 February, French ships became prizes.

On one occasion the vice-admiralty court in St. Augustine rendered a dubious decision. *Nuestra Señora del Carmen,* a sloop out of New

Orleans for the Canaries, was wrecked on Anastasia Island, and the court condemned her salvaged cargo. Spain had not yet entered the war, but news may have reached East Florida that James Willing had auctioned in New Orleans property that had been captured from West Florida planters. Also, the East Floridians possibly had heard that Francisco de Pruna, master of *Nuestra Señora del Carmen,* had taken her into Charleston harbor in January, claiming to need repairs. But, while in the rebel port, he had loaded John Rutledge's indigo for shipment to Cadiz. The East Floridians claimed that the Spanish ship was really bound for Charleston; her cargo was judged to be unsuitable for the Canary trade.[17]

The prize cargoes were welcome in East Florida, but provisioning the British ships strained the province's supplies of food and medicine. And prisoners were an additional drain on limited resources as well as a serious threat to the security of the little city of St. Augustine. Many of the sixty or seventy "private men" enlisted in the Sixtieth Regiment or joined ships' crews, but Tonyn was highly perturbed when four hundred captured Frenchmen were dumped in St. Augustine. Because France and Britain were not yet at war when the French prisoners arrived, they were not paroled but were imprisoned in the statehouse. The governor shipped them off to the West Indies and New York for exchange as fast as he could, and he requested General Prevost to keep the remainder in Fort St. Marks. The latter refused to inconvenience his regulars who were garrisoning the fort to that extent. Conditions were ripe for another quarrel (with many precedents) between governor and military officer over ultimate control of fortifications within a colony.[18]

Hearing that many Germans were among the new troops in Georgia, as well as in the long-settled areas of the state, in February Tonyn sent two German emissaries, "Carolina Palatines" who had joined the East Florida Rangers, to persuade their countrymen to desert to the British. Their efforts were successful. Eventually there was a small settlement of Germans with a church of their own near the St. Marks (or North) River between St. Augustine's outer defense line and the *Hornabeque* line.[19]

The East Florida Rangers made their headquarters at Fort Tonyn, East Florida's northernmost post. Their officers included, besides Colonel Brown, one major, four captains, four lieutenants, and a surgeon. The four companies consisted of about forty men each. On 19 February Brown reported to Tonyn that discipline had improved and that his men were ready now for any service.[20]

The Rangers had not been inactive. Raiders stole horses in St.

John's Parish, and some people in St. Andrew's Parish felt free to send boats loaded with provisions to St. Augustine.[21] At least one company of the Rangers drove off a herd of cattle from above the Altamaha, and the Georgia Executive Council ordered Colonel John Elliott of the Liberty County militia to take twenty-five men and attempt to intercept the rustlers. Thomas Gray, who was now in the pay of the state of Georgia and held a captain's commission from the assembly, was to be their guide. Some of Elliott's men flatly refused to march.[22]

Two of the Rangers, John Aarons and Rhuben Roberts, were captured; Benjamin Jones deserted.[23] Perhaps from information furnished by Jones, the Executive Council identified more than nine former residents of Georgia who were now active in the East Florida Rangers and ordered the commanding officer of the Effingham County militia to seize cattle belonging to them. Colonel Andrew Elton Wells passed the order on to Major Bonnell. When he took no action, the Executive Council remembered his lack of enthusiasm in pursuing the Rangers on an earlier occasion and ordered him to appear before it to answer for his conduct.[24]

Convinced that the Rangers were receiving assistance from Georgia residents, the Executive Council ordered stricter security measures for Savannah and its environs. All strangers were viewed with suspicion, and a nine o'clock curfew was enforced in town.[25]

On 13 March, just four days after the Georgia council had authorized free-lance plundering in northern Florida, Colonel Brown, commanding a force of one hundred Rangers and ten Indians, captured Fort Howe. Swimming the Altamaha, a chilling experience at that time of the year, when the river was a quarter of a mile wide near the fort, the British force surprised the garrison and lost only one man killed and four wounded (including Lieutenants Drew, Scott, and Williams) in the attack. Two of the defenders were killed and four wounded. The Rangers took twenty-three prisoners and two pieces of artillery and two swivels.

One Georgia refugee, Andrew Johnston, son of Doctor Lewis Johnston, distinguished himself by being the first to mount the entrenchments. Among the Indians accompanying the Rangers were Lihalgie, Stimpoy, Inatalitchie, and the Pumpkin King's two nephews. Prevost refused to be inveigled into committing his regulars this time, however, and the Rangers were not numerous enough to garrison the post. Brown could only burn the fort, abandon the site of his victory, and turn southward again with his prisoners. Prevost reported that he did not believe the destruction of Fort Howe was important. He was wrong.[26]

Now that the Georgians had no posts on the St. Marys, the Satilla, or the Altamaha—except for a small force downriver from Darien near the coast—the Rangers operated unhindered. Their raids on Georgia cattle herds were peaceful roundups. Because the backcountry was clear of opposing forces, as Whig troops were being concentrated for the invasion of East Florida, Brown encountered no difficulty in sending three small parties into Georgia and two into South Carolina to contact loyalists and to obtain information about rebel military strength and plans. He had sent one party of twelve men into South Carolina in February.[27] When these parties returned in April, he submitted a detailed intelligence report of the rebel forces' strength and of the location and condition of fortifications in Georgia and South Carolina.[28]

The secret emissaries from East Florida persuaded eleven men of Georgia's Fourth Battalion to desert. After acquiring a pilot, the deserters surprised a French vessel that was carrying a cargo of rice and indigo off Tybee Island and brought her into the St. Johns River. A French artillery officer who was serving as a captain in the Georgia Continentals was on board; he joined the other captured French officers who were incarcerated in the East Florida statehouse.[29]

Brown's reconnaissance parties, who had administered the oath of allegiance to many backcountry loyalists, reported that more than 6,000 Carolinians were willing to rise against the rebels and aid the king's troops. They counted 2,500 between the forks of the Broad and Saluda rivers, 1,000 upon the South Fork, more in the Congarees, and 2,800 on the western border between North and South Carolina.[30]

Several hundred of the Carolina loyalists immediately began to march toward St. Augustine. Although they were short of provisions, they were able bodied and well mounted, and made their way southward with astonishing rapidity. Such a large body of men could not move even in the backcountry, however, without being detected, and Whigs in every district along the way called out the militia. Although two loyalists deserted in Georgia, seven of Colonel Marbury's regiment, stationed on the Ogeechee, joined the loyalists on their march southward.[31]

Some Carolina refugees who were not well armed turned back at the Savannah River. David Fanning, later a famous partisan leader, blamed Captain John York of the Rangers for being fainthearted.

The Rangers attributed the Carolinians' timidity to their inability to procure arms and the warning earlier parties had given to local militia units, who threatened to dispute the Savannah crossings.[32]

The loyalists entered East Florida without encountering armed opposition. More than 350 Carolinians in one body reached St. Augustine in the middle of April 1778.[33] Some joined Brown's Rangers, but most were organized into a distinct corps. General Prevost formed the South Carolina Royalists, consisting of 250 men. He armed them with rifles and Brown Bess muskets and uniformed them with red coats. To forestall a command problem, he immediately put them under the command of his brother, Major James Mark Prevost.[34]

It usually has been assumed that the North Carolina Loyalist Regiment was formed in St. Augustine at about the same time. That unit, however, was not organized until a considerable number of North Carolina loyalists could reach the British lines following the conquest of Savannah.[35]

The sentiments of the Creeks were still divided. Most of the Lower Towns were still pro-American and anti-British, with the important town of Coweta divided. In February, Fine Bones, of Coweta, sent a message to Commissioner Galphin; he promised that he himself would not kill any more Americans and that he would no longer oppose the majority of the Lower Towns in their preference for neutrality. At the same time, Fine Bones warned Galphin that one party of Coweta warriors was still operating against settlers in the Ceded Lands.[36]

This Coweta party precipitated a new split between the Creeks and the Georgians by attacking a detachment of the Georgia Light Horse near the Ceded Lands and killing three soldiers. Galphin immediately stopped all trade to the entire Creek Nation.[37] The governor and council decided not to issue any land grants within the Ceded Lands.[38]

Starved for trade goods, both the Upper and Lower Creeks sent delegations to Pensacola to plead with Superintendent Stuart. Even headmen who had been strongly anti-British, such as Hycut, of Cussita, and some of the Okfuskees, promised him they would protect his agents and traders. Early in March he sent his deputies and the British traders back into the Creek country.[39]

Taitt met the Upper Creek headmen on 30 March. The Abeikas and Tallapoosas promised to protect British traders in their towns. Taitt even sent traders into towns where there were strongly disaffected factions (Great Tallassee, Okfuskee, Sugatspoges, and Corn House) in the hope of winning them over. When the Okfuskees invited the deputy to visit them, however, Taitt refused. He believed they were still too undependable, and he sent them a message that they could visit him at Little Tallassee if they were ready to go to Pensacola to pledge allegiance to the British.[40]

William McIntosh, Stuart's deputy for the Lower Towns, was under the personal protection of Hycutt, of Cussita. On 2 April he summoned the Lower Creek headmen to a meeting at the Hitchitas. Even the Fat King, of Cussita, came to this meeting and promised allegiance to the British. Cussita hunters who had sold their deerskins to Galphin's agent repossessed them to trade with the British. Because Galphin had embargoed Whig trade, the warriors considered their action justified. Most important, warriors from the Hitchitas, the Chiahas, and the Flint River promised to go to St. Augustine in May to assist a British expedition against Georgia.[41]

On 2 May four hundred Okfuskees, Tallassees, Cussitas, Hitchitas, and Apalachicolas—many of them former neutrals or even American supporters—met Stuart in Pensacola. They promised at the very least not to hinder the activities of any pro-British factions in their towns.[42]

While those delegates were talking to Stuart in Pensacola, the King of Tuckabatchee led a delegation to Savannah. Thoroughly alarmed by the threatening situation on the Indian frontier while the state was stripped of troops for the East Florida expedition, the Whigs made liberal promises. They roundly denounced white trespassers on Indian lands across the Ogeechee and gave presents of ammunition and trade goods as generously as they were able to bestow. Some Indians who managed to be present at both the Pensacola and Savannah conferences told Galphin that the Creeks had forced Stuart to agree to Indian neutrality; that they had convinced him to withdraw Taitt from their nation and to lower trade prices; and that, if more Cowetas went against the Americans, they themselves would attack Pensacola.[43]

One incident while the Pensacola meeting was in progress indicated more clearly than all the talks that the neutral faction was not beaten. Patrick Carr, one of Galphin's agents, arrived at Abeika with some trade goods, probably the first from Galphin since the general Whig embargo, and a message from Galphin to Richard Henderson asking him to urge the Creeks to side with the Americans. British traders in the area suspected Henderson of being an enemy agent and tried to seize him. A party of Okfuskees and Sugatspoges rescued him, and Carr confidently reported to Galphin that there was strong sentiment for neutrality among the Upper Creeks.[44]

Because of the Rangers' successful attack on Fort Howe, dissident Carolinians marching through Georgia to join the king's troops at St.

Augustine, and Indian ambassadors carrying tales of British machinations, all of Georgia was thrown into a state of alarm. On 27 March South Carolina dispatched a flag of truce with forty-five prisoners of war to St. Augustine.[45] Information as well as exchanged prisoners undoubtedly came back to Charleston.

The Executive Council of Georgia issued orders to improve regulation of the militia. Drafts of one-third of each regiment or battalion were to be designated, and in rotation were to keep themselves ready for service on one hour's warning.[46] Four days later, the council ordered two-thirds of the militia to be activated and, as the commanding officer in each county thought best, either to march into barracks or to pursue the Carolinians.[47] A volunteer company of horse and one of artillery were to be formed out of the Chatham County militia.[48]

On 16 April the Executive Council requested Governor John Houstoun to assume all executive power "appertaining to the Militia or the defence of the State against the present danger which threatens it or in annoyance of the Enemy." Experience had shown that it was sometimes impossible to assemble the Executive Council as quickly as necessary during an emergency, so the governor agreed to accept complete executive authority in military matters. Also, a special session of the assembly had been called to meet in Augusta on 27 April, and that body could negate the council's decision if it chose to do so. Then the council adjourned to meet in Augusta on the same day as the assembly.[49]

The Georgians were firmly convinced that the British were about to invade their state from East Florida,[50] and the American offensive against East Florida finally got underway. By 9 April the Georgia Continentals reached the Midway district, by 12 April they were at General McIntosh's plantation, the next day they arrived at McClennon's plantation, and on 14 April they camped at burned-out Fort Howe.[51] Colonel Elbert commanded there, the rendezvous for the southern expedition.

Tonyn had decided in March that the most effective preventive measures he could take were to secure the inland passage and to destroy the Georgia galleys. Consequently, the *Galatea* (Captain Jordan), the *Hinchinbrook* (Lieutenant Ellis), and the *Rebecca* (Captain Mowbray) sailed northward along the coast. The *Galatea* could not cross the St. Marys bar, and even the *Hinchinbrook* and the *Rebecca* were too large to chase the rebel galleys through the maze of waterways south of the Altamaha. The only solution seemed to be for East Florida to build galleys that would be better armed than those of the rebels. The British left a few men to garrison Fort Frederica, on St.

Simons Island, where Brown had sent his wounded from Fort Howe. A lethal fever decimated the *Galatea*'s crew. Forty of them were ill at one time and at least seven died. Jordan sent some of his sick men to Mr. Martin's house on Jekyll Island. While the British ships were on this frustrating service, Lieutenant Ellis and a seaman drowned in a small-boat accident; the loss of such an experienced officer was a heavy blow to East Florida.[52]

On 15 April Elbert decided to attack the three British ships: the *Hinchinbrook*, the privateer *Rebecca*, and a prize brig, anchored near Frederica on St. Simons Island. The next day, he marched a detachment of three field officers, six captains, eighteen subalterns, twenty-four sergeants, six drummers, two fifers, and three hundred rank and file to Darien. There they boarded three galleys: the *Washington, Lee,* and *Bulloch.* Captain Young commanded an artillery detachment with two field pieces, which boarded a flatboat.[53]

Leaving detachments of troops on board the galleys, the main body of Continentals landed at Pike's Bluff, about a mile and a half from Frederica, on the night of 18 April. Elbert immediately dispatched about a hundred men, commanded by Lieutenant Colonel Rae and Major Roberts, to enter the town; there they captured two sailors and three marines from the *Hinchinbrook*. About ten o'clock the next morning, the galleys attacked the ships, which soon surrendered. Mowbray tried to destroy the *Rebecca* before he abandoned her, but both she and the *Hinchinbrook* were captured by the rebels. The Continentals suffered no casualties. Nine of the *Hinchinbrook*'s crew were captured, but all the other British, including Captain Mowbray, escaped. While Elbert was preparing to attack the *Galatea*, anchored at the north end of Jekyll Island, she escaped. The cargo of the *Hinchinbrook* included three hundred uniforms that were intended for Colonel Pinckney's South Carolina Continental regiment and had been captured in the *Hatter* off Charleston. The campaign to the southward had begun with an important American victory.[54]

The defeat at St. Simons left East Florida with no naval defense except the *Galatea*. Consequently, Governor Tonyn, with the advice of his council and the recommendation of naval officers, purchased three vessels for provincial service. The *Germain* was large enough to cruise in open water; the others were brigs that were to be converted into galleys. Tonyn promised to donate his share of prizes, to which he was entitled as vice-admiral, toward the vessels' expenses. He noted that such vessels would be very useful indeed, not only for East Florida's defense, but also for an offensive operation from that province into Georgia. Private citizens donated and fitted out as privateers the armed sloops *Ranger* and *Tonyn's Revenge*. A bounty of ten milled dollars was offered to every seaman who volunteered to serve on the provincial vessels and galleys. The governor proclaimed an embargo on all vessels within East Florida.[55]

Tonyn and Prevost finally had submitted their quarrel over command of the East Florida Rangers to General Sir William Howe to settle.[56] Prevost doubted the legality of Tonyn's commissions for the Rangers. Tonyn requested the removal of Major James Mark Prevost, General Prevost's brother and a supporter of the Drayton faction. The governor believed that the major was a bad influence on his brother; because only three incomplete companies of his Second Battalion were in St. Augustine, his services there were not essential.[57]

Having received fresh news of the impending invasion, however, General Prevost decided not to wait for word from the commander in chief and took matters into his own hands. On 18 April he informed the governor that no regular troops would assist the Rangers who were defending the St. Marys border unless Lieutenant Colonel Brown agreed to submit to the command of Major Glazier of the regular British army. Three days later, for emphasis, Prevost ordered all the British regulars to return to the south side of the St. Johns. Neither Tonyn nor Brown had an alternative to acquiescence. Brown did request permission to resign his commission, but Tonyn, of course, refused to accept that. Brown's force, well mounted but hopelessly outnumbered, remained on the border, and, assisted only by some of the recently embodied Carolina refugees, delayed as long as possible the invading army's passage across the river.[58]

Prevost had an excuse for the withdrawal of the regulars:

> The misfortune happened to the armed vessels in the inland Navigation and probability that the Galatea will soon quit that station, rendering the conveyance of provisions to the post of the Rangers very precarious, and being apprehensive that your additional numbers would soon create a scarcity of Provisions.[59]

Tonyn called out the militia and demanded assistance in the form of Negroes, horses, carriages, and boats. Prevost requested that the militia perform guard duty in town and garrison the forts at Picolata and Matanzas. Some of the inhabitants were dilatory about rendering any service.[60]

East Florida was running short of provisions. By the time the American forces crossed the border into his province in June, Tonyn would reckon that he had provisions in store for only three weeks.[61]

Prevost cut off provisions for the Rangers and the provincial marines. Brown later said that he—and undoubtedly his Rangers—lived for four weeks on rice and palmetto cabbage.[62]

Governor Tonyn eagerly anticipated the arrival of his Indian allies;[63] it was a long and disheartening wait. Because the Whig trade embargo was in effect, Red Shoes, Mad Dog, of Tuckabatchee, and others went to Great Tallassee in April to persuade Opeitley Mico and his neutral followers to travel to Pensacola to talk to Stuart in May.[64] Mad Dog had real neutrality in mind, but a group of Okfuskees went much further. They promised that, if the Lower Creeks aided the British, they would attack British settlers near Pensacola and Mobile to even the score.[65]

Then the Creeks began to complain of the long march from their country to the Georgia-Florida border and of the scarcity of provisions. The 1777 corn crop had been a failure, following the bad crop of 1776. News of the Franco-American alliance had reached the Creeks, and the Tallassee King heard via Coweta that the Spaniards would soon take St. Augustine and Pensacola. He immediately vowed to kill Taitt if the deputy did not leave the nation.[66] Choctaws reported to Stuart that Don Bernardo de Galvez, the Spanish governor at New Orleans, had told them that West Florida would be returned to Spain some time in May 1778.[67] Galphin, who was almost keeping "open house" at his post on the Ogeechee, heard that many Indians believed rumors that France and Spain would soon repossess the Gulf Coast.[68]

When Stuart heard that a rebel army was actually invading East Florida, he ordered Taitt and McIntosh to send parties of warriors to aid St. Augustine and to raid the frontier. Most of the Creeks decided to postpone action until after the new harvest and the Green Corn Dance, in late July or early August. One party from Okfuskee and one from Coweta went out raiding. Tonyn had expected 1,700 Creek warriors; one hundred with Perryman appeared. Once again, the Seminoles were the governor's most dependable allies.[69]

This extraordinarily large number of warriors coming to the assistance of East Florida may have been a misunderstanding on Tonyn's part. As Alexander Skinner, Stuart's agent in St. Augustine, understood the matter, 1,500 or 1,600 Indians would arrive, but that number would include women and children, who would return to their homes as soon as they had obtained enough provisions from the British to subsist while the warriors were actively aiding the king's troops. Skinner himself did not expect even a quarter of the number mentioned.[70]

Perryman and other headmen told Tonyn that more Creeks were

ready to come to East Florida's aid when McIntosh and Taitt arrived
in the nation with peace talks from Stuart.[71] Tonyn blamed Stuart for
the Creeks' inactivity; Stuart denied any guilt and blamed Galphin.
The British offered a reward of £500 for Galphin—dead or alive.[72]

Prevost refused to take the invasion threat as seriously as Tonyn,
but he did take some precautions for East Florida's defense. Although
he did not support or even feed them, he ordered the Rangers and
some of the Carolina refugees, part of whom were Light Horse, to
remain at the St. Marys. He regarded the St. Johns as the real
boundary of East Florida, and he had built a small fortification on its
north side. An armed vessel was stationed on the south side; also,
some batteries had been erected at the crossing points on the river
(almost certainly Cowford and Hester's Bluff). A number of Negroes
were employed in repairing St. Augustine's defense lines.[73]

The British and provincial naval force did not fare well. The
Galatea lost her rudder and sailed directly to New York.[74] East Florida
privateers cruised as far north as Charleston harbor, but two met
disaster there. Captain George Osborne had gone to sea again in the
eight-gun sloop *Ranger,* with a crew of thirty-five. Adam Bachop
captained the sloop *Tonyn's Revenge,* which was equipped with twelve
carriage guns and swivels and carried seventy-two men. Probably
Captain Mowbray commanded the *Germain.* On 22 June the Connecticut ship *Defense* (Captain Samuel Smedley), her tender, and a French
armed sloop *Volant* (Captain Daniel) captured the *Tonyn's Revenge* and
the *Ranger.* Both sloops were subsequently condemned in the admiralty court at Charleston.[75]

While General Robert Howe was marching to the Altamaha rendezvous, Colonel McGirth led a raiding party into the Midway district.
Meeting a superior force, the British irregulars retreated hastily back
into East Florida.[76]

Brown sent Captain James Moore to collect horses on the Satilla
and then, with seventy-six Rangers and some Indians, to join a group
of loyalists, circle behind the rebel troops, and attack their rear.[77] A
report reached the American camp on 29 June that Moore had been
killed and twenty of his men captured near Augusta.[78] The next day,
Brown wrote to Tonyn that, according to an unconfirmed report
from a Georgian, Moore and nine of his company had been killed.[79]
Late in the summer, Ensign Schodde of the Sixtieth Regiment, who
had voluntarily accompanied a war party of Indians and then joined
Moore's detachment, straggled into St. Augustine with a detailed
account: Moore had been betrayed, and some of his men had deserted. After the captain had been wounded and captured, he was

murdered in cold blood. Some of the other captives survived, and Schodde escaped.[80]

A "considerable" reinforcement reached the American camp on 26 April. Presumably, this was a four-hundred-man volunteer force from the Georgia militia.[81] Governor Houstoun had issued a proclamation calling upon volunteers to meet him at a state camp that had been established at Burke County. He himself was to command this contingent; the state would furnish provisions and ammunition; plunder would be retained by the captors.[82] Houstoun and a group of his volunteers did not reach the main body of troops until after 12 June.[83] Commodore Oliver Bowen, of the Georgia navy, commanded the expedition's naval units.

On 3 May detachments of South Carolina troops reached camp.[84] Colonel Charles Cotesworth Pinckney commanded six hundred men from the First, Third, and Sixth South Carolina Continental Regiments. Colonel Andrew Williamson, leading eight hundred South Carolina militiamen, was en route, [85] but they proceeded so slowly they did not even cross the Altamaha until July.[86] There was also a detachment of thirty matrosses from the South Carolina artillery. On 10 May the troops of the Carolina Continental battalions were formed into a brigade with Colonel Pinckney as colonel commandant. The South Carolina artillery joined the Georgia artillery under the command of Major Roman.[87]

General Howe reached the fort named in his honor on 9 May;[88] there he waited for the two or three thousand troops that he expected to join his expedition. Colonel Elbert's Georgia Continentals, numbering about 500, had been encamped at Fort Howe for nearly a month.[89]

The Georgia Brigade also underwent some reorganization. Because of deaths, resignations, and promotions, several officers were shifted about. For the First Regiment, Lieutenant Colonel Rae, of the Third, became colonel; Captain Habersham, major. For the Second Regiment, Major Roberts of the Third was promoted to lieutenant colonel; Captain Porter, to major. For the Third Regiment, Lieutenant Colonel Stirk of the Second became colonel, replacing Screven, who had resigned on 21 March; Major McIntosh of the First, lieutenant colonel; and Captain Lane, major. For the Fourth Regiment, Major Pannell of the Second was advanced to lieutenant colonel.[90]

Each battalion was to be formed into ten equal companies, two of which were to be grenadiers and light infantry. These two companies were to be composed of picked men, each armed with a good musket and bayonet, as were the Light Dragoons. The Light Infantry and the

Light Dragoons were to be formed into one corps of Light Troops under the command of Lieutenant Colonel Harris, of the First Regiment. All the grenadier companies would be one corps under the command of Captain Moore, of the Second Regiment.[91]

This expedition was the best equipped of the Whig invasions of East Florida. Armaments of all sorts were in better supply than they had been. Even artillery was available. Negroes were hired or impressed to help with pioneer work. Indians, commanded by Captain Gray, accompanied the force.[92] Nevertheless, such amenities as tents, camp kettles, canteens, and medicines were in uncomfortably short supply.[93]

While the troops remained encamped at Fort Howe until 27 May, morale deteriorated steadily. Temperatures were unseasonably warm. An enemy party fired on a militia detachment on 24 April. Alarms, probably false, occurred on the nights of 14 and 16 May, but by 22 May scouting parties of enemy Indians were known to be in the vicinity.[94] Captain James Mercer, a former trader, deserted from St. Augustine and reached Savannah on 21 April. He declared that the British force in East Florida was formidable. Besides the regular garrison, hundreds of backcountry loyalists were already there and more were coming; the Creek warriors were on the way to join the British; and General Prevost had left St. Augustine and was marching northward, probably to attack the Americans on the Altamaha.[95]

Desertions increased as the weather grew hotter. Only one Georgia Continental, John Mason, of the Second Regiment, deserted in April; he received a hundred lashes. Between 16 and 23 May, however, the number of deserters soared. The officers of one court-martial devised a punishment that was unique for Georgia. John Brown, John Baptist Curchon, James Johnson (or Johnston), and Thomas Campbell (Fourth Regiment) were sentenced to "run the gauntlet thro their respective brigades." On 21 May Sergeant Tyrrell of the Fourth Georgia Battalion, who had been convicted of mutiny and of trying to persuade others to desert, was shot; General Howe announced that he had resolved "never to pardon any future desertions." A whole group of men deserted the next day. Some returned voluntarily, and others were captured. Gray's Indians brought in the scalp of one, and another was assumed to have died in the woods. James Lister and Cornelius Fitzgerald, of the First Battalion, were hanged; James Neigle, William Carpenter, Daniel McKay, Claudius Morrison, Joseph Clair, Joseph Powell, Richard Savage, John Royal, and William Conner, all privates in the Fourth Battalion, were shot.[96]

In commenting on these desertions, both Colonel Pinckney and

General Moultrie stated that Colonel White's Fourth Battalion was composed chiefly of British deserters. When these men joined the Georgia Battalion, presumably during the recruitment drives in the north, they probably never thought they might find themselves fighting other British regulars, their former comrades in arms, in East Florida. John Fauchereaud Grimké, of South Carolina, said, "This Lister had been a Sergeant in Burgoynes light horse and deserted from them after the battle of German-Town: He served as a volunteer in the 2d: Cont: Geo: Battalion."[97]

Grimké also noted that two of the men who were sentenced to run the gauntlet on 16 May were French. Their French officers protested that the two Frenchmen would prefer death to such disgrace. The soldiers, however, disagreed and chose the gauntlet.[98]

Eight Irishmen succeeded in deserting by water on 26 May. They had been sent to reconnoiter in Frederica Sound and to the southward. The lieutenant in command landed first, whereupon the boatmen pulled away from shore. Dr. Blunt, a surgeon in the "Fleet," was released and returned to the rebel camp.[99]

Long delayed in waiting for provisions, equipment, and military stores coming from South Carolina by water,[100] the Georgia and South Carolina Brigades finally started breaking up camp at Fort Howe on 25 May and crossed the Altamaha. From 28 May through 6 June, the Georgians camped at Reid's Bluff, on the south side of that river three miles downstream from Fort Howe. Rains were so heavy during this time that the ammunition was seriously endangered. Provisions ran short. Enemy Indians lurked about the camp and kept the men closely confined within the lines. The only cheerful note was General Howe's announcement on 1 June that France had publicly acknowledged the independence of the United States of America. Thirteen cannon were fired in celebration, and an issue of grog was served to the men.[101]

On the morning of 4 June, a party of about sixteen Indians killed and partially scalped a gunsmith named Seeds on the road between Fort Howe and Reid's Bluff. The bodies of the man and his mare were found by Major Romans and Captain Young of the artillery, who had crossed the Altamaha just ten minutes after Seeds. Some privates on a honey-hunting expedition saw the Indians, pursued them into a swamp, but failed to capture them.[102]

Sickness increased at an incredible rate. On 6 June one officer estimated that three hundred men had become so ill that they were moved out of the camp at Reid's Bluff to a hospital at Darien. A week later, he noted that only seven hundred Continentals were effectives;

half the soldiers in the South Carolina Brigade were sick. Hospitals were established at St. Catherines, Sapelo, Darien, and Sunbury.[103]

The only contest of arms was a skirmish near Cowford on the north side of the Satilla on 17 June. An American scouting party, consisting of Colonel Harris and some light infantry as well as Colonel Habersham and some mounted volunteers, encountered a detachment of the East Florida Rangers. The Rangers lost eight good horses, five saddles and bridles, their blankets, and one of them was taken prisoner. The rest of the East Florida company escaped through a swamp. The prisoner claimed that Brown commanded three hundred men and had provisions for three months; at least one Georgia officer, Joseph Habersham, believed that report was a gross exaggeration.[104]

Like its predecessors, this American expedition had never really become organized. The usual order of march was the Georgia Brigade in the vanguard, the South Carolina Brigade sometimes as far behind as the next river, and detachments of the Georgia militia and volunteers scattered along behind them. No one was sure where Williamson and the South Carolina militia were—except that they were a long way in the rear. Food and equipment were scarce, and the Continentals and militia quarreled over what little was available. The leaders, mainly Howe and Houstoun, rarely conferred and usually disagreed when they did.[105] By the time the Georgia Brigade crossed the Satilla River and camped on its southern bank on 21 June, some soldiers were without shoes. Again, hides for moccasins were issued.[106]

By 23 June the American naval force had anchored at Wright's landing, on the St. Marys; within three days the Continentals had encamped at Armstrong's, farther upstream on the Georgia side of that river. General Howe proposed to surprise the Rangers by a sudden attack, and he requested General Screven, who was now commanding part of the Georgia militia, to detach a body of mounted men under Major Parker to assist the Continentals. Screven replied that he had positive orders not to let the Georgia militia cross the Satilla River; he would forward Howe's dispatches to Governor Houstoun, who was still encamped at Reid's Bluff, on the Altamaha.[107]

The Georgia and South Carolina Continentals crossed the St. Marys River on 28 June. Three horsemen reconnoitering the new camp were challenged by a picket of the First Brigade (Georgia Continentals). They immediately galloped off, and the sentinel fired upon them. A light horseman pursued one of the fleeing trio so closely that he was forced to drop his baggage, including his coat, in order to escape into a swamp. The contents of the baggage revealed that the Americans had nearly captured Lieutenant Colonel Brown himself.[108]

While the last of the South Carolina Continentals were crossing the St. Marys, Governor Houstoun and his Georgia militia arrived on the north bank. The army paused for three or four hours while the governor and General Howe argued about who should have supreme command of the expedition and whether to attack the Rangers at Fort Tonyn or Prevost's regulars who were posted fifteen or twenty miles away on the St. Augustine highway. The two men could not agree. Each retained his own command. Houstoun opted to attack the British regulars. He insisted that George Mills, St. Marys' most famous rebel and the only reliable guide available, leave the Continentals and guide the militia. At four o'clock in the afternoon, the Continentals started marching toward Fort Tonyn, ten miles downstream.[109]

The delay had given the Rangers time to burn Fort Tonyn and to secure some of their supplies and equipment; they abandoned the rest. On 29 June the Continentals camped at the site. Brown's force lingered in the area, camping in nearby Cabbage Swamp and annoying the enemy as much as possible; the Rangers were virtually trapped. A detachment of regulars (the grenadiers of the Second Battalion and the Light companies of the Sixteenth Regiment and Fourth Battalion of the Sixtieth Regiment) and the newly formed South Carolina Royalists manned a small ditched redoubt of logs and brush that guarded the Alligator Creek Bridge, about fourteen miles from Fort Tonyn over that tributary of the Nassau River.[110]

One young officer from South Carolina described the laurels won in this American expedition to the southward:

> We have now with great toil and difficulty, thro' parching Lands and uncultivated wilds, frequently in the Meridian Heat, Marched near 300 Miles to this Place, and the Reward of our trouble has been to find in a half demolished Stockade Fort, a few devils Cloaths, Blankets, and trifling Necessaries buried under ground or thrown into the River, and to have the Soul Soothing Satisfaction of knowing that the Fame and Terror of our Maiden Arms have made a petty Partizan, with far Inferior numbers, Decamp from a Post not tenable ag[ains]t Field Pieces.[111]

Major Graham of the Sixteenth and two hundred regulars as well as some of McGirth's Rangers moved northward to join Brown's forces at Cabbage Swamp. When scouting Rangers encountered a group of rebel flankers, some firing occurred but no casualties resulted. The

Americans "changed the direction of their route." When Graham and Brown met, the whole force encamped. Graham shortly received orders to retreat, however, and his force returned to Alligator Bridge before night.[112]

An American detachment had come by water and taken a position on the Nassau River. On the same day, 29 June, an inhabitant who had escaped from the Americans camped at Nassau Bluff, seventeen miles east of Alligator Creek Bridge—presumably at Niel Rain's house—reached the British post and informed Major Prevost that only Colonel White and ninety of the Fourth Georgia Battalion and Captain Nash and fourteen dragoons were at the bluff. A British detachment led by Captain Murray, consisting of twenty of his company, twenty of the Sixteenth's Light Infantry, and Captain York of the South Carolina Dragoons, immediately moved out eastward and crossed Mills's and Thomas's swamps. Colonel White's force decamped. The British force dined on roast beef and biscuit that Colonel White had intended for his men, then fell back to a swamp two miles in the rear to camp for the night.[113]

In the little settlement at Nassau Bluff, Murray found an American sympathizer, a doctor, and his two daughters who had been left stranded by the retreating rebels. Two loyalist families declared that Colonel White had treated them kindly while they were prisoners, so Murray allowed the doctor and his daughters to depart with their baggage.[114]

The next day, 30 June, Murray's detachment rejoined the British force at Alligator Creek Bridge. Graham's men had returned the previous evening, and Brown's Rangers and Indians were encamped in a swamp about six miles in front of the main body. During the morning, while Brown was marching toward Alligator Creek Bridge, a rebel detachment surprised his rear. General Screven led more than a hundred mounted Georgia militia chasing the Rangers through the regular British army outposts. Because conventional uniforms were scarce among both the East Florida Rangers and the Georgia militia, the British regulars assumed that all the mounted men were Rangers. Discovering their mistake, the regulars fired on the Americans. Colonel Elijah Clarke led an attack on the British flank; he was shot through the thigh and barely escaped capture. The Rangers formed on the Americans' flank, and the Georgia militia withdrew.

More than thirteen Americans were killed, nine of whom, including an ensign and a black man, were left on the field; and several were wounded. One British regular was killed and several wounded. The Rangers' Captain Smith and Lieutenant Johnson as well as three others were wounded. The Americans captured one lieutenant from the Royal South Carolinians. A dozen or more South Carolina Royalists took the opportunity to desert in the confusion of the battle, and they soon reached the Georgia militia's camp. The Battle of Alligator Creek Bridge was the last battle in the last American invasion of East Florida.[115]

In the morning, 1 July, Major Prevost, Colonel Brown, Captain Murray, and a party of South Carolina dragoons moved about ten miles northward and surprised an American work detail that was repairing a bridge. The rebels fled on horseback. Pursuit by the British was unsuccessful; they burned the bridge and carried off the tools.[116]

That day, Major Prevost moved his advance corps, about a third of the total British force in East Florida, back from Alligator Creek to Six Mile Creek and left Indians to observe the enemy's movements. As they passed through the swamps, the British blocked the road with felled trees. Rangers supplied horses, cattle, and provisions. Two frigates guarded the mouth of the St. Marys and cruised along the coast.[117]

By 1 July the American army was out of rice.[118] The main body of the American militia and Continentals was encamped about eight miles apart on opposite sides of the St. Marys. Governor Houstoun urged General Howe to have his Continentals ready to march with the militia to attack the British at Alligator Creek on 2 July. Howe promptly agreed on the condition that Houstoun supply the Continentals with rice; an expected supply galley had failed to arrive. The governor replied that he did not have enough provisions within his own camp for the next day's rations. The American attack did not take place.[119] By the time provisions arrived on 2 July, the Continentals had been without bread for three days.[120]

Not surprisingly, tempers frayed rapidly. On 2 July two of the Georgia Brigade's officers fought a duel. Colonel (Francis?) Harris was seriously wounded.[121]

In his tent on 3 July, General Howe held an informal council with Governor Houstoun, Commodore Bowen, Colonel Elbert, and Colonel Pinckney.[122] No results were evident.

The American soldiers sickened quickly in their miserable camps. By early July the number of effective Continentals was less than half what it had been at Fort Howe. The horses were dying of starvation.[123]

On 6 July the Georgia militia finally crossed the St. Marys and joined the Continentals on its south side, much to the satisfaction of the latter. Their number had been reduced to four hundred effectives; the combined force of Major Prevost and Colonel Brown was at least equal and possibly superior to that. A British attack on any part of the American army while it was separated from the others could have been devastating.[124]

Colonel Williamson reached the St. Marys on 8 July; his South Carolina militia were just crossing the Satilla. One thousand strong, they did not cross the St. Marys until 10 July. Houstoun, Howe, Williamson, and Bowen took the opportunity to confer. Howe, Continental commander of the Southern Department and senior officer, claimed command of the expedition by right and by order of the Continental Congress; he and his Continental officers wanted to retreat immediately. Governor John Houstoun refused to relinquish ultimate authority over his Georgia militia; he wanted to cross the St. Johns and attack the British in their stronghold. Colonel Andrew Williamson, probably following Houstoun's lead, refused to take orders from the Continental general; he was willing to march as far as the St. Johns, but not to cross it. Commodore Bowen refused to take orders from any land officer; he favored retreat.[125]

The Americans' lack of organization and discipline showed up in many small disasters. Nearly a dozen Georgians, most of them from the Fourth Battalion, deserted. A scouting party of picked men from Williamson's corps lost their horses and risked capture because they refused to obey the two Continental captains who were commanding them. Several of the sick died in camp; others were evacuated by water. Colonel George Walton straggled into the governor's camp with 150 Georgia militia on 10 July.[126]

HMS *Perseus*, commanded by Captain George Keith Elphinstone, reached the mouth of the St. Johns and opened communications with General Prevost on 11 July. The *Perseus* and the sloop *Otter*, under Lieutenant John Wright, had convoyed a ship carrying food for the East Florida garrison, and Elphinstone's orders directed him to defend East Florida and to remain on that station as long as his provisions held out or until an intended reinforcement reached St. Augustine. Tonyn immediately put Captain Mowbray's *Germain* as well as the galleys *Dreadnought* and *Thunderer* under Elphinstone's command. The *Germain* and the *Thunderer* were stationed off Sisters Creek; the *Dreadnought* farther downstream toward the St. Johns bar; and the *Otter* guarded that bar and the Nassau Inlet, to the northward. The schooner *Fortune* was variously employed.[127]

General Howe called a council of war in the camp at Fort Tonyn on 11 July. Only Continental officers were present. Howe made the following points: the British had been drawn out of Georgia and their advance base, Fort Tonyn, destroyed; the roads to the southward were virtually impassable; the enemy clearly did not intend to make any stand north of the St. Johns; at least forty more horses were needed for a further advance; the physicians and surgeons believed that either continuing at the St. Marys or advancing farther southward would destroy the health of most of the soldiers; the galleys could not pass through the Amelia Narrows; and, even if they could, the British naval force at the St. Johns was superior. The council concurred with Howe's first point and agreed that nothing between the St. Marys and the St. Johns was important enough to warrant military action in that area. In view of the weakness of the army and the sickness of the troops, the council unanimously resolved not to attempt to cross the St. Johns but to retreat from the St. Marys. The council especially mentioned the divided command as a weakness of the army.[128]

Houstoun, Howe, and Williamson conferred again on 12 July, but the meeting broke up without any real conclusion. Rangers harassed the Americans' pickets that night and the next. On the 13th Howe sent a copy of the minutes of the council of war on 11 July to Governor Houstoun. The Continentals were determined to leave the field.[129]

On 14 July General Howe and Colonel Elbert started leading the Continentals able to march out of East Florida.[130] The Continentals' sick and wounded retreated by water. Georgia's troops landed at Sunbury, and the South Carolina Continentals at Port Royal.[131] The militia forces under Houstoun and Williamson had no choice but to join the retreat. By 25 July Colonel Williamson, on his way back to South Carolina, was encamped at Cat Head Creek, on the Altamaha.[132]

VII

1778: British Initiative

A s usual, Governor Tonyn wanted to take the offensive and pursue the retreating rebels, but General Prevost refused to do so. Nor was Captain Elphinstone enthusiastic about attacking; many of his crew were sick with scurvy, and he himself was not well.[1]

Tonyn charged that Superintendent Stuart—or at least his deputies—had ordered the Creeks to remain neutral.[2] Stuart steadfastly denied this charge and claimed that the Indian raids he had instigated against the Georgia frontier had been instrumental in the rebel army's abandonment of its invasion of East Florida. He claimed that Tonyn's direct interference with the Creeks upset his negotiations and control of the Southern Indian Department. Stuart wrote to the governor demanding that all future requisitions for Indian assistance to St. Augustine should be made through him, at Pensacola, and he wanted Germain to issue orders to that effect to Tonyn. General Prevost took Stuart's side in this dispute.[3]

As soon as the invasion emergency ended, the governor and the general resumed their dispute over command of the East Florida Rangers. General William Howe had written to both Tonyn and Prevost on 1 May 1778, and the letters probably reached St. Augustine late in June. They stated: "all Troops within a Province by whomever raised or paid, must while embodied be Subject to one supreme Command, . . . This Command being invested in Brigadier General Prevost at Present." Howe added that provisions should be issued to the Rangers and paid for in the same way as for regular troops.[4]

Captain Elphinstone, in the *Perseus*, had arrived with more dispatches from the north on 3 July. Sir William Howe had resigned, and Sir Henry Clinton had succeeded him in commanding His Majesty's army in North America. Clinton approved Howe's opinion that General Prevost should command the Rangers as well as other military forces in his area.[5]

Tonyn had no alternative "for the present" to yielding the Rangers' command to Prevost, but he continued his appeal to Germain about the matter.[6] Germain warmly commended the Rangers' achievements, indicated that he hoped Colonel Brown would not resign, and repeated that the rule regarding regular and provincial rank that had been established in the last war was still the guide.[7] He hesitated, however, to intervene directly in the details of military matters by countermanding the orders of two successive commanders in chief.

Although Prevost was determined to control the Rangers, like most regular army men, he scorned irregulars. At the end of the invasion, he stated that the Rangers "probably were never so numerous as represented"; that they were "reduced by desertion and otherwise to fifty or Sixty Men"; that they were reluctant to obey his orders to retreat from Fort Tonyn because they still had the idea that they were not under his command; that Governor Tonyn wanted command of the Rangers for "more reasons than one"; and that the invasion had caused the suspension of the "predatory excursions of his Rangers mmeaning [sic] in any public view."[8]

Documentary corroboration is lacking for most of these charges by Prevost, but they are too serious to be dismissed without consideration. He insinuated that the governor and his Rangers were making private profit at government expense. If Tonyn exaggerated the number of Rangers enlisted, he and Brown could have misappropriated government funds meant for their support. That a market for stolen goods existed in wartime St. Augustine is a reasonable assumption; if the "predatory excursions" of the Rangers were resulting in private plunder, those men could have acquired considerable amounts of money. There is nothing to indicate that either of these things happened; however, there is no particular reason to doubt that Prevost suspected they were happening. If he had obtained proof to substantiate such charges, he hardly would have hesitated to make direct accusations instead of none-too-subtle hints. His contemporaries believed that he was jealous of Brown and disliked Tonyn; thus, his desire for control of the Rangers has been attributed to malice, hurt pride, and a commendable desire to improve military efficiency. Considering that his brother, Major Prevost, held a public sale of goods that had been plundered in Georgia later in 1778, Prevost's motive may have been simple greed.

Because the East Florida Rangers had no practical alternative to retreating from Fort Tonyn when the Georgia and South Carolina Continentals crossed the St. Marys, they were probably not reluctant to do so, but their force at Fort Tonyn may not have amounted to more than sixty or seventy men on that day, 28 June. Brown had sent at least one large detachment into Georgia to harass the advancing rebel army, and no evidence indicates it had returned when the Rangers abandoned the fort. Some of Brown's officers, and probably some of their followers, had transferred to the South Carolina Royalists. The rebels killed, wounded, and captured an undetermined number of Rangers. Illness must have taken a heavy toll. As the rebels learned, the area in which the Rangers concentrated their efforts was highly malarial, and the Rangers had no special immunity. Because of the inadequate diet occasioned by Prevost cutting off their food supply, the effects of ailments caused by heat, dirt, and bad water must have intensified.

Brown had accepted Prevost's command of the Rangers, however unhappy he was about it; but, as Tonyn had warned, many of the men may have believed that the change in command meant that the terms of their enlistment had been abrogated, that the government had broken its contract with them, and that they were now free agents. Certainly, stoppage of their provisions would have been a powerful stimulus to desertion, but Brown's reports do not indicate any Rangers had actually done so.

What probably irritated Prevost the most was seeing regular army officers, particularly his brother, Major Prevost, in a position where they might have to take orders from a provincial lieutenant colonel, specifically Thomas Brown, whom Prevost described as "a Young man entirely unacquainted with Military matters tho' otherwise Zealous and deserving." A regular lieutenant colonel, Lewis V. Fuser, was present in the garrison, but he was often too ill for field service. General Prevost constantly denigrated the achievements of the East Florida Rangers, and he continued to question the legality of Brown's commission from Governor Tonyn.[9]

To try to circumvent the rule about regular and provincial rank, General Prevost took upon himself to appoint his brother, Major Prevost of the Second Battalion, Sixtieth Regiment, to act temporarily as lieutenant colonel in East Florida. The general recommended to the new commander in chief that this promotion for his brother be approved and made permanent instead of local. Major Prevost also sent his memorial to Clinton. He had been a captain for ten years, and, when he had twice failed to purchase a majority, he had retired on half-pay. At the beginning of the rebellion, he had reentered the army and attained the rank of major, but he had been passed over again when many promotions had been made in August 1777.[10] James Mark Prevost was restless in the king's service.

If the general's brother had hoped to have his command of the South Carolina Royalists made permanent, those hopes also were dashed. Clinton approved of the South Carolina refugees, up to the number of four hundred, being formed into a provincial corps, and he appointed their officers: Alexander Innes, colonel; Joseph Robinson, lieutenant colonel; and Euan McLaurin, major. He requested General Prevost to consult Robinson and to send him a list of other persons qualified for commissions. James Penman, Tonyn's bitter enemy, was named "Agent for Paying the corps of Carolina Royalists," an appointment certainly dependent on Prevost's recommendation.[11] General Prevost could do nothing about the command of the Carolina Royalists except to urge that Colonel Innes or "a proper person to command the Corps" be present with them.[12]

Clinton was surprised to learn that the provincial corps that had been organized by Tonyn, Stuart, and Prevost in the Floridas were being compensated in quite a different manner than provincial corps in the north. The Florida provincials were being paid more than the king's regular troops or other provincial corps. Clinton informed Prevost that all the Florida provincial forces—except the East Florida Rangers, if Tonyn had special orders from Whitehall regarding them—must accept the same terms as other provincial forces or else the government could not employ them. Clinton's letter crossed one from Prevost to him requesting directions about extra pay for the two troops of Light Horse in the Carolina Royalists who were supplying their own horses, saddles, and arms.[13]

Prevost and Tonyn finally agreed about one thing: the provincial forces in the Floridas were not being overpaid. The cost of necessities was high; the men received no monetary bounty for enlisting; they lacked barracks and quarters; they furnished and maintained their own horses and horse accoutrements; and they were on perpetual service along or beyond the frontier. The government supplied them with little besides their weapons and some clothing. Their pay was one shilling per day, usually in arrears, and both the governor and the general tried to convince Clinton that this was not extraordinarily high recompense for such extraordinary service.[14]

General Prevost felt obliged to justify his past conduct to the new commander in chief. Probably the numerous refugees who had recently arrived from the northward were pressuring him to help them to regain their positions and property. Certainly the fact that several hundred men had been willing and able to march several hundred miles to join the king's soldiers and take up arms to help restore royal government in Georgia and the Carolinas indicated that royalist support was strong in those provinces. Prevost probably began to wonder if he had been too cautious in the past.

He informed Clinton that his orders had restricted him to defensive operations and that his resources were too limited to permit him to act otherwise. According to Prevost, Tonyn was so glory-hungry that he had entertained "wild schemes" of conquering Georgia with such an inadequate force. It now seemed to Prevost, however, that British prospects were improving. The invasion had demonstrated how weak the rebel forces in Georgia actually were. Clinton had promised a reinforcement of 1,500 to 2,000 men. Prevost reasoned that, if Georgia were conquered, the rebels would be pushed so far from East Florida's boundaries that a naval force could protect that colony.[15] Darien was uninhabited by the end of June,[16] so British forces from East Florida would meet little or no opposition south of the Midway district.

Nevertheless, Prevost did not seriously contemplate taking the offensive until the promised reinforcements arrived and he had positive orders to move. Tonyn requested the general to establish new posts and to protect the formal boundaries of East Florida.[17] Prevost would not budge.

In August a rebel privateer landed part of her crew at New Smyrna, about seventy miles south of St. Augustine, and stole between twenty and thirty Negro slaves. Tonyn requested Prevost to send a party to guard the southern settlements and to prevent such raids in the future, but the general seemed to be in no hurry to comply. Elphinstone immediately ordered Lieutenant Wright of the *Otter* to the scene.[18]

Wright reached Mosquito Inlet the following day, but he could not find the raider. When a storm arose, he stood out to sea, but his *Otter* wrecked at Cape Canaveral, about 105 miles south of St. Augustine, on 25 August. All hands survived, but the loss of the ship was a heavy blow to East Florida's defenses.[19]

Despite rebel raiders, Tonyn believed East Florida was secure enough now to warrant increasing settlement in the territory between the St. Johns and the St. Marys. Also, increased settlement in that area would add to East Florida's security, and that area contained the best undeveloped land in the province. After the governor's repeated requests, George III on 26 January 1778 issued additional instructions directing him, with the advice of his council, to grant lands, including those previously granted but not yet settled according to the terms of the grant, to deserving refugees.[20] A township on the St. Marys had been laid out much earlier—although there is no indication that any lots actually had been taken up—and both a customs collector and a pilot had functioned in the vicinity.[21] To protect the port, the governor wanted to fortify the south end of Cumberland Island. After inspecting the inlet, Elphinstone, captain of the *Perseus,* and engineer Moncrief agreed with him. Prevost was the only person who could issue the necessary orders, however, and he did not do so.[22] Not until December did the governor actually grant lands according to his new instructions.[23]

Meanwhile, the Georgians had been trying to recover and reorganize after their most recent disaster. When the Georgia Continentals reached home, they were detached for garrison duty. By the end of summer, a new barracks large enough for all the troops in town had been completed at Savannah.[24]

Georgia's Executive Council made some adjustments in the state's military forces. The five independent companies that had replaced the minute battalions had proved to be an even worse disappointment. Less than 70 men, instead of the 250 expected, had served on the southern expedition, and most of them had deserted. The Executive Council ordered its clerk to notify any officers he could find that those companies were dissolved.[25] Major Wilder was found and court-martialed. But, when the Rangers and Indians increased their activities, the council decided to try again. This time, it ordered six companies to be raised, "one for each of the settled Counties within the state," though they would serve wherever they were needed within the state. Each company was to have one captain, two lieutenants, two sergeants, and twenty privates. Enlistments were for four months, rations were supplied, pay was double that of the old minute battalions, and a bounty of land as well as of money would be awarded to those who served out their time.[26]

The Executive Council approved of and decided to augment the artillery company that had been raised out of the Chatham County militia. The duties of the unit were also expanded: it was ordered to act as a fire company for Savannah.[27]

While the southern expedition was still in progress, the Georgia assembly had passed a new revenue act. Besides taxes on both real and personal property, it levied a poll tax of five shillings on every white male between fifteen and sixty years of age except those who could prove by certificate that they had served "during the expedition under his Honour the Governor," five shillings on each slave, and forty shillings on every free Negro, mulatto, or mestizo above fifteen years of age. The tax was double for nonresidents and those who had religious objections to personal military service—"minors, widows, and sequestered Estates excepted."[28]

Following the recommendation of the Continental Congress, Georgia's Executive Council proclaimed an embargo on the export of all provisions. The state's embargo on the export of salt was consistently renewed.[29]

On 24 July two of Georgia's delegates to the Continental Congress, John Walton and Edward Telfair, formally signed the Articles of Confederation for the state. The assembly had approved the articles, proposing four amendments, on 26 February, but had neglected for several months to notify the Continental Congress or the state's representatives there.[30] Georgia's need for Continental assistance was so obvious that she was hardly apt to quibble about any measure proposed by Congress.

The state enjoyed only a brief respite during the anticlimactic lull after the campaign. When the neutral Okfuskees who had visited Galphin in Ogeechee Old Town in June returned to the Upper Creeks, they called a council of headmen. Except for McGillivray, only neutrals attended this meeting. The Okfuskees, inspired by Galphin, proposed an immediate attack on British traders in the nation in retaliation for other Creeks' aid to the British and attacks on the Georgia frontier. Will's Friend and the White Lieutenant, of Okfuskee, opposed attacks on any traders, British or American. They believed that it was in the best interest of the entire Creek Confederacy that all traders should be protected in both their person and property. Because the council of neutrals was divided, the pro-American faction agreed to keep quiet until all the war parties had returned to the nation.[31]

Not only were nearly five hundred Seminoles ranging west and north of the St. Johns,[32] but also both Upper and Lower Creeks had a few parties out. Three bands of Okfuskees had gone to raid the settlements. A party of Cowetas drove off cattle and horses belonging to whites. Their pursuers stumbled upon the encampment of some friendly Cussitas and killed, among others, the two sons of Chief White Skin, who had been pro-American.[33]

Whig commissioner Galphin's nephews, David Holmes and Timothy Barnard, now acting in the British interest, led parties from the Lower Towns toward St. Augustine. To increase their prestige, Stuart had appointed Holmes as an extra commissary and Barnard as an extra assistant commissary in the Southern Indian Department. Accompanied by ten white men and twenty-two Upper Creeks, these two, acting as captain and lieutenant of the band, left Pensacola on 15 July, and collected Lower Creek warriors on their way eastward. After they had reached the St. Johns, they learned that the American invasion force had retreated back across the St. Marys and dispersed.

Most of the warriors moved on to the Altamaha to raid Georgia's frontier; some visited Governor Tonyn in St. Augustine and then returned home. Holmes and Barnard reached St. Augustine with the Black (Creek?) Factor and fifty-two warriors on 29 August.[34]

The neutrals tried to prevent more parties going out. Early in August, McGillivray's half-breed cousin, McPherson, was at Coweta raising a large party to aid the British, and William McIntosh was collecting Chiahas and Hitchitas to go to St. Augustine. Cussitas threatened McIntosh personally and warned the Cowetas that, if they raided Georgia settlements, the Cussitas would attack loyalists who were settled near Pensacola.[35] Unable to stop the war parties, the Fat King, of Cussita, sent a runner to Ogeechee Old Town to warn Galphin that Lower Creek warriors intended to raid Georgia's frontier.[36]

Upper Creek war parties, declining to be led by Taitt and his white associates, set out on their own to harass the Carolina and Georgia frontiers. One band attacked a group of rebels at a fort on the Ogeechee River and killed the captain and seven men. When this war party destroyed several plantations, inhabitants in the vicinity deserted their settlements. Because so many pro-British Creeks were absent on raids, Stuart feared for Taitt's safety in the midst of the neutrals and advised his deputy to visit Pensacola until the pro-British warriors returned.[37]

A band of 132 warriors from the lower Chattahoochee towns—part of the force collected by Holmes and Barnard—raided down the Altamaha. Another Lower Creek party captured and burned a Georgia fort on the Satilla River and carried off forty horses.[38] Indians inflicted even more damage in Wilkes County, farther north. Bands of Upper and Lower Creek warriors—eight hundred according to British deputy McIntosh and two hundred according to neutral Opeitley Mico, of Tallassee—raided the Ceded Lands above the Broad River. On 9 August they massacred twenty or thirty whites, killed livestock, plundered, and burned buildings.[39]

The First Georgia Battalion was hurried from Savannah to the northwest, and the Light Dragoons stationed at Ebenezer were ordered to Augusta.[40] Both Georgia and South Carolina called out the frontier militia companies.[41] When the Cherokees warned in late August that the Americans were preparing a counteroffensive, the Creek raids ceased.[42]

Instead, Georgia took direct action against loyalist women. Many loyalists, including some who had joined the East Florida Rangers, had left their families behind when they fled from the state. Some of these families were living in "small huts or settlements" on the Ogeechee. On 31 August the assembly ordered that they be moved to "safe" locations on forfeited estates; the commissioners running the plantations could watch them and prevent them from communicating with East Florida. If the women and children were "dissatisfied therewith," they would be deported to St. Augustine.[43]

By late August, both sides had accumulated enough prisoners to warrant an exchange. On 26 August Georgia's Executive Council decided to send a flag of truce to St. Augustine. The sloop *Rebecca*, Mowbray's former command, was the vessel selected. The council ordered the trustees of forfeited estates in Liberty County to furnish Captain Job Pray with four slaves from the estate of one Mr. Porteus; it was impossible to get free white seamen.[44]

When the war parties returned in September and October, the Creeks again were on the brink of civil war. Some Okfuskees and Cussitas, as they had threatened to do, retaliated by killing some loyalists near Pensacola. Opeitley Mico and the Fat King, of Cussita, threatened to assassinate Emistiseguo. These two told Galphin they would even attack a Creek war party that was assembling on the Ocmulgee to raid in Georgia.[45] The rumor circulated that Superintendent Stuart was plotting the assassination of the "belligerent" neutrals who had killed the West Florida loyalists and threatened Emistiseguo. Some neutrals talked of seceding from the Creek Confederacy.[46]

Among the Lower Towns, Cussita contained the strongest neutral faction. Patrick Carr wrote from there to Galphin that, if the Americans would send trade goods to them, the neutrals would stand fast even if bloodshed occurred. When Timothy Barnard demanded the return of the loyalists' property plundered in West Florida, the Fat King, of Cussita, refused; he would return nothing until the raids against the Americans ceased.[47]

The extremists even looked forward to foreign intervention to settle the tribe's internal quarrels. The Lower Creeks, hoping for Spanish intervention, had sent an emissary to Cuba. One group of neutral headmen declared that nine towns, including the Yuchis, Hitchiti, Swaglees, and Great Tallassee, would welcome an American army.[48] Barnard believed that Caligies, Otassies, Tallassees, half of Tuckabatchee, and half of Okfuskee—and probably many other towns—would desert the British if the Americans actually appeared in force in the Creek Nation.[49]

As the neutrals became increasingly pro-American, they became increasingly impoverished. British traders were afraid to enter those towns, and the Americans had stopped even their feeble trade to all

Creeks because of the summer raids. Ten headmen, including Patuoy Mico, the Cussita King, and Opeitley Mico, made another trip to confer with Galphin.[50] He contemplated lifting the trade ban only to keep the Creeks divided until the Americans could attack them. When the headmen visited him in December, he talked blandly about a great peace meeting that would be held in the spring.[51]

Before reports of the latest crisis in Georgia reached Philadelphia, the Continental Congress had been concerned about the situation there. The back pay due to the state's troops was paid by that summer, but no surplus existed. In September, Congress voted more money, another $1,000,000 for Georgia's military expenses.[52]

Both General Robert Howe and Henry Laurens, president of Congress, proposed yet another campaign to conquer East Florida.[53] Not only were Indian raids devastating the frontiers, but also the East Florida Rangers were penetrating South Carolina and carrying off Negroes and horses. Some of the Rangers, including George Aaron, Laurens's former overseer, were captured, but the raids continued.[54] "Persons from Florida in armed boats" had taken forty-four Negroes from Sapelo Island.[55] According to the Carolinians and the Georgians, the only way to stop these raids by both Indians and Rangers was to take possession of St. Augustine and Pensacola—and they expected Congress to pay all the expenses involved.[56]

This proposed campaign was to take place in the early winter, a more favorable season for southern military operations. Brigadier General William Moultrie, hero of the Battle of Sullivan's Island, had written to Laurens before all the South Carolina troops reached home in July and described the end of that expedition. At that time, he proposed a plan for a campaign to be undertaken in November, "when the weather is moderate, and not very cold." The force required was three thousand men, a small train of artillery, and some battering cannon to reduce Fort St. Marks. Bateaux convoyed by galleys would land the troops, provisions, artillery, and camp equipment at the St. Johns, thirty miles north of St. Augustine, where they would rendezvous with the cattle herds that would have been driven down by mounted troops and light infantry. The men would be fresh, fit for action, and well able to endure the short march to St. Augustine.[57]

Congress approved the plan and authorized the expedition.[58] Governor Tonyn had already learned the details of the proposed invasion. He immediately engaged Captain Moncrief, the army engineer, to build additional armed boats for East Florida's defense.[59]

During Congress's deliberations on southern affairs, on 25 September, it decided to replace Robert Howe with General Benjamin Lincoln as Continental commander of the Southern Department.[60] Howe had had the misfortune to preside over calamitous military activities, during which he had quarreled with many rebel leaders, both military and civilian. Nevertheless, at least one member of Congress attributed his recall to his activity on the dueling ground rather than the battlefield. Howe and Christopher Gadsden, a prominent Charlestonian, had clashed over command of South Carolina's Continentals, and according to rumor they also quarreled about a woman. They fought a duel, and Howe slightly wounded Gadsden; both men maintained their honor. After this affair, however, Howe would be persona non grata with many South Carolinians and Georgians; and lack of local cooperation, already deplorably evident, would be exacerbated.[61]

News of his recall reached Howe in October, much to his chagrin, but he did not receive the official message from Congress until November. By that time, he had received an urgent message from Georgia. He wrote to Congress that he was delaying his return northward so that he could assist that state.[62]

Since the beginning of the war, rumors had circulated continually in South Carolina and Georgia of an impending British invasion by combined land and sea forces. Early in October a ship from St. Augustine came to the Savannah River for an exchange of prisoners.[63] These cartels, as well as serving their nominal purpose, were usually information-gathering expeditions. From 17 October through the next month, an unusual amount of military activity took place within Georgia: shifting troops; issuing clothing, blankets, and supplies; and storing food provisions in magazines at Sunbury, Savannah, Augusta, Brownsboro, Wrightsboro, Ebenezer, Telfair, Tenats, Lawson's Fort, New Savannah, Colemans, and Heard's and Denis's forts.[64] The Georgia assembly ordered Colonel Elbert to go to South Carolina to "negotiate" with that state about affairs of mutual interest. During his absence, command of the Georgia Continentals devolved on Colonel White.[65] All these activities were equally appropriate for either offensive or defensive operations.

The Georgia assembly busied itself with several matters. On 30 October it enacted legislation abolishing the boards of commissioners who had administered the confiscated estates of loyalists and put such real estate, goods, and chattels up for sale at public auction by the county sheriffs.[66] Two weeks later, the assembly passed an act stipulating that nonresidents who did not return within twelve months and take the required oaths would have their estates confiscated and specifically confiscating the estate of William Knox, former Georgian and then undersecretary of state for the colonies.[67] The state needed ready cash. At the same time, "an act for the better ordering and regulating the Militia of this State" was enacted.[68]

On 19 November the Georgia Executive Council received dispatches from Henry Laurens in Congress informing it of an imminent invasion.[69] The British were adopting a defensive policy in the north and offensive strategy in the south. Whitehall's reasoning was based on reports from southern officials and loyalists. Numerous loyalists in Georgia and the Carolinas eagerly awaited British support to take up arms and overthrow the rebel tyranny. When the dispersed loyalists returned, civil government could be reestablished. Other rebellious colonies would see the blessings these restored provinces enjoyed under a British peace, desire to emulate them, and return to British rule.[70]

Orders for invasion of the southern colonies had been issued the preceding spring. An estimated two thousand troops would be necessary to conquer Savannah and five thousand troops to take Charleston. If not enough troops were available to attack both cities simultaneously, Savannah, the easiest to capture, should be attacked first. General Prevost was to march northward with a detachment of the St. Augustine garrison, the East Florida Rangers, and a war party of Indians to attack Georgia's southern frontier, while Superintendent Stuart directed an Indian army against Augusta. Immediate contact should be made with backcountry loyalists; thus, coastal rebels would be isolated. Operations were to begin as soon as northern campaigns were finished and troops were available. Winter was the ideal time for a southern campaign, and the climate precluded major northern military activities during that season anyway. If enough troops were available, Virginia and Maryland could be attacked at the same time as Georgia and South Carolina.[71]

Precise plans for the campaign were made in the fall, when Moses Kirkland, a loyalist from up-country South Carolina and former confederate of Thomas Brown, was in New York. Kirkland submitted a proposal that involved the East Florida forces acting in conjunction with one from New York. Prevost was to march against south Georgia when the troops from the north landed on the coast. Augusta was to be taken immediately so that contact could be maintained with backcountry loyalists and Indians and the rebels would be isolated from the hinterland. If Indians farther north attacked the Virginia and North Carolina frontiers, those states could not send aid to South Carolina and Georgia.[72]

A British peace commission, including Lord Carlisle, General Sir Henry Clinton, and William Eden, was in New York during the year, and it proposed an experiment. Just enough military force would be used in the southern colonies to enable the loyal subjects to restore their civil government and to secure their persons and property. Redress of grievances should be undertaken by the courts instead of the army. Lieutenant Colonel Archibald Campbell, commander of the southern expedition, was given commissions as civil governor as well as commander in chief of Georgia and South Carolina and authorized to delegate these commissions to other persons if he chose to do so. If this procedure proved to be satisfactory, then it could also be used in other recovered areas.[73]

At New York, Clinton assembled an invasion force of three thousand men. Lieutenant Colonel Archibald Campbell, of the Seventy-first Scottish Regiment, commanded at least two battalions of that regiment, two regiments of Hessians (Woellworth and Wissenbach), three battalions of New York Loyalists, one of New Jersey Loyalists, and a detachment of Royal Artillery. Commodore Hyde Parker commanded the naval force that would accompany the transports.[74] Clinton ordered Prevost to march to the St. Marys and be ready to cooperate with Campbell when the northern troops landed. Stuart was ordered to send a large body of Creeks toward Augusta.[75]

Preparations for such a major military effort could not be conducted in complete secrecy, but rumors of just such a campaign had circulated so frequently in the past that now there was some hesitance about accepting these new reports. A South Carolina loyalist who had been in New York informed Henry Laurens of the impending invasion; Laurens considered the source and doubted its accuracy.[76]

Congress did take precautions. Virginia was requested to send one thousand troops and North Carolina three thousand to aid South Carolina and Georgia. North Carolina complied with the request. When two thousand more troops were requested later, she sent those also.[77] Laurens proposed that Congress abandon the East Florida campaign that was being prepared, but Congress did not follow his recommendation.[78]

The rumors had reached Charleston by 11 November. Although General William Moultrie tried to appear nonchalant, the measures that he immediately proposed for Charleston's defense indicate he took the reports seriously.[79] When the Georgia Executive Council received Laurens's warning on 19 November, it took what precautionary measures it could.[80]

Because of the tremendous increase in population, both civilian refugees and military personnel, St. Augustine was running short of provisions. When the British invasion force arrived, St. Augustine would have to be its first supply base, and even more food would be needed. Consequently, in November General Prevost ordered a party of Light Troops, commanded by Major Mark Prevost, to collect cattle in the Newport and Midway settlements. At the same time, he sent a diversionary force, under Colonel Fuser, through the inland waterway to "present itself" before Sunbury. Midway Church is only thirty miles below Savannah; the East Florida Rangers and Georgia's troops had picked south Georgia clean.[81]

Prevost's force of one hundred regulars and three hundred Rangers and Indians, with a 4½-inch Coehorn mounted on a Congreve carriage, entered the Georgia settlements north of the Altamaha on 19 November.[82] They met no opposition on their march from St. Augustine until they reached the point where the Savannah-Darien road crossed Bulltown Swamp. There, on 24 November, Colonel John Baker and some mounted militia confronted them. After a short skirmish, the Americans retreated. Of the Georgians, Colonel Baker, Captain Cooper, and William Goulding were wounded.[83] Another skirmish occurred at North Newport (now Riceborough) bridge.[84]

Colonel John White, commander of the Continental troops stationed at Sunbury and of detachments operating in south Georgia, assembled one hundred Continentals and militia and prepared to make a stand at Midway. His intention was to delay Prevost until reinforcements from Savannah could reach Midway. White sent an express to Elbert and detached a party of mounted militia, commanded by Major William Baker, to harry the enemy's flanks. Then he constructed a "slight breastwork" across the only road, a causeway, near Midway Meeting House; placed two pieces of light artillery; and waited for the advancing British force.[85]

General James Screven and twenty militia joined Colonel White on the morning of 24 November. Because their combined force was too slender to halt Prevost's march, they decided to abandon the breastwork and try to ambush the British at a point about a mile and a half south of Midway Meeting House, where thick woods were near the road.[86]

The Rangers were familiar with the terrain they were traveling, but they grossly overestimated the number of troops facing them. Believing that between six hundred and nine hundred men were going to attack them, they also decided to try an ambush—and at the same location chosen by the Americans. Brown selected thirty-two Rangers whose "spirit and activity" he could trust and stationed them in the woods by the road. When the Americans arrived, the Rangers listened to General Screven and Colonel White harangue their men to spur them to action. Then the Rangers fired. General Screven and Captain Strothers were wounded in the first fire. The Americans, mistaking this small party for the entire British force, retreated precipitately. Despite careful attention by the British surgeons, Screven died the following day. Six East Florida Rangers were wounded.[87]

The Battle of Midway is one more instance where American and British accounts diverge widely. More than one historian has pondered the possibility that on several occasions more than one battle may have occurred at the same place on the same day. Hugh M'Call, followed by Georgia's other nineteenth-century historians, does not mention Brown on the expedition at all and gives the credit—or blame—for the Midway ambush to one of the McGirth brothers, subordinate officers in Brown's Rangers.

M'Call, without giving any sources, describes an extended contest at Midway: Colonel Prevost brought up his regulars to reinforce the retreating Rangers. A shot from one of the field pieces killed his horse, and the British faltered. Major Roman de Lisle, comanding the American artillery, and Major James Jackson believed they were victorious. But Prevost remounted, the British recovered, and the Americans retreated toward Midway. At this point, Colonel White tried a trick. He prepared a letter as though it had been written by Colonel Elbert ordering him to retreat to draw the British still farther and informing him that a large body of cavalry had crossed the Ogeechee and was coming up to attack Prevost from the rear. This letter was dropped in such a way as to ensure its reaching Prevost, and the Georgians were convinced it had much to do with halting the British advance. Elbert had sent White's express to Howe at Zubly's Ferry, on the Savannah, and marched himself with two hundred men to the Ogeechee, where he met White's retreating force.[88]

M'Call says that two American doctors were permitted to attend General Screven, but that they saw immediately that his wound was mortal.[89] Correspondence between Colonels White and Prevost indicates that one of the East Florida Rangers shot Screven after he was already disabled to revenge the manner of Captain Moore's death.[90] Charles C. Jones, following Dr. David Ramsay, a Charlestonian and probably the first southerner to rush into print after the war, states that the British slaughtered the wounded General Screven when they captured him. In a later work, Jones gives a summary of varying Whig accounts of Screven's death.[91]

His scouts having reported that Fuser was not at Sunbury, Prevost collected his force and leisurely made his way southward again. After the battle, he burned Midway Meeting House, the symbol of Georgia's rebellious spirit that was then used for storing arms and ammunition. The British "liberated" all the livestock and other movables along their homeward march. Slight skirmishes happened along the way. St. John's Parish was devastated.[92] Prevost's booty sold for £8,000 at a public sale on the north side of the St. Marys.[93] The troops brought into East Florida from Georgia about two thousand head of cattle and two hundred Negroes.[94]

By 27 November General Howe and an advance force reached Zubly's Ferry, on the Savannah. From there, he wrote a frantic letter to Moultrie urging him to hasten troops and supplies from South Carolina. For once the gentlemen of Charleston assented that Carolina's best line of defense was deep in Georgia, and they eagerly responded to Howe's directions.[95]

Colonel Fuser, delayed by head winds, did not reach Sunbury with his five hundred well-supplied troops and artillery until after Prevost had started southward. Lieutenant Colonel John McIntosh commanded some local militia and 127 Continentals at Fort Morris. On 1 December Fuser anchored off Colonel's Island (sometimes called Bermuda Island), where he landed, disposed his armed vessels in the Midway and the back river, and marched his troops and field pieces up to the land side of the fort. Because all but five of the inhabitants of Sunbury had fled to the fort, the British occupied the town without a shot being fired. Investigating a lighted house, Captain Murray found it inhabited by the doctor and his two daughters from Nassau Bluff. The doctor, considering himself to be on parole, had not felt it necessary to seek refuge in the fort as the townspeople had done.

Fuser informed McIntosh that four armies were moving against Georgia; that the fort's defenders were in a hopeless position; and that, if they did not resist, the parish's inhabitants and their property would be safe. McIntosh refused to surrender the fort; his reply was, "Come and take it." Inasmuch as Fuser had been ordered to divert attention away from Prevost's foraging party and had learned that Prevost had accomplished his purpose and was returning home, he declined to assault the mud fort. The Americans were convinced they had frightened the British away from Sunbury. As Fuser passed down the inland waterway, he left some of his regulars on St. Simons to repair the military works at Frederica.[96]

Southerners were confused about the implications of the invasion from East Florida. South Carolinians feared that the attack on Georgia had been a device to lure South Carolina troops out of the state and direct attention elsewhere while the main British force attacked Charleston.[97]

After talking to a British deserter from a transport at Tybee, Howe decided that the number of British troops coming from New York was too small for a serious attack on South Carolina and that the invasion force was surely aimed at Georgia.[98] The Georgia Executive Council sent two agents, Lyman Hall and George Walton, to confer with General Benjamin Lincoln, who had reached Charleston by 7 December, and talked about making military preparations.[99] General Howe was at Sunbury by 8 December; he could only deplore Georgia's defenseless condition. Lincoln urged North Carolina to rush its troops southward.[100]

The large British force for the southern campaign had left New York on 12 November, but a heavy gale drove the fleet back to Staten Island and damaged several ships. On 27 November the fleet sailed again. After a rough passage southward, it was off Charleston on 17 December.[101]

Howe's troops numbered less than 1,000, including 600 or 700 Georgia and South Carolina Continentals and some militia. Colonel Elbert commanded his Georgians and General Isaac Huger the South Carolinians. Colonel George Walton led about 100 Georgia militia.[102] General Lincoln had started marching 1,200 North and South Carolina troops southward from Charleston on 27 December.[103] Because of the river on one side and swamps on the others, Savannah was an easy city to defend, a natural citadel in a sea of mud. It was, however, a difficult site from which to retreat.

On 19 December, Tonyn received dispatches that had been written by Lieutenant Colonel Archibald Campbell and Commodore Hyde Parker on 5 December.[104] The British invasion force was then off Cape Hatteras. Campbell had three thousand troops under his command, and he expected many loyalists from the backcountry to join his force. To facilitate his army's advance inland and a junction with the loyalists, he wanted Governor Tonyn to advise the loyalists of the invasion and Superintendent Stuart to have the Indians attack the Georgia frontier. Parker wanted Tonyn to send his provincial naval force, especially small vessels suitable for the inland passage, and pilots to join the fleet.[105]

Tonyn immediately dispatched the best pilot available as well as Captain Mowbray's *Germain,* Captain White's armed brig *Spitfire,* the armed sloop *Delight,* the galley *Thunderer,* the other provincial vessels, and small craft. The governor wrote Parker that he would find Florida's little navy either in St. Simons Sound or cruising off Tybee

Island.[106] Tonyn also immediately complied with Campbell's requests. East Florida had no printing press, but Tonyn dispatched couriers with authenticated copies of Campbell's proclamation to backcountry loyalists.[107]

Bewailing the fact that he had not been notified in time to have the Indians waiting on the frontiers of Georgia, Tonyn sent expresses to Stuart and the deputies to get the war parties moving.[108] The express did not reach Stuart, in Pensacola, until late January 1779. On 1 February he ordered David Taitt to lead Creek warriors to join the British on the Upper Savannah River, but this party did not set out until 4 March.[109]

The governor sent Alexander Skinner, whom he had appointed as provincial commissary of Indian affairs, to collect the Latchoway Seminole warriors. That party proceeded to Fort Barrington (Howe), where they expected to join a group of loyalists. Not finding anyone there and not knowing what was happening on the coast, Skinner left the Indians at the fort while he made two trips to Savannah for information. A band of Creeks, who had been out hunting and thus knew nothing about current affairs, believed him to be a rebel and shot him by mistake; he lived about seventeen hours. The Latchoway warriors finally went down the Altamaha and camped for three days waiting for intelligence. When they still neither saw nor heard of redcoats in the vicinity, they remembered Galphin's warning that the British would lure them into a trap and destroy them. Suspecting that the trap was about to be sprung, they returned home.[110]

When the British fleet anchored off Tybee Island on 23 December, its leaders learned from two local residents how weak the opposing force really was. Colonel Archibald Campbell landed his troops at John Giradeau's plantation (usually called Brewton's Hill) downriver from Savannah on 29 December. An aged Negro named Quamino Dolly led part of the British force around Howe's defenses by a seldom-used path through the swamps. The British entered the city almost unopposed. As soon as the Americans realized they had been outflanked, they fled.

So little fighting occurred that the city suffered almost no damage. Some looting of private property and public papers did take place, and the Whigs charged that British troops bayoneted American soldiers who tried to surrender. The South Carolina Brigade retreated in good order and escaped across the Spring Hill causeway. Georgians who could swim abandoned their weapons and struggled across creeks and rivers; many drowned trying to escape. Colonel Campbell reported that about 100 Americans died and 453 were captured; the rebels lost more than half their force and much military equipment at Savannah. The British took Georgia's capital with a loss to their force of seven soldiers killed and nineteen wounded and one sailor killed and five wounded.[111] Georgia's delegates to the Continental Congress charged General Howe with incompetency at Savannah. He was later acquitted with honor by a court-martial.[112]

Instead of returning to St. Augustine from Sunbury, Lieutenant Colonel Fuser's force had been ordered to wait at Cumberland Island for Brigadier General Prevost, who was moving northward with more than nine hundred men to join Campbell. The military force entering south Georgia included the detachment of the Sixteenth Regiment, nearly all the Sixtieth Regiment, the small detachment of Royal Artillery, the South Carolina Royalists, the East Florida Rangers, and the East Florida Volunteers. Three companies of New Jersey Volunteers, led by Lieutenant Colonel Isaac Allen, whose transport had separated from Campbell's fleet, joined the invading army. Only four companies, numbering about two hundred men of the Third Battalion of the Sixtieth Regiment, commanded by Major Beamsley Glazier, were left behind to garrison East Florida.[113]

Some of the troops—probably most of the infantry—were transported along the inland waterway from Cumberland Island, and they experienced severe food shortages. They had little rice with them, and their foraging yielded only oysters. A gale scattered the flotilla on 2 January 1779; and, for three days, four boatloads of men on Little Cumberland Island subsisted on alligator meat and Madeira from a wrecked ship. They "feasted" on horse meat when they reached Jekyll.[114]

General Prevost detached Major Graham with three companies of the Sixteenth and Captain Murray's Light Company of the Fourth Battalion of the Sixtieth Regiment to "liberate" rice stores on Broughton Island and to forage for cattle on Sapelo Island. This force easily captured the seven-man guard at the south end of Sapelo. Taking to their boats again in the moonlit night, they moved up the inland waterway. There was no one to oppose them at either the indigo works or the salt depot, so a thirty-man detail walked quietly in the shade of the avenue leading up to the house (probably David Montaigut's house, turned into a "fort" but without even a palisade). Ensign Schoedde captured all the men in the guardhouse without making any noise; then, "Sergeant Dornself and two men changed clothes with the prisoners and very cooly mounted the stairs to the look-out at the top of the house and relieved the Sentry." The British then awakened Lieutenant David Montaigut, the "Commandant," and the other occupants of the house. Two Georgia officers went with two British officers to hunt cattle and horses, and, by two o'clock in the afternoon, twenty-six head of cattle had been brought in and slaughtered for the army.[115]

This detachment moved on, joined a party under Major Prevost that was accompanied by Captain Moncrief, the engineer, and began the siege of Fort Morris, at Sunbury. One of their guides, a Ranger, reconnoitered too near the fort and was killed.[116] Major Joseph Lane, commander of the fort, had been ordered on 29 December to evacuate his post. Instead, he retired inside the fortification with about 120 Continentals and some of the town's inhabitants and tried to hold out until reinforcements could reach him.[117]

The following morning, the garrison sent twenty-three horses out of the fort, and the British easily captured new mounts. One Roderick McIntosh, a loyalist much in his cups, escaped the restraint of his servant Cyrus (or Jim), walked up to the fort's gate, and began to taunt the garrison. The Americans fired upon the old man and wounded him in the face. When General Prevost arrived that day with the rest of the troops, two eight-inch howitzers, and a Coehorn, the besiegers settled down to serious work. Rebel galleys in the river were able to fire into the town when the tide was high, and the fort kept up a bombardment.[118]

On the third day of the siege, 10 January, the Americans tried a small and unsuccessful sally. While driving them back, three men in Major Graham's Sixteenth were slightly wounded. The Royal Artillery shelled the galleys until they were forced to withdraw and attempt to cross the bar. A shell that hit the officers' mess hall within the fort caused 9 casualties and destroyed about fifty stands of arms. At this point, the Americans offered to capitulate. Their offer was refused, and the British bombardment resumed. After two more shells fell within the fort, the rebels hauled down their colors and surrendered at discretion. General Prevost reported that 1 of his privates was killed and 3 wounded. A rebel captain and 2 men were killed and 6 wounded. When the fort surrendered, the British took 212 prisoners, including officers.[119]

The British secured Sunbury before they moved on to Savannah. They captured a ship in the Sunbury harbor, a sloop, and two galleys; another galley blew up crossing the bar or was deliberately burned by the rebels. The fort's garrison and the vessels' crews plus other prisoners brought in by the Rangers numbered between three and four hundred. The grenadiers of the Fourth Battalion escorted the prisoners along the inland waterway to Savannah. Lieutenant Colonel

Allen and his Jersey Volunteers were left at Sunbury to garrison the post; McIntosh was appointed as captain of the fort, which was renamed Fort George. General Prevost, escorted by a party of Campbell's dragoons, led his flank companies overland while the Rangers scoured the country before the advancing column.[120]

The end of that march, when General Prevost joined Lieutenant Colonel Campbell in Savannah on 17 January 1779,[121] was the end of the Georgia-Florida contest in the American Revolution. When the two officers met, Campbell sized up Prevost: "a worthy man, but too Old and unactive for this Service. He will do in Garrison."[122] Months later, Governor Tonyn of East Florida was still pleading for the ordnance stores, especially gunpowder, that he had requested in 1776.[123]

VIII

Conclusions

Few Georgians could reasonably hope to gain more economically than they would lose by rebellion. When Georgia severed her ties with Great Britain, the value of the lost imperial connection became obvious. That colony needed British imports, British markets, and British shipping. The threat of Britain's military might and the lure of Britain's trade had kept the Indians at bay. Taxpayers in England had paid Georgia's governmental expenses. As Georgians struggled to cope with their new domestic responsibilities, they were unable to contribute anything to the common cause except their traditional strategic value. Again, Georgia was a border colony; therefore, she was a buffer zone.

Prominent citizens had found their aspirations blocked by men from Britain in places of honor and profit and by British prohibitions of development of Indian lands. These local gentlemen were scattered throughout the colony. Many were connected with wealthy Carolinians who invested in lands in both Georgia and East Florida. Such men bitterly resented British attacks on both their purses and their pride. Small merchants and "mechanics" who were clustered in Savannah and worked on a narrow profit margin were aided by their proximity to each other in organizing to express their grievances. Some of their problems were endemic to their socioeconomic situation, but they found it easy to blame all their discontent on Britain.

Georgia's center of radical Whiggery was the flourishing Congregationalist community at Midway and Sunbury, in St. John's Parish. Maintaining close ties with their coreligionists in Massachusetts, these people sympathized passionately with aggrieved Bostonians. Nearby Darien, settled in 1735 by Highland Scots, was the center of a prosperous Presbyterian community. A disproportionate number of new settlers on the Ceded Lands were poor Scotch-Irish immigrants from colonies to the northward. Some of them were congenitally averse to accepting any authority or paying for their land.

These frustrated elements in the population—gentlemen office-seekers, land investors, small tradesmen, organized dissenters, and poor white frontiersmen—provided most of Georgia's revolutionary leadership. Perhaps an equal number of Georgia citizens adhered to the British Empire from principle and recognition of benefits. The majority of Georgians wanted most of all to be left alone to pursue their private concerns.

The absence of any regular British military force in Georgia in 1774 and 1775 must be considered as a factor in Georgians' decision to join the rebellion. Governor Wright and other British officials lacked any established force—except the undependable militia—to use for enforcing law and order. Georgians had repeatedly insisted they needed British regulars to help defend the colony against Indians. When incidents of violence began after news of Lexington reached Savannah, loyalists had no protection from mob violence. British forces finally appeared on the Savannah River in 1776, but they made it clear they were there merely to procure provisions, not to protect the citizens from either external or internal enemies; their orders precluded any extended stay in the vicinity.

Under the circumstances, it would have been surprising if Georgians had not pondered the ancient idea of the *reciprocity* of the obligations of allegiance and defense. Some of the colonists who were sincerely loyal were just as sincerely opposed to becoming sacrificial victims. The lack of action by the British garrison in East Florida, the defeat of the British fleet at Charleston in June 1776, and the nonappearance of any other British force for more than two years afterward would have discouraged the most ardent loyalists. They had good reason to feel abandoned.

Long before armed conflict began in their area, Georgia rebels had established an effective paragovernmental organization. The rebel leadership had little difficulty, when the need arose, in gaining control of the province's military resources, both the organized militia and virtually all the military supplies within the colony.

Conservative citizens in Georgia, the majority, expectantly waited for the traditional forces of law and order to go into effect. They did not. When the king's military might did not appear to protect their lives and property, or even royal officials and stores, Georgians either submitted to the "Committee" or fled to a safer province. Treatment given to loyalists who tried to protect themselves or express their opinions—or even "to remain neuter"—discouraged emulation. The loyalists had waited too long to take the law into their own hands and organize for their own protection. As individuals and families hastily sought refuge, Georgia became increasingly prorebel by default, and East Florida became even more loyal by immigration and by the effects of the refugees' horror tales.

The rebels began the violence. Despite economic persecution and even physical torment, the records do not indicate that the king's friends in Georgia and East Florida retaliated—or even attempted to defend themselves—in 1775. Thomas Brown seems to be the only loyalist who attempted armed resistance to a rebel mob. Not until 1776 did the loyalists fight back, and then it was the country people, not the city dwellers, who thought they had a chance to defeat their enemies.

Scattered settlement characterized the southernmost colonies. St. Augustine, Savannah, and the smaller towns were centers of settlement surrounded by wilderness. Frontier conditions produced personal and social attitudes that differed from those commonly held in urban areas. The boredom that accompanied isolation made the inhabitants overreact to any notable event. Frontier conditions produced callousness to suffering beyond the norm in an unmerciful age. Men lived at a distance from their neighbors. That distance could protect a nonconforming individual from daily abrasive contact with those who wished him ill, but it also prevented hope of help if his neighbors decided that action was worth the effort. The situation tended to produce extremes of opinion, and during the American Revolution extremists on both sides participated in numerous incidents of violence of peculiarly repulsive cruelty when no moderates were nearby to interfere. Unless they bragged of their exploits, no one would even know they had been involved.

Both the Georgia Continentals and the regular British soldiers in East Florida were a major disappointment to civilians, who expected much from them. Both sides received considerable outside assistance, but the sources of such assistance were so far distant that local leadership, initiative, and resources were of primary importance.

Little relationship existed between the northern and southern campaigns during the early years of the American Revolution. Both contemporary and historical interest focuses on the struggle in the north, where larger numbers of troops were involved. The entrance of France and Spain into the war and a stalemate in the northern theater were at least as important as reasoning by dispossessed loyalists in effecting reorientation of British strategy in 1778. More concern for the southern theater by either side at an earlier stage would have secured a sure base. If Great Britain had done in 1776 what she did in 1778, or had executed the plans of 1778, the results would have been different.

Lee, Howe, and Prevost steadily opposed undertaking offensive operations. Military leadership on each side considered its force insufficient for success. Persons on the scene or only recently removed regularly stated that more troops would be required for effective operations than either side could or would commit for the purpose. In both Georgia and East Florida it was the civilian authorities, not the military, who were enthusiastic about "conquering" the opponent and who made major efforts to do so.

Civilian governors stressed the advantages of their own province. Georgia had a much larger civilian population. It also had a stronger economy, especially in essential foodstuffs, and a better transportation system. On the other hand, East Florida maintained comparatively uninterrupted imports. Clothes, guns, and ammunition continued to reach East Florida in larger proportions than they did Georgia. East Florida had an additional advantage in relatively centralized authority, which was a superior administrative organization for prosecuting a war. Georgia had four governors in three years, none of whom had much political experience or any military experience. East Florida had the same governor throughout the war, and Patrick Tonyn was a strong civil administrator with a military background.

Great Britain's Sixtieth Regiment, the Royal Americans, seemed like the ideal military force for action on the southern frontier. At the beginning of the war, however, the regiment was only a shadow of what it had been. Too many of its officers were not on the scene, and many of those who were lacked experience. Most of the recruits were totally untrained, and a large proportion of them could not understand English well enough to follow orders. Thus, the training process was long and frustrating. Problems with supply and acclimatization increased the soldiers' misery. Desertion was impractical, considering St. Augustine's isolation and the Germans' language barrier. Wholesale apathy among both men and officers was not surprising.

Augustine Prevost was not the sort of vigorous leader who could surmount such problems. Experienced in traditional warfare, he did perform admirably in the 1779 siege of Savannah. Yet, undiplomatic, uninnovative, and in poor health, he did not effectively use available resources nor improve on temporary advantages.

Something can be said for his determination to remain on the defensive. For more than two years, he commanded the only garrison of the British army between Philadelphia and Pensacola, and he had been warned that he could not expect assistance. St. Augustine was the only port—such as it was—for British ships between New York and Jamaica. Not one of Prevost's men could be considered expendable. As had always been the case, St. Augustine's strategic value was much greater than its intrinsic value. While Governor Tonyn took a broader view, Prevost understandably concentrated on military priorities, and conquest of the area between the St. Marys and the Altamaha was not one of them. The conquest might have been effected at several times, especially following the American invasion of 1778, but Prevost did not possess sufficient manpower to garrison any "foreign" posts or to defend the area against an attempt to retake it. Considering the circumstances of American affairs, Prevost might have been able to hold a line at the Altamaha, but he believed he could not afford the risk.

On the other hand, Prevost's refusal to defend the plantation area between the St. Marys and the St. Johns was shortsighted. St. Augustine continued to receive food supplies from outside, but they were not dependable enough to prevent real want for both the civilian and military population. On several occasions, starvation was too close. Tonyn was right in his assessment that, if the productive hinterland was under enemy control, St. Augustine might fall easily.

Georgia leaders and their followers were inexperienced in virtually every phase of military activities. Few men could remember the War of Jenkins' Ear; Lachlan McIntosh and his brother had been under-age for the militia when they participated in that conflict. The French and Indian War had touched Georgia lightly indeed, and relations with the Indians had been remarkably peaceful. Because Georgia was a frontier colony, most male inhabitants were accustomed to riding horses and hunting, but the leaders were unprepared for the problems of strategy and administration they encountered. And they learned too slowly.

No surplus population was available with which to form an army. Men in military service meant that same number of men removed from the productive labor force and inevitable decline in food production. Shortage of manpower and even building tools meant that military posts were scattered too widely and undermanned. Even large garrisons could be overwhelmed, and they could not assist each other.

Morale and discipline of troops declined steadily. The population of Georgia was small enough so that "everybody knew everybody." Factions formed not so much over issues as over personal quarrels. Men quickly lined up behind their chosen leaders. Families frequently divided on the questions of the day; cliques rarely did so. Citizens-turned-soldiers were averse to being away from their families and home districts for long periods of time, and that problem became worse as the war dragged on and civilian security declined.

The American Revolution along the southern frontier was a very *personal* war. Virtually the entire merchant-large planter group knew each other all too well. Long-simmering frustrations, resentments, and animosities became unrestrained in disorderly times. Georgia's society was still so structured that, rather than dividing along lines of class-consciousness, each individual leader carried his coterie of followers along with him in his political affiliations. Many of the state's leaders were young and inexperienced in the art of government. The older ones lacked experience in exercising the large powers they now possessed. The wrenching problems of disunity under pressure surprised themselves more than it did outside observers.

Both East Florida and Georgia experienced conflicts between civil and military authorities and among factions that seriously hampered the war effort. Three factors prevented the conflicts within East Florida from reaching the disastrous state they did in Georgia: most of the men in East Florida's power positions had long years of experience with discipline, both internal and external, that to some extent prevented their letting personal differences impede public affairs; these leaders were subject to a higher authority to which they could appeal for settlement of policy problems; and Tonyn successfully used those routes of appeal to neutralize the civilian leadership of the dissident faction. Georgia's leaders settled their differences personally and directly. One civil leader was permanently removed and one military leader was temporarily removed from the scene. The resulting bitterness caused cleavage from top to bottom in Georgia's inhabitants and contributed greatly to the state's weakness.

Georgians missed their best opportunity to conquer East Florida in the 1776 campaign. At that time, the Continental military force available was superior in numbers to the adversary. Problems with supply, transportation, and leadership conflicts were roughly equal for both sides. The American leaders learned too slowly, from experience, to use the resources available to them; East Florida leaders improved comparatively rapidly in this area. The campaigns themselves, as well as the raids between campaigns, weakened Georgia instead of strengthening its military position. Time allowed improvement in fortifications and organization, but irreplaceable manpower had been depleted by the end of 1778.

The broken, thinly settled terrain of both Georgia and East Florida, especially the area between the Altamaha and the St. Johns, facilitated the operation of guerrilla bands. Slashing raids were more successful than movements of massive armies. Mounted irregulars could outmaneuver regular foot soldiers. The political sentiments of isolated settlers were easily ascertained. Friends could provide information, supplies, and hiding places. Enemies could not hope for help to reach them in time.

Experience had taught Englishmen in North America that the best frontier defense below the fall line was naval patrol in the rivers and coastal waters and land patrols between forts at the limit of settlement. Both the Georgians and the East Floridians adopted this traditional system.

Neither side could maintain completely effective naval patrols. Generally, the East Floridians were more successful because the British navy provided them some assistance. When naval vessels were not in the vicinity, command of the "seas" usually depended on who could obtain the most local cooperation—or who was willing to spend the most money at that particular time. Both sides succeeded in making daring raids that resulted in the destruction of more civilian than military property.

The East Floridians were far more successful than the Georgians in their land defense, and the credit must be given to the East Florida Rangers. One reason for that success was that East Florida had less to defend. It was totally impractical for a large force from Georgia to invade Florida from the west. Thus, the St. Marys line, with scouting patrols on one flank, was all that the Rangers had to guard. On the other hand, the land frontier of Georgia was very long, and the resources available were inadequate for its defense. Forts were too far apart and too lightly garrisoned to relieve each other in emergencies, and not enough mounted men were available for the constant patrolling and sorties that were necessary. Red and white enemies either slipped, or rode with impunity, through Georgia's defensive lines.

Southerners of both political persuasions quickly realized that mounted men armed with rifles were the ideal military force for their terrain. Commanders who doubted, or had no choice, saw their foot soldiers bogged down in sand or swamps and dying from a large assortment of fevers and other subtropical ailments. Whatever they were called—Light Horse, Rangers, Scouts—such a force was recognized by men on the scene as essential. Georgia's Regiment of Horse was one of the first cavalry units formed by Americans, and the East Florida Rangers were not far behind them.

Substantial differences existed between the two corps, however. The East Florida Rangers may have been better mounted. Indians constantly made horse-raiding excursions against the Georgia frontiers, and because of the disruption of normal trade patterns, it is reasonable to assume that the Creeks sold some of those horses to East

Floridians. Both the Rangers and their Indian allies probably rode many Georgia-bred horses. Also, the Alachua Indians had an outstanding reputation as horse breeders and kept large herds. This band was a devoted ally of the British, and it probably contributed to the Rangers' supply of mounts.

On paper the Georgia Regiment of Horse was numerically far superior to the East Florida Rangers. In fact, the numbers available for actual service fluctuated considerably. The Rangers never numbered much more than two hundred, and the attrition rate was heavy. The Georgia Horse was at times so depleted by desertion, insubordination and its aftermath, factional struggles, and lack of mounts that its effective numbers were not much greater.

The personnel of the two units were comparable. Men on both sides were experienced horsemen and novices at war. In view of East Florida's small population, most of the Rangers must have been refugees. Probably Georgians predominated during the first two years with some Carolinians; a few Minorcans joined in 1778. Neither the Rangers nor the Georgia Horse enjoyed any advantage in acclimatization or knowledge of the terrain north of the St. Marys. South of that river, however, the Rangers quickly gained a distinct advantage.

Both Prevost and McIntosh complained regularly to the point of monotony about the lack of discipline among these horse soldiers. The East Florida Rangers, however, developed an effective substitute perhaps better suited to their particular military duties: esprit de corps. There is no evidence of factional quarrels within the corps and, considering the difficulty of the service and compared to other units on both sides, the desertion rate was negligible. The Georgia Horse lacked that sort of spirit. Plagued with a succession of colonels—three in three years: McIntosh, Baker, and Marbury—who were heavily involved in party strife within the civil elite, grossly underpaid and ill supplied, the Georgia Horse had little to inspire them. On the other hand, the Rangers knew that the East Florida governor backed them solidly, and young Lieutenant Colonel Brown was a dynamic leader. If most of the Rangers were refugees, they had a strong personal motive of reconquest and personal revenge. The typical Ranger had endured physical pain and indignity, had seen his property despoiled, and had been driven from his home without his family. Concomitantly, the corps consisted of a few men, highly motivated, adequately supplied, comparatively well-disciplined, mobile, and unencumbered by families—the ideal components of a guerrilla force in an area that favored guerrilla tactics.

Unlike most regular British officers, Governor Tonyn did not denigrate the importance of irregular military forces nor of civilian attitudes and cooperation. He made extraordinarily good use of these resources that were available to him. Tony and Brown adopted and used guerrilla tactics more effectively than did the rebels. They actually tried to instigate a counterrevolution against the Whigs in Georgia. The East Florida Rangers could hardly have operated so effectively, especially in the more settled parts of Georgia, without considerable assistance from local residents. Considering the steady and ample evidence of active loyalism in the southern colonies, Whitehall had good reason to believe that, once the British army had squashed rebel tyrants and armed the loyalists, the local population, assisted by a small and hopefully temporary British regular force, could restore and maintain the traditional forms of colonial government. Historians have recognized the strategic importance of the southern colonies after the colonial alliance with France in 1778, but they have underplayed how really active southern loyalists had been.

Neither side utilized one resource as well as it might have: Indian warriors. Most tribes had every reason to side with the British, but estimates by both contemporaries and historians vary as to the usefulness of that asset. Historians' opinions vary from grudging agreement that at least the Indians kept the rebel militia from opposing the British on the coast to claiming that warriors cost the British more than they were worth or were even a positive nuisance. Contemporary accounts indicate that colonials were more afraid of Indians than of the best troops Europe could produce. Creek warriors killed and wounded more rebels in Georgia than did British regulars from St. Augustine in 1776, 1777, and 1778. Both Stuart and Galphin wished to prevent a general attack by Indians upon the frontier, but sought Indian aid for specific military activities.

The fact remains that the Creeks were independent of absolute control by either group of whites. Rival factions seemed to be on the verge of civil war, but they refrained from shedding each other's blood. With generations of practice in playing off European nations against each other, the Creeks were once again displaying their diplomatic skills, walking the narrow path between disasters, and waiting to see which side gained the advantage. Only the Latchoway Seminoles, driven by Cowkeeper's heritage of anti-Spanish passion, saw the British as the best or only bulwark against any enemy. It is impossible today to determine whether reports of civil war within the Creek Nation were real or merely propaganda. Certainly the majority of the tribesmen, like most southern whites, would have preferred neutrality. Some venal individuals were willing to take presents from anybody, knowing that the promises extracted in return would never be kept.

Galphin was extraordinarily successful in playing upon these sentiments among the Creeks. He was handicapped by the obvious policy differences within Georgia itself: the conciliatory policy of Continental and state leaders versus the aggressive policy of the frontiersmen. His biggest disadvantage was the Americans' inability to supply the Indian trade.

The British also faced serious difficulties. Their logistical problem was hopeless; lines of authority were unclear; and Pensacola was inaccessible for reds and whites alike. The disaster that befell the Cherokees in 1776–77 dispirited all the southern Indians, and the attitudes of some British officers alienated Indian allies who served with them. British troops in Pensacola or St. Augustine were too far away to help if the rebels attacked the Creeks. The failure of Great Britain to mount an offensive in the south disillusioned many Indian leaders, but the neutrals subsided when a large British army appeared and took Savannah with ease.

Historians have disagreed as to whether or not Superintendent John Stuart hesitated to unleash the Indians, despite orders to do so from his superiors.[1] Tonyn was correct when he said that Stuart was "old and infirm" and distracted by the fact that the rebels held his family and property as hostages.[2] Nevertheless, perhaps those who criticized Stuart for not being more successful at rousing the southern Indians failed to take into consideration factors beyond his control: disunity, even warfare, among the various tribes; loose organization and factionalism within each tribe; the Creeks' traditional policy of neutrality regarding white contests; difficulties in supplying the Indian trade during wartime; and the prestige of prominent and respected traders who joined the rebels. Although Stuart had enormous influence over the southern Indians, he did not have control over them. They were still a proud and independent people. Certainly Governor Tonyn was naive in believing that Indian management was simple.[3] The fact remains, however, that Stuart was not as effective a war leader as he had been a peacetime administrator. He, his deputies, Governor Tonyn, and Colonel Brown did succeed in gaining substantial assistance for the British from the Indians. Precisely who deserved credit for what will remain a matter of controversy.

Aside from personal factors, Creek warriors aided the British for two reasons: they believed that British power could restrain land-hungry "Virginians" and enforce the land treaties; trade, which only the British could supply, had become a necessity instead of a luxury.

Cross-cultural contacts during the war increased Creek assimilation of the white socioeconomic culture. Headmen had dealt with Stuart and his agents, but the ordinary warrior before the war rarely saw a white man except a trader or a packhorseman. One of the few things upon which contemporaries agreed was that traders and packhorsemen were not "flowers of western civilization." The same could be said for the common soldier in the British army, but bands of warriors led by Philetougi, Perryman, and others lived in close and continual association with Brown and other white men whose attitudes and practices were more admirable. Georgians' hopes for inculcating in the Creeks an "idea of property" were ludicrous. This tribe's theories of real property were as strong, though different, as any held by the whites; hence, the conflict over land. Because of the growth of the trade in deerskins, the Creeks had become a fiercely acquisitive society; hence, the vital importance to them of continued trade. The war increased the disparity in wealth of individuals. Some warriors were more successful than others in acquiring plunder, including livestock and slaves.

The necessities of war in such a large geographical area affected Creek politics. Contact with European military methods and the experience and training Creek leaders received during the American Revolution contributed to their ability to stand off the Georgians for another generation. McGillivray was able to achieve amazing centralization of the Upper and Lower Creeks' political system. However, military activities contributed to Seminole separatism. At the beginning of the war, they refused to act without the approbation of the Creek national council. The attitude of the Seminoles changed before the war was over. Internal disagreements became more pronounced, and too many miles separated them from other Creeks for a council to be held before every major decision was made. And the decisions could not wait. By the end of the war, the whites and the Indians themselves regarded the Seminoles as a tribe related to, but separate from, the Creeks.

With the benefit of hindsight after the British had taken Savannah, Georgians concluded that Prevost had invaded their state in November 1778 with the intention of cooperating with Campbell and that the force from East Florida had retreated because the one from New York had not yet arrived. This interpretation seems ill-founded. Not until 19 December did Tonyn or Prevost know for certain that the invasion fleet was actually en route from New York and was nearing its destination. General Prevost had not demonstrated any eagerness to take offensive action without direct orders to do so, and he hardly rushed up to Savannah when those orders arrived. Also, if he had expected to meet Lieutenant Colonel Campbell on the Georgia coast in November, he certainly would have led the expedition instead of sending his brother to command it. On the basis of available evidence, the primary purpose of the November invasion seems to have been foraging, though reconnaissance and a "softening up" operation were certainly useful achievements also.

British logistical problems, though not fatal in this instance, were glaringly evident during the invasion of Georgia in December 1778. Until he reached Tybee, Campbell possessed no information about the military situation in Georgia. The force moving north from East Florida did not make contact with that of Campbell until well into January. Skinner, leading an Indian war party through the woods, could not find either of the British forces. Stuart received orders to "cooperate" a month after Savannah had fallen.

The most serious effect of lack of accurate information was inadequate preparation for provisioning the British troops. Georgia had been a prosperous agricultural colony in 1776; British officials who planned the invasion did not realize that agricultural production had declined so drastically by 1778. The army of invasion expected to live off the land, but the plantations were so devastated that the land could not support it.

Lack of provisions, caused by wartime disruption of agricultural routine, upset the plans of the British. Their hopes for a two-pronged offensive up the coast of South Carolina and through the backcountry were rendered impossible by the necessity for staying near Savannah, the only base from which outside suppliers could provision the army and navy. Southern loyalists, particularly Brown and Kirkland, had warned that even successful attacks on the coast would be of little avail. If the rebels could secure the backcountry, they could endure indefinitely. To crush the rebellion, the coast and backcountry must be attacked simultaneously and while the latter was still predominantly loyal.

To subsist their own military personnel, the British invaders had no choice but to "requisition" civilian property. And they were not careful enough about *which* civilians' property. Undoubtedly, some British soldiers viewed all inhabitants still in Georgia in 1778 as rebels and felt that the province should be treated like any foreign conquest.

Equally as certain, many Georgians who were basically loyal to the British king or who would at least have submitted quietly came to consider the British troops, who should have been their saviors, as their enemies. In a historical context, the conquest of Savannah in December 1778 seems to have been an extraordinarily tame affair. Few of the local residents, however, had anything in their past experience to help them cope with such a traumatic experience. A kilted Scotchman or a German soldier rummaging through their household possessions was equated with the sack of great cities.

Three years of war devastated both persons and property on the southern frontier. Both armies ate whole herds of livestock. Loyalists who could come home found their property either ruined or in other hands. If the occupants had bought the property in good faith, a long and expensive court battle loomed. Forceful eviction was more likely. But military occupants could not be expelled, though this problem was not as serious early in 1779 as it was after the Franco-American siege. Country property of patriots suffered from raids by Rangers and Indians. The loss of manpower was staggering. A significant portion of the slave-labor force was removed or dispersed. Although the number of battle casualties was surprisingly small, the number of deaths from disease while on military service was exorbitant. Even if contemporary estimates of deaths in military service are exaggerated, Georgia's known population in 1775 was too small for such a loss not to disrupt the entire socioeconomic system. Prisoners of war were another temporary loss, and many refugee loyalists were slow to return or did not do so at all. Whole districts were virtually depopulated; contemporaries clearly indicate that population in the four parishes south of the Altamaha declined drastically. It would be difficult to find a resident of Georgia, of either political persuasion, who was materially better off early in 1779 than he had been early in 1776.

East Floridians as a whole fared better than their counterparts across the border. The increased military presence and influx of prosperous refugees stimulated the infant economy. Some residents of St. Augustine may have starved, and many of them must have experienced hunger, but property values soared, and some people gained substantial wealth. Country people near the border suffered from American raids and invasions, and the plantations at Mosquito Inlet were severely damaged. Caring for refugees, regardless of their origin, placed an intolerable strain on East Florida's resources. The war disrupted the young colony's steady progress, and as usual the "meaner sort" generally fared worst in the subsequent upheavals. There were, however, notable exceptions. For example, building skills were at a premium.

At the beginning of the war, Georgia and East Florida encountered similar problems with supply, terrain, climate, and factionalism. Georgia had more manpower. East Florida had more experienced leaders, and part of her manpower was more strongly motivated. Leadership and motivation were the critical differences.

Notes

ABBREVIATIONS

A.O.	Audit Office, Public Record Office, London, England.
C.O.	Colonial Office, Public Record Office, London, England.
CRG	Allen D. Candler, et al., eds., *The Colonial Records of the State of Georgia* (39 vols., published and unpublished, Atlanta: various printers, 1904–).
FHQ	*Florida Historical Quarterly*.
GHQ	*Georgia Historical Quarterly*.
GHSC	*Collections of the Georgia Historical Society*.
JCC	Worthington Chauncey Ford, ed., *Journals of the Continental Congress, 1774–1789* (34 vols., Washington, D.C.: U.S. Government Printing Office, 1904–37).
NCCR	William L. Saunders, ed., *The Colonial Records of North Carolina* (10 vols., Raleigh: published under the supervision of the Public Libraries, by order of the General Assembly, 1886–90).
NCSR	Walter Clark and Stephen B. Weeks, eds., *The State Records of North Carolina* (20 vols., Raleigh and other cities, various state printers, 1895–1914).
NDAR	William Bell Clark and William James Morgan, eds., *Naval Documents of the American Revolution* (8 vols.–, Washington, [D.C.]: U.S. Government Printing Office, 1964–80–).
RRG	Allen D. Candler, ed., *The Revolutionary Records of the State of Georgia* (3 vols., Atlanta: Franklin-Turner Co., 1908).
SCHGM	*South Carolina Historical and Genealogical Magazine*.
SCHM	*South Carolina Historical Magazine*.
WMQ	*William and Mary Quarterly*.

NOTE

In quotations from documents in this volume, archaic abbreviations of places and names have usually been spelled out. Except for this type of change, the original orthography, capitalization, and punctuation have been retained.

Many of the documents are available only in manuscript or microfilm, and those that have been printed sometimes appear in more than one source. For example, the transcript of "Report of Sir James Wright on the Condition of the Province of Georgia," 20 September 1773, enclosed in Wright to Dartmouth, No. 8, 20 December 1773, Colonial Records of Georgia, XXXVIII, Pt. I–A, 103–36 (available on microfilm from the Georgia Department of Archives and History, Atlanta), has been printed in *Collections of the Georgia Historical Society*, Vol. III. "The Proceedings and Minutes of the Governor and Council of Georgia, October 4, 1774, through November 7, 1775, and September 6, 1779, through September 20, 1780," edited by Lilla M. Hawes for the *Georgia Historical Quarterly*, Vols. XXXIV and XXXV, has been reprinted as Vol. X of the *Collections of the Georgia Historical Society*.

Chapter I

1. Royal Proclamation, 7 October 1763, Samuel Eliot Morison, ed., *Sources and Documents Illustrating the American Revolution, 1764–1788, and the Formation of the Federal Constitution* (2d ed., Oxford, England: Clarendon Press, 1929), pp. 1–2; James Wright's commission as governor of Georgia, 20 January 1764, *CRG*, IX, 215; A Further Commission to George Johnstone Esquire, governor of West Florida, For Enlarging the Province of West Florida, 6 June 1764, James A. Padgett, ed., "Commissions, Orders, and Instructions Issued to George Johnstone, British Governor of West Florida, 1763–1767," *Louisiana Historical Quarterly*, XXI (October 1938), 1034–35; Peter Chester's commission as governor of West Florida, 10 January 1770, C.O., Class 5, vol. 619 (hereafter cited, for example, 5/619); Patrick Tonyn's Commission as governor of East Florida, 14 June 1773, Leonard Woods Labaree, ed., *Royal Instructions to British Colonial Governors, 1670–1776* (2 vols., 1935; reprint ed., New York: Octagon Books, 1967), II, 826.

2. James C. Bonner, *Atlas for Georgia History* (1969; reprint ed., Fort Worth: Miran Publishers, 1975), pp. 30–31; Louis De Vorsey, Jr., *The Indian Boundary in the Southern Colonies, 1763–1775* (Chapel Hill: University of North Carolina Press, 1966), pp. 149–57, 185, 190–203, 232; William Gerard de Brahm, *De Brahm's Report of the General Survey in the Southern District of North America*, ed. by Louis De Vorsey, Jr. (Columbia: University of South Carolina, for the South Carolina Tricentennial Commission, 1971), pp. 199, 254–57, Plate 15. East Florida's southern boundary for white settlement is incorrect on De Brahm's map. The Treaty of Augusta (1763) is printed in *CRG*, XXVIII, Pt. I, 456–60, and in Charles C. Jones, Jr., *History of Georgia* (2 vols., Boston: Houghton, Mifflin and Company, 1883), II, 43–46. The Journal of that Congress, including the Treaty, printed by Peter Timothy of Charles Town, S.C., is the *CRG*, XXXIX, 293–94. James Grant and John Stuart to Board of Trade, 9 December 1765, enclosing Journal of the Picolata Congress, 15–18 November 1765, and Treaty of Picolata, 18 November 1765, C.O. 5/540.

3. *CRG*, XXVIII, Pt. I, passim; Antonio De Arredondo, *Arredondo's Historical Proof of Spain's Title to Georgia: A Contribution to the History of One of the Spanish Borderlands*, ed. by Herbert E. Bolton (Berkeley: University of California Press, 1925), pp. 81, 98–110; Labaree, *Royal Instructions*, II, 608–9; Marguerite Bartlett Hamer, "Edmund Gray and His Settlement at New Hanover," *GHQ*, XIII (March 1929), 1–12, 52–55.

4. Journals of the East Florida Council, 13 October 1766–25 June 1767, C.O. 5/548; 6 July 1767–25 June 1768, C.O. 5/549; 24 July 1773 [*sic*]–20 July 1773, C.O. 5/553; Return of Grants of Land passed in His Majesty's Province of East Florida from the 20th of June 1765 to the 22d of June 1767, C.O. 5/541; List of Applications for land in East Florida, C.O. 5/542. Note the size of some estates in East Florida, the smallest being 5,000 acres, listed by De Brahm, *Report*, pp. 255–56. See also Robert L. Gold, *Borderland Empires in Transition: The Triple-Nation Transfer of Florida* (Carbondale: Southern Illinois University Press, 1969), p. 120.

5. Rowland Berthoff and John M. Murrin, "Feudalism, Communialism, and the Yeoman Freeholder: The American Revolution Considered as a Social Accident," in *Essays on the American Revolution*, ed. by Stephen G. Kurtz and James H. Hutson (Chapel Hill and New York: published for the Institute of Early American History and Culture at Williamsburg by the University of North Carolina Press and W. W. Norton and Company, 1973), pp. 264–70.

6. For land-granting policies and practices in East Florida, see Charles Loch Mowat, *East Florida as a British Province, 1763–1784*, University of California Publications in History, Vol. XXXII (Berkeley and Los Angeles: University of California Press, 1943), 54–64. See also Percy Scott Flippin, "Royal Government in Georgia, 1752–1776: The Land System," *GHQ*, X (March 1926), 1–25; David R. Chesnutt, "South Carolina's Penetration of Georgia in the 1760's: Henry Laurens as a Case Study," *SCHM*, LXXIII (October 1972), 194–208; George C. Rogers, Jr., "The East Florida Society of London, 1766–1767," *FHQ*, LIV (April 1976), 479–96.

7. The statistics for colonial trade are admirably summarized in Merrill Jensen, ed., *American Colonial Documents to 1776*, Vol. IX of *English Historical Documents*, ed. by David C. Douglas (12 vols., London: Eyre and Spottiswoode, 1953–75), 389–411. See also "an Account of the Imports . . . [and Exports] of the Several Parts of America . . . [for 1771]" in Stella H. Sutherland, *Population Distribution in Colonial America* (New York: Columbia University Press, 1936), pp. 276–330. The best printed summary of Georgia's trade immediately before the American Revolution is the *Report of Governor Sir James Wright to Lord Dartmouth on the Condition of the Colony, September 20, 1773, GHSC*, III (Savannah, 1873), 164–67, 175–76. Many discerning descriptions of plantations and cowpens in both colonies are included in John Bartram, "Diary of a Journey through the Carolinas, Georgia, and Florida from July 1, 1765, to April 10, 1766," annotated by Francis Harper, *Transactions of the American Philosophical Society*, XXXIII, Pt. I (1942), 1–120, and William Bartram, *The Travels of William Bartram*, Naturalist's Edition, ed. by Francis Harper (1791; New Haven: Yale University Press, 1958).

8. For Georgia, De Brahm estimated 16,000 whites and 13,000 blacks. De Brahm, *Report*, p. 162. Governor Wright estimated 18,000 whites and 15,000 blacks. *Report of Sir James, GHSC*, III, 167. For East Florida, De Brahm estimated 1,688 whites and more than 900 blacks. De Brahm, *Report*, pp. 180–86.

9. *Report of Sir James, GHSC*, III, 165.

10. Patrick Tonyn to Lord George Germain, No. 39, 8 May 1777, C.O. 5/557.

11. Evarts B. Greene and Virginia D. Harrington, *American Population before the Federal Census of 1790* (New York: Columbia University Press, 1932), pp. 183, 186; Thomas Brown to Tonyn, ca. 24 February 1776, C.O. 5/556. One historian estimates that in 1774 Savannah had 560 houses and a population of 3,500. Barrett Wilkins, "A View of Savannah on the Eve of the Revolution," *GHQ*, LIV (Winter 1970), 578–79. These figures seem too high. A German observer estimated that Savannah had about 600 houses in 1779, S. D. H———n to ———, 16 January 1779, Ray W. Pettengill, trans., *Letter from America, 1776–1779, Being Letters of Brunswick, Hessian, and Waldeck Officers with the British Army during the Revolution* (Boston: Houghton Mifflin Company, 1924), p. 202.

12. De Brahm, *Report*, pp. 144–46; De Vorsey, *Indian Boundary*, pp. 159–60; Harold E. Davis, *The Fledgling Province: Social and Cultural Life in Colonial Georgia, 1773–1776* (Chapel Hill: University of North Carolina Press for the Institute of Early American History and Culture, 1976), pp. 22–26; Ralph C. Scott, Jr., "The Quaker Settlement of Wrightsborough, Georgia," *GHQ*, LVI (Summer 1972), 210–23; E. R. R. Green, "Queensborough Township: Scotch-Irish Emigration and the Expansion of Georgia, 1763–1776," *WMQ*, 3d Ser., XVII (April 1960), 183–99.

13. James Wright to Board of Trade, 1 October 1762, 10 June 1763, *CRG*, XXVIII, Pt. I, 383, 446; Wright to Earl of Halifax, 8 December 1763, 25 October 1764, *CRG*, XXXVIII, Pt. I, 67–68, 79–80; Wright to Edward Sedgwick, 30 August 1764, *CRG*, XXXVII, Pt. I, 75–76; Charles C. Jones, Jr., *The Dead Towns of Georgia, GHSC*, IV (Savannah: By the Society, 1878), 35, 151, 155, 171.

14. Henry Ellis to Board of Trade, 11 March, 5 May 1757, *CRG*, XXXVIII, Pt. I, 11, 16; Wright to Board of Trade, 23 December 1760, *CRG*, XXXVIII, Pt. I, 297; Jones, *Dead Towns*, p. 229.

15. De Brahm estimated in the early 1770s that the Georgia militia numbered 2,500 and the Creek warriors more than 3,000. De Brahm, *Report*, pp. 162, 166. In works published in 1775, both Adair and Romans estimated the number of Creek warriors as 3,500. James Adair, *Adair's History of the American Indians*, ed. by Samuel Cole Williams (1775; Johnson City, Tenn.: Watauga Press, 1930), p. 274; Bernard Romans, *A Concise Natural History of East and West Florida* (1775; New Orleans: Pelican Publishing Company, 1961), p. 62. Governor Wright reported the Georgia militia at 2,828 and the Creek warriors at 4,000 in 1773. *Report of Sir James, GHSC*, III, 167, 169; Wright to William Legge, Earl of Dartmouth, No. 5, 16 August 1773, *CRG*, XXXVIII, Pt. I–A, 90. Wright believed the Seminoles (Creeks in East Florida) numbered 800 gunmen. Wright to Halifax, No. 21, 5 October 1768, *CRG*, XXXVII, Pt. II, 369.

16. Adair, *American Indians*, p. 275; Bartram, *Travels*, pp. 240–41; Stuart to [Hillsborough], No. 19, 27 January 1770, C.O. 5/71, Pt. I.

17. Edmond Atkin, *Indians of the Southern Colonial Frontier: The Edmond Atkin Report and Plan of 1755*, ed. by Wilbur R. Jacobs (Columbia: University

of South Carolina Press, 1954), p. 63; Adair, *American Indians*, p. 456, passim; Bartram, *Travels*, p. 326; David H. Corkran, *The Creek Frontier, 1540–1783*, The Civilization of the American Indian Series (Norman: University of Oklahoma Press, 1967), p. 53; Robert Spenser Cotterill, *The Southern Indians: The Story of the Civilized Tribes before Removal*, The Civilization of the American Indian Series, Vol. XXXVIII (Norman: University of Oklahoma Press, 1954), p. 17.

18. James Oglethorpe's report on the Proceedings of the assembled estates of all the lower Creek nation, on Saturday, the eleventh day of August, one thousand seven hundred and thirty-nine, Hugh M'Call, *The History of Georgia, Containing Brief Sketches of the Most Remarkable Events Up to the Present Day (1784)* (2 vols., 1811–16; reprint ed., 2 vols. in 1, Atlanta: A. B. Caldwell, 1909), I, 254; Stuart to Germain, No. 5, 23 August 1776, C.O. 5/77; Bartram, *Travels*, pp. 325–26; William Bartram, "Observations on the Creek and Cherokee Indians, 1789," ed. by E. G. Squier, *Transactions of the American Ethnological Society*, III, Pt. 1 (1852), 36–37.

19. Atkin, *Report*, p. 62; Adair, *American Indians*, pp. 277, 309–10.

20. For the evolution of official British opinion disapproving of "western" settlements, see the following letters in Clarence Edwin Carter, ed., *The Correspondence of General Thomas Gage, 1763–1775*, Yale Historical Publications, Manuscripts and Edited Texts, Vols. XI and XII (2 vols., New Haven: Yale University Press, 1931, 1933): Thomas Gage to Lord Barrington, Private, 7 May 1766, II, 350; Hillsborough to Gage, No. 3, 15 April 1768, II, 61–66; Gage to Hillsborough, Nos. 48 [misnumbered], 51, and 61, 18 August, 10 November 1770, 4 June 1771, I, 226, 274–81, 300; Hillsborough to Gage, No. 51, 5 February 1772, II, 140; and Gage to Barrington, Private, 5 August 1772, II, 615–16. See also Labaree, *Royal Instructions*, II, 473–74, 476–80.

21. Halifax to Sir Jeffery Amherst, Commander in Chief of His Majesty's Forces in North America, Separate, 19 October 1763, Carter, ed., *Correspondence of Gage*, II, 5; Adair, *American Indians*, pp. 275–76, 285–86, 288–89, 293–300, passim; Corkran, *Creek Frontier*, pp. 27, 249. For a thorough examination of Stuart's career, see John Richard Alden, *John Stuart and the Southern Colonial Frontier: A Study of Indian Relations, War, Trade, and Land Problems in the Southern Wilderness, 1754–1775*, University of Michigan Publications, History and Political Science, Vol. XV (Ann Arbor: University of Michigan Press, 1944). Fear of an Indian confederacy demolishing the weakest colonies is a constantly recurring theme in the correspondence of the governors of Georgia and the Floridas.

22. Gage to William Petty, Earl of Shelburne, 13 June 1767, Carter, ed., *Correspondence of Gage*, I, 143.

23. Assembly Resolutions, 25 March 1765, *CRG*, XIV, 252–53, XVII, 199–200; Assembly Committee of Correspondence to Colonial Agent William Knox, 15 April 1765, *GHSC*, VI, 30–33.

24. *Georgia Gazette*, 7 November 1765; Assembly Committee of Correspondence to Colonial Agent William Knox, 15 April, 18 July 1765, *The Letters of Hon. James Habersham, 1756–1775*, *GHSC*, VI (Savannah: By the Society, 1904), 32, 40–41 (hereafter cited as *GHSC*, VI); James Habersham to Knox,

28 October 1765, 29 January 1766, ibid., 44–46, 56; Habersham to George Whitefield, 27 January, 7 February 1766, ibid., 54–55, 57; Habersham to Daniel Roubadeau, 17 December 1766, ibid., 58; Wright to Conway, 31 January 1766, *CRG*, XXXVII, Pt. I, 103–9; Wright to Conway, 7 February 1766, *CRG*, XXXVII, Pt. I, 101–11; Wright to Conway, 10 March, 24 June, 23 July 1776, *CRG*, XXXVII, Pt. I, 116–17, 97–98, 129–30; Wright to Board of Trade, 15 January, 7 February 1766, quoted in Flippin, "Royal Government," *GHQ*, VIII (March 1924), 91–93; Journal of the [Georgia] Commons House of Assembly, 25 October 1765–22 July 1766, *CRG*, XIV, 270–74, 300–1, 304–6, 315–17, 370–72, 374–75, 377–81; Proceedings and Minutes of the [Georgia] Governor and Council, 31 October, 12, 22 November, 6, 16, 18 December 1765, 3 February, 16 June 1766, *CRG*, IX, 435–60, 470–540; *Georgia Gazette*, 25 April, 2, 9 May, 13, 27 June, 1, 8, 15 August, 5, 19, 26 September, 3, 10, 17, 24, 31 October, 7, 14, 21 November 1765; *South Carolina Gazette and Country Journal*, 21 January, 1, 29 April 1766.

25. *Georgia Gazette*, 25 June 1766.

26. Wright to Commons House, 20 January, 27 October 1767, 2 February 1768, *CRG*, XIV, 412–14, 479–80, 514–23; Commons House to Wright, 18 February, 26 March 1767, *CRG*, XIV, 441–42, 474–77; Journal of the Commons House, 29, 30 October 1767, 27–29 January, 3 February, 7 April 1768, *CRG*, XIV, 483–86, 505–12, 525–26, 580; Journal of the Upper House of Assembly, 20 January 1767, *CRG*, XVII, 311–13, 27 October 1767, *CRG*, XVII, 279–80; Tax Act, 11 April 1768, *CRG*, XIX, Pt. I, 44–45; Wright to Shelburne, 6 April 1767, *CRG*, XXXVII, Pt. I, 177–79, 188–89; Shelburne to Wright, No. 8, 18 July 1767, *CRG*, XXXVII, Pt. I, 213–14; Wright to Shelburne, No. 9, 15 August 1767, enclosing extracts of Wright to Gage, 2 April, Gage to Wright, 16 May, Wright to Gage, 20 July, Wright to Fuser, 6 August, and Wright to Gage, 6 August 1767, *CRG*, XXXVII, Pt. I, 240–52; Wright to Hillsborough, 23 May 1768, *CRG*, XXXVII, Pt. I, 284–85; Gage to Shelburne, 27 May 1767, Carter, ed., *Correspondence of Gage*, I, 140; Gage to Hillsborough, Nos. 3, 8, and 13, 16 June, 18 August, 9 September 1768, Carter, ed., *Correspondence of Gage*, I, 176, 187, 192; Hillsborough to Gage, No. 3, 15 April 1768, Carter, ed., *Correspondence of Gage*, II, 63–66; *Georgia Gazette*, 4 November 1767; Wright to Gage, 25 February 1767, Gage to Wright, 12, 24 June 1768, Thomas Gage Papers, William L. Clements Library, University of Michigan, Ann Arbor, Michigan.

27. Grant to [Hillsborough], Nos. 34 and 35, 16 January, 27 March 1770, C.O. 5/551; Grant to Hillsborough, No. 40, 1 October 1770, to Hillsborough, No. 43, 12 December 1770, C.O. 5/545; John Moultrie to Dartmouth, No. 28, 28 September 1773, C.O. 5/553. See also Carter, ed., *Correspondence of Gage*.

28. *CRG*, XIV, 592–93, 595–96, 643–59; Wright to both Houses, 15 November 1768, *CRG*, XVII, 454; Wright to Hillsborough, [no number], 23 May 1768, No. 12, 6 August 1768, and No. 26, 24 December 1768, *CRG*, XXXVII, Pt. I, 282, 352–53, Pt. II, 380–81; Hillsborough to Wright, No. 17, 15 September 1768, *CRG*, XXXVII, Pt. I, 332–33; *Georgia Gazette*, 14 October 1767, 31 August, 28 December 1768. Governor Wright lucidly explained his

view of the problem in a letter to Hillsborough, No. 34, 15 August 1769, *CRG*, XXXVII, Pt. II, 409–13.

29. Georgia's Non-Importation Resolutions, *RRG*, I, 8–11; Wright to Hillsborough, Nos. 37, 38, and 41, 20 September, 8 November 1769, 1 March 1770, *CRG*, XXXVII, Pt. II, 417–18, 423, 436; Wright to Hillsborough, Nos. 43 and 44, 10, 11 May 1770, *CRG*, XXXVII, Pt. II, 441–42, 447; *Georgia Gazette*, 19, 26 July, 6, 13, 20, 27 September, 4 October, 8 November 1769; *South Carolina Gazette*, 21, 28 June, 13, 27 December 1770.

30. *CRG*, X, 945–46; XI, 253–59, 302, 333–34; XV, 43, 46–49, 86–87, 119, 123–24, 126–28, 153, 155, 157, 159–70, 170–71, 175, 194, 202, 206–7, 298–300; XVII, 579–82, 585–86, 590; Tax Act, *CRG*, XIX, Pt. I, 161–98; [Georgia] Council Minutes, 27 November 1769, in Wright to Hillsborough, No. 44, 11 May 1770, *CRG*, XXXVII, Pt. II, 450–51; Address of the [Georgia] Council to Wright, and Wright's reply, 12 March 1770, in Wright to Hillsborough, No. 44, 11 May 1770, *CRG*, XXXVII, Pt. II, 453–57; Wright to [Hillsborough], 26 December 1768, quoted in Flippin, "Royal Government," *GHQ*, VIII (December 1924), 245; Wright to Hillsborough, No. 44, 11 May 1770, *CRG*, XXXVII, Pt. II, 446; Hillsborough to Wright, Nos. 32 and 35, 31 July, 11 December 1770, *CRG*, XXXVIII, Pt. II, 461–62, 488; Wright to Hillsborough, No. 49, 8 October 1770, *CRG*, XXXVII, Pt. II, 483; Wright to Hillsborough, No. 55, 28 February 1771, *CRG*, XXXVII, Pt. II, 520–21; *Georgia Gazette*, 14, 21, 28 March, 16 May 1770. For the act extending Georgia laws into this territory and defining parish boundaries (25 March 1765), see *CRG*, XVIII, 689–91.

31. Wright to Dartmouth, No. 4, 10 August 1773, *CRG*, XXXVIII, Pt. I–A, 83; Dartmouth to Wright, No. 6, 28 October 1773, *CRG*, XXXVIII, Pt. I–A, 93.

32. James Habersham to Hillsborough, No. 1, 3 August 1771, *CRG*, XXXVII, Pt. II, 549–50; Habersham to Hillsborough, No. 11, 30 April 1772, *CRG*, XXXVII, Pt. II, 622–36; Hillsborough to Habersham, Nos. 39 and 45, 4 December 1771, 7 August 1772, *CRG*, XXXVII, Pt. II, 552–53, XXXVIII, Pt. I–A, 1–3; Wright to Hillsborough, Nos. 55 and 56, 28 February, 2 March, 30 April 1771, *CRG*, XXXVII, Pt. II, 520–27, 535–38; Journal of the [Georgia] Upper House, 21–25 April 1772, *CRG*, XXXVII, Pt. II, 637–46; W[illiam] W[right] Abbot, *The Royal Governors of Georgia, 1754–1775* (Chapel Hill: University of North Carolina Press for the Institute of Early American History and Culture, 1959), pp. 154–59; Kenneth Coleman, *The American Revolution in Georgia, 1763–1789* (Athens: University of Georgia Press, 1958), pp. 33–38.

33. Correspondence regarding the preliminaries to the cessions is voluminous. Most detailed is Stuart's correspondence with Hillsborough, 1771–72, and with Dartmouth, 1772–73, including numerous enclosures, in C.O. 5/72–74. Habersham's correspondence with Hillsborough and Dartmouth, 1771–72, also with enclosures, is in *CRG*, XXXVII, Pt. II, and XXXVIII, Pt. I–A. Governor Wright's correspondence with Dartmouth about the cessions, 1772–73, is in *CRG*, XXXVIII, Pt. I–A. See also Stuart to Peter Chester, 30

August 1771, C.O. 5/72; Memorial of Traders to Creek and Cherokee Nations to Gov. James Wright, [? June] 1771, K. G. Davies, ed., *Documents of the American Revolution, 1770–1783: Colonial Office Series* (21 vols., Shannon, Ireland: Irish University Press, 1972–81), III, 125–27; Representation of the Board of Trade to His Majesty upon a Memorial of the Governor of Georgia, 9 November 1772, *CRG*, XXXVIII, Pt. I–A, 15–26 (an excellent map is enclosed, p. 30); *CRG*, XV, 425–26, 439, 442, 444; *CRG*, XVII, 692–93, 704, 707–8, 714; De Vorsey, *Indian Boundary*, pp. 162–70.

34. Proclamation by Sir James Wright, 11 June 1773, A.O., Class 13, bundle 34 (hereafter cited, for example, 13/34); Wright to Dartmouth, No. 3, 17 June 1773, *CRG*, XXXVIII, Pt. I–A, 60–62; Wright and Stuart to Dartmouth, No. 9, 14 June 1773, *CRG*, XXXVIII, Pt. I–A, 65; Treaty of Augusta, 1 June 1773, *CRG*, XXXVIII, Pt. I–A, 66–72; Copy of a Release and Discharge from the Traders to the Indians, 1 June 1773, *CRG*, XXXVIII, Pt. I–A, 73–74; copy of a Declaration and Discharge from the Traders against any Claim on the Crown or Province on Account of their Debts and Demands, etc., 1 June 1773, *CRG*, XXXVIII, Pt. I–A, 75–78; maps, *CRG*, XXXVIII, Pt. I–A, 89, 268. Excellent maps of these Indian land cessions in Georgia are in Bonner, *Atlas*, p. 30; Coleman, *Revolution in Georgia*, p. 6; De Vorsey, *Indian Boundary*, pp. 164, 176–77, 232; Berry Fleming, comp., *Autobiography of a Colony: The First Half-Century of Augusta, Georgia* (Athens: University of Georgia Press, 1957), p. 111.

35. Stuart's correspondence with Dartmouth and enclosures, 1774–75, C.O. 5/75–76; Wright's correspondence with Dartmouth and enclosures, 1774, *CRG*, XXXVIII, Pts. I–A and I–B; John Moultrie's and Tonyn's correspondence with Dartmouth, 1774, C.O. 5/554–55; East Florida Council Minutes, 2 February–26 December 1774, C.O. 5/571; Draft of a Circular from Dartmouth to Lt. Gov. Bull, Gov. Tonyn, Gov. Chester, 6 July 1774, C.O. 5/75; *CRG*, XII, 405–10; *CRG*, XVII, 469–74, 769–74; Wright's proclamation of 24 October 1774, *Georgia Gazette*, 2 November 1774; Mr. Seymour to the Society for Propagating the Gospel in Foreign Parts, 24 February 1774, Fleming, comp., *Augusta*, p. 114; Gage to Dartmouth, No. 10, 29 August 1774, Carter, ed., *Correspondence of Gage*, I, 368–69; *Georgia Gazette*, 19 October 1774.

36. *Georgia Gazette*, 2 November 1774; [Georgia] Council Minutes, 17 October 1774, Lilla Mills Hawes, ed., "The Proceedings and Minutes of the Governor and Council of Georgia, October 4, 1774, through November 7, 1775, and September 6, 1779, through September 20, 1780," *GHQ*, XXXIV (September 1950), 206; C.O. 5/556, passim; Wright to Dartmouth, Nos. 31 and 32, 24 October, 16 November 1774, *CRG*, XXXVIII, Pt. I–B, 348–54, 357; Tonyn to Dartmouth, No. 9, 14 December 1774, and enclosures, C.O. 5/555; Stuart to Dartmouth, Nos. 25 and 29, 3 January, 27 July 1775, and enclosures, C.O. 5/76; Dartmouth to Stuart, No. 59, 3 March 1776, C.O. 5/76; East Florida Council Minutes, 26, 27 December 1774, C.O. 5/571; Stuart to Gage, 18, 25 January 1775, and enclosures, Gage Papers.

37. Extract of a letter from Georgia, to a Gentleman in New York, 7 September 1774, and Extract of a letter from Savannah, Georgia, to a

gentleman in Philadelphia, 9 December 1774, Peter Force, ed., *American Archives*, 4th and 5th Ser. (9 vols., Washington, [D.C.]: M. St. Clair and Peter Force, 1837–53), I, 773, 1033–34.

38. *RRG*, I, 11–13; Force, ed., *Archives*, 4th Ser., I, 549; Wright to Dartmouth, No. 23, 29 July 1774, *CRG*, XXXVIII, Pt. I–A, 293–94; George White, *Historical Collections of Georgia: Containing the Most Interesting Facts, Traditions, Biographical Sketches, Anecdotes, Etc. Relating to Its History and Antiquities, from Its First Settlement to the Present Time* (New York: Pudney and Russell, 1854), p. 44; *Georgia Gazette*, 3 August, 7 September 1774; Charlestown, South Carolina, 1 August 1774, Force, ed., *Archives*, 4th Ser., I, 638–39.

39. *RRG*, I, 12–17; *Georgia Gazette*, 7 September 1774; Wright's proclamation, 5 August 1774, *CRG*, XXXVIII, Pt. I–A, 299–300; Letter from St. John's parish in Georgia (extract), 2 September 1774, Force, ed., *Archives*, 4th Ser., I, 766–67; Charlestown, South Carolina, Force, ed., *Archives*, 4th Ser., I, 638–39; Extract of a letter from Philadelphia, 3 September 1774, *Georgia Gazette*, 21 September 1774. The Georgia resolutions are printed in Force, ed., *Archives*, 4th Ser., I, 700–701.

40. Wright to Dartmouth, No. 30, 13 October 1774, *CRG*, XXXVIII, Pt. I–B, 333; *Georgia Gazette*, 7, 21, 28 September, 12, 16 October 1774; *RRG*, I, 17–34; White, *Collections*, pp. 48–49, 283–84, 412–13, 437–38, 603–6.

41. Wright to Dartmouth, No. 26, 24 August 1774, *CRG*, XXXVIII, Pt. I–A, 303; *Georgia Gazette*, 24 August, 7 September 1774.

42. Wright's Proclamation of 11 November 1774, *Georgia Gazette*, 16 November 1774; Wright to Dartmouth, No. 34, 13 December 1774, *CRG*, XXXVIII, Pt. I–B, 361; Wright to Dartmouth, No. 54, 18 July 1775, *CRG*, XXXVIII, Pt. I–B, 512.

43. Jensen, ed., *Colonial Documents*, pp. 813–16; *JCC*, I, 75–80; *Georgia Gazette*, 7, 14, 21, 28 December 1774, 11 January 1775; Extract of a letter from Savannah to a gentleman in Philadelphia, 9 December 1774, Force, ed., *Archives*, 4th Ser., I, 1033–34; *RRG*, I, 37–42; *Georgia Gazette*, 14 December 1774; White, *Collections*, pp. 554–56.

44. *CRG*, XXXVIII, Pt. I–B, 375–88; *RRG*, I, 34–37, 42–57; Force, ed., *Archives*, 4th Ser., I, 1152–60, 1162–63; White, *Collections*, pp. 50–63, 521–22; Letter of Noble Wimberly Jones, Archibald Bullock, and John Houstoun to the President of the Continental Congress, 6 April 1775, *RRG*, I, 63–66; Georgia Council Minutes, 3, 9, 10 February 1775, Hawes, ed., "Minutes of the Governor and Council," *GHQ*, XXXIV (September 1950), 211–12, 214–15; Georgia Council Minutes, 17 July 1775, *CRG*, XXXVIII, Pt. I–B, 521; Wright to Dartmouth, No. 36, 1 February 1775, *CRG*, XXXVIII, Pt. I–B, 371–74; Wright to Dartmouth, No. 54, 18 July 1775, *CRG*, XXXVIII, Pt. I–B, 512–13; *Georgia Gazette*, 25 January, 1 February 1775; *South Carolina Gazette*, 27 February 1775.

45. Log of His Majesty's Schooner *St. John*, 15 February 1775, *NDAR*, I, 91; Wright to Dartmouth, No. 39, 24 February 1775, and relevant affidavits, *CRG*, XXXVIII, Pt. I–B, 395–414; Wright's proclamation, 21 February 1775, *CRG*, XXXVIII, Pt. I–B, 415–17; Georgia Council Minutes, 21 February

1775, Hawes, ed., "Minutes of the Governor and Council," *GHQ,* XXXIV (September 1950), 215–16.

46. Wright to Dartmouth, No. 42, 24 April 1775, *CRG,* XXXVIII, Pt. I–B, 426–27; *South Carolina Gazette,* 27 February, 6 March 1775; *RRG,* I, 37–39, 54–55, 58–62; *JCC,* II, 45–47; Force, ed., *Archives,* 4th Ser., I, 1161–63; II, 1829–30.

47. Henry Laurens to John Laurens, 18 February 1775, *NDAR,* I, 93; James Habersham to Clark and Milligan, 7 April 1775, *GHSC,* VI, 235; Wright to Dartmouth, No. 42, 24 April 1775, *CRG,* XXXVIII, Pt. I–B, 426; 17 May 1775, *JCC,* II, 54. For South Carolina's action of 8 and 16 February 1775, see *South Carolina Gazette,* 6 March 1775; *RRG,* I, 57–58; and Force, ed., *Archives,* 4th Ser., I, 1163. For Pennsylvania's action of 27 April 1775, see Force, ed., *Archives,* 4th Ser., II, 421; and Minutes of the Committee of the City and Liberties of Philadelphia, 27 April 1775, *NDAR,* I, 233. For Maryland's action of 24 April–3 May 1775, see Force, ed., *Archives,* 4th Ser., II, 380. For Virginia's action of 19 June 1775, see Force, ed., *Archives,* 4th Ser., II, 1221; and Minutes of the Baltimore Committee, 22 May 1775, *NDAR,* I, 506–7.

48. Noble Wimberly Jones, Archibald Bullock, and John Houstoun to the President of the Continental Congress, 6 April 1775, *RRG,* I, 63–66.

49. *Georgia Gazette,* 29 March 1775; Wright to Dartmouth, No. 42, 24 April 1775, *CRG,* XXXVIII, Pt. I–B, 426–27; *JCC,* II, 44–45, 47–50; Force, ed., *Archives,* 4th Ser., II, 1829.

50. Wright to Dartmouth, No. 42, 24 April 1775, *CRG,* XXXVIII, Pt. I–B, 427; *Georgia Gazette,* 29 March 1775; Noble W. Jones to Committee for Receiving Donations for the Distressed Inhabitants of Boston, 1 June 1775, White, *Collections,* pp. 63–64.

51. Wright's proclamation of 11 May 1775, *Georgia Gazette,* 17 May 1775; Wright to Dartmouth, No. 54, 18 July 1775, *CRG,* XXXVIII, Pt. I–B, 513–14; Georgia Council Minutes, 17 July 1775, *CRG,* XXXVIII, Pt. I–B, 521–22; Georgia Council Minutes, 2, 11 May 1775, Hawes, ed., "Minutes of the Governor and Council," *GHQ,* XXXIV (September 1950), 224–25. On 8 November, Wright prorogued the assembly until 16 January 1776, by which time royal authority was nil. Wright's proclamation of 8 November 1775, *Georgia Gazette,* 15 November 1775.

52. Wright's proclamation of 12 May 1775, *Georgia Gazette,* 17 May 1775; Georgia Council Minutes, 12 May 1775, Hawes, ed., "Minutes of the Governor and Council," *GHQ,* XXXIV (September 1950), 225–26; Wright to Dartmouth, No. 46, 12 May 1775, *CRG,* XXXVIII, Pt. I–B, 439; M'Call, *History,* II, 286–87. Without giving his source, M'Call names "Dr. Noble W. Jones, Joseph Habersham, Edward Telfair, William Gibbons, Joseph Clay, John Milledge, and some other gentlemen" as the raiders.

53. *Georgia Gazette,* 7 June 1775; Wright to Dartmouth, No. 48, 9 June 1775, enclosing depositions of Thomas Johnston, Peter Edwards, Andrew Law, Thomas Gunnersall, William Tongue, and Matthew White, all dated 7 June 1775, and the warrant for the arrest of Joseph Habersham, Peter Bard,

and_____Platt, 10 June 1775, *CRG*, XXXVIII, Pt. I–B, 446–65. These deponents repeatedly identified Joseph Habersham as the leader of the Sons of Liberty.

54. Wright to Dartmouth, No. 49, 17 June 1775, *CRG*, XXXVIII, Pt. I–B, 467; *Georgia Gazette*, 14, 21, 28 June 1775; *RRG*, I, 232–34; Coleman, *Revolution in Georgia*, pp. 55–56.

55. Bullock to President of the Continental Congress, 8 July 1775, *JCC*, II, 192–93; *South Carolina Gazette*, 7 September 1775. The Proceedings of the Georgia Provincial Congress are in *RRG*, I, 229–59.

56. Thomas Skinner to James Hare (extract), 18 September 1775, William Moss to John and Thomas Hodgson (extract), 17 August 1775, C.O. 5/134.

57. Jensen, ed., *Colonial Documents*, p. 815. Not until several months later did the Continental Congress recommend to the provincial governing bodies that they arrest loyalists "whose going at large may . . . endanger the safety of the colony, or the liberties of America." 6 October 1775, *JCC*, III, 280.

58. Charleston Council of Safety to Georgia Council or Congress, 14 December 1775, White, *Collections*, pp. 86–87; Georgia Council of Safety, 24 December 1775, *RRG*, I, 81; Laurens to Col. [Richard] Richardson, 19 December 1775, to Col. Stephen Bull, 23 December 1775, and to the Committee for St. Helena, 31 December 1775, *NDAR*, III, 191, 222, 325–26.

59. Wright to Dartmouth, No. 55, 29 July 1775, *CRG*, XXXVIII, Pt. I–B, 523–24; Depositions of John Hopkins and others, 25 July 1775, *CRG*, XXXVIII, Pt. I–B, 526–33, 536–38; Wright to Dartmouth, Nos. 56 and 57, 7, 17 August 1775, *CRG*, XXXVIII, Pt. I–B, 542, 546; Journal of his Majesty's Schooner *St. John*, 5 July 1775, *NDAR*, I, 824.

60. Thomas Brown, contemporary members of his family, and copyists were not particular about the spelling of this surname. Later generations have insisted upon the final "e".

61. [George?] Beckwith to Lieutenant Colonel Hope, 37th Regiment, Trinidad, 24 September 1803, Browne Family Papers, Private Collection, London, England; The Supplemental Memorial of Lieutenant Colonel Thomas Brown and Agent for Indian Affairs in the Southern District of America formerly of the Province of Georgia by his Agent and Attorney Jonas Brown of Kingston upon Hull Merchant to the Honorable The Commissioners for inquiring into the Losses and Services of the American Loyalist, n.d., A.O. 13/34; Muster-Rolls of Lieutenant Colonel Brown's Indented Servants sent from Great Britain to Georgia and the Expenses of the same, 1 January 1788, A.O. 13/34; A Schedule of the Real and Personal Estate which belonged to Lieutenant Colonel Brown of the King's Rangers and afterwards Agent for Indian Affairs in the Southern District of America of which he was Dispossessed in the Year 1775 and was afterwards Confiscated by an Act of the Georgia Legislature passed the _____ day of _____, n.d., A.O. 13/34; Thomas Brown to Jonas Brown, 10 November 1775, copy in author's possession, but location of original unknown. This letter is to Thomas Brown's father, Jonas Brown, not to his brother, Jonas Brown.

Letters from Thomas Brown to his relatives in England were addressed to Whitby and Kingston-upon-Hull.

62. This account of the circumstances and events of Brown's torment is taken from the following sources: *Georgia Gazette*, 30 August 1775; Thomas Brown to Jonas Brown, 10 November 1775, author's copy; Thomas Brown to Lord North, 4 June 1783, C.O. 5/82; Deposition of Thomas Brown, New Providence, Bahama Islands, 26 November 1787, A.O. 13/34; Supplemental Memorial of Thomas Brown, n.d., A.O. 13/34; Brown to Cornwallis, 16 July 1780, Cornwallis Papers, Alderman Library, University of Virginia, Charlottesville.

63. According to a statement—not written by Thomas Brown—in the Browne Papers, the skull fracture necessitated trepanning. Brown may have wished to plead "temporary insanity" as an excuse for the promises he made to his tormentors in the next several hours. In Thomas Brown to Jonas Brown, 10 November 1775, author's copy, a person unknown added the note that the mob vandalized the house and outbuildings and removed "upwards of 20 stand of arms." In that letter, Brown refrained from telling his father that he had shot a man.

64. *Georgia Gazette*, 30 August 1775. An Indian trader who chose the rebel side later said that Thomas Graham was the most active man in tarring and feathering Brown. A party of ten Indians killed Graham in 1782. Patrick Carr to John Martin, Gov. of Ga., 22 August 1782, "Letters of Patrick Carr, Terror to British Loyalists, to Governors John Martin and Lyman Hall, 1782 and 1783," *GHQ*, I (December 1917), 339.

65. He was "Scalpt in three Places burnt in the Soals of his feet." Deposition of Thomas Brown, New Providence, Bahama Islands, 26 November 1787, A.O. 13/34. Tonyn stated that some of Brown's toes were actually burned off. Tonyn to Germain, No. 32, 7 January 1777, C.O. 5/557. Brown himself said that he could not put his feet on the ground for six months. Brown to Cornwallis, 16 July 1780, Cornwallis Papers.

66. Georgia Council Minutes, 15 August 1775, including Grierson to Wright, John Wilson (Secretary of St. Paul's Parish Committee) to Colonel James Grierson, and Grierson to Wilson, all dated 6 August 1775, *CRG*, XXXVIII, Pt. I–B, 583–87; Wright to Dartmouth, No. 57, 17 August 1775, *CRG*, XXXVIII, Pt. I–B, 564–65; Wright to Dartmouth, No. 58, 16 September 1775, *CRG*, XXXVIII, Pt. I–B, 595–96. The best published account of Brown's activities in 1775 is in Gary D. Olsen, "Loyalists and the American Revolution: Thomas Brown and the South Carolina Backcountry, 1775–1776," Pt. I, *SCHM*, LXVIII (October 1967), 201–19.

67. Depositions of James Kitching, Customs Collector, and Isaac Antrobus, Comptroller and Searcher, 29 June, 4 July 1775, *CRG*, XXXVIII, Pt. I–B, 483–92; Georgia Council Minutes, 4 July 1775, *CRG*, XXXVIII, Pt. I–B, 493–94.

68. Georgia Council Minutes, 4 July 1775, *CRG*, XXXVIII, Pt. I–B, 494–95; Depositions of George Baillie, Commissary General of the Province of Georgia, Thomas Moodie, Deputy Secretary of the Province of Georgia,

and John Menzies and Joseph Goldwire, Writing Clerks in the Secretary's Office, all dated 5 July 1775, *CRG*, XXXVIII, Pt. I–B, 497–501; Deposition of George Baillie, 26 July 1775, *CRG*, XXXVIII, Pt. I–B, 533–34; Deposition of George Macmichen, 26 July 1775, *CRG*, XXXVIII, Pt. I–B, 535; Wright to Dartmouth, No. 54, 18 July 1775, *CRG*, XXXVIII, Pt. I–B, 514–15.

69. Wright to Dartmouth, Nos. 52 and 53, 8, 10 July 1775, *CRG*, XXXVIII, Pt. I–B, 480–81, 503; Memorial of James Jackson and Andrew McLean to Governor Wright, 21 March 1776, *CRG*, XXXVIII, Pt. II, 96; Deposition of Richard Maitland, Master, John Fullerton, First Mate, and Samuel Burnett, Second Mate of the ship *Philippa*, 21 September 1775, *CRG*, XXXVIII, Pt. I–B, 606–16; Deposition of Robert Smith and others, 26 September 1775, *CRG*, XXXVIII, Pt. I–B, 631–33; Daniel DeSausure to Henry Laurens, President of the South Carolina Council of Safety, 18 July 1775, *NDAR*, I, 920; Journal of the South Carolina Council of Safety, 18, 19 July 1775, *NDAR*, I, 920–21, 931–32; *London Chronicle*, Tuesday, August 22, to Thursday, August 24, 1775, in *NDAR*, II, 686; Patrick Tonyn to Dartmouth, No. 22, 21 July 1775, C.O. 5/555.

70. East Florida Council Minutes, 7, 19, 21 August 1775, C.O. 5/571; Tonyn to Gage, 14 September 1775, to Vice Admiral Samuel Graves, 14 September 1775, and to Dartmouth, No. 25, 24 August 1775, and enclosures, C.O. 5/555; Tonyn's proclamation of 21 August 1775, *Georgia Gazette*, 6 September 1775; Wright to Dartmouth, No. 57, 17 August 1775, *CRG*, XXXVIII, Pt. I–B, 563–64; South Carolina Council of Safety's Orders and Commission to Clement Lempriere, and Journal—Sloop *Commerce*, R[obert] W[ilson] Gibbes, comp., *Documentary History of the American Revolution,* . . . (3 vols.: I and II, New York: D. Appleton and Co., 1855–57; III, Columbia, S.C.: n.p., 1883), I, passim; William Moultrie, *Memoirs of the American Revolution, So Far As It Related to the States of North and South Carolina, and Georgia*, Eyewitness Accounts of the American Revolution (1802; reprint ed., 2 vols. in 1, New York: New York Times and Arno Press, 1968), I, 78–79; [Henry Laurens] to Clement Lempriere, 27 July 1775, Daniel De Saussure to Laurens, 29 July, 2 August 1775, Laurens to the Committee at Beaufort, Port Royal, 12 August 1775, and Council of Safety in Charleston to William Henry Drayton, 13 August 1775, in "Papers of the First Council of Safety of the Revolutionary Party in South Carolina, June–November 1775," *SCHGM*, I (January, April 1900), 66, 68, 73–74, 127, 133.

71. Wright to Dartmouth, No. 59, 23 September 1775, *CRG*, XXXVIII, Pt. I–B, 600–601; Stuart to Major Small, 2 October 1775, Force, ed., *Archives*, 4th Ser., IV, 317; Henry Laurens to John Laurens (extract), 26 September 1775, *NDAR*, II, 217.

72. J. Leitch Wright, Jr., *Florida in the American Revolution*, sponsored by the American Revolution Bicentennial Commisson of Florida (Gainesville: University Presses of Florida, 1975), p. 27.

73. Wright to Dartmouth, No. 53, 10 July 1775, *CRG*, XXXVIII, Pt. I–B, 503–5; Wright to Dartmouth, No. 57, 17 August 1775, *CRG*, XXXVIII, Pt. I–B, 562; Wright to Dartmouth, 3 January 1776, *CRG*, XXXVIII, Pt. II,

63–65; 15 July 1775, *JCC*, II, 185; Force, ed., *Archives*, 4th Ser., II, 1567–69; Vice Admiral Samuel Graves to Sir James Wright, Governor of Georgia, 22 August 1775, *NDAR*, I, 1204; Lord William Campbell, Governor of South Carolina, to Vice Admiral Samuel Graves, 30 June 1775, *NDAR*, I, 792; Campbell to Gage, 1 July 1775, *NDAR*, I, 800–802; Gage to Captain Cooper, 14th Regiment, 29 July 1775, C.O. 5/555. Wright's letters to General Gage and Admiral Graves, and the letters substituted by the Charleston Committee and dated 27 June 1775 are in *CRG*, XXXVIII, Pt. II, 26–31; Force, ed., *Archives*, 4th Ser., II, 1109–11; *NDAR*, I, 764–66; Gibbes, comp., *Documentary History*, I, 98–102.

Regular packet-boat service between London and Charleston ceased in the fall. J. Pownall to Anthony Todd, 28 September 1775, C.O. 5/135; J. Pownall to Tonyn, 4 October 1775, C.O. 5/555.

74. Wright to Dartmouth, No. 48, 9 June 1775, *CRG*, XXXVIII, Pt. I–B, 447; Wright to Dartmouth, No. 49, 17 June 1775, *CRG*, XXXVIII, Pt. I–B, 469; Wright to Dartmouth, No. 53, 10 July 1775, *CRG*, XXXVIII, Pt. I–B, 504–5; Wright to Dartmouth, No. 54, 18 July 1775, *CRG*, XXXVIII, Pt. I–B, 515.

75. *Georgia Gazette*, 16 August, 20 September 1775; Dartmouth to Wright, No. 22, 2 August 1775 (royal permission for Wright to return to England), *CRG*, XXXVIII, Pt. I–B, 479; Dartmouth's circular to the governors of New Hampshire, Massachusetts Bay, New York, New Jersey, Virginia, North Carolina, South Carolina, Georgia, and the deputy governors of Pennsylvania and Maryland, 8 November 1775, C.O. 5/76; Tonyn to Gage, 14 September 1775, C.O. 5/555; Wright to Dartmouth, No. 57, 17 August 1775, *CRG*, XXXVIII, Pt. I–B, 562–65; Wright to Dartmouth, No. 58, 16 September 1775, *CRG*, XXXVIII, Pt. I–B, 595–98; Wright to Dartmouth, No. 59, 23 September 1775, *CRG*, XXXVIII, Pt. I–B, 601; Wright to Dartmouth, No. 61, 14 October 1775, *CRG*, XXXVIII, Pt. II, 1–5; Wright to Dartmouth, No. 62, 1 November 1775, *CRG*, XXXVIII, Pt. II, 13; Wright to Dartmouth, No. 64, 9 December 1775, *CRG*, XXXVIII, Pt. II, 36–37; Depositions of Martin Strohaker, 2 September 1775, Thomas Larre, 11 Savannah [September?] 1775, Isaac Roberts, 12 September 1775, and Richard Bissell, 12 September 1775, *CRG*, XXXVIII, Pt. I–B, 603–27; Depositions of Robert Smith and others, n.d., [in Wright to Dartmouth, No. 60, 26 September 1775], *CRG*, XXXVIII, Pt. II, 628–47; Joseph Farley to Anthony Stokes, Chief Justice of Georgia, 13 October 1775, *CRG*, XXXVIII, Pt. II, 6; Records of the Georgia General Court and Pleas Office, 16, 17 October 1775, *CRG*, XXXVIII, Pt. II, 7–12; Enclosures in Wright to Dartmouth, No. 64, 9 December 1775, *CRG*, XXXVIII, Pt. II, 41–50; Orders of the Georgia Provincial Congress, 30 November, 5, 6 December 1775, C.O. 5/115. The surviving Proceedings of the Georgia Council of Safety, 3 November 1775–22 February 1777, are printed in *RRG*, I, 68–227.

When a recruiter for South Carolina regiments was jailed in Savannah, a mob released him. Wright to Dartmouth, No. 56, 7 August 1775, and enclosures, *CRG*, XXXVIII, Pt. I–B, 541–42, 544–45, 548–61.

For a summary of the breakdown in Georgia's legal system, see Anthony Stokes's memorial to the Treasury, 5 January 1778, *CRG*, XXXIX, 35–41, and C.O. 5/116.

76. Journal of the Georgia Council of Safety, 3 November 1775, *RRG*, I, 68; Journal of Georgia's Provincial Congress, 7, 11 July 1775, *RRG*, I, 240–41, 248–49; 13, 15 September 1775, *JCC*, 140–42, 251–52; John Adams' Notes of Debates, *JCC*, III, 478–82, 484–85, 490–504; Diaries of Richard Smith and John Adams, 11–15 September 1775, Edmund C. Burnett, ed., *Letters of Members of the Continental Congress* (8 vols., Washington, D.C.: Carnegie Institution of Washington, 1921–36), 192–96; Edith Duncan Johnston, *The Houstouns of Georgia* (Athens: University of Georgia Press, 1950), pp. 204–7.

77. Tonyn to Gage, [14 September 1775], C.O. 5/555; Tonyn's proclamation of 2 November 1775, C.O. 5/556.

Colonial land offices had been closed by instructions dated 3 February 1774. Additional Instructions to Gov. Tonyn, 3 February 1774, in East Florida Council Minutes, 30 May 1774, C.O. 5/571. Nevertheless, on 5 July 1775 Dartmouth authorized Governor Tonyn to make gratuitous grants of land, exempt from quitrents for ten years, to loyalist refugees in East Florida and to use the colony's contingent fund to relieve indigent refugees. Dartmouth to Tonyn, No. 9, 5 July 1775, C. O. 5/555; extracts in East Florida Council Minutes, 1 November 1775, C.O. 5/571.

78. Tonyn to Dartmouth, Private, No. 14, 25 October 1775, C.O. 5/555. For the adventures of one spy in East Florida, Capt. Adam M'Donald, of South Carolina, see Moultrie, *Memoirs*, I, 72–73.

79. Georgia Council Minutes, 4 July 1775, Hawes, ed., "Minutes of the Governor and Council," *GHQ*, XXXIV (December 1950), 291; Tonyn to Dartmouth, No. 19, 1 July 1775, C.O. 5/555. Eight hundredweight equals 896 pounds. British weights, in use in the united colonies, allowed 28 pounds to the quarter and 4 quarters to the hundredweight. *NDAR*, III, 1391.

80. Tonyn to Dartmouth, No. 26, 15 September 1775, to Dartmouth, Private, No. 11, 20 September 1775, and Receipts Office of Ordnance, East Florida, 31 August 1775, C.O. 5/555.

81. State of His Majesty Forces in the province of East Florida . . . , 1 March 1774, C.O. 5/554; Return of His Majesty's Forces in the Province of East Florida . . . , 20 July 1775, Tonyn to Dartmouth, Private, No. 10, 22 July 1775, to Dartmouth, No. 26, 15 September 1775, Lord Dunmore, governor of Virginia, to Tonyn, 29 August 1775, to Major Furlong of the 14th Regiment, 24 August 1775, Gage to Maj. Furlong, 14th Regiment, or Officer Commanding at St. Augustine, 27 July 1775, to Capt. Cooper, 14th Regiment, 29 July 1775, Tonyn to Gage, [14 September 1775], to Dunmore, n.d., to Dartmouth, Private, No. 11, 20 September 1775, State of the 14th Regiment of Infantry, in the province of East Florida, St. Augustine, 30th September 1775, and Return of Ammunition Issued to His Majesty's 14th Regiment of Infantry, between the 13th August 1775 and 25th Instant, C.O. 5/555; Tonyn to Dartmouth, No. 35, 24 December 1775, Return of three Companys of the 16th Regiment of Foot Commanded by Captain Collin

Graham Detached to St. Augustine, 24 December 1775, and Tonyn to Dartmouth, No. 37, 14 January 1776, C.O. 5/556; John Stuart to Maj. Small, 2 October 1775, and Maj. Furlong to Gage, 5 October 1775, Force, ed., *Archives,* 4th Ser., IV, 318, 319; "British Regiments in St. Augustine, 1768–1784," *El Escribano,* VII (April 1970), 43–44; East Florida Council Minutes, 17 July, 12 September, 21 December 1775, C.O. 5/571.

82. Vice Admiral Samuel Graves to Lt. John Graves, H.M. Schooner *St. Lawrence,* 15 September 1775, Lt. Graves to Vice Admiral Graves, 3 October 1775, Frederick George Mulcaster to Brigadier James Grant (extract), 3 October 1775, Tonyn to Vice Admiral Graves, 3 October 1775, and List of British ships . . . , 29 September 1775, *NDAR,* II, 107, 286–89, 742.

83. Gage to Graves, 8 September 1775, *NDAR,* II, 47.

84. Wright had originally requested one hundred troops and one ship, but by the time he had received notice that they were available, both he and his council had decided that such a small force would be merely an irritant. Georgia Council minutes, 25 July 1775, *CRG,* XXXVIII, Pt. I–B, 566; Dartmouth to Gage, No. 14, 28 January 1775, Carter, ed., *Correspondence of Gage,* II, 183–84; Dartmouth to Wright, No. 18, 1 February 1775, *CRG,* XXXVIII, Pt. I–B, 364; Gage to Dartmouth, No. 27, 19 April 1775, Carter, ed., *Correspondence of Gage,* I, 395; Wright to Dartmouth, No. 47, 25 May 1775, *CRG,* XXXVIII, Pt. I–B, 445; Wright to Dartmouth, No. 50, 17 June 1775, enclosing Gage to Wright, 16 April 1775, *CRG,* XXXVIII, Pt. I–B, 471–73; Gage to Capt. Cooper, 14th Regiment, 29 July 1775, C.O. 5/555; Lords Commissioners of the British Admiralty to Vice Admiral Samuel Graves, 28 January 1775, *NDAR,* I, 389.

85. Journal of the Council of Safety, 11 December 1775, *RRG,* I, 71–72; Georgia Council Minutes, 1 August, Hawes, ed., "Minutes of the Governor and Council," *GHQ,* XXXIV (December 1950), 299–301; Georgia Council Minutes, 15 August 1775, *CRG,* XXXVIII, Pt. I–B, 567–83; Wright to Dartmouth, No. 57, 17 August 1775, *CRG,* XXXVIII, Pt. I–B, 562–63; Wright to Dartmouth, No. 58, 16 September 1775, *CRG,* XXXVIII, Pt. I–B, 595. See also Gordon B. Smith, "The Georgia Grenadiers," *GHQ,* LXIV (Winter 1980), 405–15.

86. 4, 9 November 1775, *JCC,* III, 325, 343; Samuel Adams to James Warren, 4 November 1775, Joseph Hewes to Samuel Johnston, 9 November 1775, Burnett, ed., *Letters,* I, 247, 251.

87. Stuart to Dartmouth, No. 16, 13 February 1775, C.O. 5/75.

88. James Habersham to Philotheos Chiffelle, 16 June 1775, Force, ed., *Archives,* 4th Ser., II, 1007–8; Journal of His Majesty's Schooner *St. John,* Lieut. William Grant, Commanding, 16, 17, 18 June 1775, *NDAR,* I, 697, 712, 715; Lt. William Grant to Vice Admiral Samuel Graves, 18 June 1775, *NDAR,* I, 716–17; Wright to Dartmouth, No. 51, 20 June 1775, *CRG,* XXXVIII, Pt. I–B, 475; Extract of a letter from Charleston, 27 June 1775, Force, ed., *Archives,* 4th Ser., II, 1111–12; Tonyn to Dartmouth, No. 19, 1 July 1775, C.O. 5/555; Stuart to Dartmouth, No. 28, 21 July 1775, to the Committee at Charlestown, 18 July 1775, Charlestown Committee of Intelligence to Stuart,

21 July 1775, and Stuart to William Henry Drayton, 18 July 1775, C.O. 5/76; Lord William Campbell to Dartmouth, No. 1, 2 July 1775, Davies, ed., *Documents of the Revolution*, XI, 34–35; John Richard Alden, ed., "John Stuart Accuses William Bull," *WMQ*, 3d Ser., II (July 1945), 315–20.

89. Wright to Dartmouth, No. 52, 8 July 1775, *CRG*, XXXVIII, Pt. I–B, 481; George Galphin to Council of Safety in Savannah, 9 August 1775, "Papers of the First Council of Safety," *SCHGM*, I (April 1900), 123–24. They appointed three other commissioners to the Cherokees. Wright to Stuart, 6 July 1775, in Stuart to Dartmouth, No. 28, 21 July 1775, C.O. 5/76.

90. Stuart to Dartmouth, No. 32, 17 December 1775, C.O. 5/77; Talk from the Rebel Commissioners to the Creeks, 13 November 1775, *NCCR*, X, 330–31; George Galphin's Commission, 2 October 1775, "Papers of the First Council of Safety," *SCHGM*, II (April 1901), 99–100; 12, 19, 21 July 1775, *JCC*, II, 174–77, 192, 194; Corkran, *Creek Frontier*, pp. 288–89, 292.

91. Taitt to Stuart, 20 September 1775, C.O. 5/77; Brown to Tonyn, ca. 24 February 1776, C.O. 5/556; Tonyn to Dartmouth, Private, No. 11, 20 September 1775, enclosing Tonyn to Gage, 20 September 1775, C.O. 5/555; Talk from the Indian commissioners of the Southern District to the Creeks, 13 November 1775, *NCCR*, X, 330–31.

92. Substance of a message sent by Mr. George Galphin into the Creek Nation, [June 1775], and the answer, C.O. 5/76; Taitt to Stuart, 1 August 1775, Stuart to Dartmouth, No. 31, 26 October 1775, C.O. 5/76; Tonyn to Dartmouth, No. 38, 16 February 1776, C.O. 5/556; Georgia Council Minutes, 31 October 1775, Hawes, ed., "Minutes of the Governor and Council," *GHQ*, XXXIV (December 1950), 310–11; Wright to Germain, No. 4, 27 March 1776, enclosing James Jackson to Wright, 23 March 1776, and Memorial of James Jackson and Andrew McLean, 21 March 1776, *CRG*, XXXVIII, Pt. II, 91–97.

93. Stuart to Gage, 15 September 1775, Force, ed., *Archives*, 4th Ser., III, 714–15; Gage to Stuart, 12 September 1775, Taitt to Stuart, 1 August 1775, and Stuart's instructions to Henry Stuart, 25 October 1775, C.O. 5/76; Stuart to Dartmouth, No. 32, 17 December 1775, Superintendent's Talk to the Lower Creek Indians at a Meeting held at the Cowford, 4 December 1775, Stuart to Cameron, 16 December 1775, and Stuart to Taitt, 15 December 1775, C.O. 5/77. See also Gage to Barrington, Private, 12 June 1775, and Dartmouth to Gage, Separate, 2 August 1775, Carter, ed., *Correspondence of Gage*, II, 684, 204.

94. In the autumn, Stuart proposed to end the Creek-Choctaw War in order to free those tribes to act against the rebels. Stuart to Dartmouth, No. 31, 25 October 1775, C.O. 5/76; Stuart to Dartmouth, No. 33, 6 January 1776, Taitt to Stuart, 20 October 1776, and Talk from Niaha Thlaco (Secondman of Little Tallassee), 20 October 1775, C.O. 5/77.

95. Adair, *American Indians*, pp. 16, 84, 118, 165–66, 435, 442–43, 448–53, 459–60; Bartram, "Observations," pp. 23–25, 34–41, 52–57; Bartram, *Travels*, pp. 133, 231–33, 284–89, 313–15, 325–26, 330–32; De Brahm, *Report*, pp. 110, 112–13; Romans, *Natural History*, p. 45. The most convenient "Compara-

tive Town Census" for the Creeks, 1738–1832, is in John R[eed] Swanton, *Early History of the Creek Indians and Their Neighbors,* Smithsonian Institution Bureau of American Ethnology, Bulletin 73 (Washington, [D.C.]: U.S. Government Printing Office, 1922), pp. 434–37.

96. The most detailed analysis of the Creek clan system is in John R[eed] Swanton, "Social Organization and Social Usages of the Indians of the Creek Confederacy," *Forty-Second Annual Report of the Bureau of American Ethnology* (Washington, [D.C.]: U.S. Government Printing Office, 1928), pp. 107–241.

97. Wright to Dartmouth, No. 51, 20 June 1775, *CRG,* XXXVIII, Pt. I–B, 475–77; Wright to Dartmouth, No. 59, 23 September 1775, *Letters from Governor Sir James Wright to the Earl of Dartmouth and Lord George Germain, Secretaries of State for America, from August 24, 1774, to February 16, 1782, GHSC,* III (Savannah: By the Society, 1873), 212 (hereafter cited as *GHSC,* III); Wright to Dartmouth, No. 62, 1 November 1775, *CRG,* XXXVIII, Pt. II, 13–14; Stuart to Gage, 15 September 1775, Force, ed., *Archives,* 4th Ser., III, 714–15; Stuart to Dartmouth, No. 30, 17 September 1775, Taitt to Stuart, 1 August 1775, and Stuart's talk to the great and small Medal Chiefs and Rulers of the Cowetas, Tallapusees, Abuchkas, and Alebamons, [15 August 1775], C.O. 5/76; Talk of Emistisiguo to Stuart, 20 September 1775, C.O. 5/77; Georgia Council minutes, 25 July, 31 October 1775, Hawes, ed., "Minutes of the Governor and Council," *GHQ,* XXXIV (December 1950), 198, 311–12.

98. In the summer of 1776, Stuart reported that "about four hundred good white men Traders and packhorsemen" who could be called into military service were then living within the Indian nations of his district. Stuart to Germain, No. 6, 23 August 1776, C.O. 5/77. Caleb Swan, deputy agent for the Creeks, reported that nearly three hundred whites were living among the Creeks in 1791. Caleb Swan, "Position and State of Manners and Arts in the Creek Nation, in 1791," in Henry R. Schoolcraft, *Information Respecting the History, Condition, and Prospects of the Indian Tribes of the United States: Collected and Prepared Under the Direction of the Bureau of Indian Affairs per Act of Congress of March 3rd 1847,* Vol. V (6 vols., Philadelphia: Lippincott and Co., 1855), 263. Considering that Stuart's figures include whites living with the Cherokees, Choctaws, Chickasaws and smaller tribes, as well as the Creeks, but do not include temporary refugees, the numbers of whites living within the Creek Nation appear to have remained fairly consistent over a fifteen-year period at least.

99. Taitt to Stuart (extract), 13 April 1775, Substance of a message sent by Mr. George Galphin into the Creek Nation, [June 1775 and the answer], C.O. 5/76.

100. Stuart to Taitt, 29 August 1775, Gibbes, comp., *Documentary History,* I, 158; Stuart to McKay and McLean, 30 August 1775, "Papers of the First Council of Safety," *SCHGM,* I (October 1900), 293; Extract from an Intercepted Letter of Frederick George Mulcaster to Governor Grant, 29 September 1775, Gibbes, comp., *Documentary History,* I, 197; Tonyn to Dartmouth, No. 26, 15 September 1775, to Gage, [14 September 1775], C.O. 5/555. See

also Georgia Council Minutes, 31 October 1775, Hawes, ed., "Minutes of the Governor and Council," *GHQ,* XXXIV (December 1950), 310–11.

101. Tonyn to Dartmouth, No. 26, 15 September 1775, to Dartmouth, Private, No. 11, 20 September 1775, C.O. 5/555.

102. Talk to Gov. Wright given at Usitchee town, 7 September 1775, *CRG,* XXXVIII, Pt. II, 17–18; George Galphin to Council of Safety at Charleston, 15 October 1775, Laurens to Galphin, 22 October 1775, "Papers of the First Council of Safety," *SCHGM,* III (January 1902), 7–10.

103. Tonyn to Dartmouth, Private, No. 11, 20 September 1775, to Gage, 20 September 1775, C.O. 5/555.

104. Tonyn to Dartmouth, Private, No. 14, 25 October 1775, C.O. 5/555.

105. Examinations of Thomas Gray, 2, 10 October 1775, C.O. 5/555. Governor Tonyn ordered that Gray be paid just over £22 for his information. General Account of sundry extra Indian expences from the 25th June 1775 to the 24th June 1776, C.O. 5/557.

106. Tonyn to Dartmouth, Private, No. 18, 18 December 1775, Tonyn's Talk to the Creek Nation, 6 December 1775, Kaligie . . . of the Chihaw's Talk, 7 December 1775, C.O. 5/556; Tonyn's Talk to . . . the Pumpkin King and Kaligy of the Chihaws, and Pumpkin King and Kaligie's reply to Tonyn, both dated 8 December 1775, C.O. 5/556; Stuart to Dartmouth, No. 32, 17 December 1775, Stuart's Talk to the Lower Creeks, 4 December 1775, and Stuart to David Taitt, 15 December 1775, C.O. 5/77; Journal of H.M. Schooner *St. Lawrence,* 4–11, 27 November, 10 December 1775, *NDAR,* II, 995–96, 1168, III, 43; East Florida Council Minutts [*sic*], 3 November 1775, including Tonyn to Maj. Furlong, 3 November 1775, and Tonyn to Lt. Graves Commanding His Majesty's Schooner *St. Lawrence,* 3 November 1775, C.O. 5/571.

107. Stuart to Taitt, 15 December 1775, to Cameron, 16 December 1775, C.O. 5/77. The South Carolina loyalists had signed a truce at Ninety-Six on 22 November. Journal of the South Carolina Council of Safety, 4, 5 December 1775, Henry Laurens to Major Andrew Williamson (extract), 4 December 1775, *NDAR,* II, 1275–76, 1299–1300.

108. *RRG,* I, 81.

109. Memorial of Jermyn Wright and supporting documents, 1787, Wilbur Henry Siebert, *Loyalists in East Florida, 1774–1785,* Publications of the Florida Historical Society, No. 9 (2 vols., Deland, Fla.: Florida State Historical Society, 1929), II, 168–74.

110. Tonyn to Germain, No. 18, 18 July 1776, C.O. 5/557; Memorial for Jermyn and Charles Wright to Lord George Germain, n.d., C.O. 5/116. The location of Wright's house and landing is shown in De Brahm's "Plan of St. Marys' Inlet," De Brahm, *Report,* Plate 16 facing p. 200.

Secondary sources mention an attack on Fort Wright in February 1776. Tonyn's correspondence, usually detailed about such matters, does not mention one at that time, and the Whig accounts seem confused with one later in the year. On the other hand, Wright himself said that he first bore arms in

February 1776. Memorial of Jermyn Wright, 27 April 1784, Hugh Edward Egerton, ed., *The Royal Commission on Losses and Services of American Loyalists, 1783–1785*, Mass Violence in America Series (1915; reprint ed., New York: Arno Press and the New York Times, 1969), p. 115.

111. Governor Wright's interview with Noble W. Jones and Joseph Clay, 18 January 1776, Joseph Valence Bevan Papers, Georgia Historical Society, Savannah, Georgia; *Georgia Gazette*, 24 January 1776; Journal of the [Georgia] Council of Safety, 7–16 January 1776, *RRG*, I, 86–101. An excellent brief summary of the actions by this British fleet in the Savannah River is in the Extract of a letter from General Howe to Lord George Germain, 7 May 1776, Force, ed., *Archives*, 4th Ser., V, 1233, and in Extract of a Letter, dated on board the brig *Allerton*, Cockspur, in Georgia, 24 March [1776], *NDAR*, IV, 493–94.

112. Journal of the Council of Safety, 18–19 January 1776, *RRG*, I, 101–5; Journal of the South Carolina Council of Safety, 30 January 1776, *NCSR*, XI, 271; Memorial of Lieut. Governor John Grahame to Germain, n.d., *GHSC*, III, 376–77; Martin Jollie to Tonyn, 13 February 1776, C.O. 5/556.

113. *Georgia Gazette*, 7 February 1776; Journal of H.M.S. *Raven*, Captain John Stanhope, and Journal of H.M.S. *Scarborough*, Captain Andrew Barkley, 12 February 1776, *NDAR*, III, 1239; Wright to Council, 13 February 1776, *RRG*, I, 269–72; Captain Andrew Barclay to Wright, 19 February 1776, in Journal of the Council of Safety, 21 February 1776, *RRG*, I, 107; Memorial of Sir James Wright to Lord George Germain, 19 February 1778, *CRG*, XXXIX, 27; Lachlan McIntosh to Washington, 8 March 1776, Lilla Mills Hawes, ed., *The Papers of Lachlan McIntosh, 1774–1779*, *GHSC*, XII (Savannah: By the Society, 1957), 1 (hereafter cited as *GHSC*, XII).

114. Wright to Council, 13 February 1776, *RRG*, I, 269–72; Captain Andrew Barkley, R.N., to Major General Henry Clinton, 23 February 1776, *NDAR*, IV, 60; Clinton to Wright, 20 March 1776, *NDAR*, IV, 428.

115. The best collection of documents pertaining to the "battle of the riceboats" as well as prior and subsequent events is in *NDAR*, III, IV. The most readable account is Harvey H. Jackson, "The Battle of the Riceboats: Georgia Joins the Revolution," *GHQ*, LXVIII (Summer 1974), 229–43.

116. Memorial of Sir James Wright, Baronet, Governor of the Province of Georgia, and several other Gentlemen late Inhabitants of that Province, and others who have property therein, n.d., [in Wright to Germain, 6 January 1779], *CRG*, XXXVIII, Pt. II, 138; Bull to Laurens, 13 March 1776, Gibbes, comp., *Documentary History*, I, 266.

117. Memorial of Lieutenant Governor John Grahame to Germain, n.d., *GHSC*, III, 376–77; Captain Andrew Barkley, R.N., and Major James Grant to Anthony Stokes, 14 March 1776, *NDAR*, IV, 435; Georgia Council of Safety to Captain Barkley and Major Grant, 16 March 1776, Force, ed., *Archives*, 4th Ser., V, 603; McIntosh to Washington, 8 March 1776, *GHSC*, XII, 3; Wright to Germain, No. 2, 20 March 1776, *CRG*, XXXVIII, Pt. II, 78–80; Master's Log of HM Armed Vessel *Cherokee*, Journal of HM Sloop

Tamar, Captain Edward Thornbrough, and Journal of HMS *Scarborough,* Captain Andrew Barkley, all dated 30–31 March 1776, *NDAR,* IV, 600–603.

HM Sloop *Raven* and HM Armed Vessel *Cherokee* were stationed at the mouth of the Savannah River when the fleet left. Disposition of His Majesty's Ships and Vessels in North America Under the Command of Vice Admiral Schuldham, 24 April 1776, *NDAR,* IV, 1226.

Chapter II

1. 27 February, 1 March 1776, *JCC,* IV, 174, 180–81; John Hancock, President of Congress, to Charles Lee, 1 March 1776, Burnett, ed., *Letters,* I, 370–71; Hancock to John Armstrong, Armstrong to Hancock, both dated 2 March 1776, Force, ed., *Archives,* 4th Ser., V, 43; Washington to McIntosh, 4 June 1776, Force, ed., *Archives,* 4th Ser., VI, 709.

2. 4 November 1775, *JCC,* III, 325–27.

3. A list of the original officers for the eight companies of this battalion appeared in *Georgia Gazette,* 7 February 1776, and is also printed in White, *Collections,* p. 94. For Gwinnett's disappointment, see Maj. Joseph Habersham to William Drayton, n.d., Gibbes, comp., *Documentary History,* I, 259; Joseph Clay to Henry Laurens, 16 October 1777, *Letters of Joseph Clay, Merchant of Savannah, 1776–1793, . . . , GHSC,* VIII (Savannah: By the Society, 1913), 50 (hereafter cited as *GHSC,* VIII); Charles Francis Jenkins, *Button Gwinnett, Signer of the Declaration of Independence* (1926; reprint ed., Spartanburg, S.C.: Reprint Company, 1974), pp. 72, 94.

4. 4 November 1775, *JCC,* III, 322.

5. Journal of the Council of Safety, 14, 16 May, 8 June 1776, *RRG,* I, 124, 128, 137.

6. McIntosh to Washington, 16 February 1776, White, *Collections,* pp. 92–93; McIntosh to Washington, 28 April 1776, *GHSC,* XII, 4–5; Armstrong to Hancock, 7 May 1776, Force, ed., *Archives,* 4th Ser., V, 1219–20; Armstrong to Maj. Gen. Charles Lee, 8 May 1776, *Charles Lee Papers,* Vol. V. of *Collections of the New York Historical Society,* II, *1776–1778* (New York: By the Society, 1872), 11; Lt. Col. Samuel Elbert to Lee, 14 May 1776, *GHSC,* XII, 6; Elbert to Lee, 28 May 1776, *GHSC,* XII, 7–8; Lee to Hancock, 6 June 1776, *Lee Papers,* II, 54; Committee reports, 25 March, 29 May 1776, *JCC,* IV, 235–400.

7. Journal of the [Georgia] Council of Safety, 2, 9 January, 23 May, 21 June 1776, *RRG,* I, 84–86, 93–94, 130, 144; Laurens to Bull, 13 January 1776, *NDAR,* III, 787.

8. Archibald Bullock's "Permission to Thomas Young to Load Rice on Board the Snow *Georgia,*" 26 April 1776, *NDAR,* IV, 1274; Journal of the Council of Safety, 8, 9 August 1776, 22 February 1777, *RRG,* I, 174–76, 178, 227–28; Tonyn to British naval commander at Savannah River, 5 August 1776, C.O. 5/556; Tonyn to Admiral Lord Richard Howe, No. 16, 25

December 1776, C.O. 5/557. In 1785 the Georgia legislature passed an act of clemency that relieved Young of the penalties of the Act of Confiscation and Banishment, but fixed certain financial and political liabilities for him; he could not vote or hold office for fourteen years. Just two years later, the legislature granted him all the rights of citizenship. *RRG*, I, 612–13, 617.

9. 1 January 1776, *JCC*, IV, 15; Richard Smith's diary, 1–2 January 1776, Burnett, ed., *Letters*, I, 293–94.

10. Tonyn to Gage, [14 September 1775], to Dartmouth, Private, No. 11, 20 September 1775, and to Gage, 20 September 1775, C.O. 5/555; C. Shirreff to Maj. William Shirreff, 25 September 1775, Force, ed., *Archives*, 4th Ser., III, 788; C. Shirreff to Gen. Robertson, 25 September 1775, ibid., 789; John Moultrie, Lt. Gov. of East Florida, to General Grant, 4 October 1775, Force, ed., *Archives*, 4th Ser., IV, 336; Tonyn to Dartmouth, No. 37, 14 January 1776, Martin Jollie to Tonyn, 13 February 1776, C.O. 5/556.

11. The rebels captured some military stores that the British had to leave behind. Manifesto of Commodore Eseck Hopkins, sent on shore at New Providence, 3 March 1776, Force, ed., *Archives*, 4th Ser., V, 46; Eseck Hopkins to Hancock, 9 April 1776, ibid., 823–24; Inventory of Stores taken at Ft. Montague (3 March 1776) and Ft. Nassau (4 March 1776), ibid., 824; Extract of a letter from the Captain of Marines [Samuel Nicholas], on board the ship *Alfred*, . . . 10 April 1776, ibid., 846–47; Tonyn to Germain, No. 5, 8 March 1776, Lt. William Grant to Tonyn, 7 March 1776, Tonyn to Germain, No. 6, 18 March 1776, and Montfort Browne to Tonyn, 4 March 1776, C.O. 5/556; Journal of H.M. Schooner *St. John*, Lt. William Grant, 2–7 March 1776, *NDAR*, IV, 173–75, 225; Journal of Continental Brig *Andrew Doria*, Captain Nicholas Biddle, 1–4, 6–16 March 1776, *NDAR*, IV, 153, 171, 373; Journal prepared for the King of France by John Paul Jones, *NDAR*, IV, 133–34; Grant to Vice Admiral Molyneux Shuldham, 8 March 1776, to Philip Stephens, 18 March 1776, and John Brown to Vice Admiral Clark Gayton, 22 March 1776, C.O. 5/124; Thomas Atwood to Dartmouth, 22 March 1776, *NDAR*, IV, 464–67; Montfort Browne to Germain, 5 November 1776, *NDAR*, VII, 48–51.

12. Tonyn to Germain, No. 3, 5 March 1776, Return to Recruits . . . 60th or Royal American Regiment, . . . 11 May 1776, C.O. 5/556; Lewis [William George] Butler and Stewart Hare, *The Annals of the King's Royal Rifle Corps*, Vol. I: Lewis [William George] Butler, *The Royal Americans* (London: Smith, Elder and Co., 1913), 208.

13. Butler, *Royal Americans*, pp. 2–4, 16–21, 23, 159–62, 199, 288–89, 297, 369–70.

14. East Florida Council Minutes, 2, 6 February, 30 March 1776, C.O. 5/571.

15. A List of Sundry Articles to be delivered at Pensacola in February by Mr. James Penman merchant, n.d., C.O. 5/60; Minutes of the Council of West Florida, 28 November 1775, *NDAR*, II, 1186–87; Stuart to Dartmouth, No. 35, 19 January 1776, Emistisiguo to Stuart, 2 March 1776, C.O. 5/77; Memorial of James Jackson and Andrew McLean to Governor Wright, 21

March 1776, *CRG*, XXXVIII, Pt. II, 95–99; A Talk from the Headmen and Warriors of the lower Creek Nation, . . . 23 March 1776, C.O. 5/77.

16. Stuart to Clinton, 15 March 1776, C.O. 5/77.

17. East Florida Council Minutes, 2 February 1776, C.O. 5/571; Tonyn to Dartmouth, No. 39, 16 February 1776, to Clinton, 17 February 1776, C.O. 5/556.

18. Martin Jollie to Tonyn, 13 February 1776, Tonyn to Dartmouth, No. 39, 16 February 1776, and to Clinton, 17 February 1776, C.O. 5/556.

19. Precis Prepared for the King of Events Leading up to the Expedition Against the Southern Colonies, 22 October, 30 November, 31 December 1775, [Extract], *NDAR*, II, 769–74, III, 398–400, 465–67; Sandwich to Graves, Private, 25 August 1775, *NDAR*, II, 687–89; J. Pownell to Wright, 4 October, 7 November 1775, *CRG*, XXXVIII, Pt. I–B, 509, 594; Dartmouth to General William Howe, 22 October 1775, Headquarters Papers of the British Army in America, Colonial Williamsburg Foundation, Williamsburg, Virginia, No. 68; Dartmouth to William Campbell, Governor of South Carolina, 7 November 1775, Headquarters Papers, No. 81; Dartmouth to Martin, governor of North Carolina, No. 22, 7 November 1775, Headquarters Papers, No. 82; Germain to Howe, 8 November 1775, Headquarters Papers, No. 80; Philip Stephens to Rear Admiral Molyneux Shuldham, 11 November 1775, *NDAR*, III, 360–61; Germain to Howe, 18 November 1775, Headquarters Papers, No. 85; Germain to Clinton, 6 December 1775, Headquarters Papers, No. 87; Germain to Tonyn, No. 1, 23 December 1775, C.O. 5/555; Germain to Wright, No. 1, 23 December 1775, *CRG*, XXXVIII, Pt. I–B, 649; Germain to Martin, No. 1, 23 December 1775, *NDAR*, III, 445–46; Germain to Dunmore, No. 1, 23 December 1775, *NDAR*, III, 444–45; Germain to Gov. Robert Eden, [of Maryland], No. 1, 23 December 1775, *NDAR*, III, 446.

20. Wright to Dartmouth, 3 January 1776, *CRG*, XXXVIII, Pt. II, 63–65; Narrative of Sir Henry Clinton, 6 January–12 February 1776, *NDAR*, III, 1231–32; Brown to Stuart, 24 February 1776, Clinton Papers, William L. Clements Library, University of Michigan, Ann Arbor, Michigan; Brown to Tonyn, ca. 24 February, C.O. 5/556; Extract of a letter from Frederick George Mulcaster to Governor Grant, 29 September 1776, Gibbes, comp., *Documentary History*, I, 197.

21. Stuart to Dartmouth, Nos. 32, 34, and 35, 17 December 1775, 8, 19 January 1776, C.O. 5/77.

22. For an astute analysis of the "concerted plan" for reducing the southern colonies that was formulated by Thomas Brown and Governor Tonyn as well as for a convincing argument that the plan was not put into operation because Superintendent Stuart did not deliver the message to Clinton, see Gary D. Olsen, "Loyalists and the American Revolution: Thomas Brown and the South Carolina Backcountry, 1775–1776," Pt. II, *SCHM*, LXIX (January 1968), 44–56, especially 50. For the theory that Stuart presented the plan and then sabotaged it, see James H. O'Donnell III, *Southern Indians in the American Revolution* (Knoxville: University of Tennessee Press, 1973), pp. 35–36.

23. Printed in *RRG*, I, 274–77.

24. Speech by Council of Safety (30 April 1776) and Bulloch's reply (1 May 1776), *RRG*, I, 114–16, 277–78.

25. 20 May 1776, *JCC*, IV, 367.

26. 27 January, 29–30 April, 6 May 1776, *JCC*, IV, 96–98, 317–19, 329–30; 6 July 1776, *JCC*, IV, 1065; Secret Committee to Silas Deane, 1 March 1776, Burnett, ed., *Letters*, I, 372.

27. 8 March 1776, *JCC*, IV, 191.

28. Richard Smith's Diary, 8 March 1776, Burnett, ed., *Letters*, I, 382.

29. 25 May 1776, *JCC*, IV, 394–96; 17 June 1776, *JCC*, V, 452; President of Congress [John Hancock] to Washington, 18 June 1776, Burnett, ed., *Letters*, I, 496–97.

30. Talk from the Headmen and Warriors of the Lower Creek Nation . . . At the Cussitas, 23 March 1776, C.O. 5/77.

31. Tonyn to Taitt, 20 April 1776, C.O. 5/556.

32. Tonyn to Taitt, 30 March, 20 April 1776, Brown to Tonyn, 2 May 1776, C.O. 5/556.

33. Robert Rae to Samual Thomas, 3 May 1776, C.O. 5/77.

34. Tonyn to Taitt, 20 April 1776, Brown to Tonyn, 2, 8 May 1776, and Taitt to Tonyn, 3, 8 May 1776, C.O. 5/556.

35. Brown to Tonyn, 2, 8 May 1776, Taitt to Tonyn, 3 May 1776, C.O. 5/556.

36. Ibid.; Taitt to Tonyn, 8 May 1776, Tonyn to Taitt, 20 April 1776, C.O. 5/556.

37. Talk from the Rebel Commissioners to the Creeks, 13 November 1775, C.O. 5/77; Talk delivered by the Commissioners . . . as Related by Lecoffee, who was present at Augusta, Interpreted by Samuel Thomas, and the Chawokly Warrior's answer, [May 1776], C.O. 5/77; Robert Rae to Samuel Thomas, 3 May 1776, C.O. 5/77; Taitt to Tonyn, 3 May 1776, C.O. 5/556; Stuart to Germain, No. 3, 20 May 1776, Taitt to Stuart, 7 July 1776, C.O. 5/77.

Taitt pointed out that having some Indians go to Augusta and collect presents might be good, rather than bad, for the king's service; it would drain the rebels of things they had even less supply of than the Indians did. The British agent had planted spies, the Chavulky Warrior and Lacuffe, in the Creek contingent at the Augusta congress. Taitt to Tonyn, 3, 8 May 1776, C.O. 5/556; Taitt to Stuart, 7 July 1776, C.O. 5/77.

38. Brown to Tonyn, 8 May 1776, Tonyn to Clinton, 8 June 1776, C.O. 5/556.

39. Stuart to Germain, No. 5, 23 August 1776, C.O. 5/77.

40. Journal of the Council of Safety, 14–16 May 1776, *RRG*, I, 122–23, 125, 128. For Thomas Fee's murder of the Upper Creek Mad Turkey, on 24 March 1774, see Wright's Proclamation, [n.d., dated page (245) not filmed], *CRG*, XXXVIII, Pt. I–A, 244; Wright to Dartmouth, No. 21, 24 May 1774, *CRG*, XXXVIII, Pt. I–A, 286; East Florida Council Minutes, 30 May 1774, C.O. 5/571.

41. Talk delivered by the Commissioners . . . as Related by Lecoffee, who was present at Augusta, Interpreted by Samuel Thomas, and the Chawokly Warrior's answer, n.d., in Stuart to Germain, No. 5, 23 August 1776, and Taitt to Stuart, 7 July 1776, C.O. 5/77. The law that applied in this case was signed by Governor Wright on 20 June 1774 and was entitled "An Act Declaring that to Murder any free Indian in amity with this province is equally penal with the Murdering of any white person and that to Rescue a Prisoner Committed for such Offence is Felony," CRG, XIX, Pt. II, 36–37.

42. Taitt to Stuart, 7 July 1776, C.O. 5/77; Samuel Thomas to Stuart, 19 September 1776, C.O. 5/78.

43. Brown to Stuart, 29 September 1776, David Holmes to Stuart, 26 September 1776, C.O. 5/78.

44. Copy of a talk from the Committee in Savannah [signed by Archibald Bullock] to the Lower Creeks, [? June 1776], C.O. 5/77; Conference with the Georgia Deputies, n.d., in Lee to Hancock, 2 July 1776, Lee Papers, pp. 116–17; Report of the Georgia Deputies, Journal of the Council of Safety, 5 July 1776, RRG, I, 154, 303.

45. M'Call, History, p. 317.

46. Journal of the Council of Safety, 15–16 May 1776, RRG, I, 125, 128; George Galphin to Timothy Barnard, 18 August 1776, to James Burges, 28 August 1776, C.O. 5/78; Galphin to Willie Jones, 26 October 1776, Force, ed., Archives, 5th Ser., III, 648–50; Samuel Thomas to Stuart, 29 September 1776, Daniel McMurphy to John Burges, n.d., in Stuart to Germain, No. 10, 26 October 1776, Copy of a Talk from George Galphin to the Creek Indians, n.d., in Stuart to Germain, No. 10, 26 October 1776, and Copy of a Talk from Daniel McMurphy to Sinittahaugey and the Rest of the Headmen at the forks, n.d., in Stuart to Germain, No. 10, 26 October 1776, C.O. 5/78; Petition to His Excellency General Lee . . . of the Inhabitants of . . . the ceded lands in the Province of Georgia, 31 July 1776, Lee Papers, pp. 181–82.

47. Journal of H.M. Schooner St. John, 1 April 1776, NDAR, IV, 702.

48. Ibid., 2 April 1776, 702–03.

49. Ibid., 3–7 April 1776, 703.

50. Ibid., 11–14 April 1776, 825. Tonyn intended to condemn the St. John's three prizes, along with two vessels from the Dutch West Indies that had engaged in illicit commerce, in the admiralty court at St. Augustine. Tonyn to Germain, No. 12, 22 April 1776, C.O. 5/556.

The same day that the St. John left St. Marys, the rebels were discomfited to the northward. HM Sloop Raven, stationed off Cockspur Island at the mouth of the Savannah River, sighted a sail outside the bar. Captain John Stanhope manned and armed the pilot boat and sent her out. At eleven o'clock that night, she returned with a Jamaica brig, the Live Oak, whose master was a man named Foster, that was bound for Sunbury with twenty-nine puncheons of rum and sugar. Journal of H.M. Sloop Raven, 14 April 1776, NDAR, IV, 824–25.

51. Providence Gazette, 7 January 1775, and Table showing the Guard Ships in the English Parts and the Ships Cruising in Various Seas, as of 6

March 1775, in M. Garnier to Count de Vergennes, 6 March 1776, both in *NDAR*, I, 428.

52. List of British ships . . . , 29 September 1775, *NDAR*, II, 742; Capt. Henry Bryne, R.N., to Vice Admiral James Young, 21 May 1776, *NDAR*, V, 197. The *Hinchinbrook* had taken dispatches from the north to St. Augustine and Pensacola in February and March, then returned to St. Augustine to relieve the *St. Lawrence* on that station. Vice Admiral [Samuel] Graves to Captain Andrew Barkley, H.M.S. *Scarborough*, 26 December 1775, *NDAR*, III, 256; Tonyn to Germain, No. 3, 5 March 1776, C.O. 5/556.

53. Tonyn to Germain, No. 12, 22 April 1776, C.O. 5/556; Bryne to Young, 21 May 1776, *NDAR*, V, 197; *New York Packet*, Thursday, 18 July 1776, *NDAR*, V, 367.

54. Journal of H.M. Schooner *Hinchinbrook*, Lt. Alexander Ellis, 22–23 April 1776, *NDAR*, IV, 1242–43; Bryne to Young, 21 May 1776, *NDAR*, V, 197; *New York Packet*, Thursday, 18 July 1776, *NDAR*, V, 367. For the orders under which the British naval officers acted, see Lord Dartmouth to the Lords Commissioners of the British Admiralty, 22 October 1775, *NDAR*, II, 769.

55. Journal of H.M. Schooner *Hinchinbrook*, Lt. Alexander Ellis, 24 April 1776, *NDAR*, IV, 1243; Bryne to Young, 21 May 1776, *NDAR*, V, 197.

56. Bryne to Young, 21 May 1776, *NDAR*, V, 197.

57. Tonyn to Germain, No. 12, 22 April 1776, to Clinton, 21 May 1776, C.O. 5/556. There is a distinct possibility that the secrecy surrounding the sailing of both the *Hind* and the *Hinchinbrook* was occasioned by fear of a leak in the governor's council.

58. Commodore Sir Peter Parker to Philip Stephens, 15 May 1776, *NDAR*, V, 110–11.

59. Tonyn to Germain, No. 12, 22 April 1776, C.O. 5/556; Butler, *Royal Americans*, pp. 208–9, 298, 361.

60. C. Shirreff to Tonyn, 14 May 1776, C.O. 5/556. These barracks had been completed in 1771. Gage to Hillsborough, No. 64, 3 September 1771, Carter, ed., *Correspondence of Gage*, I, 307.

There were actually two barracks, besides the fort, in St. Augustine. Both were on the south side of town. One, constructed around the buildings of the church and friary of St. Francis, was completed by May 1771. The other "new" barracks was completed by August 1771. It had deliberately been constructed as cheaply as possible, and this was the building that was already "ruinous." Charles L. Mowat, "St. Francis Barracks, St. Augustine: A Link with the British Regime," *FHQ*, XXI (January 1943), 266–80.

61. Tonyn to Germain, No. 14, 19 May 1776, C.O. 5/556.

62. Estimates of Expences to be done immediately to His Majesty's Barracks at St. Augustine, 14 May 1776, C.O. 5/556.

63. C. Shirreff to Tonyn, 14 May 1776, Tonyn to Germain, No. 14, 19 May 1776, C.O. 5/556. The Treasury Lords directed that Tonyn's draft on them for barracks repairs be paid. Germain to Tonyn, 6 November 1776, C.O. 5/556.

64. Tonyn to Germain, No. 14, 19 May 1776, C.O. 5/556.

65. Journal of the [Georgia] Council of Safety, 1, 14, 16 May 1776, *RRG*, I, 118, 123–24, 127–28.

66. Journal of the Council of Safety, 5 July 1776, ibid., 151–53.

67. Memorial of Thomas Nixon, London Merchant, to Lords of the Treasury, 6 February 1776, Headquarters Papers, No. 123; Thomas Nixon to John Robinson, 1 March 1776, Headquarters Papers, No. 131; Nixon to Lords of the Treasury, 7 March 1776, Headquarters Papers, No. 134; John Robinson to General Howe, 1 May 1776, Headquarters Papers, No. 171; Brown to Tonyn, 24 February 1776, C.O. 5/556.

68. Journal of the Council of Safety, 5 July 1776, *RRG*, I, 151–53; Henry Laurens to John Laurens, 14 August 1776, *Lee Papers*, p. 218.

69. Tonyn to Germain, No. 13, 19 May 1776, C.O. 5/556.

70. East Florida Council Minutes, 20 May 1776, C.O. 5/571; Tonyn to Clinton, No. 7, 21 May 1776, C.O. 5/556.

71. Ibid.; Tonyn to Lt. Grant Commanding His Majesty's Armed Schooner *St. John*, to Col. Prevost Commanding His Majesty's Troops at St. Augustine, and to John Bethune, all dated 20 May 1776, in East Florida Council Minutes of 20 May 1776, C.O. 5/571; Tonyn to Clinton, Private, No. 10, 8 June 1776, C.O. 5/556; Tonyn to Germain, No. 18, 18 July 1776, C.O. 5/557.

72. Journal of H.M. Schooner *St. John*, Lt. William Grant, 27 May 1776, *NDAR*, V, 327; Tonyn to Clinton, Private, No. 10, 8 June 1776, to Germain, Private, No. 1, 10 June 1776, C.O. 5/556; General Account of extra Contingent Expences incurred for the service of His Majesty's Province of East Florida from the 25th June 1775 to the 24th June 1776, C.O. 5/557.

73. Journal of H.M. Schooner *St. John*, 29 May 1776, *NDAR*, V, 327–28; Tonyn to Clinton, Private, No. 10, 8 June 1776, to Germain, Private, No. 1, 10 June 1776, C.O. 5/556.

74. Journal of H.M. Schooner *St. John*, 31 May 1776, *NDAR*, V, 328; Tonyn to Clinton, Private, No. 10, 8 June 1776, to Germain, Private, No. 1, 10 June 1776, C.O. 5/556.

75. Journal of H.M. Schooner *St. John*, 4 June 1776, *NDAR*, V, 465; Memorial of William Chapman and accompanying documents, 13, 21 March 1787, Siebert, *Loyalists*, II, 215–20.

76. Journal of H.M. Schooner *St. John*, 31 May, 1, 2 June 1776, *NDAR*, V, 328, 465; Tonyn to Clinton, Private, No. 10, 8 June 1776, to Germain, Private, No. 1, 10 June 1776, C.O. 5/556.

77. Tonyn to Clinton, Private, No. 10, 8 June 1776, to Germain, Private, No. 1, 10 June 1776, C.O. 5/556; Journal of the Council of Safety, 2 July 1776, *RRG*, I, 148; Journal of H.M. Schooner *St. John*, 11 July 1776, *NDAR*, V, 1031.

78. Lt. Col. Samuel Elbert to Lee, 14 May 1776, *GHSC*, XII, 6.

79. Tonyn to Germain, No. 18, 18 July 1776, C.O. 5/557.

80. Journal of H.M. Schooner *St. John*, 1–30 June, 1–5 July 1776, *NDAR*, V, 465–66, 611–12, 654, 761–62, 844, 929, 942.

81. Journal of the Council of Safety, 14–16 May, 20 June 1776, *RRG*, I, 123, 128, 141–42. "Gaskins" may have been Gascoigne Bluff, on St. Simons Island; one Capt. Woodruff seized a St. Augustine sloop that was loaded with rum, sugar, and osnabergs as well as a schooner (both of which vessels the Council of Safety ordered to be released) in the Sapelo River. Journal of the Council of Safety, 19 June 1776, *RRG*, I, 140.

82. Wright, *Florida*, p. 38.

83. *Report of Sir James, GHSC*, III, 168–69.

84. Journal of the Council of Safety, 8 June, 30 July 1776, *RRG*, I, 136, 169; J. Kitching to Tonyn, [9 August ?] 1776, C.O. 5/556. The fort may not have been entirely new, though Governor Wright's Report of 1773 did not mention a fort at Sunbury. After a tour of inspection through the southern part of his province, Governor Ellis, Wright's predecessor, had observed that he was pleased that "the inhabitants [of the Midway District] had . . . erected a Battery of 8 guns at Sunbury in a very proper situation for defending the River." Henry Ellis to the Board of Trade, 20 May 1758, *CRG*, XXVIII, Pt. I, 155. Two years later, the Georgia governor reported that "A very good Logg Fort is built at Sunbury." Ellis to Board of Trade, 25 August 1760, *CRG*, XXVIII, Pt. I, 285.

85. Journal of the Council of Safety, 20 June 1776, *RRG*, I, 142.

86. Gage to Barrington, 21 May 1767, Carter, ed., *Correspondence of Gage*, II, 419.

87. Grant to Halifax, 6 December 1764, C.O. 5/548; Grant to Shelburne, No. 4, 19 April 1767, C.O. 5/541; General Account of sundry Expences Incurred for Indians from the 25th of June 1773 to the 24th of June 1774, C.O. 5/554.

88. Tonyn to Clinton, to Brown, and to Prevost, all dated 29 May 1779, C.O. 5/559; Brown to Carleton, 11 January 1783, Headquarters Papers, No. 6737; Tonyn to Carleton, 14 January 1783, Headquarters Papers, No. 6752; Memorial of Lt. Col. Brown, n.d., in McArthur to Carleton, 9 January 1783, Headquarters Papers, No. 10050.

89. Tonyn to Clinton, Private, No. 10, 8 June 1776, to Germain, Private, No. 1, 10 June 1776, C.O. 5/556; Journal of H.M. Schooner *St. John*, 19 June 1776, *NDAR*, VI, 654; General Account of extra Contingent Expences incurred for the service of His Majesty's Province of East Florida from the 25th June 1775 to the 24th June 1776, C.O. 5/557.

90. Brown to Cornwallis, 16 July 1780, Cornwallis Papers; Prevost to Clinton, 30 July 1779, Headquarters Papers, No. 2151.

91. Extract of a letter from Lieutt Colonel Stiell [*sic*] of the 3rd Battalion of the Royal American or 60th Regiment to His Excellency Sir Basil Keith, 21 May 1776, *NDAR*, V, 196.

92. Tonyn to Clinton, Private, No. 10, 8 June 1776, C.O. 5/556; "Memoir of Major Patrick Murray, Who Served in the 60th from 1770 to 1793," in Butler, *Royal Americans*, pp. 298–99.

93. Germain to Tonyn, No. 2, 14 June 1776, C.O. 5/556.

94. Tonyn to Clinton, Private, No. 10, 8 June 1776, C.O. 5/556.

95. Ibid.

96. Journal of the Council of Safety, 25 June, 1 July 1776, *RRG*, I, 145, 148; McIntosh to Lee, 7 July 1776, *GHSC*, II, 51. It was probably about this time that William Bartram, the naturalist, embarked on a reconnaissance mission between the Altamaha and the St. Marys for Colonel Lachlan McIntosh. Bartram, *Travels*, pp. 416–17; Francis Harper, "William Bartram and the American Revolution," in *Proceedings of the American Philosophical Society*, XCVII, No. 5 (1953), 573–74.

97. Lachlan McIntosh, Jr., to Lachlan McIntosh, Sr., 22, 27 July, 14, 24 August 1776, *GHSC*, XII, 52–56.

98. Lachlan McIntosh, Jr., to Lachlan McIntosh, Sr., 14 August 1776, ibid., 54.

99. Journal of the Council of Safety, 11 July 1776, *RRG*, I, 160.

100. Journal of the Council of Safety, 28 May 1776, *RRG*, I, 131; Force, ed., *Archives*, 4th Ser., VI, 718.

101. Journal of the Council of Safety, 26 June 1776, *RRG*, I, 146–47.

102. Journal of the Council of Safety, 26 July 1776, ibid., 167.

103. East Florida Council Minutes, 20 June 1776, C.O. 5/571; Petition of Refugees from South Carolina and Georgia to Governor Patrick Tonyn, n.d., in Tonyn to Germain, No. 16, 20 June 1776, C.O. 5/557.

104. The American Prohibitory Act, 22 December 1775, Jensen, ed., *Colonial Documents*, p. 853; Prize Instructions, 2 May 1776, W. G. Perrin, ed., *The Keith Papers, Selected from the Letters and Papers of Admiral Viscount Keith*, Vol. LXII of Publications of the Navy Records Society, I (n.p.: Navy Records Society, 1926), 26–29.

105. 23 March, 6 April 1776, *JCC*, IV, 229–33, 257–59.

106. Tonyn to Germain, No. 16, 20 June 1776, C.O. 5/557.

107. Tonyn to John Pownal, 15 August 1776, C.O. 5/556.

108. The whole story is told in C.O. 5/546, 555, 556, and 571. For Drayton's earlier quarrel with Lieutenant Governor John Moultrie, see C.O. 5/545, 552, 553, 554, and 571.

109. A copy of the contract between Bryan and the Creeks is in C.O. 5/555 and 556.

110. When the Georgia assembly had transmitted an address to the king through its agent instead of through Governor Wright, Secretary of State Hillsborough wrote that "His Majesty considers the transmission of this Address, through any other Channel than that of His Governor, as irregular and disrespectful." Hillsborough to Wright, No. 21, 23 March 1769, *CRG*, XXXVII, Pt. II, 395.

111. Germain to Tonyn, 14 June 1776, C.O. 5/556.

112. Turnbull remained in London for months after Drayton's departure. For his unsuccessful campaign to have Tonyn replaced, see *Journal of the Commissioners for Trade and Plantations, 1704–1782* (14 vols., London: H.M. Stationery Office, 1920–50), XIV, 47, 57, 73, 75–76; and E[paminodes] P. Panagopoulos, *New Smyrna: An Eighteenth-Century Greek Odyssey* (Gainesville: University of Florida Press, 1966), pp. 138–44.

113. Documentation of the Cherokee attacks in 1776 and the aftermath is voluminous. See Stuart's correspondence with Germain, including enclosures, 1776, C.O. 5/77, 78, and 94, much of which, with some additions, is printed in *NCCR*, X; Davies, ed., *Documents of the Revolution*, XII; and Philip M. Hamer, ed., "Correspondence of Henry Stuart and Alexander Cameron with the Wataugans," *Mississippi Valley Historical Review*, XVII (December 1930), 451–59. See also Stuart to Howe, 16 June 1777, enclosing Joseph Vann to Alexander Cameron, n.d., Headquarters Papers, Nos. 586 and 587; R[obert] Rae to Governor A[rchibald] Bullock, 3 July 1776, enclosing depositions of Aaron Smith, 1 July 1776, and David Shettroe, 30 June 1776, Force, ed., *Archives*, 4th Ser., V, 1228–29; George Galphin to Willie Jones, 26 October 1776, Force, ed., *Archives*, 5th Ser., III, 648; 30 July 1776, *JCC*, V, 616–17; North Carolina Delegates [to Continental Congress] to North Carolina Council of Safety, [30 July 1776?], and Elbridge Gerry to Joseph Trumbull, 8 October 1776, Burnett, ed., *Letters*, II, 30, 121. The best secondary work on the war faction within the Cherokee tribe is James Paul Pate, "The Chickamauga: A Forgotten Segment of Indian Resistance on the Southern Frontier" (Ph.D. dissertation, Mississippi State University, 1969).

114. East Florida Council Minutes, 8 July 1776, C.O. 5/571; Tonyn to Germain, No. 18, 18 July 1776, C.O. 5/557.

115. Ibid.

116. Tonyn to Germain, No. 18, 18 July 1776, C.O. 5/557.

117. East Florida Council Minutes, 8 July 1776, C.O. 5/571.

118. 9 July 1776, ibid.

119. Tonyn to Germain, No. 18, 18 July 1776, C.O. 5/557.

120. Journal of H.M. Schooner *St. John*, 1–5 July 1776, *NDAR*, V, 929, 942. This may have been the British raid described as having occurred on the Ogeechee River. Charleston, South-Carolina, 2 August 1776, Force, ed., *Archives*, 5th Ser., I, 719.

121. Journal of H.M. Schooner *St. John*, 4–5 July 1776, *NDAR*, V, 929, 942.

122. According to a Whig report, on 2 July Col. Lachlan McIntosh and part of his Continental regiment reconnoitered the position. They got within two miles of the St. Marys before they were fired upon by an outpost. Returning the loyalists' fire, they killed one man and took nine prisoners. When the fort fired an alarm signal, the *St. John* dispatched one lieutenant and nine men in a barge, all of whom the rebels captured. Extract of a letter from Charlestown, South Carolina, 27 July 1776, Force, ed., *Archives*, 4th Ser., VI, 1230. The report of this attack is confused with the rebel attack on Wright's Fort on 11 July. The *St. John's* journal does not mention any attack on 2 July 1776. Quite possibly a skirmish occurred well upstream between a rebel detachment sent to reconnoiter and one of the fort's outposts.

123. Journal of H.M. Schooner *St. John*, 11, 13 July 1776, *NDAR*, V, 1031, 1069; Tonyn to Germain, No. 18, 18 July 1776, C.O. 5/557.

124. Journal of H.M. Schooner *St. John*, 11–12 July 1776, *NDAR*, V, 1031, 1052; Tonyn to Germain, No. 18, 18 July 1776, C.O. 5/557; Charlestown,

South-Carolina, 2 August 1776, Force, ed., *Archives*, 5th Ser., I, 719; McIntosh to Lee, 29 July 1776, *GHSC*, XII, 10–11.

Jermyn Wright said that the rebels murdered one of his slaves, captured seven others, and also carried away three free Negro servants. Deposition of Jermyn Wright, 5 April 1777, C.O. 5/116. The Council of Safety determined that the three servants, a woman and her two children, could not be sold but ordered that Wright's captured slaves be sold at vendue in Savannah. Journal of the Council of Safety, 31 July 1776, *RRG*, I, 169. These three Negroes may be those who were released to one John Torrence nearly a year later. 6 June 1777, "Minutes of the Executive Council, May 7 through October 14, 1777," transcribed by Margaret Godley, *GHQ*, XXXIII (December 1949), 330.

125. Journal of H.M. Schooner *St. John*, 11–12 July 1776, *NDAR*, V, 1031, 1052.

126. 13–16 July 1776, ibid., 1069, 1106–7.

127. "A List of Ships and Vessels Under the Command of Commodore Sir Peter Parker and the Ships and Vessels Stationed at Cape Fear, Savannah and St. Augustine, 10 July 1776," and "Disposition of His Majesty's Ships and Vessels Employed in North America Under the Command of the Vice Admiral the Viscount Howe," 13 August 1776, *NDAR*, V, 1023–24, VI, 167–69.

128. Tonyn to Commanding Officer of His Majesty's Ships, Savannah River, 5 August 1776, C.O. 5/556.

129. Tonyn to Germain, No. 18, 18 July 1776, C.O. 5/557.

130. Minutes of the Boston Committee of Correspondence, Inspection and Safety, 15 August 1776, Dr. David Cobb to Robert Treat Paine, 19 August 1776, *NDAR*, VI, 191, 233. The *Perkins*, under Captain Jenkins, sailed from St. Augustine on 24 July and was captured off the Virginia capes on 4 August. *Whitehall Evening Post*, Thursday, November 7 to Saturday, November 9, 1776, *NDAR*, VII, 733.

131. State of the 14th Regiment of Infantry, in the Province of East Florida, 30 September 1775, C.O. 5/556; "Memoir of Murray," in Butler, *Royal Americans*, p. 229; Return of three Companys of the 16th Regiment of Foot Commanded by Captain Collin Graham Detailed to St. Augustine, 24 December 1775, C.O. 5/556; Butler, *Royal Americans*, pp. 208–9, 298–99, 316–62, 368.

132. McIntosh to Lee, 29 July 1776, *GHSC*, XII, 10–11; John Rutledge, president of the South Carolina General Assembly, to Lee, 20 August 1776, *Lee Papers*, pp. 237–38; Tonyn to Germain, No. 18, 18 July 1776, C.O. 5/557.

133. Petition of John Berwick, Proceedings of the General Assembly of the State of South-Carolina, 25 September 1776, Force, ed., *Archives*, 5th Ser., III, 26.

134. Journal of H.M. Schooner *St. John*, 26 July 1776, *NDAR*, V, 1251; Tonyn to Admiral Howe, 25 December 1776, C.O. 5/557; Deposition of Jermyn Wright, 5 April 1777, C.O. 5/116.

135. Journal of H.M. Schooner *St. John*, 27 July 1776, *NDAR*, V, 1251.

136. Kitching to Tonyn, 9 August 1776, C.O. 5/556. Orders for the reduction of Wright's Fort were given on 30 July to Colonels McIntosh and Screven and Captains Baker and Woodruffe. Journal of the Council of Safety, 30 July 1776, *RRG*, I, 168; Deposition of Jermyn Wright, 5 April 1777, C.O. 5/116.

137. Kitching to Tonyn, 9 August 1776, C.O. 5/556.

138. Tonyn to Commanding Officer of His Majesty's Ships in Savannah River, 5 August 1776, C.O. 5/556.

139. John Martin to [?] Anderson, 5 August 1776, Grant to Tonyn, 6 August 1776, C.O. 5/556; Journal of H.M. Schooner *St. John,* 5 August 1776, *NDAR*, VI, 73. Mr. Martin escaped from Jekyll and went to St. Augustine. Tonyn to Germain, No. 20, 15 August 1776, C.O. 5/556.

140. Journal of H.M. Schooner *St. John,* 5 August 1776, *NDAR,* VI, 73; Grant to Tonyn, 7 August 1776, C.O. 5/556; Tonyn to Admiral Howe, 25 December 1776, C.O. 5/557; Deposition of Jermyn Wright, 5 April 1777, C.O. 5/556.

141. Stephen Egan to Tonyn, 5 August 1776, C.O. 5/556.

142. Ibid.; Journal of H.M. Schooner *St. John,* 5 August 1776, *NDAR*, VI, 73.

143. List of British Ships . . . , 29 September 1775, *NDAR*, II, 742; Disposition of His Majesty's Ships and Vessels in North America Under the Command of Vice Admiral Molyneux Shuldham, 6 July 1776, *NDAR,* V, 949; Journal of H.M. Schooner *St. John,* 6 August 1776, *NDAR*, VI, 89; Grant to Capt. Colin Graham, 6 August 1776, to Tonyn, 7 August 1776, C.O. 5/556.

144. Tonyn to Bishop, 6 August 1776, C.O. 5/556; East Florida Council Minutes, 6 August 1776, C.O. 5/571; Tonyn to Germain, No. 20, 15 August 1776, C.O. 5/556; Tonyn's Certificate for Captain George Osborne, 4 December 1776, C.O. 5/557. The *Lady William* belonged to Lord William Campbell, British governor of South Carolina.

145. Journal of H.M. Schooner *St. John,* 7 August 1776, *NDAR*, VI, 109; Grant to Tonyn, 7 August 1776, C.O. 5/556.

146. Journal of H.M. Schooner *St. John,* 7 August 1776, *NDAR*, VI, 109.

147. East Florida Council Minutes, 9 August 1776, C.O. 5/571; Tonyn to Germain, No. 20, 15 August 1776, C.O. 5/556.

148. Captain Thomas Bishop to Tonyn, 9 August 1776, Tonyn to Germain, Private, No. 3, 23 August 1776, Ç.O. 5/556.

149. Kitching to Tonyn, n.d., and 9 August 1776, C.O. 5/556; Master's Bond of the Georgia Schooner *George,* [14 June 1776], *NDAR*, V, 536–37; Journal of the Council of Safety, 9 August 1776, *RRG*, I, 178–79.

150. Tonyn to Germain, No. 20, 15 August 1776, C.O. 5/556; Memorial for Jermyn and Charles Wright to Lord George Germain, n.d., Deposition of Jermyn Wright, 5 April 1777, C.O. 5/116. One East Floridian charged that the depredations in Georgia of "Messrs. Moore and Clarke, at the head of a body of plunderers," had provoked the Georgia attack across the St. Marys. Extract of a Letter to a Gentleman in London, dated St. Augustine, 20 August 1776, Force, ed., *Archives,* 5th Ser., I, 1076.

151. East Florida Council Minutes, 15 August 1776, C.O. 5/571; "Memoir of Murray," in Butler, *Royal Americans*, p. 299.

152. Tonyn to Germain, No. 20, 15 August 1776, C.O. 5/556; Tonyn to Admiral Howe, 25 December 1776, C.O. 5/557. Tonyn blamed Grant more than Graham for the fiasco on the border, and Grant was subsequently removed from command of the *St. John*. Tonyn to Germain, No. 43, 18 September 1777, C.O. 5/557.

Chapter III

1. Journal of the Council of Safety, 18 June 1776, *RRG,* I, 139.

2. 5 July 1776, ibid., 150–54; Conference with the Georgia Deputies, n.d., in Lee to President of Congress, 2 July 1776, *Lee Papers,* pp. 114–17; Report of the Georgia Deputies, 5 July 1776, *RRG,* I, 299–303.

3. Lee to Hancock, 2 July 1776, *Lee Papers,* pp. 109–10. On the subject of Continental cavalry for the southern provinces, see also Lee to Cornelius Harnet, President of the Council of Safety of North Carolina, 24 July 1776, *Lee Papers,* p. 164.

4. Lee to Bullock, to McIntosh, both dated 18 July 1776, *Lee Papers,* pp. 144–45.

5. McIntosh to Lee, 25 July 1776, *Lee Papers,* pp. 168–69; McIntosh to Lee, 26 July 1776, *GHSC,* XII, 10; Bullock to Lee, 26 July 1776, *Lee Papers,* p. 171.

6. Lee to Rutledge, 19, 20, 22, 23, 24, 27 July 1776, *Lee Papers,* pp. 149–50, 156–60, 163, 173.

7. Lee to Rutledge, 27 July 1776, *Lee Papers,* p. 173.

8. Ibid., p. 174.

9. Congress had decided as early as May that the Continental establishment should be increased in Georgia and South Carolina. 29 May 1776, *JCC,* IV, 400.

10. Resolutions of 5, 8, 24 July, 16 September 1776, *JCC,* V, 521–22, 528, 606–7, 762. See also Hancock to Rutledge, 24 July 1776, Force, ed., *Archives,* 5th Ser., I, 555; Hancock to Convention of the State of Georgia, 24 July 1776, in Journal of the Council of Safety, 30 August 1776, *RRG,* I, 194–99. Between 8 August and 10 December 1776, $62,000 was advanced to the Georgia delegates for the use of Continental forces in that province. 8, 28 August, 16 September, 1 November, 10 December 1776, *JCC,* V, 639, 711, 761, VI, 917, 1017.

11. Journal of the Council of Safety, 8 August 1776, and Proclamation by President Archibald Bullock, n.d., *RRG,* I, 174, 280–81; Force, ed., *Archives,* 5th Ser., I, 882; White, *Collections,* pp. 200–201.

12. James Grant Forbes, *Sketches, Historical and Topographical, of the Floridas; More Particularly of East Florida* (facsimile reproduction of the 1821 edition, Gainesville: University of Florida Press, 1964), p. 23.

13. Lee to Richard Peters, Secretary to the Board of War and Ordnance, 2 August 1776, to Rutledge, 1, 3, 6 August 1776, to Board of War and Ordnance, 7 August 1776, *Lee Papers*, pp. 186–89, 199, 200–205; Resolutions of 18 June and 24 July 1776, *JCC*, V, 461–63, 607. The South Carolina assembly did not formally acquiesce in this arrangement until 20 September 1776. Moultrie, *Memoirs*, I, 187. Moultrie declared that Jonathan Bryan's report in July on the weakness of the St. Augustine garrison influenced Lee's decision to attack. Moultrie, *Memoirs*, I, 184.

14. Tonyn to the Commanding Officer of His Majesty's Ships, Savannah River, 5 August 1776, C.O. 5/556.

15. Extract of a Letter from Charleston, S.C., 7 August 1776, Force, ed., *Archives*, 5th Ser., I, 805; Robert Howe to Lee, 10 August 1776, Henry Laurens to John Laurens, 14 August 1776, *Lee Papers*, pp. 207–8, 227.

16. Orders issued on the expedition to Georgia, etc., 7 August 1776, *Lee Papers*, p. 251; Williamsburg, Va., 13 September 1776, Force, ed., *Archives*, 5th Ser., I, 959. The North Carolina Continentals for the Georgia-Florida expedition numbered 81 of the First Regiment, 75 of the Second Regiment, and all except 37 of the Third Regiment. General Return of the [North Carolina] Brigade Commanded by Colonel Moore, 20 October 1776, *NCCR*, X, 858–59. See also "Monthly Return of the Forces in South-Carolina, for July 1776," Force, ed., *Archives*, 5th Ser., I, 631–32; and Extract of a Letter from Charlestown, South-Carolina, 31 July 1776, ibid., 685.

17. Master's Log of H.M. Armed Vessel *Cherokee*, 14 August 1776, *NDAR*, VI, 189; Tonyn's Certificate for Capt. George Osborne, 4 December 1776, and Memorial of George Osborne, 14 January 1777, C.O. 5/557; Proceedings of the General Assembly of the State of South Carolina, 4 October 1776, Force, ed., *Archives*, 5th Ser., III, 44.

18. Lee to Lt. Berrian, to Colonel Bull, and to President Rutledge, all dated 18 August, *Lee Papers*, pp. 231–33.

19. Conference with the Ga. Council of Safety, 19 August 1776, ibid., pp. 233–35.

20. 18 August 1776, Robert Howe's Orderly Book (Library of Congress microfilm), p. 20; Orders issued on the expedition to Georgia, etc., 18, 21 August 1776, *Lee Papers*, pp. 253–55. Moultrie identifies William Harden as captain of the Beaufort artillery company at this time. Moultrie, *Memoirs*, I, 124.

21. Moultrie, *Memoirs*, I, 185–86.

22. Lee to Colonel Moultrie, 30 July 1776; Orders issued on the expedition to Georgia, etc., 21, 23 August 1776, *Lee Papers*, pp. 180, 253–54; Journal of the Council of Safety, 20, 22, 24, 28 August, 29 September 1776, *RRG*, I, 183–86, 189, 191, 204; Moultrie, *Memoirs*, I, 184; Jones, *History of Georgia*, II, 248.

23. 23 August 1776, Howe's Orderly Book, p. 21; McIntosh to Lee, 26 August 1776, Lilla Mills Hawes, ed., *Lachlan McIntosh Papers in the University of Georgia Libraries*, University of Georgia Libraries Miscellanea Publications, No. 7 (Athens: University of Georgia Press, 1968), pp. 16–17.

24. Lee to Patrick Henry, 29 July 1776, to Richard Peters, Secretary to the Board of War and Ordnance, 2 August 1776, to Board of War and Ordnance, 7 August 1776, to the President and Council of the State of Georgia, 23, 24 August 1776, and to General John Armstrong, 27 August 1776, *Lee Papers*, pp. 179, 190, 203–25, 238–41, 246.

25. 8 August 1776, *JCC*, V, 638; Hancock to Lee, 8 August 1776, *Lee Papers*, pp. 205–6; Hancock to Washington, 8 August 1776, Force, ed., *Archives*, 5th Ser., I, 832; Lee to Rutledge, 29 August 1776, *Lee Papers*, p. 236; Lee's Orders, 9 September 1776, *Lee Papers*, pp. 258–59; Charlestown, [S.C.], Wednesday, 11 September 1776, Force, ed., *Archives*, 5th Ser., II, 285.

26. East Florida Council Minutes, 15, 16 August 1776, C.O. 5/571; Tonyn to Germain, No. 21, 21 August 1776, C.O. 5/556. The government paid for some items, including 257 cartridge boxes, of the East Florida militia's equipment. General Account of extraordinary Expences incurred for the Subsistence of Distressed Refugees from Virginia, Carolina and Georgia, and other extra Contingencies from the 24th June 1776 to the 24th June 1777, in Tonyn to Germain, No. 43, 18 September 1777, C.O. 5/557.

27. For Dodd, see Siebert, *Loyalists*, I, 38.

28. East Florida Council Minutes, 9, 15 August 1776, C.O. 5/571; Tonyn to Germain, Private, No. 3, 26 August 1776, C.O. 5/556; Tonyn to Taitt, 3 September 1776, C.O. 5/78; Tonyn to Germain, No. 25, 9 September 1776, C.O. 5/556.

29. Tonyn to Germain, Private, No. 3, 26 August 1776, Captain Thomas Bishop to Tonyn, 9 August 1776, and Tonyn to Germain, Nos. 24 and 25, 8, 9 September 1776, C.O. 5/556; Tonyn to Howe, 8 October 1776, C.O. 5/94; Tonyn to Howe, 25 December 1776, C.O. 5/557; East Florida Council Minutes, 5 September 1776, C.O. 5/571; Prevost to Howe, 9 September 1776, Headquarters Papers, No. 265.

30. Tonyn to Germain, No. 24, 8 September 1776, C.O. 5/556; Journal of H.M. Schooner *St. John*, 29 August 1776, *NDAR*, VI, 367; Charlestown, [S.C.], Wednesday, 11 September 1776, Force, ed., *Archives*, 5th Ser., II, 285.

Turpin's vessel may have been the eighteen-gun privateer that left South Carolina on 12 August 1776 in the hope of capturing two ships expected from London that were laden with military supplies and dry goods for St. Augustine. William Bull, Jr., to Joseph Pringle, 13 August 1776, *NDAR*, VI, 176.

Captain Joseph Turpin commanded the armed brigantine *Comet*, which belonged to South Carolina. Minutes of the South Carolina Council of Safety, 11 February 1776, *NDAR*, III, 1220. On 16 September he quit the service of the South Carolina navy because of dissatisfaction with the system of awarding prize shares. On 21 September the South Carolina General Assembly recorded that he was "absent and gone to Georgia without leave." Journal of the South Carolina General Assembly, 21 September 1776, *NDAR*, VI, 941–42.

31. Journal of H.M. Schooner *St. John*, 30 August 1776, *NDAR*, VI, 367; Tonyn to Germain, No. 24, 8 September 1776, C.O. 5/556. The *Comet* and her

prize reached Charleston on Thursday, 5 September 1776. Charlestown, [S.C.], Wednesday, 11 September 1776, Force, ed., *Archives,* 5th Ser., II, 285.

32. Tonyn to Prevost, to Grant, both dated 5 September 1776, C.O. 5/556; East Florida Council Minutes, 5 September 1776, C.O. 5/571; Tonyn to Germain, No. 24, 8 September 1776, C.O. 5/556; Prevost to Howe, 9 September 1776, Headquarters Papers, No. 265.

33. Tonyn to Germain, No. 25, 9 September 1776, C.O. 5/556.

34. Brown to Stuart, 29 September 1776, C.O. 5/78. Brown does not make clear whether this particular raid was carried out by the Georgians in August or by an advance party of the "grand expedition" in September. Considering the time when British troops at Cowford reported an American force on the north side of that river, September is the likelier date.

The planter specifically mentioned by Brown was probably David Curvoisieux. De Brahm, *Report,* p. 181. One Francis Courvoisie was paid £8 for ferriage and boat repairs at the St. Johns Ferry. General Account of Contingent Expenses, incurred for the Service of His Majesty's Province of East Florida, from the 25th June 1776, to the 24th June 1777, in Tonyn to Germain, No. 43, 18 September 1777, C.O. 5/557. Major Patrick Murray mentions a "Monsieur Courvoixier, a Swiss" who had a house "on the left bank [of the St. Johns] where the river at the Cowford is only 1600 yards over." "Memoir of Murray," in Butler, *Royal Americans,* p. 299.

35. State of His Majesty's Forces in the Province of East Florida, St. Augustine, 8 September 1776, C.O. 5/556.

36. Ibid.; Prevost to Howe, 9 September 1776, Headquarters Papers, No. 265.

37. Tonyn to Prevost, 27 January 1777, C.O. 5/557.

38. Tonyn to Germain, No. 50, 19 January 1777, C.O. 5/546; Tonyn to Cornwallis, 12 July 1778, Cornwallis Papers; Tonyn to Clinton, Private, 27 May 1780, Headquarters Papers, No. 2768.

39. East Florida Council Minutes, 8 July 1776, C.O. 5/571; Tonyn to Germain, Private, No. 2, 19 July 1777/6 [*sic*], C.O. 5/557.

40. Panagopoulos, *New Smyrna,* p. 144.

41. Tonyn to Germain, No. 23, 8 September 1776, C.O. 5/556; Andrew Turnbull to Arthur Gordon (extract), Robert Bisset to Tonyn, both dated 1 September, C.O. 5/556; Tonyn to Prevost, 5 September 1775 [*sic*], in East Florida Council Minutes, 5 September 1776, C.O. 5/571; Tonyn to Howe, 8 October 1776, C.O. 5/94; Tonyn to Germain, No. 25, 9 September 1776, C.O. 5/556. It had been reported at the Spanish court in 1773 that the Minorcans wanted "to throw off the yoke of Great Britain." A. M. Brooks, comp., *The Unwritten History of Old St. Augustine,* trans. by Annie Averette ([St. Augustine]: n.p., [1909]), p. 223.

42. East Florida Council Minutes, 11 September 1776, C.O. 5/571; Dunmore to Tonyn (extract), 31 July 1776, C.O. 5/557; List of prisoners sent to St. Augustine in His Majesty's Sloop *Otter,* C.O. 5/557; Capt. Andrew Snape Hamond, R.N., to Capt. Matthew Squire, H.M.S. *Otter,* 31 July 1776, *NDAR,* V, 1315; Vice Admiral Richard Lord Howe to Philip Stephens, 31 August

1776, *NDAR*, VI, 376; Narrative of Captain Andrew Snape Hamond, *NDAR*, VI, 173–74; Journal of H.M. Sloop *Otter*, Capt. Matthew Squire, 24 August, 10 September 1776, *NDAR*, VI, 295, 775; Protest of John Bynoe, Master of the British Brigantine *Betsy*, 24 August 1776, *NDAR*, VI, 296; John Mitchell, Jr., to Alexander Mitchell, 15 September 1776, *NDAR*, VI, 850; Disposition of His Majesty's Ships and Vessels Employed in North America Under the Command of Vice Admiral the Viscount Howe, 18 September 1776, *NDAR*, VI, 893; Capt. Andrew Snape Hamond, R.N., to Vice Admiral Shuldham, 29 November 1776, *NDAR*, VII, 319–20.

43. Journal of H.M. Ship *Active*, Capt. Anthony Hunt, 31 August 1776, *NDAR*, VI, 379; East Florida Council Minutes, 18 September 1776, including Tonyn to Capt. Squire, Commanding His Majesty's Ship *Otter*, same date, C.O. 5/571.

44. East Florida Council Minutes, 20 September 1776, C.O. 5/571; Prevost to Howe, 9 September 1776, Headquarters Papers, No. 265.

45. George Logan to Samuel Lawford, 3 September 1776, *NDAR*, VI, 668; East Florida Council Minutes, 11 September 1776, C.O. 5/571.

46. East Florida Council Minutes, 11 September 1776, C.O. 5/571.

47. Journal of H.M.S. *Sphynx*, Capt. James Reid, 28–30 September 1776, *NDAR*, VI, 1074–75; Master's Log of H.M. Armed Vessel *Cherokee*, Lt. John Fergusson, 4–5 October 1776, *NDAR*, VI, 1141; Capt. James Reid to Admiral Howe, 26 October 1776, *NDAR*, VI, 1422–23; McIntosh to Howe, 1 October 1776, *GHSC*, XII, 12.

48. Tonyn to Germain, Nos. 23 and 26, 8 September, 18 October 1776, C.O. 5/556, 557. In September a Savannah vessel brought the news to St. Augustine that General Washington had been killed in New York, but the story was doubted in East Florida. John Mitchell, Jr., to Alexander Mitchell, 15 September 1776, *NDAR*, VI, 849.

49. Tonyn to Germain, No. 27, 30 October 1776, C.O. 5/557; Moultrie, *Memoirs*, I, 186; M'Call, *History*, pp. 323–24; Jones, *History of Georgia*, II, 249–50.

50. Extract of a Letter to a Gentleman in London, dated St. Augustine, 20 August 1776, Force, ed., *Archives*, 5th Ser., I, 1076; Brown to Stuart, 29 September 1776, C.O. 5/78.

51. Hawes, ed., *McIntosh Papers*, pp. 68–69; 3–4 September 1776, Howe's Orderly Book, pp. 22–24; Tonyn to Germain, No. 25, 9 September 1776, C.O. 5/556.

52. October 1776, *JCC*, V, 850; William Ellery to Governor Cooke, 11 October 1776, Force, ed., *Archives*, 5th Ser., II, 990; Tonyn to Germain, No. 27, 30 October 1776, C.O. 5/557.

53. General John Armstrong to Hancock, 7 October 1776, Force, ed., *Archives*, 5th Ser., II, 924–25.

54. Journal of the Council of Safety, 28 August 1776, *RRG*, I, 190–91; Lee to the President and Council of the State of Georgia, 28 August 1776, *Lee Papers*, pp. 247–48; Resolves of the St. Andrews Parochial Committee, 10 September 1776, with List of Torys, *GHSC*, XII, 56–57.

55. Lee to the Board of War and Ordnance, 27 August 1776, *Lee Papers,* pp. 242–44.

56. Lee to the President and Council of the State of Georgia, 28 August 1776, *Lee Papers,* pp. 247–48; Journal of the Council of Safety, 28, 29 August, 22 October 1776, *RRG,* I, 190–91, 193, 210–11; Howe to Bulloch (extract), 20 September 1776, quoted in Jenkins, *Gwinnett,* pp. 97–98; Howe to John Rutledge, President of South Carolina, 6 October 1776, Proceedings of the General Assembly of the State of South-Carolina, 19 October 1776, Force, ed., *Archives,* 5th Ser., III, 52, 80; Proclamation by John Rutledge, President of South Carolina, 4 November 1776, *South Carolina and American General Gazette,* 14–21 November 1776.

57. 16 September 1776, *JCC,* V, 761; Jenkins, *Gwinnett,* pp. 94–96; McIntosh to Laurens, 30 May 1777, Jenkins, *Gwinnett,* p. 254.

58. Samuel Elbert, Colonel of the Second Georgia Battalion, to Lieutenant Colonel John Stirk and Major Seth John Cuthbert, 2 October 1776, *Order Book of Samuel Elbert, Colonel and Brigadier General in the Continental Army, October, 1776, to November, 1778: GHSC,* V, Pt. II (Savannah: By the Society, 1902), 6–7 (hereafter cited as *GHSC,* V, Pt. II); Proclamation by Archibald Bulloch, 12 July 1776, *RRG,* I, 279–80; 16 September, 21 November 1776, *JCC,* V, 762–63, VI, 971; Hancock to Washington, 24 September 1776, to the Assemblies of the Several States, 24 September 1776, Force, ed., *Archives,* 5th Ser., II, 488, 489.

59. Howe to [North Carolina] Council of Safety, 2 August 1776, *NCCR,* X, 718; Journal of the [North Carolina] Council of Safety, 13 August 1776, *NCCR,* X, 700; General Orders by General Lee, 8 September 1776, *NCCR,* X, 795–96; Resolutions of 25 October 1776, *NCCR,* X, 880; Richard Caswell, Governor of North Carolina, to General Howe, 7 March 1777, *NCSR,* XI, 409; *Virginia Gazette* (Purdie), 23 August, 6 December 1776; *Virginia Gazette* (Dixon and Hunter), 27 September 1776.

60. 19 November 1776, *JCC,* VI, 966; Hancock to the States, 20 November 1776, Force, ed., *Archives,* 5th Ser., III, 776–77; William Kennon, Continental Commissary General, to General Lee, 7 December 1776, *Lee Papers,* pp. 333–35.

61. Journal of the [Georgia] Council of Safety, 16 July, 9, 23, 28 August, 18 October 1776, *RRG,* I, 162, 178–79, 188, 191–92, 208; Lee to the Governor at Cape Francois, 29 August 1776, *Lee Papers,* pp. 255–58; 20 September, 1 November 1776, *JCC,* V, 788, VI, 917–18. See also Robert Rhodes Crout, "Pierre-Emmanuel de la Plaigne and Georgia's Quest for French Aid during the War of Independence," *GHQ,* LX (Summer 1976), 177–79.

62. McIntosh to the Georgia Congressional Delegates, 17 December 1776, *GHSC,* XII, 24–25.

63. Tonyn to Prevost, 13 January 1777, C.O. 5/557.

64. Howe to the Chairman of the Georgia Convention, 3 December 1776, *NDAR,* VII, 360–62; same dated 7 December 1776, in Jenkins, *Gwinnett,* pp. 209–10; McIntosh to the Georgia Congressional Delegates, 17 December 1776, *GHSC,* XII, 24–25.

65. Tonyn to Admiral Howe, 25 December 1776, C.O. 5/557. On 28 November 1776 Lachlan McIntosh wrote an unduly optimistic letter to his son John in Jamaica. C. M. Destler, ed., "An Unpublished Letter of General Lachlan McIntosh," *GHQ*, XXIII (December 1939), 394–95. The real purpose of this letter may have been to counteract adverse accounts of the rebel cause then circulating in the British West Indies.

66. Journal of the Council of Safety, 2 May 1776, *RRG*, I, 119–21.

67. Bullock to the Georgia Provincial Congress, 5 June 1776, Force, ed., *Archives*, 4th Ser., VI, 719; McIntosh to George Walton (from Savannah), 11 July 1776, *GHSC*, XII, 8; Journal of the Council of Safety, 25 July, 2, 8 August 1776, *RRG*, I, 166, 173, 177.

68. Journal of the Council of Safety, 28 August 1776, *RRG*, I, 191.

69. Joseph Clay to Messrs. Bright and Pechin and Capt. Hazard, 7 December 1776, *GHSC*, VIII, 13–15.

70. Journal of the Council of Safety, 30 May 1776, *RRG*, I, 134; Johnston, *Houstouns*, pp. 295–97.

71. McIntosh to Robert Howe, 1 [or 2] October 1776, *GHSC*, XII, 11–12; Tonyn to William Howe, 8 October 1776, C.O. 5/94; Tonyn to Germain, No. 27, 30 October 1776, C.O. 5/557.

72. Tonyn to Germain, No. 27, 30 October 1776, C.O. 5/557.

73. McIntosh to Howe, 2 October, to Colonel Mewhlengburg, 7, 8 October 1776, and to Howe, 22 October 1776, *GHSC*, XII, 13–15; Journal of the Council of Safety, 7 October 1776, *RRG*, I, 205–6.

74. Master's Log of H.M. Armed Vessel *Cherokee*, 5 October 1776, *NDAR*, VI, 1141.

75. Captain James Reid, R.N., to Vice Admiral Richard Lord Howe, 26 October 1776, *NDAR*, VI, 1422–23.

76. Journal of H.M. Armed Schooner *Hinchinbrook*, 27 October 1776, *NDAR*, VI, 1430, n. 2.

77. Captain James Reid to Vice Admiral Richard Lord Howe, 26 October 1776, Journal of H.M.S. *Lively*, 1 November 1776, Journal of Ambrose Serle, 7 November 1776, and Vice Admiral Richard Lord Howe to Philip Stephens, 27 November 1776, *NDAR*, VI, 1432, VII, 10, 77, 305.

78. Master's Log of H.M. Armed Vessel *Cherokee*, 15 October 1776, *NDAR*, VI, 1284; East Florida Council Minutes, 17 October 1776, C.O. 5/558.

79. Navy Board to Capt. Thomas Pickering, 2 November 1776, Journal of the South Carolina Navy Board, *NDAR*, VII, 23; Journal of the South Carolina Navy Board, 4, 7, 11 November 1776, *NDAR*, VII, 43, 81–82, 110; Master's Log of H.M. Armed Vessel *Cherokee*, 14 November 1776, *NDAR*, VII, 159–60; Libel in East Florida Court of Vice Admiralty Against the American Prize Ship *Friendship*, [31 December 1776], *NDAR*, VII, 672; Proceedings of the Navy Board of South-Carolina, 30 November, 5 December 1776, Force, ed., *Archives*, 5th Ser., III, 1537. The Proceedings do not indicate when or where the *Comet* captured her prizes.

80. Lachlan McIntosh to Howe, to William McIntosh, both dated 22 October 1776, *GHSC*, XII, 15; General Account of Sundry Expences in-

curred for Indians, from the 25th June 1776 to the 24th June 1777, in Tonyn to Germain, No. 43, 18 September 1777, C.O. 5/557.

81. McIntosh to William McIntosh, 22 October 1776, McIntosh's Orders, 24 October 1776, and McIntosh to Howe, 29 October 1776, *GHSC*, XII, 15–18. This plan had been outlined by Lee in August. Lee to the Board of War and Ordnance, 27 August, *Lee Papers*, pp. 242–44; Lee to the Board of War and Ordnance, 24 August, Force, ed., *Archives*, 5th Ser., I, 1131–32.

82. McIntosh to Howe, 29 October 1776, McIntosh to _____, 29 October 1776, Copy of Letter [from McIntosh] to President [Bulloch], 1 November 1776, and McIntosh to Howe, 19 November 1776, *GHSC*, XII, 9, 11, 57–58, 19.

83. Stuart to Howe, 4 March 1777, C.O. 5/94; Stuart to Germain, No. 15, 10 March 1777, Stuart to William Knox, Undersecretary of State for the Southern Department, 10 March 1777, and Stuart's Circular letter to Captains Daniel Wiedner, James Macdonald, Cressian Reynard, etc., of North Carolina, 9 February 1777, C.O. 5/78.

84. McIntosh to Howe, 19 November 1776, to Major Marbury, 25 November 1776, and to Lieutenant Colonel [Joseph] Habersham, 27 November 1776, *GHSC*, XII, 19–21.

85. McIntosh to Henry Laurens, 8 November 1776, to Lieutenant Wilson, 4th Company of Light Horse, 13 December 1776, *GHSC*, XII, 21–22.

86. McIntosh to William McIntosh, 22 October 1776, to Henry Laurens, 8 November 1776, and to Howe, 19 November 1776, ibid., 15, 21, 19.

87. Tonyn to Howe, 8 October 1776, C.O. 5/94; Tonyn to Germain, No. 27, 30 October 1776, C.O. 5/557.

88. Howe to Germain, No. 32, Separate, 30 November 1776, *Report on the Manuscripts of Mrs. Stopford-Sackville, of Drayton House, Northamptonshire*, Historical Manuscripts Commission, Vol. II (2 vols., n.p.: published for H.M. Stationery Office, 1904, 1910), 49–50.

89. Tonyn to William Knox, 1 November 1776, to Admiral Richard Howe, 25 December 1776, to General William Howe, 25 December 1776, and to Germain, No. 26, 18 October 1776, C.O. 5/557.

90. Howe to Prevost, 25 August 1776, Headquarters Papers, No. 257; Tonyn to Germain, No. 27, 30 October 1776, to Howe, 25 December 1776, C.O. 5/557. For Spanish construction of St. Augustine's defensive lines between 1706 and 1762, see Verne E. Chatelain, *The Defenses of Spanish Florida, 1565 to 1763*, Carnegie Institution of Washington Publication 511 (Washington, D.C.: Carnegie Institution of Washington, 1941), pp. 82–93.

91. Tonyn to Germain, No. 27, 30 October 1776, to Howe, 25 December 1776, C.O. 5/557.

92. Tonyn to Germain, No. 28, [31 October 1776; actually dated 31 November, an obvious error, because No. 27 is dated 30 October and No. 29 is dated 1 November], and enclosed Demand for Ordnance Stores, for use of His Majesty's Garrison, and Forts in East Florida, together with the State the 30 September 1776, C.O. 5/557.

93. Tonyn to Germain, No. 31, 7 December 1776, C.O. 5/557.

94. Tonyn to Germain, No. 27, 30 October 1776, Petition of Georgia refugees in East Florida, n.d., in Tonyn to Germain, No. 29, 1 November 1776, C.O. 5/557.

95. Tonyn to Germain, No. 29, 1 November 1776, enclosing The humble Address and Petition of Several Refugees . . . from the Province of Georgia, and List of Lands Granted in East Florida . . . Particularizing Those which are actually settled, and Tonyn's reply to the petitioners, C.O. 5/557.

96. Tonyn to Germain, No. 26, 18 October 1776, C.O. 5/557.

97. Tonyn to Germain [possibly intended for Earl of Dunmore], 24 December 1776, enclosing Anthony Lawson (Lt. Col.) Parole of Honour, 23 November 1776, Affidavit of John Mitchell and James Cuthbert in behalf of William Westcott, 28 December 1776, and Release to the Earl of Dunmore from William Westcott, 28 December 1776, C.O. 5/557.

98. An Account of the Exports from the Province of East Florida from January 1775, to January 1776, An Account of the Exports from the Province of East Florida from January 1776 to January 1777, C.O. 5/546; Tonyn to Germain, No. 29, 1 November 1776, to Germain, No. 27, 30 October 1776, to General Howe, 25 December 1776, and to Admiral Howe, 25 December 1776, C.O. 5/557.

In mid-summer Tonyn had forecast a bountiful crop that year. Tonyn to Germain, No. 18, 18 July 1776, C.O. 5/557. Obviously, the depredations of the Georgians had not been nearly as damaging as they had hoped.

99. Tonyn to Germain, Nos. 26, 27, and 31, 18, 30 October, 7 December 1776, to Admiral Howe, 25 December 1776, and to General Howe, 25 December 1776, C.O. 5/557.

100. Tonyn to Howe, October 1776, C.O. 5/94.

101. Stuart to Germain, No. 6, 23 August 1776, C.O. 5/77; Stuart to Germain, No. 13, 23 January 1777, C.O. 5/78; Germain to Stuart, No. 1, 5 September 1776, C.O. 5/77; Germain to Stuart, 7 February 1777, C.O. 5/78; Stuart to Howe, 30 August 1776, Howe to Stuart, 13 January 1777, C.O. 5/94; Tonyn to Germain, No. 26, 18 October 1776, C.O. 5/557.

102. Tonyn to Germain, No. 27, 30 October 1776, C.O. 5/557.

103. Taitt to Stuart, 7 July 1776, C.O. 5/77; Stuart to Germain, No. 10, 26 October 1776, C.O. 5/78.

104. Stuart to Germain, No. 10, 26 October 1776, and enclosures, Stuart to Germain, Nos. 12 and 13, 24 November 1776, 23 January 1777, C.O. 5/78; Henry Laurens to John Laurens, 14 August 1776, Lee Papers, p. 225; A[ndrew] Williamson to W. H. Drayton, 22 August 1776, Gibbes, comp., Documentary History, II, 32; Extract of a letter from Charleston, South Carolina, 21 July 1776, Force, ed., Archives, 4th Ser., VI, 1230, 5th Ser., I, 481; James Creswell to William Henry Drayton, 27 July 1776, Force, ed., Archives, 5th Ser., I, 610; William Ellery to Governor Nicholas Cooke, 11 October 1776, Force, ed., Archives, 5th Ser., II, 990; Galphin to Willie Jones, 26 October 1776, Force, ed., Archives, 5th Ser., III, 649.

105. Samuel Thomas to Stuart, 19 September 1776, David Holmes to Stuart, 26 September 1776, Brown to Stuart, 29 September 1776, and Talk

from the Chavucley Warrior in behalf of himself and the Head Men of the Lower Creek Nation, 28 September 1776, all enclosed in Stuart to Germain, No. 10, 26 October 1776, C.O. 5/78; Stuart to Germain, No. 7, 16 September 1776, C.O. 5/230.

Samuel Thomas said that news of the rebel invasion of East Florida did not reach the Lower Creeks (he was writing from Cussita) until 19 September. Samuel Thomas to Stuart, 19 September 1776, in Stuart to Germain, No. 10, 26 October 1776, C.O. 5/78. By that time, the invasion had collapsed.

Howe's orders, dated 23 May and 25 August, directing Stuart "to engage the Indians for the Defense of the Floridas" and to send all the Indians possible to the assistance of the invaded colonies, had not reached Stuart by 30 August. Howe to Stuart, 23 May, 25 August 1776, 13 January 1777, C.O. 5/94. Stuart mentioned in his dispatch No. 12 to Germain dated 24 November 1776 (but not No. 10, 26 October 1776), that he had received those orders from Howe. Stuart to Germain, No. 12, 24 November 1776, C.O. 5/78.

Tonyn wrote to Germain that he could have sent a large body of Creek warriors to devastate Georgia, but he had refrained from doing so because he did not know how such a procedure would fit in with the commander in chief's overall plan. Tonyn to Germain, No. 27, 30 October 1776, C.O. 5/557.

106. Galphin to Timothy Barnard, 18 August 1776, Galphin to the Creek Indians, n.d., Holmes to Stuart, 26 September 1776, and Stuart to Germain, No. 10, 26 October 1776, C.O. 5/78.

107. Extract of a letter from a friend in Georgia, quoted in Brown to Tonyn, 8 November 1776, C.O. 5/557.

108. Stuart to Germain, No. 20, 6 October 1777, C.O. 5/79. Alexander McGillivray's father was Lachlan McGillivray, a Scotch trader, and his mother was Sehoy Marchand, half French and half Creek. Through his mother, McGillivray was connected to the powerful Wind clan. The British commissary, David Taitt, had married one of his sisters in 1768. Cotterill, *Southern Indians*, p. 41, n. 8. Louis LeClerc de Milford, a French adventurer, married another of his sisters sometime later. McGillivray's father had sent him to Charleston to be educated, and he had worked for a short time in the counting house of Samuel Elbert in Savannah. John Walton Caughey, ed., *McGillivray of the Creeks*, The Civilization of the American Indian Series, Vol. XVIII (Norman: University of Oklahoma Press, 1938), pp. 4, 15–16. Lachlan McGillivray was a loyalist, and, when the Georgians proscribed him and confiscated his property, he sailed back to Scotland. Consequently, Alexander McGillivray returned to the Creeks with a hatred of Americans, especially Georgia rebels.

109. Niaha Thlaco to Stuart, 20 October 1775, C.O. 5/77; Stuart to Dartmouth, Nos. 31 and 33, 25 October 1776, 6 January 1776, C.O. 5/76 and 5/77; Stuart to Clinton, 15 March 1776, to Germain, No. 4, 6 June 1776, C.O. 5/77; Stuart to Germain, No. 10, 26 October 1776, C.O. 5/78; Howe to Stuart, 23 May 1776, C.O. 5/94; Peter Chester, Governor of West Florida, to Germain, No. 19, 25 October 1776, C.O. 5/593; Tonyn to Germain, No. 31, 7 December 1776, C.O. 5/557.

110. Stuart to Germain, Nos. 10 and 12, 26 October 1776, 24 November 1776, C.O. 5/78.

111. Stuart to Germain, No. 10, 26 October 1776, C.O. 5/78.

112. General Lee's Talk to the Head Men of the Lower Creeks, 1 September 1776, Jonathan Bryan to the Headmen and Warriors of the Creek Nation, 1 September 1776, David Holmes to Stuart, 26 September 1776, and Brown to Stuart, 29 September 1776, all enclosed in Stuart to Germain, No. 10, 26 October 1776, C.O. 5/78.

113. McIntosh to Howe, 22 October 1776, *GHSC*, XII, 14-15. General Howe refused to take Gray's rebuff very seriously. Howe to Gwinnett, 26 October 1776, Jenkins, *Gwinnett*, pp. 205-7. Galphin and Rae had proposed that some of the Creek headmen be invited to visit the Continental Congress at Philadelphia. On 19 August that body resolved that Galphin and Rae should escort the headmen to Philadelphia and that Congress would defray the expenses of the journey. 19 August 1776, *JCC*, V, 670.

114. George Galphin to Willie Jones, 26 October 1776, including depositions of George Barnes, John Lambeth, and Joseph Ironmonger, 21 October 1776, Force, ed., *Archives*, 5th Ser., III, 648-51; Stuart to Germain, No. 15, 10 March 1777, C.O. 5/78.

115. Brown to Tonyn, 8 November 1776, C.O. 5/557.

116. Emistisico to Stuart, 19 November 1776, Stuart's Circular letter to Captains Daniel Wirdman, James McDonald, Cressian Reynard, etc., of North Carolina, 9 February 1777, Stuart to Germain, Nos. 13 and 15, 23 January, 10 March 1777, and to William Knox, Undersecretary of State for the American Department, 10 March 1777, C.O. 5/78; Stuart to Howe, 22 December 1776, 4 March 1777, C.O. 5/94.

117. William McIntosh to Alexander Skinner, Commissary of Indian Affairs at St. Augustine (extract), 9 November 1776, Brown to Tonyn, 8 November 1776, C.O. 5/557. This William McIntosh, a British Indian agent for the Lower Creeks, was the second cousin, not the brother, of General Lachlan McIntosh.

118. Tonyn to Germain, No. 30, 27 November 1776, C.O. 5/557.

119. Panton to Tonyn, 18 January 1776, C.O. 5/556; Talk from the Cussita Town to Stuart, 6 February 1777, Stuart to Germain, No. 15, 10 March 1777, and to William Knox, Undersecretary of State for the American Department, 10 March 1777, C.O. 5/78.

120. Stuart tried to ransom the prisoners, two boys. Stuart to Howe, 22 December 1776, C.O. 5/94.

121. Tonyn to Germain, No. 31, 7 December 1776, C.O. 5/557.

122. McIntosh to William McIntosh, 12 December 1776, *GHSC*, XII, 21-22. Fort Barrington must have been in ruins by 1776; McIntosh said one Mr. Heard was to lay it out.

123. McIntosh to Lt. Col. William McIntosh or Major Marbury, 12 December 1776, to Howe, 13 December 1776, and to George Walton, 15 December 1776, *GHSC*, XII, 22-24.

124. McIntosh to Lt. Colonel [William] M'Intosh, 19 December 1776, McIntosh to Howe, 27 December 1776, *GHSC*, XII, 25, 27; General McIntosh's Talk to the Creeks, 23 December 1776, C.O. 5/78.

125. McIntosh to William McIntosh, 19 December 1776, to _____ 20 December 1776, and to Howe, 27 December 1776, *GHSC*, XII, 25–27.

126. McIntosh to Howe, 27 December 1776, [McIntosh's] Orders for the Officer Commanding the De[tach]ment of Foot, Station'd at the first Landing North Side of Alatamaha, n.d., *GHSC*, XII, 28–29. The commanding officer of the detachment was probably Major Cuthbert. See McIntosh to Captain John McIntosh, 28 January 1777, *GHSC*, XII, 40.

127. McIntosh to Howe, 27, 28 December 1776, *GHSC*, XII, 28–29; Joseph Clay to Capt. Samuel Stiles, 28 January 1777, *GHSC*, VIII, 20; *South Carolina and American General Gazette*, Thursday, 2 January 1777.

On 9 January the Georgia Council of Safety ordered a man named Carey to be sent to St. Augustine with a flag of truce to arrange a general prisoner exchange and specifically to offer Beecher for Woodruff. Journal of the Council of Safety, 9 January 1777, *RRG*, I, 223.

Colonel Elbert was to see evidence of the skirmish on Sapelo Island when he led Georgia's invasion force down the inland waterway the following spring. 4 May 1776, *GHSC*, V, Pt. II, 23–24.

128. Journal of Capt. Charles S. Middleton, 20 December 1776–9 January 1777, Gibbes, comp., *Documentary History*, II, 47–53.

129. 3 January 1777, ibid., 52; McIntosh to [Howe?], 30 December 1776, *GHSC*, XII, 29; McIntosh to Howe, 7 January 1776, *GHSC*, XII, 31–32.

Chapter IV

1. McIntosh to Howe, 30 December 1776, to Lieutenant Ignatius Few, 30 December 1776, to Lieut. Colo. Wm. McIntosh, 2 January 1777, and to Howe, 7 January 1777, *GHSC*, XII, 29–32.

2. McIntosh to William McIntosh, 2 January 1777, to Howe, 7 January [2 letters], to [William McIntosh?], 7 January 1777, to William McIntosh and Major Marbury, 8 January 1777, and to Col. Samuel Elbert, 8 January 1777, ibid., 30–34.

3. Journal of the Council of Safety, 8 January 1777, *RRG*, I, 221.

4. McIntosh to Howe, 7 January 1777, to Captain Jeremiah Bugg, 8 January 1777, to [William McIntosh?], 7 January 1777, to Elbert, 17 January 1777, to Howe, 24 January 1777, and to Noble Wimberly Jones, Speaker of the Convention of Georgia, 15 February 1777, *GHSC*, XII, 32–34, 36, 38, 41. Marbury apparently reconsidered his resignation; about 8 February he again threatened to resign if anyone were promoted over his head as lieutenant colonel of the Light Horse. McIntosh to Noble Wimberly Jones, 15 February 1777, *GHSC*, XII, 41.

5. McIntosh to Elbert, 17 January 1777, *GHSC*, XII, 36.

6. McIntosh to Washington, 13 April 1777, ibid., 46.

7. McIntosh to Elbert, 8 January 1777, to Lyman Hall, Dr. [Nathan] Brownson, and George Walton, 23 January 1777, and to Howe, 24 January 1777, ibid., 34–38.

8. McIntosh to Colonel William Kennon, 26 January 1777, ibid., 39.

9. McIntosh to Wm. McIntosh and Major Marbury, 8 January 1777, to Lyman Hall, Dr. [Nathan] Brownson, and George Walton, 23 January 1777, ibid., 34–37.

10. McIntosh to Captain Richard Winn, 10 January 1777, to Elbert, 17 January 1777, ibid., 35–36.

11. McIntosh to Howe, 24, 25, 26 January 1777, to Capt. Caldwell, 25 January 1777, ibid., 38–39.

12. McIntosh to [Howe?], 26 January 1777, to [Captain Caldwell?], 26 January 1777, and to Capt. John M'Intosh, 28 January 1777, ibid., 39–40; Tonyn to Germain, No. 35, 2 April 1777, C.O. 5/557. One loyalist reported that the rebel galley was burned by Captain Squire's *Otter*. Memorial of Stephen Haven, 26 June 1784, Egerton, ed., *Royal Commission*, p. 141.

13. Tonyn to Germain, No. 35, 2 April 1777, C.O. 5/557.

14. William Henry Drayton and John Smith to Noble Wimberly Jones, Speaker of the Convention of Georgia, and W. Jones to William Henry Drayton and John Smith, both dated 22 January 1777, Gibbes, comp., *Documentary History*, II, 74; William Henry Drayton to Humphrey Wells, 8 June 1777, White, *Collections*, pp. 203–4.

15. Drayton to Wells, 8 June 1777, White, *Collections*, pp. 203, 205. See also Jenkins, *Gwinnett*, p. 104.

16. The Continental Congress had recommended the preceding spring that the colonies form state governments for themselves. Resolutions of 10, 15 May 1776, *JCC*, IV, 342, 357–58.

Georgia's constitution of 1777 is printed in *RRG*, I, 282–97. For a clear analysis of this constitution, see Coleman, *Revolution in Georgia*, pp. 79–85, and Albert B. Saye, *New View-Points in Georgia History* (Athens: University of Georgia Press, 1943), pp. 166–95. On pages 169–70 of the latter (also Jenkins, *Gwinnett*, pp. 108–10) is printed the surviving fragment of the convention's journal, which records the personnel of a Committee of Form and is concerned with the final revision and adoption of the constitution.

17. *RRG*, I, 284–86.

18. Lyman Hall to Roger Sherman, 16 May 1777, Jenkins, *Gwinnett*, pp. 227–28.

19. McIntosh to George Walton, 15 December 1776, *GHSC*, XII, 24.

20. John Wereat to George Walton, 30 August 1777, ibid., 66–73; Joseph Clay to Messrs. Bright and Pechin, 2 July 1777, to Laurens, 16 October 1777, *GHSC*, VIII, 35, 47–49.

21. Halifax to Grant, 9 February 1765, C.O. 5/548; Shelburne to Gage, 13 September 1766, Carter, ed., *Correspondence of Gage*, II, 45–46.

22. Dartmouth to North American Governors (circular), 15 April 1775, C.O. 5/76, and in East Florida Council Minutes, 17 July 1775, C.O. 5/571.

23. Tonyn's titles as enumerated in his commission were: Captain General, Governor, Commander in Chief and Vice Admiral in and over His Majesty's Province of East Florida. East Florida Council Minutes, 9 March 1774, C.O. 5/571. The Commission of Patrick Tonyn, Governor of East Florida, 14 June 1773, is printed in Labaree, *Royal Instructions*, II, 825–35.

24. Grant to Shelburne, No. 4, 19 April 1767, C.O. 5/541.

25. General Account of sundry Expenses incurred for Indians from the 25th of June 1773 to the 24th of June 1774, C.O. 5/554.

26. Tonyn to Prevost, 29 May 1779, C.O. 5/559.

27. General Account of extra Contingent Expences incurred for the service of His Majesty's Province of East Florida from the 25th June 1775 to the 24th June 1776, General Accompt of Sundry Extraordinary Expences incurred for raising and Paying a Corps of four Troops of East Florida Rangers from 24th June 1776 to 24th June 1777, and Estimate of the Expences of One Troop of East Florida Rangers for one Day, C.O. 5/557.

28. Germain to Tonyn, No. 13, 9 July 1779, C.O. 5/559; Memorial of Lt. Col. Thomas Brown to Sir Guy Carleton, 11 January 1783, Headquarters Papers, Nos. 6737 and 10050.

29. General Accompt of Sundry Extraordinary Expences incurred for raising and Paying a Corps of four Troops of East Florida Rangers from 24th June 1776 to 24th June 1777, Governor Tonyn's Instructions and Orders to the Officers of the Rangers, 30 January 1777, Brown to Tonyn, 20 February 1777, and Tonyn to Prevost, 13 January 1777, C.O. 5/557; Journal of Captain Charles S. Middleton, 27 December 1776, Gibbes, comp., *Documentary History*, II, 49–50.

30. Stuart to [Hillsborough], Nos. 20 and 22, 30 April, 2 May 1770, C.O. 5/227; Carter, ed., *Correspondence of Gage*, I, x–xi; Alden, *Stuart*, pp. 154–55.

31. Stuart to Germain, No. 6, 23 August 1776, C.O. 5/77; Tonyn to Prevost, 23 January 1777, C.O. 5/557.

32. Howe to Stuart, 13 January 1777, C.O. 5/94.

33. Tonyn to Prevost, 13 January 1777, Return of Provisions in Store, 3 February 1777, and Tonyn to Germain, No. 35, 2 April 1777, C.O. 5/557. See also Nicholas Rogers to Silas Deane, 12 April 1777, *NDAR*, VIII, 331–32.

34. Tonyn to Germain, No. 35, 2 April 1777, enclosing Prevost to Tonyn, 11, 16, 21, 23 January, Tonyn to Prevost, 13, 17, 19, 23, 27 January 1777, and Return of the Working Tools received for the Kings Works at St. Augustine, 23 January 1777, C.O. 5/557. This correspondence was copied into the East Florida Council Minutes, 13–27 January 1777, in Tonyn to Germain, No. 48, 26 December 1777, C.O. 5/558.

35. Tonyn to Prevost, 19 January 1777, Prevost to Tonyn, 23 January 1777, C.O. 5/557.

36. Tonyn to Prevost, 27 January 1777, C.O. 5/557.

37. Tonyn to Prevost, 17 January 1777, Tonyn's Talk to Perryman and all the Creek Indians on the Scouting Party with the Rangers, 12 January 1777, Tonyn to Lt. Williams of the Rangers, 24 January 1777, and Tonyn's Talk to Perryman and the Creek Indians, 24 January 1777, C.O. 5/557. These three

groups of Indians belonged to the Hitchiti-speaking element in the Creek Confederacy.

38. Tonyn to Prevost, 23 January 1777, to Lt. Williams of the Rangers, 24 January 1777, and Tonyn's Talk to Perryman and the Creek Indians, 24 January 1777, C.O. 5/557. To ensure that no possible misunderstanding or hesitation occurred about using Indians as a military force to aid the British, General Howe had "earnestly recommended" to Gov. Tonyn that he "use every possible means to employ them in the Defence of the Province [East Florida], or against the Invaders in their own Country if you find it more conducive to your Safety." Howe to Tonyn (extract), 25 August 1776, Headquarters Papers, No. 258.

39. Tonyn to Germain, No. 35, 2 April 1777, C.O. 5/557.

40. Prevost to Tonyn, 23 January 1777, Tonyn to Prevost, 27 January 1777, and Talk from Governor Tonyn to Perryman and the Creek Indians, 31 January 1777, C.O. 5/557. This probably was the period when "the Troops were reduced to live mostly upon fish they caught in this Harbour." Tonyn to John Robinson, Secretary to Lords of the Treasury, n.d., in Tonyn to Germain, No. 81, 25 September 1779, C.O. 5/559.

41. Tonyn to Prevost, 27 January 1777, Governor Tonyn's Instructions and Orders to the Officers of the Rangers, 30 [or 31?] January 1777, Tonyn to John Hambly the Indian Interpreter, 31 January 1777, Talk from Governor Tonyn to Perryman and the Creek Indians, 31 January 1777, and Gov. Tonyn to Lt. Col. Brown of the East Florida Rangers, 5 February 1777, C.O. 5/557.

42. Mowat, *East Florida*, p. 111.

43. Tonyn to John Hambly, the Indian Interpreter, 31 January 1777, C.O. 5/557; "Memoir of Murray," in Butler, *Royal Americans*, pp. 299–300.

44. "Memoir of Murray," in Butler, *Royal Americans*, p. 300.

45. McIntosh to Washington, 13 April 1777, *GHSC*, XII, 46.

46. Tonyn to Germain, No. 35, 2 April 1777, enclosing Lt. Col. Brown of the East Florida Rangers to Gov. Tonyn, 20 February 1777, and List of the Garrison of Fort McIntosh on St. Illa River surrendered Prisoners of War this 18th February 1777, C.O. 5/557; McIntosh to Howe, to Colonel Scriven, both dated 19 February 1777, *GHSC*, XII, 41; McIntosh to Washington, 13 April 1777, *GHSC*, XII, 46; Joseph Clay to John Burnley, 24 February 1777, *GHSC*, VIII, 20–21; M'Call, *History*, pp. 325–26; "Memoir of Murray," in Butler, *Royal Americans*, pp. 300–302.

McCall states that Cunningham and McGirth were Brown's immediate subordinates and that Cussupa led the Indians. In his letter to Screven, McIntosh says, "I am just inform'd by Express that fort McIntosh upon Satilla is besiged by Col. Brown (little Brown). . . ." This is one of the two descriptions of Brown yet found by this writer.

Brown mentions the regulars' camp at the "Old Fort," and Murray describes the temporary fortification erected by them at the "burnt Fort." Brown to Tonyn, 20 February 1777, C.O. 5/557; "Memoir of Murray," in Butler, *Royal Americans*, p. 300. This fort may have been one constructed by the Georgia Light Horse when they were stationed between the Satilla and St. Marys and destroyed by them when they moved back across the Satilla late in 1776.

47. Hostages, and Articles of Capitulation betwixt Colonel Fuser and His Majesty's 60th Royal American Regiment of Foot, and Richard Winn Esqr. Commander of Ft. McIntosh on Santilla River the 18th February 1777, C.O. 5/557; M'Call, *History,* pp. 327–28.

48. "Memoir of Murray," in Butler, *Royal Americans,* pp. 301–2.

49. Brown to Tonyn, 20 February 1777, C.O. 5/557.

50. Ibid.; "Memoir of Murray," in Butler, *Royal Americans,* p. 302.

51. McIntosh to Capt. Bostick, to Capt. Habersham, both dated 20 February 1777, *GHSC,* XII, 42; Journal of the Council of Safety, 21, 22 February 1777, *RRG,* I, 224–25.

52. McIntosh to Washington, 13 April 1777, *GHSC,* XII, 46.

53. Brown to Tonyn, 20 February 1777, C.O. 5/557; "Memoir of Murray," in Butler, *Royal Americans,* pp. 300–302. Murray states that the British remained on the Satilla for ten days while the Rangers collected cattle, which subsequently sold for "3d. per pound in the public market" at St. Augustine, but he does not mention any military activity at all during this time.

54. 21 February 1777, Howe's Orderly Book, pp. 43–44; *GHSC,* V, Pt. II, 9; Howe to Moultrie, 23 February 1777, *NCSR,* XI, 706–7; Journal of the South Carolina Navy Board, 23–27 February 1777, *NDAR,* VII, 1311–14; John Bennett, comp., "A List of Noncommissioned Officers and Private Men of the Second South Carolina Continental Regiment of Foot," *SCHGM,* XVI (January 1915), 27–28.

Moultrie said that he dispatched a total force of six hundred men under the command of Marion from Charleston on 28 February, but that the enemy had retreated before the Carolinians reached Savannah. Moultrie, *Memoirs,* I, 189. Moultrie confuses dates in his account of actions during the British invasion.

South Carolina recalled all her Continental troops, at least seven hundred men, when the North Carolina Continentals were ordered to march northward from South Carolina to reinforce General Washington. Moultrie, *Memoirs,* I, 190–91.

55. Journal of the Council of Safety, 21, 22 February 1777, *RRG,* I, 224–25; Jones, *History of Georgia,* II, 264.

56. Howe to Moultrie, 16 March 1777, Moultrie, *Memoirs,* I, 191–92; McIntosh to Lt. Colonel [Francis?] Harris, 23 March 1777, to Col. Sumpter, 2 [?] March 1777, *GHSC,* XII, 42–43; Howe to Moultrie, 23 February 1777, to Hancock, 26 February 1777, *NCSR,* XI, 706–9; Jenkins, *Gwinnett,* pp. 139, 141–42.

57. A State of Military and Naval Force of the Province of South Carolina and Georgia, n.d., in Tonyn to Germain, No. 35, 2 April 1777, C.O. 5/557.

58. Gwinnett to John Hancock, 28 March 1777, Jenkins, *Gwinnett,* p. 218.

59. Joseph Clay to Messieurs Bright and Pechin and Capt. McDaniel, 8 April 1777, *GHSC,* VIII, 25; A State of the Military and Naval Force of the

Provinces of South Carolina and Georgia, n.d., in Tonyn to Germain, No. 35, 2 April 1777, C.O. 5/557.

60. McIntosh to Lt. Col. Harris, 25 March 1777, to Colonel Sumter, 2 [4?] March 1777, and to Howe, 2 April 1777, *GHSC*, XII, 42–43, 45; Gwinnett to Hancock, 28 March 1777, Jenkins, *Gwinnett*, pp. 217–21; George Washington to Howe, 4 July 1777, John C. Fitzpatrick, ed., *The Writings of George Washington from the Original Manuscript Sources, 1745–1799* (39 vols.; Washington, [D.C.]: U.S. Government Printing Office, 1931–40), VIII, 343; Jenkins, *Gwinnett*, pp. 138–42.

Alexander Chesney says that the South Carolinians who were to garrison Fort Howe reached that post on 25 March. Chesney, *The Journal of Alexander Chesney, a South Carolina Loyalist in the Revolution and After*, ed. by E. Alfred Jones, Ohio State University Studies, Contributions in History and Political Science, No. 7 (n.p.: Ohio State University, 1921), p. 8.

61. Resolutions of 5 February 1777, *JCC*, VII, 90–91; Washington to Howe, 17 March 1777, 4 July 1777, Fitzpatrick, ed., *Writings of Washington*, VII, 297–98, VIII, 343; Howe to Hancock, 26 February 1777, *NCSR*, XI, 708–9; Gwinnett to Hancock, 28 March 1777, Jenkins, *Gwinnett*, p. 220; Moultrie, *Memoirs*, I, 188–89.

62. 1 January 1777, *JCC*, VII, 8–9; Tonyn to Germain, Private, No. 2, 19 July 1776/7 [*sic*], C.O. 5/557; Resolve of the Rebel Congress and extract of Tonyn's letter to Germain (enclosure No. 19), in Tonyn to Germain, No. 35, 2 April 1777, C.O. 5/557; President of Congress (John Hancock) to President of Georgia (Archibald Bullock), 8 January 1777, Burnett, ed., *Letters*, II, 208–9; Gwinnett to Hancock, 28 March 1777, Jenkins, *Gwinnett*, pp. 215–17; Jenkins, *Gwinnett*, pp. 135–38.

63. McIntosh to Walton, 15 December 1776, *GHSC*, XII, 23–24.

64. McIntosh to Colonel Sumpter, 2 [4?] March 1777, to Gwinnett, 28 March 1777, and "Papers Respecting the Augustine Expedition in April 1777," *GHSC*, XII, 43–44, 61.

65 McIntosh to Gwinnett, 28 March 1777, to Howe, 2 April 1777, and "Papers Respecting the Augustine Expedition in April 1777," *GHSC*, XII, 44–45, 61.

66. McIntosh to Washington, 13 April 1777, *GHSC*, XII, 46; Howe to Moultrie, 16 March 1777, Moultrie, *Memoirs*, I, 191–92.

67. McIntosh to Washington, 13 April 1777, to Gwinnett, 17 April 1777, to Elbert, 26 April 1777, and "Papers Respecting the Augustine Expedition in April 1777," *GHSC*, XII, 45–48, 61–63, *GHSC*, V, Pt. II, 15–21; Lyman Hall to Roger Sherman, 1 June 1777 (continuation of letter begun 16 May 1777), Jenkins, *Gwinnett*, pp. 228–29; John Adam Treutlen, governor of Georgia, to Hancock, 19 June 1777, Jenkins, *Gwinnett*, p. 245; Jenkins, *Gwinnett*, pp. 144–45; "Extract of a Letter from Savannah in Georgia, Dated April 3 [1777]," *NDAR*, VIII, 268.

68. Tonyn to Germain, Nos. 35 and 38, 2 April, 5 May 1777, to Stuart, 15 April 1777, C.O. 5/557; Tonyn to Howe (extract), 28 April 1777, Prevost to Howe, 23 April 1777, C.O. 5/94; East Florida Council Minutes, 23 April 1777,

in Tonyn to Germain, No. 48, 26 December 1777, C.O. 5/558; Gwinnett to Provost [sic], 11 April 1777, C.O. 5/94.

69. Howe to Prevost, 15 January 1777, Headquarters Papers, No. 380; Queries to Lt. Col. Robert Bissett, 16 December 1777, C.O. 5/546. Howe also warned the governor that he could not "at this Time extend [his] views" beyond his own province. Howe to Tonyn, 15 January 1777, C.O. 5/94.

70. Tonyn to Taitt, 20 April 1777, Headquarters Papers, No. 497; Tonyn to Howe (extract), 28 April 1777, C.O. 5/94; Tonyn to Germain, No. 38, 5 May 1777, C.O. 5/557.

71. Tonyn to Germain, No. 38, 5 May 1777, Taitt to Tonyn, 23 May 1777, C.O. 5/557.

72. McIntosh to Howe, 2 April 1777, GHSC, XII, 44.

73. William Knox to Philip Stephens, 26 February 1777, Stephens to Knox, 6 March 1777, and Knox to Stephens, 26 March, 3 April 1777, NDAR, VIII, 611, 644, 714, 740; Prevost to Howe, 23 April 1777, Tonyn to Howe (extract), 28 April 1777, C.O. 5/94.

74. Howe to Prevost (extract), 3 May 1777, C.O. 5/94.

75. General Intelligence Observations, [ca. 21 October 1777], Paul Wentworth to [the Earl of Suffolk], 9 August 1777, B. F. Stevens, ed., Facsimiles of Manuscripts in European Archives Relating to America, 1773–1783, with Descriptions, Editorial Notes, Collations, References, and Translations (25 vols., Holborn, England: Malby and Sons, 1889–95), III, 277, VII, 705. For Prevost genealogy, see Edward G. Williams, "The Prevosts of the Royal Americans," Western Pennsylvania Historical Magazine, LVI (January 1973), 1–38.

76. Tonyn to Germain, No. 38, 5 May 1777, C.O. 5/557; Copy of a Circular Letter from His Excellency Governor Tonyn, to the Gentlemen Resident and on the Plantations on saint John's River on the Rebel Invasion of the Province of East Florida in May 1777, C.O. 5/546; Memorandum of Sir James Wright, n.d., [endorsed "Received August 1777"], CRG, XXXVIII, Pt. II, 126; East Florida Council Minutes, 31 April 1777, in Tonyn to Germain, No. 48, 26 December 1777, C.O. 5/558.

77. Tonyn to Germain, Nos. 35, 38, 39, and 42, 2 April, 5, 8 May, 26 July 1777, Three Memorials of Patrick Tonyn, all dated 19 July 1777, in Tonyn to Germain, No. 42, 26 July 1777, Certificates of the Hawke's damage 25–26 July 1777, and General Account of sundry Expences incurred for Naval Services in His Majesty's Province of East Florida, 21 July 1777, C.O. 5/557; East Florida Council Minutes, 24 April 1777, in Tonyn to Germain, No. 48, 26 December 1777, C.O. 5/558; Disposition of Richard Lord Howe's Fleet in North America, 15 January 1777, NDAR, VII, 965; "Gazette of the State of South-Carolina, 9 April 1777," NDAR, VIII, 308; Vice Admiral Richard Lord Howe to Philip Stephens, 31 March 1777, NDAR, VIII, 231–32.

78. Memorandum from Sir James Wright, n.d., [endorsed "Received August 1777"], CRG, XXXVIII, Pt. II, 124.

79. GHSC, V, Pt. II, 21–25.

80. Memorandum from Sir James Wright, n.d., [endorsed "Received August 1777"], CRG, XXXVIII, Pt. II, 124–25; GHSC, V, Pt. II, 19; M'Call, History, p. 340.

81. M'Call, *History,* pp. 340–41.

82. Elbert to McIntosh, 25 May 1777, *GHSC,* XII, 64; *GHSC,* V, Pt. II, 25–29; M'Call, *History,* p. 343.

83. Tonyn to Germain, No. 40, 16 June 1777, C.O. 5/557.

84. M'Call, *History,* p. 341. Henry Barefield was paid eighteen shillings by the East Florida government for provisions for a party of Indians returning from the St. Marys. General Account of Sundry Expences incurred for Indians, from the 25th June 1776 to the 24th June 1777, C.O. 5/557.

85. Brown to Tonyn, 15 May 1777, C.O. 5/557; Major Prevost to Colonel Prevost (extract), 15 May 1777, C.O. 5/94.

86. Brown to Tonyn, 15 May 1777, C.O. 5/557; M'Call, *History,* p. 341; Tonyn to Germain, No. 40, 16 June 1777, C.O. 5/557; "Memoir of Murray," in Butler, *Royal Americans,* p. 299.

87. Brown to Tonyn, 15 May 1777, C.O. 5/557.

88. Brown to Tonyn, 18 May 1777, C.O. 5/557; Memorandum from Sir James Wright, n.d., [endorsed "Received August 1777"], *CRG,* XXXVIII, Pt. II, 124.

89. Joseph Thomas had a settlement on the Nassau River. General Account of Sundry Expences incurred for Indians from the 25th June 1776 to the 24th June 1777, C.O. 5/557.

90. Brown to Tonyn, 18 May 1777, C.O. 5/557; Prevost to Prevost, 18 May 1777 (extract), C.O. 5/94; Prevost to Howe, 14 June 1777, Headquarters Papers, No. 584; "Memoir of Murray," in Butler, *Royal Americans,* pp. 302–3; Tonyn to Germain, No. 40, 16 June 1777, C.O. 5/557; Memorandum from Sir James Wright, n.d., [endorsed "Received August 1777"], *CRG,* XXXVIII, Pt. II, 124; M'Call, *History,* pp. 341–42.

91. Elbert to McIntosh, 25 May 1777, *GHSC,* XII, 64–65; *GHSC,* V, Pt. II, 20, 25–26, 27–28; M'Call, *History,* pp. 343–44. Brown said that ten rebels had deserted and, while they were being escorted by two Rangers, the Indians killed three and drove the remaining seven into the swamp. Brown to Tonyn, 18 May 1777, C.O. 5/557. Murray said that the Black Creek Factor was responsible for the death of the prisoners, only sixteen of forty being saved. "Memoir of Murray," in Butler, *Royal Americans,* p. 303.

92. Prevost to Howe, 14 June 1777, Headquarters Papers, No. 584; Tonyn to Germain, No. 40, 16 June 1777, Tonyn's Certificate for Captain McLeod of the *Hawke,* 19 July 1777, Certificate of the *Hawke's* damage, 25–26 July 1777, Tonyn to Taitt, 12 June 1777, and Tonyn to Stuart, 16 June 1777, C.O. 5/557.

93. *GHSC,* V, Pt. II, 27–34; Elbert to McIntosh, 25 May 1777, *GHSC,* XII, 65–66.

94. Memorandum from Sir James Wright, n.d., [endorsed "Received August 1777"], *CRG,* XXXVIII, Pt. II, 124. No accounts of this invasion agree on the number of Americans taken prisoner by the British. Quite possibly confusion exists between "prisoners" and "deserters."

95. *GHSC,* V, Pt. II, 32–33; Memorial of Sir James Wright, n.d., [endorsed "Received August 1777"], *CRG,* XXXVIII, Pt. II, 124.

96. *GHSC,* V, Pt. II, 34–35, 37, 45. Elbert tried to tighten the discipline when Major Mark Prevost sent Lieutenant Skinner of the British Sixteenth Regiment with a flag of truce to demand that the articles of capitulation negotiated at Fort McIntosh be fulfilled and that prisoners, including Indians, be exchanged. Prevost warned that in the future, "Agreeable to an order of His Excellency Sir William Howe," all small parties found in arms below Georgia's southern boundary would be treated as robbers and murderers. He further stated ". . . it is indecent that Harmless and Innocent Planters should find themselves the object of these Excursions, and that the Sending of any Parties to take or assassinate any Particular Individual is never Countenanced and is Contrary to the rules of war, Dictates of Humanity, and when ever they are taken no quarter given to them." Elbert was convinced that Skinner's primary purpose was to gain information about the rebels' strength and position. Ibid., 35–37.

97. Elbert to McIntosh, 26 May 1777, *GHSC,* V, Pt. II, 31.

98. Elbert to Howe, 18 July 1777, ibid., 45–46.

Chapter V

1. Howe to Augustine Prevost, 1 April 1777, C.O. 5/94.

2. Tonyn to Germain, No. 40, 16 June 1777, C.O. 5/557; Prevost to Howe, 14 June 1777, Headquarters Papers, No. 584.

3. Prevost to Tonyn, 29 June 1777, Tonyn to Prevost, 5 July 1777, C.O. 5/557.

4. Prevost to Howe, 14 June 1777, Headquarters Papers, No. 584; Prevost to Tonyn, 4 July 1777, C.O. 5/557.

5. Tonyn to Prevost, 5 July 1777, C.O. 5/557. For the relevant paragraphs of Governor Tonyn's commission, see Labaree, *Royal Instructions,* II, 832. See also Germain to Peter Chester, governor of West Florida, No. 3, 27 May 1776, C.O. 5/619.

6. Germain to Howe, No. 9, 19 April 1777, C.O. 5/94.

7. Three memorials to Patrick Tonyn, all dated 19 July 1777, Certificate of the *Hawke*'s damage, 25–26 July 1777, and Tonyn to Germain, No. 42, 26 July 1777, C.O. 5/557; Memorandum from Sir James Wright, n.d., [endorsed "Received August 1777"], *CRG,* XXXVIII, Pt. II, 126.

8. Memorandum of Sir James Wright, n.d., [endorsed "Received August 1777"], *CRG,* XXXVIII, Pt. II, 125; Jenkins, *Gwinnett,* pp. 150–51.

9. Gwinnett to John Hancock, 28 March 1777, John Adam Treutlen, governor of Georgia, to Hancock, 19 June 1777, Jenkins, *Gwinnett,* pp. 216–17, 243; John Wereat to George Walton, 30 August 1777, *GHSC,* XII, 67–68; M'Call, *History,* pp. 333, 335–38. A good secondary account of McIntosh's troubles that is favorable to him is in Johnston, *Houstouns,* pp. 348–65.

Gwinnett complained that three of McIntosh's relatives on the council were responsible for his having been released on bail. The charges against McIntosh included one that he had associated with other St. Andrew's Parish planters, Sir Patrick Houstoun and George Baillie, to send three rice ships (a brig, a schooner, and a sloop) from Sunbury to Dutch Guiana in May 1776. William Panton, the Tory Indian trader, had joined the group, sailed with the vessels, and commandeered them. He ordered the sloop to the St. Johns and the schooner to St. Augustine. After obtaining new papers for the brig, he took that vessel to the British West Indies, sold her cargo there, and brought a return cargo to St. Augustine. Evidence is lacking that McIntosh knew of Panton's plans; Panton declared that McIntosh was innocent.

10. John Adam Treutlen to Hancock, 19 June, 6 August 1777, Jenkins, *Gwinnett,* pp. 244–49; "Part of G[eorge] McIntosh's Journal," in Hawes, ed., *McIntosh Papers,* pp. 94–95; M'Call, *History,* pp. 338–39; Jenkins, *Gwinnett,* pp. 159–62, 165–67. See also "Minutes of the Executive Council, May 7 through October 13, 1777," *GHQ* (March, June 1950), 19–35, 106–25, passim.

McIntosh's estate had been confiscated for the use of the state of Georgia, and a party of soldiers were billeted there. Much property was destroyed. John Wereat to George Walton, 30 August 1777, *GHSC,* XII, 72; L. McIntosh to Walton, 13 July 1777, Jenkins, *Gwinnett,* p. 260; Wright to [Germain], 8 October 1777, *CRG,* XXXVIII, Pt. II, 128; "Part of G[eorge] McIntosh's Journal," in Hawes, ed., *McIntosh Papers,* pp. 94–95.

Congress considered the case during the period 2–10 October 1777, decided that the evidence was insufficient for a trial, and released McIntosh. 2, 4, 9, 10 October 1777, *JCC,* VIII, 757–58, IX, 764–65, 787–90.

11. Lyman Hall to Roger Sherman, 1 June 1777 (continuation of letter begun 16 May 1777), Jenkins, *Gwinnett,* pp. 228–29; Jenkins, *Gwinnett,* pp. 152–53.

12. Hall to Sherman, 1 June 1777 (continuation of letter begun 16 May 1777), Jenkins, *Gwinnett,* pp. 229, 152–57; M'Call, *History,* pp. 333–34.

13. 1, 6 August 1777, *JCC,* VIII, 597, 616; Wereat to Walton, 30 August 1777, *GHSC,* XII, 66–73; Walton to Washington, 5 August 1777, Laurens to McIntosh, 11 August 1777, Burnett, ed., *Letters,* II, 439, 444; Washington to Walton, 6 August 1777, Fitzpatrick, ed., *Writings of Washington,* IX, 25–26; McIntosh to Laurens, 30 May 1777, McIntosh to Walton, 14 July 1777, Jenkins, *Gwinnett,* pp. 253–61; Petitions from the Georgia Assembly and Inhabitants of Chatham County to the Continental Congress, 13 September, 1 July 1777, Jenkins, *Gwinnett,* pp. 265–71; M'Call, *History,* pp. 334–35; Jenkins, *Gwinnett,* pp. 159–68.

Two letters and a petition from Ann, Button Gwinnett's widow, to John Hancock, president, and members of the Continental Congress, two dated 1 August 1777 and one undated but endorsed "Received 28 September 1777," are printed in Jenkins, *Gwinnett,* pp. 233–40. They contain highly interesting charges against the McIntosh family and their adherents, but most of the information has not been corroborated from other sources.

14. 27 June 1777, "Minutes of the Executive Council," *GHQ,* XXXIV (March 1950), 27; M'Call, *History,* p. 351.

15. 14 July 1777, "Minutes of the Executive Council," *GHQ,* XXXIV (March 1950), 31.

16. Orders by Gen. McIntosh, 18 June 1777, *GHSC*, V, Pt. II, 37–38.

17. 12 July 1777, "Minutes of the Executive Council," *GHQ*, XXXIV (March 1950), 30; 8, 10 October 1777, *JCC*, IX, 783, 792–93; R. Howe to Gov. Caswell of N.C., 10 April 1777, Col. I. [*sic*] White to Gov. Caswell of N.C., 30 November 1777, Richard Caswell to Thos. Craike Comr. Stores, and to Col. J. White 4th Georgia Batt'n, both dated 6 December 1777, *NCSR*, XI, 446, 685–87, 692; Richard Caswell, Governor of North Carolina, to the General Assembly, 9 April 1777, Senate Journal, State of N.C., 17, 23 April, 5 December 1777, and Journal of the House of Commons, State of N.C., 5, 6 December 1777, *NCSR*, XII, 445, 23, 35, 171–72, 339, 348; Minutes of the North Carolina Council, 4 March 1777, *NCSR*, XIII, 915–16.

18. Elbert to Howe, 18 July 1777, *GHSC*, V, Pt. II, 46.

19. General Orders by Genl. McIntosh, 24 July 1777, ibid., 48–49.

20. McIntosh to Walton, 14 July 1777, Jenkins, *Gwinnett*, p. 259; 18 October 1777, *JCC*, IX, 820–21; James Lovell to William Whipple, 3 November 1777, Burnett, ed., *Letters*, II, 540. See also Crout, "Georgia's Quest for Aid," *GHQ*, LX (Summer 1976), 179–82.

21. Elbert to Howe, 18 July 1777, *GHSC*, V, Pt. II, 46.

22. Regimental Orders, 2d Battalion, 21 July 1777, ibid.

23. An Act for opening a land-office, and for the better settling and strengthening this state, *CRG*, XIX, Pt. II, 53–58; Gov. John A. Treutlen's Proclamation of 12 June 1777, *RRG*, I, 313; Clay to Laurens, 16 October 1777, *GHSC*, VIII, 47–48.

24. Certificate of Philip Minis signed by Col. William Kennon, Commissary General, 17 May (or February) 1777, "The Minis Family," *GHQ*, I (March 1917), 46–47; Treutlen to Hancock, 6 August 1777, Jenkins, *Gwinnett*, pp. 249–50; Elbert to Howe, 16 August 1777, in Tonyn to Germain, No. 43, 18 September 1777, C.O. 5/557; Clay to Edward Telfair, 10 August 1777, to Messrs. Bright and Pechin, 19 September 1777, *GHSC*, VIII, 37, 39; Gov. John Adam Treutlen's proclamations of 12 June, 21 July, 21 November 1777, *RRG*, I, 312, 316, 319–20; 12 June, 3, 21 July, 19 August, 6 October 1777, "Minutes of the Executive Council," *GHQ*, XXXIV (March 1950), 21, 28, (June 1950), 106–7, 114, 123; An Act to amend the several Acts for regulating the Pilotage of Vessels into the several Ports of the then Province now State of Georgia, 7 June 1777, and An Act to regulate and extend the Trade and Commerce of this State and to establish an Insurance Office for the encouragement thereof and also to restrain the Selling of Merchandize by Public Auction within the Same, 16 September 1777, *CRG*, XIX, Pt. II, 45–50, 72–80.

"One yard of bad linen costs 15 to 20 shill." Anna Barbara Rabenhorst to Henry Muhlenberg, 26 September 1777, Andrew W. Lewis, ed., "Henry Muhlenberg's Georgia Correspondence," *GHQ*, XLIX (December 1965), 431.

25. 25 July, 1, 5, 6, 15 August 1777, *JCC*, VIII, 579, 596–97, 606–7, 616, 644–46; Clay to Laurens, 16, 21 October 1777, *GHSC*, VIII, 48, 52; Clay to Howe, 15 October 1777, Clay to Messrs. Bright and Pechin, 21 October 1777,

GHSC, VIII, 41–45, 59; Laurens to Clay, 20 August 1777, Laurens to Isaac Motte, 26 January 1778, Burnett, ed., *Letters*, II, 458, III, 51.

Congress had already advanced substantial sums "to the delegates of Georgia, for the use of that state." 10, 15 January, 25 February, 17 April, 26 May, 19 July 1777, *JCC*, VII, 28, 39, 152, 275, VIII, 385, 567–68.

26. 6 August 1777, *JCC*, VIII, 616; 13 October 1777, *GHSC*, V, Pt. II, 57–58.

27. McIntosh to Laurens, 30 May 1777, Jenkins, *Gwinnett*, pp. 253–55; Wereat to Walton, 30 August 1777, *GHSC*, XII, 68.

28. Elbert to Capt. John Dooley, 25 August 1777, Elbert to McIntosh, 27 August 1777, *GHSC*, V, Pt. II, 52–53; John Baker, colonel of the Georgia Regiment of Horse, to McIntosh, 29 August 1777, Hawes, ed., *McIntosh Papers*, pp. 17–19.

29. Treutlen to the officers commanding the troop of horse and minute Battalions, n.d., *GHSC*, V, Pt. II, 52–53; Elbert to Noble W. Jones, 11 September 1777, *GHSC*, V, Pt. II, 55.

30. Elbert to [McIntosh], 9 September 1777, *GHSC*, V, Pt. II, 54–55.

31. Elbert to McIntosh, Elbert to Capt. Bard, both dated 27 August 1777, *GHSC*, V, Pt. II, 53–54; Baker to McIntosh, 29 August 1777, Hawes, ed., *McIntosh Papers*, p. 19.

32. 5, 13, 15 August 1777, "Minutes of the Executive Council," *GHQ*, XXXIV (June 1950), 110–13; Clay to Laurens, 16 October 1777, *GHSC*, VIII, 51.

33. Clay to Laurens, 21 October 1777, *GHSC*, VIII, 54.

34. Walton's testimony, *Proceedings of a General Court Martial, . . . for the Trial of Major General Howe, December 7, 1781, . . .* , *Revolutionary Papers*, Vol. XII of *Collections of the New York Historical Society*, II (New York: By the Society, 1879), 254.

35. 19, 22, 25, 30 July 1777, *JCC*, VIII, 566–67, 570, 579, 590; Charles Tomson, Notes of Debates, 24, 25 July 1777, Laurens to L. McIntosh, 11 August 1777, Laurens to John Rutledge, President of South Carolina, 12 August 1777, and Laurens to Clay, 20 August 1777, Burnett, ed., *Letters*, II, 421–23, 443–44, 445–47, 458.

36. 14 July 1777, "Minutes of the Executive Council," *GHQ*, XXXIV (March 1950), 31–32; Form of the Remonstrance and Petition of the Inhabitants of in [*sic*] the State of Georgia, Form of the Address and Petition of the Inhabitants of in [*sic*] the State of Georgia, and Proclamation by His Honor John Adam Treutlen, esq., Captain-General, Governor and Commander-in-Chief, in and Over the State of Georgia, 15 July 1777; Gibbes, comp., *Documentary History*, II, 81–84. See also Wright to [Germain], 8 October 1777, *CRG*, XXXVIII, Pt. II, 128–30.

37. To His Honor, John Adam Treutlen, Esq., Captain-General, Governor and Commander-in-Chief of the State of Georgia, and to Those Members of His Executive Council Who Advised the Above Proclamation, 1 August 1777, Gibbes, comp., *Documentary History*, II, 84–87.

38. Brown to Tonyn, 12 December 1777, Queries [by the Council] to Lieutenant Colonel Brown, n.d. [December 1777], Capt. Euan McLaurin to Brown, 9 December 1777, Queries [by the Council] to Mr. Yonge, Attorney at Law, 15 December 1777, Queries to Capt. George Osborne, 16 December 1777, and Tonyn to Germain, No. 33, 9 March 1777, C.O. 5/546; Tonyn to Drayton, 28 November 1777, C.O. 5/558.

39. Queries [by the Council] to Mr. Yonge, Attorney at Law, 15 December 1777, Queries [by the Council] to Capt. George Osborne, 16 December 1777, and Affidavit of James Coates, 22 September 1777, C.O. 5/546; Memorial to George Osborne, 14 January 1777, C.O. 5/557; Tonyn to Germain, No. 33, 9 March 1777, C.O. 5/546; Tonyn to Drayton, 28 November 1777, C.O. 5/558.

Thomas Palmer reported to the Georgia Council of Safety that George Barry frequently *sold* livestock to British ships. Journal of the [Georgia] Council of Safety, 28 August 1776, *RRG*, I, 190. And a George Barry (almost certainly the same person) was named in An Act for attainting such persons as are therein mentioned of high Treason, and for Confiscating their Estates, both real and personal to the use of this State . . . , 1 March 1778, *RRG*, I, 328. George Barry, of Tybee Island, filed a loyalist claim. Memorial of George Barry, 22 September 1784, Egerton, ed., *Royal Commission*, p. 208.

James Coates was taken prisoner by the Georgia rebels in December 1776, whereupon Palmer, Barry's overseer, tried to charge Coates with felony for stealing the stock. However, Georgia's grand jury refused to indict Coates, raising the question of who had actually owned the livestock enjoyed by seamen of His Majesty's ships. Affidavit of James Coates, 22 September 1777, C.O. 5/546, C.O. 5/558.

40. Memorial of George Osborne, 14 January 1777, C.O. 5/557. Captain Osborne eventually returned to sea. He and his sloop (with Captain Adam Bachop and his sloop) were captured by a Connecticut vessel and her tender and taken into Charleston on 20 June 1778. Moultrie to Howe, 22 June 1778, Moultrie, *Memoirs*, I, 224.

41. Tonyn to Germain, No. 33, 9 March 1777, Case of John Harvey under Arrest for High Treason, and Jermyn Wright a refugee from the Province of Georgia, [8?] March 1777, C.O. 5/557.

42. Drayton to Germain, 30 January 1777, and enclosures, C.O. 5/557.

43. Tonyn to Germain, No. 33, 9 March 1777, General Account of extra Contingent Expences incurred for the service of His Majesty's Province of East Florida from the 25th June 1775 to the 24th June 1776, C.O. 5/557. John Proctor was paid £8 for apprehending John and Francis Caine on suspicion of treasonable correspondence with the Georgia rebels.

44. Tonyn to Germain, No. 33, 9 March 1777, C.O. 5/557.

45. Tonyn to Germain, No. 39, 8 May 1777, C.O. 5/557.

46. Tonyn to Germain, No. 33, 9 March 1777, C.O. 5/557; to Lord Amherst, 19 January 1778, C.O. 5/558.

47. Copy of a Letter from Mr. James Penman to Captain John Mowbray, Jerico, 20 May 1777, Extract of a Paragraph of a Letter from Captain John

Mowbray to . . . Tonyn enclosing Mr. Penman's Letter of 20 May 1777, and Tonyn to Germain, No. 50, 19 January 1778, C.O. 5/546.

48. Tonyn to Germain, No. 39, 8 May 1777, C.O. 5/557.

49. Tonyn to Germain, No. 39, 8 May 1777, to William Knox, 10 September 1777, C.O. 5/557. In the latter letter, Tonyn mentions that Penman and Mann also refused to join the militia.

50. Tonyn to the East Florida Council, n.d. [November–December 1777], Copy of a letter from His Excellency Governor Tonyn to Alexander Gray and Gray's answer, both dated 11 December 1777, Queries by the Council to Mr. Gray, and Queries by Mr. Drayton to Mr. Gray, n.d. [December 1777], Deposition by Robert Payne, 15 December 1777, Queries [by the Council] to Mr. Penman, 16 December 1777, Deposition of Lieut. Col. Robert Bissett, 16 December 1777, Copy of an Extract of a Paragraph of a Letter from His Excellency Governor Tonyn to Lord George Germain, 8 May 1777, and Deposition of William Godfrey, 20 December 1777, C.O. 5/546; Tonyn to Germain, No. 39, 8 May 1777, C.O. 5/557; Tonyn to Germain, No. 50, 19 January 1778, C.O. 5/546; Tonyn to William Knox, 10 September 1777, C.O. 5/557; Tonyn to Lord Amherst, 19 January 1778, C.O. 5/558; Tonyn to Clinton, Private, 27 May 1780, Headquarters Papers, No. 2768; Tonyn to Cornwallis, 12 July 1778 [sic], Cornwallis Papers.

51. Tonyn to Germain, No. 33, 9 March 1777, C.O. 5/557; Tonyn to Germain, No. 50, 19 January 1778, C.O. 5/558.

52. Tonyn to Germain, No. 33, 9 March 1777, to Germain, No. 36, 7 April 1777, C.O. 5/557.

53. Tonyn to Howe (extract), 28 April 1777, C.O. 5/94; East Florida Council Minutes, 31 April 1777, in Tonyn to Germain, No. 48, 26 December 1777, C.O. 5/558; Tonyn to Germain, No. 39, 8 May 1777, C.O. 5/557.

54. Tonyn to Germain, No. 39, 8 May 1777, C.O. 5/557.

55. Ibid.; Henry Yonge, Jr., to Tonyn, 8 May 1777, C.O. 5/557; Tonyn to Howe (extract), 28 April 1777, C.O. 5/94; East Florida Council Minutes, 31 April 1777, in Tonyn to Germain, No. 48, 26 December 1777, C.O. 5/558.

56. Tonyn to Germain, No. 39, 8 May 1777, C.O. 5/557; East Florida Council Minutes, 31 April 1777, in Tonyn to Germain, No. 48, 26 December 1777, C.O. 5/558. Also, not until the court had acted would Turnbull's servants be legally free, and enticing away a man's servant was almost as serious a crime as stealing his slave.

57. Tonyn to Germain, No. 39, 9 May 1777, Henry Yonge, Jr., to Tonyn, 8 May 1777, and Twenty Affidavits of Turnbull's servants, 7–20 May 1777, C.O. 5/557.

58. Tonyn to Germain, No. 39, 8 May 1777, C.O. 5/557. For Dr. Turnbull's version of these events, see Andrew Turnbull to Germain, 8 December 1777, Lord George Germain Papers, William L. Clements Library, University of Michigan, Ann Arbor, Michigan.

59. Tonyn to Stuart, 15 April, 16 June 1777, C.O. 5/557.

60. Stuart to Tonyn, 21 July 1777, C.O. 5/557.

61. The land ceded belonged to the Middle and Lower Towns; only the Overhill Cherokees signed the treaty. The war faction in the tribe, led by Dragging Canoe, had moved to Chickamauga Creek in March. Cotterill, *Southern Indians*, pp. 44–45.

62. Taitt to Tonyn, 23 May 1777, Taitt to Thomas Brown, 23 May 1777, C.O. 5/557; Stuart to Germain, Nos. 13 and 17, 23 January, 14 June 1777, C.O. 5/78.

63. Taitt to Tonyn, 23 May 1777, Taitt to Brown, 23 May 1777, C.O. 5/557; Stuart to Germain, No. 17, 14 June 1777, C.O. 5/78.

64. Taitt to Tonyn, 23 May 1777, Taitt to Brown, 23 May 1777, C.O. 5/557. See also 9 June 1777, "Minutes of the Executive Council," *GHQ*, XXXIV (March 1950), 19. St. James was Thomas Gray's uncle, his mother's brother. Examination of Thomas Gray, 2 October 1775, and Deposition of Thomas Gray, 10 October 1775, C.O. 5/555.

65. Taitt to Tonyn, 23 May 1777, Tonyn to Stuart, 16 June 1777, C.O. 5/557.

66. Tonyn to Taitt, Governor Tonyn's Talk to the Headmen and Warriors of the Creek Nation, both dated 12 June 1777, Tonyn to Stuart, 16 June 1777, and Deposition of John Williams, 30 May, 6 June 1777, C.O. 5/557.

67. Stuart to Germain, No. 16, 14 April 1777, C.O. 5/78; Stuart to Howe, 13 April 1777, C.O. 5/94; Stuart to Howe, 16 June 1777, Headquarters Papers, No. 586; Stuart to Tonyn, 21, 25 July 1777, C.O. 5/557; Stuart to Prevost, 24 July 1777, Headquarters Papers, No. 629; David Holmes to Stuart, 28 July 1777, C.O. 5/557.

68. Taitt to Tonyn, 23 May 1777, to Brown, 23 May 1777, and William McIntosh to Tonyn, 29 May 1777, C.O. 5/557; 6 June 1777, "Minutes of the Executive Council," *GHQ*, XXXIII (December 1949), 330; Corkran, *Creek Frontier*, p. 305, citing Laurens Papers, 17 June 1777; Taitt to Stuart, 5 June 1777, William McIntosh to Alexander Cameron, 6 July 1777, and Taitt to Stuart, 12 July 1777, C.O. 5/78; Stuart to Tonyn, 21 July 1777, C.O. 5/557; Taitt to Stuart, 13 August 1777, Stuart to Germain, No. 18, 22 August 1777, C.O. 5/78; Stuart to Howe, 23 August 1777, Headquarters Papers, No. 649; *Gazette of the State of South Carolina*, 14 July 1777.

On 4 April 1777 the Continental Congress had authorized Galphin to invite the Creek chiefs to Philadelphia. *JCC*, VII, 224.

69. William McIntosh to Alexander Cameron, 6 July 1777, C.O. 5/78; Stuart to Howe, 23 August 1777, Headquarters Papers, No. 649; Corkran, *Creek Frontier*, pp. 305–6, citing Laurens Papers, 17 June 1777.

70. Taitt to Stuart, 3, 13 August 1777, Stuart to Germain, No. 18, 22 August, C.O. 5/78; Stuart to Howe, 23 August 1777, Headquarters Papers, No. 649.

71. Taitt to Tonyn, 23 May 1777, to Brown, 23 May 1777, C.O. 5/557; Stuart to Germain, No. 17, 14 June 1777, C.O. 5/78; Stuart to Tonyn, 21 July 1777, Taitt to Tonyn, 24 August 1777, C.O. 5/557; Howe to Peter Chester, governor of West Florida, 12 July 1777, Howe to Stuart, 12 July 1777, Howe to Lt. Col. Stiell (of the 60th Regt. of Foot Commanding His Majesty's Troops

in West Florida), 13 July 1777, and Howe to Germain, No. 65, 15 July 1777, C.O. 5/94; Chester's Proclamation, 10 January 1778, C.O. 5/79.

72. Prevost to Howe, 14 June 1777, Headquarters Papers, No. 584.

73. Germain to Howe, No. 9, 19 April 1777, C.O. 5/94; Germain to Stuart, Nos. 4 and 5, 2 April, 11 October 1777, Prevost to Stuart, 14 June 1777, C.O. 5/78.

74. Germain to Tonyn, Nos. 4 and 5, 2 April, 2 July 1777, C.O. 5/557; Germain to Stuart, No. 4, 2 April 1777, C.O. 5/78.

75. Stuart to Prevost, 24 July 1777, Distance of Indian towns in the Southern District from St. Augustine and Pensacola, n.d., in Stuart to Germain, No. 18, 22 August 1777, C.O. 5/78. See also Taitt to Stuart, 12 July 1777, and Stuart to Tonyn, 21 July 1777, C.O. 5/557.

76. Conference of Stuart, Chester, and Stiell, 10 April 1777, Stuart to Howe, 13 April 1777, C.O. 5/94; Stuart to Germain, No. 17, 14 June 1777, C.O. 5/78.

77. Tonyn to Stuart, 16 June 1777, C.O. 5/557.

78. William McIntosh to Tonyn, 29 May 1777, C.O. 5/557; Taitt to Stuart, 5 June, 12 July 1777, Stuart to William Knox, 26 July 1777, and Taitt to Stuart, 3 August 1777, C.O. 5/78; Corkran, *Creek Frontier,* pp. 304, 307.

79. Taitt to Stuart, 3 August 1777, C.O. 5/78; Corkran, *Creek Frontier,* pp. 306–7. Taitt's "Murphy" is correctly identified as Galphin's agent McMurphy in Stuart to Germain, No. 18, 22 August 1777, C.O. 5/78; and Stuart to Howe, 23 August 1777, Headquarters Papers, No. 649.

80. Stuart to Germain, No. 18, 22 August 1777, C.O. 5/78; Stuart to Howe, 23 August 1777, Headquarters Papers, No. 649.

81. Stuart to Prevost, 24 July 1777, to Knox, 26 July 1777, C.O. 5/78.

82. *GHSC,* V, Pt. II, 59; Elbert to [McIntosh], 9 September 1777, *GHSC,* V, Pt. II, 54; John Lewis Gervais to Henry Laurens, 16 August 1777, Raymond Starr, ed., "Letters from John Lewis Gervais to Henry Laurens, 1777–1778," *SCHM,* LXVI (January 1965), 22; M'Call, *History,* pp. 316–17. M'Call mistakenly dates this action in 1776. See McIntosh to N. W. Jones, 15 February 1777, *GHSC,* XII, 41: "Capt. Dooley, who is going to Virginia on the recruiting Service requests he may be supplied with Continental Money for that purpose." Taitt said this Coweta party killed five men besides Dooley and took six rifles and five horses; one Coweta was killed and three wounded in this engagement. Taitt to Tonyn, 15 August 1777, C.O. 5/557.

83. Taitt to Tonyn, 15 August 1777, C.O. 5/557; Stuart to Germain, No. 20, 6 October 1777, C.O. 5/78; M'Call, *History,* p. 348; Corkran, *Creek Frontier,* p. 307.

84. Stuart to Germain, No. 20, 6 October 1777, C.O. 5/78.

85. Taitt to Tonyn, 15 August 1777, Tonyn to Stuart, 31 August 1777, C.O. 5/557; Elbert to McIntosh, 27 August 1777, *GHSC,* V, Pt. II, 53.

86. Taitt to Stuart, 13 August 1777, C.O. 5/78; Taitt to Tonyn, 15 August 1777, C.O. 5/557.

87. Tonyn to Germain, No. 42, 26 June 1777, C.O. 5/557; Tonyn to Germain, No. 49, 29 December 1777, C.O. 5/558; Forbes, *Sketches*, p. 24. One historian of the New Smyrna colony says that the only servants "freed by the Courts were a few who had been contracted for by their parents when under age. The Court of Sessions declared the others still legally bound to serve the proprietors of New Smyrna and ordered them back to the settlement." Carita [Corse] Doggett, *Dr. Andrew Turnbull and the New Smyrna Colony of Florida* (Jacksonville, Fla.: Drew Press, 1919), p. 163, citing Sackville Mss. America, 1755–7, No. 100, and also Lansdowne Mss. Vol. 66, pp. 725–27.

88. 5 August 1777, "Minutes of the Executive Council," *GHQ*, XXXIV (June 1950), 109; Clay to Laurens, 29 September 1777, *GHSC*, VIII, 40–41; Tonyn to Stuart, 31 August 1777, C.O. 5/557; East Florida Council Minutes, 21 August 1777, in Tonyn to Germain, No. 48, 26 December 1777, C.O. 5/558.

89. Elbert to McIntosh, 27 August 1777, *GHSC*, V, Pt. II, 53; Baker to McIntosh, 29 August 1777, Hawes, ed., *McIntosh Papers*, p. 18; M'Call, *History*, pp. 348–49.

Tonyn reported that the Cowkeeper led the Indians in this action and did not mention any whites being with them. He said eighteen rebels were killed. Tonyn to Stuart, 31 August 1777, C.O. 5/557.

It was probably this action concerning which a garbled report reached Cussita: Brown's Rangers and Indians had captured a fort on the Altamaha, killing ten rebels and wounding six in the process. David Holmes and Thomas Scott to Stuart, 19 October 1777, Headquarters Papers, No. 706.

90. Clay to Laurens, 29 September 1777, *GHSC*, VIII, 40.

91. Elbert to [McIntosh], 9 September 1777, *GHSC*, V, Pt. II, 54.

92. Clay to Laurens, 16, 21 October 1777, *GHSC*, VIII, 51, 54; 20 October 1777, *JCC*, IX, 823–24.

93. Stuart to Howe, 23 August, 6 October 1777, Headquarters Papers, Nos. 649 and 695; Stuart to Germain, No. 20, 6 October 1777, C.O. 5/79; Stuart to Germain, No. 20, 6 October 1777, C.O. 5/79; *Gazette of the State of South Carolina*, 14 July 1777; Corkran, *Creek Frontier*, p. 306; J[ames] H. O'Donnell, "Alexander McGillivray: Training for Leadership, 1777–1783," *GHQ*, LXIX (June 1965), 175.

Handsome Fellow's group may also have visited Savannah. 21, 23 July 1777, "Minutes of the Executive Council," *GHQ*, XXXIV (June 1950), 106–7; Colonel Elbert's Talk to the Creek Indians at Augusta, 13 August 1777, in Tonyn to Germain, No. 43, 18 September 1777, C.O. 5/557.

94. Wright to [Germain], 8 October 1777, *CRG*, XXXVIII, Pt. II, 127.

95. Elbert to [McIntosh], 9 September 1777, to Col. Stirk, 13 September 1777, to Howe, 17, 25 October, 16 November 1777, Headquarters, Savannah, 7, 17 November 1777, *GHSC*, V, Pt. II, 54, 58, 63, 68, 70, 72–73; Gervais to Laurens, 16 August 1777, Starr, ed., "Letters from Gervais to Laurens," *SCHM*, LXVI (January 1965), 21–22.

Dooley was allowed to resign his Continental commission; thereafter, he was a colonel in the Wilkes County (Georgia) militia. M'Call, *History*, pp. 471–72.

96. Colonel Elbert's talk to the Creek Indians at Augusta, 13 August 1777, in Tonyn to Germain, No. 43, 18 September 1777, C.O. 5/557; 12 August 1777, "Minutes of the Executive Council," *GHQ*, XXXIV (June 1950), 110.

97. Elbert to McIntosh, 27 August 1777, *GHSC*, V, Pt. II, 53; Corkran, *Creek Frontier*, p. 307; Colonel Elbert's Talk to the Creek Indians at Augusta, 13 August 1777, in Tonyn to Germain, No. 43, 18 September 1777, C.O. 5/557. This talk was made to "the Handsome Man," the Head Warrior of Tallassee, the "Handsome Mans Son, and Nephew," the Oakchoi Warrior, the Cussita Second Man, the Hallowing King "Lingee and his Son and the Palachocola Second Man."

98. Stuart to Germain, No. 20, 6 October 1777, C.O. 5/79; Stuart to Howe, 6 October 1777, Headquarters Papers, No. 695; Taitt to Germain, 6 August 1779, C.O. 5/80; Corkran, *Creek Frontier*, p. 307. Cameron had requested a "Book of Manual Exercise" and a drum to use in training the irregulars. Stuart to Cameron, 11 July 1777, C.O. 5/79.

99. McGillivray to Stuart, 21 September 1777, C.O. 5/79; McGillivray to Stuart, 25 September 1777, Headquarters Papers, No. 677; Stuart to Germain, No. 20, 6 October 1777, C.O. 5/79; Taitt to Germain, 6 August 1779, C.O. 5/80; Corkran, *Creek Frontier*, pp. 307–8.

100. Corkran, *Creek Frontier*, p. 308.

101. McGillivray to Stuart, 21 September 1777, C.O. 5/79; McGillivray to Stuart, 25 September 1777, Headquarters Papers, No. 677; Stuart to Germain, No. 20, 6 October 1777, C.O. 5/79; Stuart to Howe, 6 October 1777, Headquarters Papers, No. 695; Corkran, *Creek Frontier*, p. 308.

102. McGillivray to Stuart, 21 September 1777, C.O. 5/79; McGillivray to Stuart, 25 September 1777, Headquarters Papers, No. 677; Corkran, *Creek Frontier*, p. 308.

103. Stuart to Germain, [No. 21], 23 January 1778, C.O. 5/79; Stuart to Howe, 4 February 1778, Headquarters Papers, No. 925.

104. Corkran, *Creek Frontier*, p. 308.

105. 25 October 1777, *GHSC*, V, Pt. II, 67–68.

106. Corkran, *Creek Frontier*, p. 310.

107. Tonyn to Germain, No. 48, 26 December 1777, C.O. 5/558; Stuart to Germain, [No. 21], 23 January 1778, C.O. 5/79; Stuart to Howe, 4 February 1778, Headquarters Papers, No. 925. In this letter, Stuart indicates that Hycut (or Hycoat) was the leader of the neutral or pro-American faction among the Lower Creeks.

108. Pierre Colomb, "Memoirs of a Revolutionary Soldier," English translation, *The Collector*, LXIII (October 1950), 199–200.

109. Tonyn to Germain, No. 48, 26 December 1777, C.O. 5/558; Stuart to Germain, [No. 21], 23 January 1778, C.O. 5/79; Stuart to Howe, 4 February 1778, Headquarters Papers, No. 925; Corkran, *Creek Frontier*, p. 310.

110. David Holmes and Thomas Scott to Stuart, 19 October 1777, Headquarters Papers, No. 706.

111. M'Call, *History*, pp. 348–49; Jones, *Dead Towns*, p. 130.

112. This act, long thought to be lost, is printed in Heard Robertson, "Georgia's Banishment and Expulsion Act of September 16, 1777," *GHQ,* LV (Summer 1971), 278–81.

113. An act to amend and repeal part of "An Act for opening a land-office, and for the better settling and strengthening of this state," 16 September 1777, *CRG,* XIX, Pt. II, 70–72.

114. Elbert to Howe, 17, 25 October 1777, *GHSC,* V, Pt. II, 62–63, 68.

115. 10 October 1777, *GHSC,* V, Pt. II, 56; 20 October 1777, *JCC,* IX, 823; Washington to Howe, 13 January 1778, Fitzpatrick, ed., *Writings of Washington,* X, 301; Hawes, ed., *McIntosh Papers,* p. 20.

116. Writing from Midway on 29 August, Colonel John Baker referred to "my fort." Baker to McIntosh, 29 August 1777, Hawes, ed., *McIntosh Papers,* p. 19. He may have been referring to this fort in the Midway district. On the other hand, he could have meant a stockade around his own house in that district or even Fort Howe, the usual headquarters for the Light Horse.

117. Jones, *Dead Towns,* pp. 178–83, including a map on p. 180. Jones describes in detail the earthworks as they appeared in the last quarter of the nineteenth century.

118. Elbert to Captain Defau of the Artillery, 5 December 1777, *GHSC,* V, Pt. II, 76.

119. Savannah, 15 October, 26 November 1777, *GHSC,* V, Pt. II, 62, 73–74.

120. *CRG,* IX, Pt. II, 80–86. This measure may have been necessary for the completion of Fort Morris.

121. Elbert to Scriven, 10 October 1777, to McIntosh, Friday evening, [10 October 1777?], Savannah, 13 October 1777, and Elbert to Howe, 25 October 1777, *GHSC,* V, Pt. II, 56–57, 68.

122. 31 October, 7 November 1777, ibid., 69–70.

123. Elbert to Howe, 5, 6 December 1777, to Lt. Col. Hovenden, 6 December 1777, ibid., 77–78.

124. 3 November 1777, ibid., 69.

125. 8 December 1777, ibid., 78.

126. 8, 9 December 1777, ibid., 78.

127. *RRG,* I, 319–20.

128. Elbert to Scriven, 10 December 1777, *GHSC,* V, Pt. II, 57.

129. 13 October 1777, ibid., 57.

130. 19, 31 October, 3, 17, 20 November 1777, ibid., 64, 68–69, 73.

131. Elbert to Col. Scriven, 10 October, to George Randal, 16 October 1777, ibid., 56–57, 62.

132. 29, 31 October, 26 November 1777, ibid., 74.

133. 18 October 1777, ibid., 63. The post may or may not have been Fort Howe. Andrew Hays, William Asbey, and John Asbey, all of the Light Horse, were punished on 13 October by order of court-martial, but the records do not indicate whether or not the offense or the punishment were the same. 13 October 1777, ibid., 59.

134. Elbert to Marbury, 13 October 1777, *GHSC,* V, Pt. II, 58–59; Savannah, n.d. [14 or 15 October 1777], ibid., 60; Elbert to Howe, 15 October 1777,

ibid., 61–62. In this letter, Elbert declared that Marbury had been superseded in the Light Horse earlier by the Georgia legislature "without cause or even a hearing." Apparently, Marbury had been one of the first victims of the McIntosh-Gwinnett feud.

135. 3, 4 December 1777, *GHSC*, V, Pt. II, 75.

136. 9 December 1777, ibid., 78–79.

137. Elbert to Howe, 17 October, 17 November, 6 December 1777, ibid., 63, 72, 77; Elbert to Gen. Provost [*sic*], 27 November 1777, ibid., 74. The Floridians and the South Carolinians had exchanged some prisoners in October. *Gazette of the State of South Carolina*, 21 October 1777.

138. Elbert to Stirk, to Scriven, to Marbury, all dated 13 October 1777, and to Howe, 15 October 1777, *GHSC*, V, Pt. II, 58–59, 61.

139. Richard Eastmead to Mordecai Sheftall, 17 October 1777, ibid., 65.

140. Elbert to Scriven, After Orders, and Elbert to Lt. Col. Francis Harris, all dated 19 October 1777, ibid., 64–67. From the elaborate precautions taken to prevent the two forces mistaking each other for the enemy, it would seem the Georgia Continentals did not have—and probably never had—uniforms. Order of 5 November 1777, ibid., 70, indicates that the officers possessed uniforms, but did not always wear them.

141. Elbert to Col. [Joseph] Habersham, 5, 9 December 1777, *GHSC*, V, Pt. II, 79. Elbert said that the East Florida Rangers usually wore red cockades in their hats.

In the spring, Tonyn had reported that a group of loyalists on the Ogeechee had requested assistance from his Rangers. One officer from that region and a few men were preparing to go in May. Tonyn to Germain, Nos. 35 and 38, 2 April, 5 May 1777, C.O. 5/557. The invasion and subsequent activities during the summer would probably have delayed that party. A connection between the Ogeechee loyalists' plea and Moore's encampment is problematical.

142. 4, 8 December 1777, Elbert to Habersham, 5, 9 December 1777, and to Howe, 5 December 1777, *GHSC*, V, Pt. II, 75–79.

143. Elbert to Habersham, to Howe, both dated 5 December 1777, ibid., 76.

144. 23–31 December 1777, ibid., 80–85; 23–31 December 1777, Howe's Orderly Book, pp. 92–98.

145. Tonyn to William Knox, 10 September 1777, C.O. 5/557; Memorial of Lord William Campbell and others to Lord George Germain, [August 1777], C.O. 5/94.

146. Tonyn to William Knox, 10 September 1777, C.O. 5/557.

147. Germain to Howe, Separate, 20 May 1777, C.O. 5/94.

148. Tonyn to Germain, Private, 1 October 1777, C.O. 5/557.

149. Robert Catherwood to Robert Adair, Inspector General of British Hospitals (extract), 25 February 1777, Headquarters Papers, No. 412; Barrington to Howe, War Office, 21 May 1777, Headquarters Papers, No. 535; Robert Mackenzie to Lt. Col. George Clark, Barrack Master General, 8 October 1777, Headquarters Papers, No. 701; Robert Mackenzie to Prevost, 8 October 1777, Headquarters Papers, No. 702.

150. Prevost to Howe, 1 November 1777, Headquarters Papers, No. 728; Prevost to Tonyn, 20 December 1777, Headquarters Papers, No. 816; Tonyn to Prevost, 24 December 1777, Headquarters Papers, No. 821; Tonyn to Germain, No. 48, 26 December 1777, C.O. 5/558.

151. Germain to Tonyn, Separate, 2 April 1777, and No. 5, 2 July 1777, Tonyn to Germain, Separate, 10 September 1777, and Tonyn to Knox, 10 September 1777, C.O. 5/557.

152. Proceedings of His Majesty's Council Respecting Chief Justice Drayton, C.O. 5/558; East Florida Council Minutes, 19, 20 November, 11, 13, 15, 16 December 1777, C.O. 5/546. For Drayton's defense against Tonyn's charges, see Drayton to Knox, 18 December 1777, enclosing Drayton to Tonyn, 11 December 1778 [sic], C.O. 5/558.

153. Tonyn to Lord Amherst, 19 January 1778, C.O. 5/558. The memorial is in C.O. 5/558.

154. Tonyn to Germain, No. 49, 29 December 1777, to Knox, 26 September 1778, C.O. 5/558. See also Joseph Purcell to Tonyn, 4 May 1778, and Tonyn to Purcell, 27 May 1778, C.O. 5/558. For Turnbull's accusations against Tonyn, see Turnbull to Germain, 8 December 1777, Germain Papers.

155. Examination of John Augustus Ernest and deposition of Thomas Poplett, Siebert, *Loyalists*, II, 53.

156. After continued disputes with Governor Tonyn, both Drayton and Turnbull eventually retired to Charleston, South Carolina—Drayton in 1780 or earlier, and Turnbull, accompanied by James Penman, in 1781. There, both men were allowed to live in peace, without physical molestation, and to practice their professions (law and medicine) with honor and financial reward. Drayton died in 1790; Turnbull in 1792. Doggett, *Turnbull*, pp. 170–95; Panagopoulos, *New Smyrna*, pp. 159–72; Mowat, *East Florida*, pp. 104–6.

Chapter VI

1. Coleman, *Revolution in Georgia*, pp. 106, 141–46, 161–74, 178–85. Congress later vindicated Howe. 29 May 1778, *JCC*, XI, 553–54.

2. 13 February 1778, *JCC*, X, 159–65.

3. *GHSC*, V, Pt. II, 85–119; 1–8 January, 14, 17 February 1778, Howe's Orderly Book, pp. 98–102, 111–113.

4. 4, 16 January, 19, 12 March 1778, *GHSC*, V, Pt. II, 87, 91, 112, 114; 4 January, 10, 12 March 1778, Howe's Orderly Book, pp. 99–100, 120, 122.

5. 4, 7, 13, 19 January, 3, 12–14 February, 19, 21 March 1778, *GHSC*, V, Pt. II, 87–88, 90, 92, 98, 101–2, 117–18; 7 January, 3 February, 18, 21 March 1778, Howe's Orderly Book, pp. 101, 107–8, 125–27.

6. 19 January, 5, 9, 10 February 1778, *GHSC*, V, Pt. II, 92, 99–100; 18–19 January, 5, 10 February 1778, Howe's Orderly Book, pp. 102–3, 108, 110–11.

7. 20 January, 19 February 1778, *GHSC*, V, Pt. II, 93, 105; 20 January 1778, Howe's Orderly Book, p. 103.

8. 26 February, 6, 12–13, 16, 19 March 1778, *GHSC*, V, Pt. II, 108, 110, 113–17; 6, 13, 16, 19 March 1778, Howe's Orderly Book, pp. 118, 123, 125–26.

9. 21 January 1778, *GHSC*, V, Pt. II, 93; 21 January 1778, Howe's Orderly Book, p. 104.

10. 27 November 1777, *JCC*, IX, 971.

11. An Act for attainting such persons as are herein mentioned of high Treason, and for Confiscating their Estates, both real and personal to the use of this State; for establishing boards of Commissioners for the sale of such Estates, and for other purposes therein mentioned, 1 March 1778, *RRG*, I, 326–47; Elizabeth Lichtenstein Johnston, *Recollections of a Georgia Loyalist*, ed. by Arthur Wentworth Eaton (New York: M. F. Mansfield and Company, 1901), pp. 46–47.

12. Minutes of the Executive Council, 19 February 1778, *RRG*, II, 38–39.

13. 9 March 1778, ibid., 47–50.

14. Ibid., 50.

15. See Coleman, *Revolution in Georgia*, pp. 106–7.

16. Tonyn to Howe, 6 April 1778, Headquarters Papers, No. 1073.

17. Tonyn to Germain, No. 52, 20 March 1778, C.O. 5/558; Germain to Tonyn, No. 11, 10 February 1779, Tonyn to Germain, No. 84, 13 October 1779, enclosing copies of proceedings of Vice Admiralty Court, C.O. 5/559; Light Townsend Cummins, "Spanish Agents in North America during the Revolution, 1775–1779" (Ph.D. dissertation, Tulane University, 1977), pp. 262–65, 269.

18. Tonyn to Germain, Nos. 51, 52, and 55, 16 January, 20, 29 March 1778, C.O. 5/558; Prevost to Howe, 5 April 1778, Tonyn to Howe, 6 April 1778, Headquarters Papers, Nos. 1069 and 1073; "Memoir of Murray," Butler, *Royal Americans*, p. 303.

19. Brown to Tonyn, 19 February 1778, Tonyn to Howe, 24 February 1778, Headquarters Papers, Nos. 949 and 962; Forbes, *Sketches*, p. 88.

20. Prevost to Howe, 12 February 1778, Brown to Tonyn, 19 February 1778, Headquarters Papers, Nos. 941 and 949.

21. Minutes of the Executive Council, 9 February 1778, *RRG*, II, 26.

22. 16 February, 5, 13 March 1778, ibid., pp. 36, 46–47, 52.

23. 15 January, 17 February, 18, 25 March 1778, ibid., pp. 8, 37, 57, 63. Roberts escaped from the Sunbury jail.

24. 19 February, 13, 18 March 1778, ibid., pp. 39, 54–55, 57. Bonnell was ordered to appear before the Executive Council on 30 March; the records do not indicate he ever did so.

25. 23 February, 13 March 1778, ibid., pp. 41–43, 52–53; 14 March 1779, Howe's Orderly Book, pp. 123–24.

26. Brown to Tonyn, 13 March 1778, Tonyn to Germain, No. 52, 20 March 1778, C.O. 5/558; Prevost to Howe, 21 March 1778, Tonyn to Howe, 31 March 1778, Headquarters Papers, Nos. 1035 and 1058. Eight years later, Brown reminisced that "three-fourths of that detachment consisted of Indians" and that half the officers with him were killed or wounded in the assault on Fort Howe. Brown to David Ramsey, 25 December 1786, White, *Collec-*

tions, p. 617. Andrew Johnson became a captain in Brown's corps. He was killed during the second siege of Augusta, in 1781. Johnston, *Recollections,* pp. 13–14, 68–69.

27. Brown to Tonyn, 19 February 1778, Headquarters Papers, No. 949; Brown to Tonyn, 13 March 1778, C.O. 5/558.

28. Brown to Tonyn, 6, 16 April 1778, Headquarters Papers, Nos. 1070 and 1100; Brown to Prevost, 10 April 1778, Headquarters Papers, No. 1081. Not all this information was accurate.

29. Tonyn to Howe, 6 April 1778, Headquarters Papers, No. 1073.

30. Brown to Tonyn, 6, 16 April 1778, Headquarters Papers, Nos. 1070 and 1100; Brown to Prevost, 10 April 1778, Headquarters Papers, No. 1081.

31. Ibid.; Tonyn to Howe, 28 April, 15 May 1778, Headquarters Papers, Nos. 1133 and 1172; Minutes of the Executive Council, 7 April 1778, *RRG,* II, 72–73; Elbert to [Howe?], 14 April 1778, *GHSC,* V, Pt. II, 125–26; Howe to Moultrie, 7 April 1778, Moultrie to Howe, 10 April 1778, Rawlins Lowndes, president of South Carolina, to Moultrie, and Moultrie to Lowndes, both dated 14 April 1778, Lowndes to Moultrie, 6 April 1778, and Moultrie to Laurens, 19 April 1778, Moultrie, *Memoirs,* I, 203–8, II, 363–64, 367; Thomas Pinckney to Harriott Horry, his sister, 7 April 1778, Jack L. Cross, ed., "Letters of Thomas Pinckney, 1775–80," *SCHM,* LVIII (July 1957), 148–49.

32. Brown to Prevost, 10 April 1778, to Tonyn, 16 April 1778, Headquarters Papers, Nos. 1081 and 1100; David Fanning, *Col. David Fanning's Narrative of His Exploits and Adventures as a Loyalist of North Carolina in the American Revolution, Supplying Important Omissions in the Copy Published in the United States,* ed. by A. W. Savery (Toronto: reprint from the Canadian Magazine, 1908), p. 11.

33. Alexander Skinner to Stuart, extract, 20 April 1778, Prevost to Stuart, extract, 26 April 1778, C.O. 5/79; Brown to Cornwallis, 16 July 1780, Cornwallis Papers.

34. Prevost to Stuart, extract, 26 April 1778, C.O. 5/79; Prevost to Howe, 27 April 1778, Memorial of George Dawkins and Edward Lane on behalf of themselves and other Refugees from South Carolina, n.d., enclosed in Prevost to Howe, 27 April 1778, Headquarters Papers, Nos. 1124 and 1125; Tonyn to Germain, Nos. 54 and 55, 28, 29 April 1778, C.O. 5/558; Tonyn to Germain, No. 57, 15 May 1778, C.O. 5/558; Tonyn to Howe, 28 April, 15 May 1778, Headquarters Papers, Nos. 1133 and 1172; Brown to Cornwallis, 16 July 1780, Cornwallis Papers.

Murray says the South Carolinians were formed into two forty-man troops of rifle dragoons and four forty-five-man companies of infantry. "Memoir of Murray," in Butler, *Royal Americans,* p. 303.

35. Prevost to Clinton, 1 March 1779, C.O. 5/98; Clinton to Prevost, 28 March 1779, Headquarters Papers, No. 1863.

36. Corkran, *Creek Frontier,* p. 311, citing Patrick Carr to Galphin, 19 February 1778, Galphin Papers in Laurens Papers.

37. Stuart to Germain, No. 22, 5 March 1778, C.O. 5/79. The report that reached South Carolina indicated that five rebels were killed: a Captain

Walker and four others. Gervais to Laurens, 16 February 1778, Starr, ed., "Letters from Gervais to Laurens," *SCHM*, LXVI (January 1965), 26.

38. Minutes of the Executive Council, 25 March 1778, *RRG*, II, 62–63. The implication here is that no grants for land within the Ceded Lands had been issued since Governor Wright's departure.

39. Stuart to Germain, Nos. 22 and 24, 5 March, 2 May 1778, C.O. 5/79.

40. Taitt to Stuart, 7 April 1778, C.O. 5/79.

41. McIntosh to Stuart, 3 April 1778, Alexander Skinner to Stuart (extract), 20 April 1778, and Stuart to Germain, No. 23, 13 April 1778, C.O. 5/79.

42. Stuart to Germain, Nos. 24 and 25, 2, 19 May 1778, to William Knox, Private, 18 May 1778, C.O. 5/79; Stuart to Tonyn, 10 July 1778, C.O. 5/558.

43. Corkran, *Creek Frontier,* p. 313, citing Indian Talks to Galphin, 9 June 1778, Galphin Papers in Laurens Papers; Minutes of the Executive Council, 9 March, 3 April 1778, *RRG*, II, 51, 66–68. A Creek delegation had been in Savannah in February and had seen the rebels' preparations for the offensive against East Florida. Subayqué, a Lower Creek, delivered news of the planned attack to the Spanish at Havana on 18 March. The Spanish may have had contact with Cowkeeper in late winter or early spring. Mark F. Boyd and Jose Navarro Latorre, eds., "Spanish Interest in British Florida, and in the Progress of the American Revolution. I. Relations with the Spanish Faction of the Creek Indians," *FHQ*, XXXII (October 1953), 98, 120–23.

44. Corkran, *Creek Frontier,* pp. 313–14, citing Patrick Carr to Galphin, 10 June 1778, Galphin Papers in Laurens Papers.

45. "Account of the Loss of the Randolph as Given in a Letter from Rawlins Lowndes to Henry Laurens," *SCHGM*, X (July 1909), 173.

46. Minutes of the Executive Council, 3 April 1778, *RRG*, II, 70–71.

47. 7 April 1778, ibid., 72–73.

48. 13 April 1778, ibid., 73.

49. 13, 16 April 1778, ibid., 73, 75–77.

50. 7 April 1778, ibid., 72–73.

51. 9, 10, 12, 14 April 1778, *GHSC*, V, Pt. II, 123–25.

52. Thomas Jordan, Captain of the *Galatea,* to Tonyn, 6, 17 March, 16 April 1778, Tonyn to Germain, Nos. 52 and 54, 20 March, 28 April 1778, C.O. 5/558; Tonyn to Howe, 31 March 1778, Headquarters Papers, No. 1058.

53. April 1778, *GHSC*, V, Pt. II, 127; Elbert to Howe, 19 April 1778, Moultrie, *Memoirs,* II, 375–76.

54. 18 April 1778, *GHSC*, V, Pt. II, 127–28; Elbert to Howe, 19 April 1778, Moultrie, *Memoirs,* II, 365–76; Col. Charles C. Pinckney to Moultrie, 4 May 1778, Moultrie, *Memoirs,* II, 380; Tonyn to Germain, No. 54, 28 April 1778, Jordan to Tonyn, 19 April 1778, C.O. 5/558; East Florida Council Minutes, 2 May 1778, C.O. 5/559.

Murray states that the *Hinchinbrook* and the *Rebecca* ran aground in Raccoongut, and, when the ebb tide exposed their decks to rebel musketry, the crews were forced to take their boats. "Memoir of Murray," in Butler, *Royal Americans,* p. 303.

55. Tonyn to Germain, Nos. 54 and 57, 28 April, 15 May 1778, C.O. 5/558; East Florida Council Minutes, 25 April, 13, 20 May, 3, 8, 19 June, 8 July 1778, C.O. 5/559; Tonyn to Howe, 15 May 1778, Headquarters Papers, No. 1172.

56. Prevost to Howe, 21 February 1778, Tonyn to Howe, 24 February 1778, Headquarters Papers, Nos. 941 and 962.

57. Tonyn to Howe, 4 April 1778, Prevost to Howe, 5 April 1778, Headquarters Papers, Nos. 1068 and 1069. Recruits for the Second Battalion had been detained in St. Vincent, and General Prevost complained that the number of privates of the three companies of the Second Battalion in St. Augustine were insufficient to complete one company. Prevost to Howe, 2 March 1778, Headquarters Papers, No. 974.

58. Tonyn to Brown, 18 April 1778, Brown to Tonyn, [1 May 1778], C.O. 5/558; Tonyn to Howe, 1 May 1778, Headquarters Papers, No. 1143; Tonyn to Germain, Nos. 56 and 58, 1 May, 3 July 1778, C.O. 5/558.

59. Prevost to Glazier, 21 April 1778, C.O. 5/558.

60. East Florida Council Minutes, 13, 20, 25 May, 24 June, 8 July 1778, C.O. 5/559.

61. Tonyn to John Robinson, Secretary to the Lords of the Treasury, n.d., in Tonyn to Germain, No. 81, 25 September 1779, Return of Provisions in Store at St. Augustine at different Periods from the 25th December 1777 to the 25 December 1778, and A Calculation made by His Excellency Governor Tonyn of the time the several Species of Provisions mentioned in the annexed Return will serve 3000 men agreeable to the several Periods set down therein, C.O. 5/559; Prevost to Howe, 27 April, 7 May, 5, 13 June 1778, Headquarters Papers, Nos. 1124, 1156, 1215, and 1236.

62. Tonyn to Howe, 9 June 1778, Headquarters Papers, No. 1223; Brown to Cornwallis, 16 July 1780, Cornwallis Papers.

63. McIntosh to Stuart, 3 April 1778, C.O. 5/79; Tonyn to Howe, 6 April 1778, Headquarters Papers, No. 1073.

64. Taitt to Stuart, 13 April 1778, C.O. 5/79.

65. Stuart to Tonyn, 10 July 1778, C.O. 5/558.

66. Stuart to Germain, No. 27, 10 August 1778, C.O. 5/79.

67. Stuart to William Knox, Private, 18 May 1778, C.O. 5/79.

68. Corkran, *Creek Frontier*, p. 314, citing Henderson to Galphin, 12 June 1778, and Galphin to Laurens, 25 June 1778, both in Galphin Papers in Laurens Papers.

69. Stuart to Germain, Nos. 25, 26, and 27, 19 May, 3 June, 10 August 1778, C.O. 5/79; Tonyn to Germain, Nos. 55 and 57, 29 April, 15 May 1778, C.O. 5/558; Tonyn to Taitt, 16 May 1778, C.O. 5/80; Stuart to Tonyn, 10 July 1778, Tonyn to Stuart, 18 July 1778, C.O. 5/558.

70. Alexander Skinner to Stuart, extract, 20 April 1778, C.O. 5/79.

71. Tonyn to Howe, 28 April, 15 May, 3 June 1778, Headquarters Papers, Nos. 1133, 1172, and 1210; Tonyn to Stuart, 16 May 1778, C.O. 5/79; Tonyn to Taitt, 16 May 1778, C.O. 5/80.

72. Corkran, *Creek Frontier*, p. 314, citing Galphin to Laurens, 25 June 1778, Galphin Papers in Laurens Papers.

73. Prevost to Howe, 5, 13 June 1778, Headquarters Papers, Nos. 1215 and 1236.

74. Tonyn to Howe, 3 June 1778, Headquarters Papers, No. 1210.

75. Moultrie to Howe, 22 June 1778, Moultrie, *Memoirs*, I, 224; Wilbur H. Siebert, "Privateering in Florida Waters and Northward during the Revolution," *FHQ*, XXII (October 1943), 71–72. Three of the crew from *Tonyn's Revenge*, named Malcolm, McGuire, and Johnson, were convicted of desertion from a South Carolina regiment and were sentenced to death. Malcolm was shot, but the others were reprieved. *Gazette of the State of South Carolina*, 24 July 1778.

76. M'Call, *History*, p. 355. Brown had sent an intelligence-gathering party to the Midway settlement. Brown to Tonyn, 16 April 1778, Headquarters Papers, No. 1100. The two parties referred to by Brown and M'Call may have been one and the same.

77. Brown to Tonyn, 16 April 1778, Headquarters Papers, No. 1100.

78. John Faucheraud Grimké, "Journal of the Campaign to the Southward, May 9th to July 14th, 1778," *SCHGM*, XII (July 1911), 134.

79. Brown to Tonyn, 30 June 1778, C.O. 5/558.

80. Prevost to Clinton, 25 September 1778, Headquarters Papers, No. 1399. This was definitely James Moore; Sam Moore was still alive and active in 1782. See Minutes of the Executive Council, 22 October 1782, *RRG*, II, 385, and Carr to John Martin, governor of Georgia, 11 August 1782, "Letters of Patrick Carr," *GHQ*, I (December 1917), 338. After the attack on Fort McIntosh, Ensign Schodde seems to have been the only one of the regulars garrisoning East Florida who ever joined either Indians or Rangers for offensive operations in Georgia.

81. *GHSC*, V, Pt. II, 131; Howe to Moultrie, 12 June 1778, Moultrie, *Memoirs*, I, 233.

82. Undated proclamation in Tonyn to Germain, No. 57, 15 May 1778, C.O. 5/558.

83. Howe to Moultrie, 12 June 1778, Moultrie, *Memoirs*, I, 223.

84. *GHSC*, V, Pt. II, 136.

85. Moultrie to Laurens, 5 June 1778, Moultrie, *Memoirs*, I, 217; Howe to Moultrie, 14 April 1778, Moultrie to Laurens, 19 April 1778, to Lowndes, 18 April 1778, Major J. F. Grimkie, Howe's aide-de-camp, to Moultrie, 18 April 1778, and Moultrie to Howe, 24 April 1778, Moultrie, *Memoirs*, II, 367–69, 372, 377. See also Williamson to Col. James Williams, 19 April 1778, and Williamson to Capt. John Irvin, 21 April 1778, Gibbes, comp., *Documentary History*, II, 93–94.

86. Pinckney to Moultrie, 6 July 1778, Moultrie, *Memoirs*, I, 230.

87. 10 May 1778, Howe's Orderly Book, p. 132; *GHSC*, V, Pt. II, 138; Grimké, "Journal," *SCHGM*, XII (April 1911), 61.

88. Grimké, "Journal," *SCHGM*, XII (April 1911), 61.

89. Howe to Moultrie, 7 April 1778, Moultrie, *Memoirs*, I, 204. One participant stated that the total number of Continentals in the invasion force numbered 2,500. Colomb, "Memoirs," *Collector*, LXIII (October 1950), 200. A more reasonable figure for men and officers would be 1,200–1,300.

90. 25 May 1778, Howe's Orderly Book, pp. 146–47; 23 May 1778, *GHSC*, V, Pt. II, 153.

91. 28 May 1778, *GHSC*, V, Pt. II, 156.

92. Howe's Orderly Book, pp. 132–69; *GHSC*, V, II, 122–54; Grimké, "Journal," *SCHGM*, XII (April 1911), 67; Minutes of the Executive Council, 26 June 1778, *RRG*, II, 77–78.

93. Pinckney to Moultrie, 24 May 1778, Moultrie, *Memoirs*, I, 213–14; Howe to Moultrie, 3, 23 May 1778, Moultrie, *Memoirs*, II, 379–80, 382; Pinckney to Horry, 18 June 1778, Cross, ed., "Letters of Pinckney," *SCHM*, LVIII (July 1957), 155.

94. 15, 17, 22 May 1778, Howe's Orderly Book, pp. 137–38, 143; *GHSC*, V, Pt. II, 129, 140, 143, 145, 150; Grimké, "Journal," *SCHGM*, XII (April 1911), 62–63.

95. Deposition of James Mercer, in Grimkié to Moultrie, both dated 21 April 1778, Moultrie, *Memoirs*, II, 373–75.

96. 10, 13, 15, 18, 20–23 May 1778, Howe's Orderly Book, pp. 133, 135–46; *GHSC*, V, Pt. II, 129–30, 139, 141–42, 144, 146–47, 149–52; Grimké, "Journal," *SCHGM*, XII (April 1911), 64–67; Pinckney to Horry, 23 May 1778, Cross, ed., "Letters of Pinckney," *SCHM*, LVIII (July 1957), 149–150.

97. Pinckney to Moultrie, 24 May 1778, Moultrie, *Memoirs*, I, 212–14; Grimké, "Journal," *SCHGM*, XII (April 1911), 66.

98. Grimké, "Journal," *SCHGM*, XII (July 1911), 63.

99. Ibid., 67–68.

100. Howe to Moultrie, 23 May 1778, Pinckney to Moultrie, 24 May 1778, Moultrie, *Memoirs*, I, 212–14, II, 381–82.

101. 31 May, 1, 4 June 1778, Howe's Orderly Book, pp. 153–55, 157; *GHSC*, V, Pt. II, 154–63; Pinckney to Moultrie, 24 May 1778, Moultrie, *Memoirs*, I, 212; Grimké, "Journal," *SCHGM*, XII (July 1911), 118–21. This is the only one of the three Whig invasion forces for which the evidence is clear that personal servants accompanied officers and that some women went along on the campaign. See 5 June 1778, Howe's Orderly Book, p. 158, and *GHSC*, V, Pt. II, 161.

102. Grimké, "Journal," *SCHGM*, XII (July 1911), 119–21; Pinckney to Horry, 7 June 1778, Cross, ed., "Letters of Pinckney," *SCHGM*, LVIII (July 1959), 154.

103. Grimké, "Journal," *SCHGM*, XII (July 1911), 120–22, 126, 129; Clay to Howe, 26 June 1778, *GHSC*, VIII, 93–94.

104. 19 June 1778, Howe's Orderly Book, p. 165; 19 June 1778, *GHSC*, V, Pt. II, 166–67; Grimké, "Journal," *SCHGM*, XII (July 1911), 128; Pinckney to Horry, 18 June 1778, Cross, ed., "Letters of Pinckney," *SCHM*, LVIII (July 1957), 155; Joseph Habersham to Mrs. Isabella Habersham, 17 June 1778, U. B. Phillips, ed., "Some Letters of Joseph Habersham, 1775–1790," *GHQ*, X (June 1926), 148.

One French officer described the action of 17 June as a "general engagement" in which artillery was used. He also mentions an earlier but smaller skirmish with the Rangers and states that the Americans killed a few Rangers in the process of capturing Fort Tonyn. Colomb, "Memoirs," *Collector*, LXIII (October 1950), 200. This is not confirmed in other reports.

105. 21 June 1778, Howe's Orderly Book, p. 167; Grimké, "Journal," *SCHGM*, XII (April, July 1911), 60–69, 118–34, passim.

106. 21 June 1778, Howe's Orderly Book, p. 167; *GHSC*, V, Pt. II, 167–68.

107. Grimké, "Journal," *SCHGM*, XII (July 1911), 129–31.

108. Ibid. (July, October 1911), 132, 192; Pinckney to Horry, 1 July 1778, Cross, ed., "Letters of Pinckney," *SCHM*, LVIII (July 1957), 156–57. Pinckney refers to Brown as "the little Tory." Brown must have been diminutive in stature; that seems to be his only physical characteristic ever noted.

109. Grimké, "Journal," *SCHGM*, XII (July 1911), 133. Pinckney, writing from Fort Tonyn, says that Governor Houstoun "is encamped at our last Camp about 10 Miles higher up on this River." Pinckney to Horry, 1 July 1778, Cross, ed., "Letters of Pinckney," *SCHM*, LVIII (July 1957), 157.

110. Brown to Tonyn, 30 June 1778, C.O. 5/558; 29 June 1778, Howe's Orderly Book, pp. 171–72; Grimké, "Journal," *SCHGM*, XII (July 1911), 134; *Gazette of the State of South Carolina*, 15 July 1778; M'Call, *History*, pp. 357–59.

Murray says that Major Prevost took post at Alligator Creek Bridge "twenty-two miles from the Cowford with about 450 men. The enemy took a position at Niel Rain's 17 miles from Alligator Bridge." "Memoir of Murray," in Butler, *Royal Americans*, p. 304. One historian states that Alligator Bridge was "near the central position of today's Callahan, Florida and was only two miles north and ten miles west of where the 1777 battle of Thomas Creek occurred." Charles E. Bennett, *Southernmost Battlefields of the Revolution* ([Bailey's Crossroads, Va.: Blair, Inc., privately published], 1970), p. 28.

111. Pinckney to Horry, 1 July 1778, Cross, ed., "Letters of Pinckney," *SCHM*, LVIII (July 1957), 156.

112. Brown to Tonyn, 30 June 1778, C.O. 5/558; "Memoir of Murray," in Butler, *Royal Americans*, p. 304; Grimké, "Journal," *SCHGM*, XII (July 1911), 134. A British prisoner or deserter later told the Americans that McGirth was slightly wounded in the shoulder during the firing. Grimké, "Journal," *SCHGM*, XII (October 1911), 192.

113. "Memoir of Murray," in Butler, *Royal Americans*, pp. 304–5.

114. Ibid., p. 304.

115. Brown to Tonyn, 30 June 1778, Alexander Shaw, captain of the Fourth Battalion of the Sixtieth Regiment, to Tonyn, 1 July 1778, and Tonyn to Stuart, 3 July 1778, C.O. 5/558; Prevost to Clinton, 11 July 1778, Headquarters Papers, No. 1262; "Memoir of Murray," in Butler, *Royal Americans*, p. 305; Grimké, "Journal," *SCHGM*, XII (October 1911), 190–92; Pinckney to Horry, 1 July 1778, Cross, ed., "Letters of Pinckney," *SCHM*, LVIII (July 1957), 157; M'Call, *History*, pp. 358–59.

According to Shaw, Major Prevost thought he had been attacked by 900 rebels. M'Call says that 300 Georgia militia attacked the British and that three Americans were killed and nine wounded. Tonyn had a report that Screven had been wounded.

116. "Memoir of Murray," in Butler, *Royal Americans*, p. 306.

117. Ibid.; Prevost to Clinton, 11 July 1778, Headquarters Papers, No. 1262; Pinckney to Horry, 7 July 1778, Cross, ed., "Letters of Pinckney," *SCHM,* LVIII (July 1957), 158; Grimké, "Journal," *SCHGM,* XII (October 1911), 195.

118. 1 July 1778, Howe's Orderly Book, p. 172; *GHSC,* V, Pt. II, 173.

119. Howe to Moultrie, 5 July 1778, Moultrie, *Memoirs,* I, 229; Grimké, "Journal," *SCHGM,* XII (October 1911), 190–91.

120. Grimké, "Journal," *SCHGM,* XII (October 1911), 193; Colomb, "Memoirs," *Collector* (November 1950), 223.

121. Pinckney to Horry, 4 June [July] 1778, Cross, ed., "Letters of Pinckney," *SCHM,* LVIII (July 1957), 153; Habersham to Habersham, 5 July 1778, Phillips, ed., "Letters of Habersham," *GHQ,* X (June 1920), 149.

122. 4 July 1778, Howe's Orderly Book, pp. 175–76; *GHSC,* V, Pt. II, 174–75.

123. Pinckney to Moultrie, 6, 10 July 1778, Moultrie, *Memoirs,* I, 229, 231–32. Moultrie said that the Continental troops of Georgia and South Carolina, at first amounting to 1,100, had been reduced to 350 men who were fit for duty. Moultrie to Laurens, 26 July 1778, Moultrie, *Memoirs,* I, 238. One participant on the American side stated that the British killed 250 Americans, but more than 1,200 Americans died of illness during this campaign. Colomb, "Memoirs," *Collector,* LXIII (November 1950), 223.

124. Grimké, "Journal," *SCHGM,* XII (October 1911), 193.

125. Pinckney to Moultrie, 10 July 1778, Moultrie, *Memoirs,* I, 230–31; Grimké, "Journal," *SCHGM,* XII (October 1911), 196–98; Pinckney to Horry, 11 July 1778, Cross, ed., "Letters of Pinckney," *SCHM,* LVIII (July 1957), 159.

126. Grimké, "Journal," *SCHGM,* XII (October 1911), 198–200.

127. Tonyn to Germain, No. 58, 3 July 1778, C.O. 5/558; Howe to Elphinstone, 3 June 1778, Elphinstone to Prevost, 11 July 1778, Elphinstone to Mowbray, 16 July 1778, and Elphinstone to Lt. John Wright, 16 July 1778, Perrin, ed., *Keith Papers,* I, 101–6.

128. "At a council of war held in camp, at Fort Tonyn," 11 July 1778, Howe's Orderly Book, pp. 181–84.

129. Grimké, "Journal," *SCHGM,* XII (October 1911), 204–6.

130. 14 July 1778, Howe's Orderly Book, p. 185; 13, 14 July 1778, *GHSC,* V, Pt. II, 177–78; Grimké, "Journal," *SCHGM,* XII (October 1911), 206; Prevost to Prevost (extract), 10 July 1778, in Prevost to Elphinstone, 16 July 1778, Perrin, ed., *Keith Papers,* I, 107.

131. Pinckney to Moultrie, 23 July 1778, Moultrie, *Memoirs,* I, 237.

132. Andrew Williamson's Orders, . . . 25 July 1778, Gibbes, comp., *Documentary History,* II, 94–95.

Chapter VII

1. Prevost to Elphinstone, 16 July 1778, Tonyn to Elphinstone, 17 July 1778, Tonyn to Prevost, 17 July 1778, Prevost to Tonyn (extract), 17 July

1778, Shaw to Wright, 18 July 1778, Elphinstone to Tonyn, 19 July 1778, Elphinstone to Prevost, 19 July 1778, Prevost to Elphinstone, 20, 22 July, 9 August 1778, and Robert Cottonwood to Elphinstone, 9 August 1778, Perrin, ed., *Keith Papers*, I, 106–24; Tonyn to Stuart, 18 July 1778, to Germain, No. 59, 24 July 1778, C.O. 5/558; Tonyn to Clinton, 25 July 1778, Headquarters Papers, No. 1274.

2. Tonyn to Germain, Nos. 55, 57, and 58, 29 April, 15 May, 3 July 1778, C.O. 5/558; Tonyn to Taitt, 16 May 1778, C.O. 5/80; Tonyn to Stuart, 16 May 1778, C.O. 5/79; Tonyn to Stuart, 8 September 1778, C.O. 5/80; Germain to Stuart, No. 10, 5 August 1778, C.O. 5/79; Germain to Stuart, No. 10 [*sic*], 2 December 1778, C.O. 5/79.

3. Prevost to Stuart, 7 September 1778, Stuart to Germain, Nos. 29 and 30, 4 December 1778, 11 January 1779, and Stuart to William Knox, 9 October–26 November 1778, C.O. 5/80. Taitt later wrote to Germain denying Tonyn's charges. Taitt to Germain, 6 August 1779, C.O. 5/80. See also Commissioners for Indian Affairs to Germain, No. 6, 12 July 1779, enclosing Commissioners for Indian Affairs to Taitt and McIntosh, 30 May 1779, C.O. 5/81; Tonyn to Taitt, 28 July 1779, and Certificate by Maj. Gen. Augustine Prevost, 10 August 1779, in David Taitt to William Knox, 10 August 1779, Knox to Taitt, 25 October 1779, C.O. 5/80.

4. Howe to Prevost, to Tonyn, both dated 1 May 1778, Headquarters Papers, Nos. 1138 and 1140.

5. Germain to Howe, No. 25, 4 February 1778, Headquarters Papers, No. 919; Germain to Clinton, 4 February 1778, Clinton to Massey, Tonyn, and Prevost, Circular, 12 May 1778, to Prevost, 3 June 1778, to Tonyn, 3 June 1778, and Prevost to Clinton, 11 July 1778, Headquarters Papers, Nos. 917, 1167, 1203, 1204, and 1262.

6. Prevost to Tonyn, 20 July 1778, Tonyn to Prevost, 21 July 1778, and to Germain, Nos. 59 and 62, 24 July, 20 August 1778, C.O. 5/558.

7. Germain to Tonyn, Nos. 8 and 9, 1 July, 5 August 1778, C.O. 5/558.

8. Prevost's italics. Prevost to Clinton, 11 July 1778, Headquarters Papers, No. 1262. See also Prevost to Clinton, 25 September 1778, Headquarters Papers, No. 1399.

9. Prevost to Clinton, 25 September 1778, Headquarters Papers, No. 1399.

10. Prevost to Clinton, 11 July 1778, M. Prevost to Clinton, 31 July 1778, and Memorial of Major Mark Prevost to Clinton, 31 July 1778, Headquarters Papers, Nos. 1262, 1284, and 1285.

11. Clinton to Prevost, 3 June 1778, to Tonyn, 3 June 1778, to Prevost, 4 June 1778, List of persons recommended by Joseph Robinson for officers in the Carolina Royalists, 20 July 1778, and Prevost to Clinton, 26 July 1778, Headquarters Papers, Nos. 1203, 1204, 1211, 1269, and 1275. Several of the men named on Robinson's list had served under Colonel Brown.

12. Prevost to Clinton, 26 July, 25 September 1778, Headquarters Papers, Nos. 1275 and 1399.

13. Prevost to Clinton, 26 July 1778, Clinton to Prevost, 25 August 1778, Headquarters Papers, Nos. 1275, 1308, and 1309.

14. Prevost to Clinton, 30 September 1778, Tonyn to Clinton, 30 September 1778, Headquarters Papers, Nos. 1408 and 1409.

15. Clinton to Prevost, 3 June 1778, Prevost to Clinton, 11 July 1778, Clinton to Prevost and Tonyn, 9 September 1778, and Prevost to Clinton, 16 September 1778, Headquarters Papers, Nos. 1203, 1262, 1335, and 1361.

16. Grimké, "Journal," SCHGM, XII (July 1911), 134.

17. Tonyn to Germain, No. 59, 24 July 1778, C.O. 5/558; Tonyn to Clinton, 25 July 1778, Headquarters Papers, No. 1274.

18. Elphinstone to Wright, 19 August 1778, Perrin, ed., Keith Papers, I, 124–25; Tonyn to Germain, No. 62, 20 August 1778, C.O. 5/558; East Florida Council Minutes, 27 August 1778, C.O. 5/559.

19. Wright to Elphinstone, 26 August 1778, Elphinstone to Wright, 31 August 1778, Perrin, ed., Keith Papers, I, 130–34; Tonyn to Germain, No. 62, 20 August [sic] 1778, C.O. 5/558; Prevost to Clinton, 16 September 1778, Headquarters Papers, No. 1361. Tonyn reported that the George, an armed schooner in provincial service, was also wrecked.

20. Additional instructions, 26 January 1778, Germain to Tonyn, No. 6, 19 February 1778, C.O. 5/559. Tonyn wanted an act of Parliament or a court decision to annul the former grants in question; otherwise, he anticipated lawsuits by the patentees whose lands would be regranted to others. Tonyn to Germain, No. 61, 12 August 1778, C.O. 5/558.

21. Memorial . . . to Hillsborough, n.d., [endorsed "Received 12 February 1770"], C.O. 5/551; Grey Cooper, Treasury Chamber, to John Pownall, 6 April 1770, C.O. 5/551; East Florida Council Minutes, 26 December 1770, 20 April 1771, 21 December 1775, C.O. 5/571; Tonyn to Dartmouth, No. 32, 24 October 1775, C.O. 5/555.

The township was the area designated as "Bermudas." De Brahm, Report, p. 199 and Plate (Plan of St. Mary's Inlet) facing p. 220. This site was the same as "Hillsborough township," which had been briefly settled in 1772 by sixty people from the Isle of Skye. Mowat, East Florida, pp. 66, 126.

22. Tonyn to Elphinstone, 25 July 1778, Perrin, ed., Keith Papers, I, 121–22; Tonyn to Germain, Nos. 59 and 62, 24 July, 20 August 1778, C.O. 5/558; Tonyn to Prevost, 27 August 1778, 29 May 1779, C.O. 5/559; Tonyn to William Knox, 26 September 1778, C.O. 5/558.

23. East Florida Council Minutes, 6 December 1778, C.O. 5/559. The minutes do not specify the location of these grants, but it is reasonable to assume they were in the area Tonyn favored.

After the British conquered Georgia, Tonyn proposed to extend East Florida's territory northward to the Altamaha. He cited the historical precedent of Spanish claims and the right of conquest by the Rangers; also, Florida was loyal and deserved to be rewarded while Georgia was rebellious and should be punished. He pointed out that, if East Florida's northern boundary were the Altamaha River, then the port of St. Marys would be central to the province's productive lands. Germain was enthusiastic about settling the town and developing the port but not about moving the boundary. Tonyn to Germain, Nos. 78, 79, and 103, 1, 3 July 1779, 9 December 1780, C.O. 5/559 and 5/560; Germain to Tonyn, Nos. 11, 14, and 18, 10 February 1779, 19 January 1780, 4 June 1781, C.O. 5/559 and 5/560.

24. Minutes of the Executive Council, 25 August 1778, *RRG*, II, 85; 28 August, 19 September 1778, *GHSC*, V, Pt. II, 183, 185.

25. Minutes of the Executive Council, 5 August 1778, *RRG*, II, 83–84.

26. 31 August 1778, ibid., 96.

27. 5 August 1778, ibid., 84.

28. An Act for raising the sum of twelve thousand pounds for the use and support of the Government of the State of Georgia for the year one thousand seven hundred and seventy-eight, to be raised at certain Rates and after the Method therein mentioned, 4 May 1778, *CRG*, XIX, Pt. II, 87–99.

29. Minutes of the Executive Council, 7 July 1778, *RRG*, II, 79–80.

30. 25, 26 June, 23, 24 July 1778, *JCC*, XI, 656, 670–71, 712, 714–16; Nathaniel Scudder to the Speaker of the New Jersey Assembly, 13 July 1778, Josiah Bartlett to John Langdon, 13 July 1778, and Laurens to John Houstoun, 18 July [1778], Burnett, ed., *Letters*, III, 327, 329, 336; Edmund C. Burnett, "Edward Langworthy in the Continental Congress," *GHQ*, XII (September 1928), 220.

31. McGillivray to Stuart (extract), 6 August 1778, C.O. 5/79; Corkran, *Creek Frontier*, pp. 314–15.

32. Tonyn to Germain, Nos. 58 and 59, 3 July, 24 July 1778, C.O. 5/558; Tonyn to Clinton, 25 July 1778, Headquarters Papers, No. 1274.

33. Stuart to Tonyn, 11 July 1778, C.O. 5/558.

34. David Holmes Journal, July–September 1778, C.O. 5/80; Tonyn to Germain, No. 64, 25 September 1778, Stuart to Tonyn, 10 July 1778, and Tonyn to Stuart, 8 September 1778, C.O. 5/558. For the appointment of Holmes and Barnard, see Stuart to Tonyn, 10 July 1778, C.O. 5/558.

35. McGillivray to Stuart (extract), 6 August 1778, Stuart to Germain, No. 27, 10 August 1778, C.O. 5/79.

36. Corkran, *Creek Frontier*, p. 315, citing Galphin to J. L. Gervais, 10 August 1778, Gervais Papers in Laurens Papers.

37. Stuart to Germain, No. 27, 10 August 1778, C.O. 5/79; Taitt to Germain, 6 August 1779, C.O. 5/80.

38. David Holmes Journal, July–September 1778, C.O. 5/80; Tonyn to Germain, No. 64, 25 September 1778, C.O. 5/558.

39. McGillivray's Report of the State, Temper, and disposition of the Indians in the Upper Creek Nation, 1 September 1778, C.O. 5/80; Tonyn to Germain, No. 64, 26 September 1778, C.O. 5/558; Minutes of the Executive Council, 26 August 1778, *RRG*, II, 90; Clay to _____, 7 September 1778, *GHSC*, VIII, 109; John Houstoun, governor of Georgia, to Richard Caswell, governor of North Carolina, 20 September 1778, Houstoun to Laurens, 1 October 1778, quoted in Johnston, *Houstouns*, pp. 221–22; Corkran, *Creek Frontier*, p. 316, citing Colonel Williamson to Gervais, n.d., Gervais Papers in Laurens Papers.

40. 19, 28 August 1778, *GHSC*, V, Pt. II, 182–83.

41. Minutes of the Executive Council, 26 August, 18, 24 September 1778, *RRG*, II, 91, 102–5; Andrew Pickens to Capt. John Irvin, or in his absence to his lieutenant, 29 August 1778, Gibbes, comp., *Documentary History*, II, 96; Gervais to Laurens, 21 September 1778, Starr, ed., "Letters from Gervais to Laurens," *SCHM*, LXVI (January 1965), 36.

42. McGillivray's Report of the State, temper, and disposition of the Indians in the upper Creek Nation, 1 September 1778, C.O. 5/78; McGillivray to Stuart, 20 November 1778, Stuart to Knox, 9 October–26 November 1778, C.O. 5/80.

43. Minutes of the Executive Council, 31 August 1778, 29 September 1778, *RRG*, II, 97, 106–7.

44. 26, 31 August 1778, ibid., 89–90, 94–95.

45. Corkran, *Creek Frontier*, p. 316, citing Tallassee King's Talk to Galphin, 10 October 1778, Galphin Papers in Laurens Papers.

46. Ibid., citing Talk of Patuoy Mico to Galphin, 4 November 1778, Galphin Papers in Laurens Papers.

47. Ibid., pp. 316–17, citing Patrick Carr to Galphin, 4 November 1778, Galphin Papers in Laurens Papers.

48. Timothy Barnard to Stuart, 9 November 1778, C.O. 5/80; Corkran, *Creek Frontier*, pp. 316–17, citing Carr to Galphin, 4 November 1778, Galphin Papers in Laurens Papers. The main Spanish enthusiasts were the Yuchi-speaking element in the Tallahassee-Apalachee area. Wright, *Florida*, pp. 68–69.

49. Barnard to Stuart, 9 November 1778, C.O. 5/80.

50. Ibid.; Stuart to Knox, 9 October–26 November 1778, to Germain, No. 29, 4 December 1778, C.O. 5/80.

51. Corkran, *Creek Frontier*, p. 317, citing Galphin to Laurens, 11 November, 29 December 1778, Galphin Papers in Laurens Papers.

52. Clay to Howe, 20 June 1778, Clay to Laurens, 9 September 1778, *GHSC*, VIII, 86–87, 103–5; Laurens to Houstoun, 18 July [1778], Burnett, ed., *Letters*, III, 336–37; 21 September 1778, *JCC*, XII, 937–39.

53. Laurens to John Rutledge, 3 June 1778, to John Houstoun, 27 August 1778, Burnett, ed., *Letters*, III, 273, 384–85.

54. Clay to Laurens, 9 September 1778, to _____, 7 September 1778, *GHSC*, VIII, 106, 109; Gervais to Laurens, 21 September 1778, Starr, ed., "Letters from Gervais to Laurens," *SCHM*, LXVI (January 1965), 35.

55. Houstoun to Laurens, 1 October 1778, Johnston, *Houstouns*, p. 22. A French officer who was serving with the Georgia Continentals described an attack, presumably by the East Florida Rangers, upon "a kind of redoubt" on the Altamaha, possibly a small fortification downstream from Darien, and stated that "the general" told him to abandon the position rather than risk a single man. Colomb, "Memoirs," *Collector*, LXIII (October 1950), 201.

56. Clay to Laurens, 9 September 1778, to _____, 7 September 1778, *GHSC*, VIII, 106, 109; Gervais to Laurens, 9, 21 September 1778, Starr, ed., "Letters from Gervais to Laurens," *SCHM*, LXVI (January 1965), 34–37. See also Christopher Gadsden to William Henry Drayton, 1, 15 June 1778,

Christopher Gadsden, *The Writings of Christopher Gadsden, 1746–1805,* ed. by Richard Walsh (Columbia: University of South Carolina Press, 1966), pp. 126–27, 134.

57. Moultrie to Laurens, 26 July 1778, Moultrie, *Memoirs,* I, 238–40. The Marquis de Bretigny also presented a memorial concerning the conquest of St. Augustine to the Continental Congress. 26 August 1778, *JCC,* XI, 837.

58. 2, 10 November 1778, *JCC,* XII, 1091, 1116–21; Cornelius Harnett to Caswell, 10 November 1778, South Carolina Delegates to Lowndes, 14 November 1778, Burnett, ed., *Letters,* III, 487, 494.

59. Tonyn to Germain, No. 64, 25 September 1778, C.O. 5/558; Tonyn to Clinton, 26 September 1778, Headquarters Papers, No. 1404.

60. 25 September 1778, *JCC,* XII, 951.

61. Harnett to Caswell, 26 September, 28 November 1778, Burnett, ed., *Letters,* III, 426, 512; Gadsden to Drayton, 1 June, 4 July, 15 August, 9, 22 September 1778, to Thomas Heyward, 16 August 1778, Gadsden, *Writings,* pp. 128–29, 134–44, 147, 150–51, 152–54, 148–49; L. Van Loan Naisawald, "Major General Howe's Activities in South Carolina and Georgia, 1776–1779," *GHQ,* XXV (March 1951), 29.

62. Howe to Laurens, 9 October 1778, to President of Congress, 24 November 1778, *NCSR,* XV, 766–67; XIII, 498–99.

63. 7 October 1778, *GHSC,* V, Pt. II, 186–87; Minutes of the Executive Council, 7, 11, 19 October 1778, *RRG,* II, 107–8, 110–11.

64. 17, 24 October 1778, *GHSC,* V, Pt. II, 187–88; Minutes of the Executive Council, 27 October, 4 November, 2 December 1778, *RRG,* II, 113–16, 118, 122–23.

65. 11 November 1778, *GHSC,* V, Pt. II, 191.

66. An Act to alter and amend a clause or clauses of an act entitled "An act for attainting such person as are therein named of high treason, for confiscating their estates, both real and personal to the use of this state, for establishing boards of commissioners for the sale of such estates, and for other purposes therein mentioned," and for the better and more effectual carrying the other purposes of the said act into execution, 30 October 1778, *CRG,* XIX, Pt. II, 100–103.

67. An act to compel non-residents to return within a certain time or in default thereof, that their estates be confiscated, and for confiscating the estate of William Knox, Esq. formerly provost marshal, of the then province, now state of Georgia, 15 November 1778, ibid., 126–27.

68. 15 November 1778, ibid., 103–26.

69. Minutes of the Executive Council, 19 November 1778, *RRG,* II, 119.

70. All these points had been touched upon in earlier memorials, but Georgia's Governor Wright and Lieutenant Governor Graham submitted yet another memorial to Germain on 17 July 1778. C.O. 5/116. They had not been informed of the British plans for the immediate future. See also Tonyn to Clinton, 6 April 1778, Clinton Papers.

71. Germain to Clinton, "Most Secret," 8 March 1778, Headquarters Papers, No. 996; George III to Clinton, Secret Instructions, 21 March 1778,

Headquarters Papers, No. 1032; Germain to Clinton, No. 10, 5 August 1778, C.O. 5/96; Precis of Orders, *Manuscripts of Mrs. Stopford-Sackville*, p. 151.

72. Prevost to Howe, 18 March 1778, Headquarters Papers, No. 1025; Moses Kirkland to Clinton, 13 October 1778, to His Majesty's Commissioners, 21 October 1778, Clinton Papers.

73. Commissioners for Quieting Disorders to Germain, No. 22, Secret, 16 November 1778, Stevens, ed., *Facsimiles*, XII, No. 1216; His Majesty's Commissioners' (Carlisle, Clinton, Eden) Draft of Commission to Lieut. Col. Archibald Campbell, November 1778, and Peace Commissioners' Secret Instructions to Lieut. Col. Archibald Campbell, ca. 3 November 1778, ibid., Nos. 1202 and 1205.

74. Clinton to Germain, Nos. 24 and 26, 25 October, 8 November 1778, C.O. 5/96; James Gambier, Rear Admiral of the Blue etc., to Captain Hyde Parker, Secret Instructions, 2 November 1778, Stevens, ed., *Facsimiles*, XII, No. 1203; S. D. H_____n to _____, 16 January 1779, Pettengill, trans., *Letters*, pp. 197–98.

75. Clinton to Prevost, 20 October 1778, to Tonyn, 20 October 1778, to Stuart, 27 October 1778, and to Lieut. Colonel Archibald Campbell, 71st Regt., 8 November 1778, Headquarters Papers, Nos. 1461, 1462, 1492, and 1535; Clinton to Germain, No. 24, 25 November 1778, Headquarters Papers, No. 1477. Clinton's orders, dated 20 October, reached St. Augustine on 27 November. Prevost to Germain, 18 January 1779, C.O. 5/182.

76. Laurens to Washington, 23 September 1778, to Patrick Henry, 26 September 1778, Burnett, ed., *Letters*, III, 422–23, 425; Laurens to Caswell, 26 September 1778, *NCSR*, XIII, 234–36; Gadsden to Drayton, 14 October 1778, Gadsden, *Writings*, p. 160.

77. 25 September, 17 October 1778, *JCC*, XII, 949–50, 1021; John Mathews to Thomas Bee, 17–18 October 1778, John Penn to Caswell, 18 October 1778, Burnett, ed., *Letters*, III, 454, 455; Minutes of the meeting of the North Carolina Council, 7 November 1778, *NCSR*, XXII, 935–37; Caswell to Lowndes, 30 October, 5 November 1778, to General Griffith Rutherford, 7, 13 November 1778, to Peter Mallett, 8 November 1778, and Gen. W. Skinner to Caswell and Col. Ant. Lytle to Caswell, both dated 13 November 1778, *NCSR*, XIII, 258, 265, 267–69, 276–77, 269–70, 274, 276.

78. 2, 10 November 1778, *JCC*, XII, 1091, 1116–21; Harnett to Caswell, 10 November 1778, Laurens to Caswell, 14 November 1778, *NCSR*, XIII, 271, 279; Laurens to Washington, 20 November 1778, Burnett, ed., *Letters*, III, 500.

79. Moultrie to Lowndes, 14 November 1778, Moultrie, *Memoirs*, I, 240–42; 11–14 November 1778, "Order Book of John Faucheraud Grimké, August 1778 to May 1780," *SCHGM*, XIII (July 1912), 150–51; *Gazette of the State of South Carolina*, 11, 25 November 1778.

80. Minutes of the Executive Council, 19 November 1778, *RRG*, II, 119–20.

81. Brown to David Ramsay, 25 December 1786, White, *Collections*, p. 615. Tonyn implied that Fuser was really supposed to take Fort Morris, at

Sunbury, not merely to serve as a feint to draw the Georgians' attention away from Prevost's advancing troops. Tonyn to Germain, Separate, 19 December 1778, No. 67, 9 January 1779, C.O. 5/559. Because of the low state of the stores in St. Augustine at that time, however, it would seem that foraging was the priority and conquest was a secondary consideration. See Return of Provisions in Store at St. Augustine at different Periods from the 25th December 1777 to the 25th December 1778, and a Calculation made by His Excellency Governor Tonyn of the time the several Species of Provisions mentioned in the Annexed Return will serve 3000 men agreeable to the several Periods set down therein, C.O. 5/559. See also Clinton to John Robinson, 16 November 1778, Headquarters Papers, No. 1567.

82. Jones, *Dead Towns*, p. 185; M'Call, *History*, p. 365. Murray says that the force numbered 750 men. "Memoir of Murray," in Butler, *Royal Americans*, p. 306. That figure would include the detachment under Fuser that went by sea. Murray does not mention any Indians on this expedition, and Tonyn later implied that none were involved. Tonyn to Campbell, 23 December 1778, C.O. 5/559.

83. M'Call, *History*, pp. 364–66; Jones, *Dead Towns*, pp. 185–86.

84. Jones, *Dead Towns*, p. 186.

85. Ibid.; M'Call, *History*, p. 366.

86. Ibid.

87. Brown to Ramsay, 25 December 1786, White, *Collections*, pp. 615–16; Tonyn to Germain, Separate, 19 December 1778, C.O. 5/559; Brown to Cornwallis, 16 July 1780, Cornwallis Papers; M'Call, *History*, pp. 366–68; Jones, *Dead Towns*, pp. 186–87.

88. M'Call, *History*, pp. 367–68. See also Colomb, "Memoir," *Collector*, LXIII (October 1950), 201.

89. M'Call, *History*, p. 368.

90. White to J. Prevost, 20 November 1778, J. Prevost to White, 22 November 1778, White, *Collections*, pp. 524–25, cited as being copied from the *London Remembrancer*.

91. Jones, *Dead Towns*, p. 187; Jones, *History of Georgia*, II, 306–7, n. 2. Note the discrepancies in dates of various accounts of all the actions between 19 and 24 November 1778.

92. Houstoun to Laurens, 25 November 1778, quoted in Johnston, *Houstouns*, p. 222; Colomb, "Memoirs," *Collector*, LXIII (October 1950), 201; *Gazette of the State of South Carolina*, 25 November 1778; *South Carolina and American General Gazette*, 3, 10 December 1778; M'Call, *History*, pp. 368–69; Jones, *Dead Towns*, pp. 188–89.

93. "Memoir of Murray," in Butler, *Royal Americans*, p. 308. The question remains: who were the purchasers?

94. Tonyn to Taitt, to McIntosh, and to Stuart, all dated 20 December 1778, C.O. 5/559.

95. Howe to Moultrie, 27 November 1778, Moultrie to Howe, 28 November 1778, Moultrie, *Memoirs*, I, 243–46; 22–30 November 1778, "Order Book of Grimké," *SCHGM*, XIII (October 1912), 205–8.

96. Moultrie, *Memoirs*, I, 189; Howe to Moultrie, 8 December 1778, Moultrie, *Memoirs*, I, 247; White, *Collections*, pp. 525–26; M'Call, *History*, pp. 369, 371; Jones, *Dead Towns*, pp. 189–93; Jones, *History of Georgia*, II, 308–11; "Memoir of Murray," in Butler, *Royal Americans*, pp. 306–8. According to Murray, Fuser's forces consisted of 250 men from the Fourth Battalion of the Sixtieth Regiment and some of Brown's Rangers, and Colonel Fuser landed at Colonel's Bluff on 24 November.

97. Moultrie to Howe, 28 November 1778, Lowndes to Moultrie, 29 November 1778, Moultrie, *Memoirs*, I, 245–46; *Rivington's Gazette*, 20 January 1779, *Pennsylvania Packett*, 30 January 1779, both quoted in Frank Moore, ed., *Diary of the American Revolution: From Newspapers and Original Documents* (2 vols., New York: Charles Scribner, 1860), II, 107, 108–9.

98. Howe to Moultrie, 8 December 1778, enclosing Deposition of William Haslam, a mariner, 6 December 1778, Moultrie, *Memoirs*, I, 247–51.

99. Hall went to South Carolina; Walton did not. *Trial of Howe*, p. 250.

100. Howe to Moultrie, 8 December 1778, Moultrie, *Memoirs*, I, 247–49; Maj. Gen. Benjamin Lincoln to Caswell, 22 December 1778, *NCSR*, XIII, 332.

101. Clinton to Germain, Nos. 27 and 28, 18, 24 November 1778, C.O. 5/96; *Gazette of the State of South Carolina*, 30 December 1778; S. D. H———n to ———, 16 January 1779, Pettengill, trans., *Letters*, pp. 199–200. The *Neptune*, the ship in which William Haslam (the deserter who gave information to the Georgians) sailed, parted with her anchor in the gale and put out to sea. Therefore, she reached Tybee well ahead of the fleet. Deposition of William Haslam, 6 December 1778, Moultrie, *Memoirs*, I, 249–50; *Gazette of the State of South Carolina*, 23 December 1778.

102. Isaac Huger, Brigadier General, to Moultrie, 28 December 1778, Moultrie, *Memoirs*, I, 251–52; General Howe's Order of Battle at Savannah, 29 December 1778, Moultrie, *Memoirs*, I, 252–53. M'Call says Howe's Continentals numbered 672. He gives a good description of the city's site. M'Call, *History*, pp. 375, 377.

103. Moultrie, *Memoirs*, I, 255–56.

104. Tonyn to Germain, Separate, 19 December 1778, to Prevost, 19 December 1778, C.O. 5/559.

105. Campbell to Tonyn, 5 December 1778, Commodore Hyde Parker to Tonyn, 5 December 1778, C.O. 5/559.

106. Tonyn to Parker, 27 December 1778, to Germain, No. 72, 28 March 1779, C.O. 5/559. Months later, East Florida's inhabitants whose boats had been used by the troops were still begging for the return of their river craft or some compensation. Tonyn to Prevost, 11 February 1779, Prevost to Tonyn, 2 March 1779, and Tonyn to Prevost, 29 May 1779, C.O. 5/559.

107. Tonyn to Campbell, 23 December 1778, to Germain, No. 72, 28 March 1779, C.O. 5/559.

108. Tonyn to Prevost, 19 December 1778, to Stuart, 20 December 1778, to Taitt and McIntosh, 20 December 1778, to Campbell, 23 December 1778, and to Germain, No. 72, 28 March 1779, C.O. 5/559.

109. Stuart to Principal Chiefs, Head Men, and the Warriors of the Upper and Lower Creek Nation, 1 February 1779, Stuart's Instructions to Taitt, 1 February 1779, Stuart to Lt. Col. Archibald Campbell, 9 February 1779, Cameron and Charles Stuart to Germaine [sic], 10 April 1779, Taitt to Germain, 6 August 1779, and Charles Shaw to Germain, 7 August 1779, C.O. 5/80.

Stuart had been very ill during most of 1778, and he died on 21 March 1779. Tonyn to Stuart, 18 July 1778, C.O. 5/558; Stuart to Germain, No. 29, 4 December 1778, Cameron and Charles Stuart to Germain, 26 March 1779, C.O. 5/80; Tonyn to Knox, 29 March 1779, to Germain, Separate, 21 April 1779, C.O. 5/559.

110. Tonyn to Prevost, 19 December 1778, 2 February 1779, to Stuart, 20 December 1778, to Germain, No. 72, 28 March 1779, and to Knox, 29 March 1779, C.O. 5/559; ———— to General Lincoln, February 1799 [sic], Moultrie, Memoirs, I, 334.

111. Campbell to Germain, 16 January 1779, Return of Prisoners of War taken in Action 29 December 1778 by His Majesty's Forces under the Command of Lieutt Colonel Archibald Campbell of the 71st Regiment, Return of the Killed, Wounded, and Missing of the detachment of His Majesty's Forces Under the Command of Lieut. Coll. Archibald Campbell in the Action of the 29 december 1778, and Return of Iron and Brass Ordnance and Stores belong to the Rebels taken at Savannah in Georgia by Order of Lieutenant Colonel Archibald Campbell Commanding a Detachment of the Royal Army, 8 January 1779, C.O. 5/182; Campbell to Clinton, 16 January 1779, Headquarters Papers, No. 1679; Campbell to Earl of Carlisle, 19 January 1779, Stevens, ed., Facsimiles, I, No. 113; Captain Hyde Parker to Philip Stephens, 14–15 January 1779, Stevens, ed., Facsimiles, XII, No. 1246; S. D. H————n to ————, 16 January 1779, Pettengill, trans., Letters, pp. 199–202; 24–30 December 1778, "Order Book of Grimké," SCHGM, XIV (January 1913), 45–57; Colomb, "Memoirs," Collector, LXIII, (November 1950), 224–25; Johnston, Recollections, pp. 48–49; Trial of Howe, pp. 213–311; New Jersey Gazette, 10 February 1779, in Moore, ed., Diary of Revolution, II, 115–16; M'Call, History, pp. 377–80; Jones, History of Georgia, II, 315–22; Alexander A. Lawrence, "General Robert Howe and the British Capture of Savannah in 1778," GHQ, XXXVI (December 1952), 303–27.

112. Trial of Howe, pp. 213–311; 24 January 1782, JCC, XXII, 46.

113. Return of the Troops arrived from East Florida under the Command of Brig. General Prevost, 17 January 1779, C.O. 5/182; "Memoir of Murray," in Butler, Royal Americans, pp. 308–9; Butler, Royal Americans, p. 210.

114. Prevost to Germain, 18 January 1779, C.O. 5/182; "Memoir of Murray," in Butler, Royal Americans, p. 309.

115. "Memoir of Murray," in Butler, Royal Americans, pp. 309–10.

116. Ibid., p. 310; Prevost to Clinton, 19 January 1779, Headquarters Papers, No. 1691.

117. Moultrie to Col. C. C. Pinckney (extract), 10 January 1779, Moultrie, *Memoirs*, I, 259.

118. "Memoir of Murray," in Butler, *Royal Americans*, p. 310; Reminiscences of Captain Roderick McIntosh, . . . in John Couper to a gentleman of Georgia, 16 April 1842, White, *Collections*, pp. 472–74.

119. Prevost to Germain, 18 January 1779, C.O. 5/182; Prevost to Clinton, 19 January 1779, Headquarters Papers, No. 1691; Return of the Garrison in Fort Morris commanded by Major Lane the 10th January 1779, C.O. 5/182; Return of Brass and Iron Ordnance Stores in Fort Morris now Fort George at Sunbury in Georgia 13 January 1779, C.O. 5/182; "Memoir of Murray," in Butler, *Royal Americans*, p. 310. For a list of the names of the Sunbury garrison, see Paul McIlvaine, *The Dead Towns of Sunbury, Ga., and Dorchester, S.C.* (2d ed., Hendersonville, N.C.: privately published, 1971), pp. 47–49.

120. Prevost to Germain, 18 January 1779, C.O. 5/182; Prevost to Clinton, 19 January 1779, Headquarters Papers, No. 1691; Parker to Stevens, 14–15 January 1779, Stevens, ed., *Facsimiles*, XII, No. 1246; "Memoir of Murray," in Butler, *Royal Americans*, p. 311. M'Call says that 4 Americans were killed, 7 wounded, and 212 taken prisoner (officers and men, Continentals and militia); 24 pieces of artillery, ammunition, and provisions were also captured. Lane was later court-martialed and dismissed from the service for having disobeyed orders. M'Call, *History*, pp. 380–82.

121. Prevost to Clinton, 19 January 1779, Headquarters Papers, No. 1691; S. D. H_____n to _____, 16 January 1779, Pettengill, trans., *Letters*, pp. 203–4.

122. Campbell to William Eden, 19 January 1779, Stevens, ed., *Facsimiles*, XII, No. 1252.

123. Tonyn to Germain, Nos. 78, 87, and 91, 1 July, 27 November 1779, 5 February 1780, C.O. 5/559.

Chapter VIII

1. For the thesis that Stuart initially followed a nonaggressive policy, see Philip M. Hamer, "John Stuart's Indian Policy during the Early Months of the American Revolution," *Mississippi Valley Historical Review*, XVII (December 1930), 351–66. For the opposite interpretation, see Wright, *Florida*, pp. 32–33, 156–57, n. 3.

2. Tonyn to Clinton, 8 June 1776, C.O. 5/556.

3. Tonyn to Dartmouth, Private, No. 18, 18 December 1775, to Clinton, No. 7, 18 May 1776, C.O. 5/556.

Bibliography of
Sources Cited

Primary Sources

MANUSCRIPT MATERIALS

Bevan, Joseph Vallence. Papers. Georgia Historical Society, Savannah.

Browne Family Papers. Private Collection, London, England.

Candler, Allen D., and Knight, Lucien Larmar, eds. The Colonial Records of the State of Georgia (fewer than half of the thirty-nine volumes are still in manuscript; they are available on microfilm or at the Georgia Department of Archives and History, Atlanta).

Clinton, Sir Henry. Papers. William L. Clements Library, University of Michigan, Ann Arbor, Michigan.

Cornwallis, Sir Charles. Papers. Alderman Library, University of Virginia, Charlottesville. Microfilm of the Collection in the Public Record Office, London, England.

Gage, Thomas. Papers. William L. Clements Library, University of Michigan, Ann Arbor, Michigan.

Germain, Lord George. Papers. William L. Clements Library, University of Michigan, Ann Arbor, Michigan.

Great Britain. Public Record Office. London.

Audit Office 12 and 13, as concerned with Georgia loyalists. Georgia Department of Archives and History, Atlanta.

Colonial Office Series 5 (microfilm).

Headquarters Papers of the British Army in America (microfilm). Colonial Williamsburg Foundation, Williamsburg, Virginia.

Howe, Robert. Orderly Book (microfilm). Library of Congress, Washington, D.C.

Letter, Thomas Brown to Jonas Brown, 10 November 1775. Copy in author's possession; location of original unknown.

PUBLISHED COLLECTIONS OF DOCUMENTS

Brooks, A. M., comp. *The Unwritten History of Old St. Augustine.* Translated by Annie Averette. [St. Augustine]: n.p., [1909].

Burnett, Edmund C., ed. *Letters of Members of the Continental Congress.* 8 vols. Washington, D.C.: Carnegie Institution of Washington, 1921–36.

Candler, Allen D., ed. *The Revolutionary Records of the State of Georgia.* 3 vols. Atlanta: Franklin-Turner Co., 1908.

_____, et al., eds. *The Colonial Records of the State of Georgia.* 39 vols. Atlanta: various printers, 1904–. (More than half of the volumes have been printed, and the intention is to publish as rapidly as possible those volumes that are still available only in manuscript or typescript.)

Carter, Clarence Edwin, ed. *The Correspondence of General Thomas Gage, 1763–1775.* 2 vols. Yale Historical Publications, Manuscripts and Edited Texts, Vols. XI and XII. New Haven: Yale University Press, 1931, 1933.

Caughey, John Walton, ed. *McGillivray of the Creeks.* The Civilization of the American Indian Series, Vol. XVIII. Norman: University of Oklahoma Press, 1938.

Clark, Walter, and Weeks, Stephen B., eds. *The State Records of North Carolina.* 20 vols. Raleigh and other cities. Various state printers, 1895–1914.

Clark, William Bell, and Morgan, William James, eds. *Naval Documents of the American Revolution.* 8 vols.–, Washington, [D.C.]: U.S. Government Printing Office, 1964–80–.

Collections of the Georgia Historical Society. Published by the Society.

    III. . . . *Report of Governor Sir James Wright to Lord Dartmouth on the Condition of the Colony, September 20, 1773; Letters from Governor Sir James Wright to the Earl of Dartmouth and Lord George Germain, Secretaries of State for America, from August 24, 1774, to February 16, 1782.* Savannah, 1873.

    V. Part II. *Order Book of Samuel Elbert, Colonel and Brigadier General in the Continental Army, October, 1776, to November, 1778:* . . . . Savannah, 1902.

    VI. *The Letters of Hon. James Habersham, 1756–1775.* Savannah, 1904.

    VIII. *Letters of Joseph Clay, Merchant of Savannah, 1776–1793,* . . . . Savannah, 1913.

    XII. *The Papers of Lachlan McIntosh, 1774–1779.* Edited by Lilla Mills Hawes. Savannah, 1957.

Collections of the New York Historical Society. Published by the Society.

    V. *Charles Lee Papers,* Vol. II. *1776–1778.* New York, 1872.

    XII. *Revolutionary Papers,* Vol. II. *Proceedings of a General Court Martial, . . . for the Trial of Major General Howe, December 7, 1781,* . . . . New York, 1879.

Davies, K. G., ed. *Documents of the American Revolution, 1770–1783: Colonial Office Series.* 21 vols. Shannon, Ireland: Irish University Press, 1972–81.

Douglas, David C., ed. *English Historical Documents.* 12 vols. London: Eyre and Spottiswoode, 1953–75. Vol. IX, *American Colonial Documents to 1776,* edited by Merrill Jensen, 1955. Vol. X, *English Historical Documents, 1714–1783,* edited by D. B. Horn and Mary Ransome, 1957.

Egerton, Hugh Edward, ed. *The Royal Commission on Losses and Services of American Loyalists, 1783–1785.* Mass Violence in America Series. 1915; reprint ed., New York: Arno Press and the New York Times, 1969.

Fitzpatrick, John C., ed. *The Writings of George Washington from the Original Manuscript Sources, 1745–1799.* 39 vols. Washington, [D.C.]: U.S. Government Printing Office, 1931–40.

Fleming, Berry, comp. *Autobiography of a Colony: The First Half-Century of Augusta, Georgia.* Athens: University of Georgia Press, 1957.

Force, Peter, ed. *American Archives.* 4th Series. 6 vols. Washington, [D.C.]: M. St. Clair and Peter Force, 1837–46. 5th Series. 3 vols. Washington, [D.C.]: M. St. Clair and Peter Force, 1848–53.

Ford, Worthington Chauncey, ed. *Journals of the Continental Congress, 1774–1789.* 34 vols. Washington, D.C.: U.S. Government Printing Office, 1904–37.

Gadsden, Christopher. *The Writings of Christopher Gadsden, 1746–1805.* Edited by Richard Walsh. Columbia: University of South Carolina Press, 1966.

Gibbes, R[obert] W[ilson], comp. *Documentary History of the American Revolution, . . .* 3 vols. Vols. I and II, New York: D. Appleton and Co., 1855–57; Vol. III, Columbia, S.C.: n.p., 1883.

Hawes, Lilla Mills, ed. *Lachlan McIntosh Papers in the University of Georgia Libraries.* University of Georgia Libraries Miscellanea Publications, No. 7. Athens: University of Georgia Press, 1968.

Historical Manuscripts Commission. Published for H.M. Stationery Office. *Report on the Manuscripts of Mrs. Stopford-Sackville, of Drayton House, Northamptonshire.* 2 vols. Vol. II. N.p., 1910.

Journal of the Commissioners for Trade and Plantations, 1704–1782, Preserved in the Public Record Office. 14 vols. London: H.M. Stationery Office, 1920–50.

Labaree, Leonard Woods, ed. *Royal Instructions to British Colonial Governors, 1670–1776.* 2 vols. 1935; reprint ed., New York: Octagon Books, 1967.

Moore, Frank, ed. *Diary of the American Revolution: From Newspapers and Original Documents.* 2 vols. New York: Charles Scribner, 1860.

Morison, Samuel Eliot, ed. *Sources and Documents Illustrating the American Revolution, 1764–1788, and the Formation of the Federal Constitution.* 2d ed. Oxford, England: Clarendon Press, 1929.

Perrin, W. G., ed. *The Keith Papers, Selected from the Letters and Papers of Admiral Viscount Keith,* Vol. I. Publications of the Navy Records Society, Vol. LXII. N.p.: Navy Records Society, 1926.

Pettengill, Ray W., trans. *Letters from America, 1776–1779, Being Letters of Brunswick, Hessian, and Waldeck Officers with the British Army during the Revolution.* Boston: Houghton Mifflin Company, 1924.

Saunders, William L., ed. *The Colonial Records of North Carolina.* 10 vols. Raleigh: published under the supervision of the Public Libraries, by order of the General Assembly, 1886–90.

Stevens, B. F., ed. *Facsimiles of Manuscripts in European Archives Relating to America, 1773–1783, with Descriptions, Editorial Notes, Collations, References, and Translations.* 25 vols. Holborn, England: Malby and Sons, 1889–95.

White, George. *Historical Collections of Georgia: Containing the Most Interesting Facts, Traditions, Biographical Sketches, Anecdotes, Etc. Relating to Its History and Antiquities, from Its First Settlement to the Present Time.* New York: Pudney and Russell, 1854.

MEMOIRS AND CONTEMPORARY WORKS

Adair, James. *Adair's History of the American Indians.* Edited by Samuel Cole Williams. 1775; Johnson City, Tenn.: Watauga Press, 1930.

Atkin, Edmond. *Indians of the Southern Colonial Frontier: The Edmond Atkin Report and Plan of 1755.* Edited by Wilbur R. Jacobs. Columbia: University of South Carolina Press, 1954.

Arredondo, Antonio De. *Arredondo's Historical Proof of Spain's Title to Georgia: A Contribution to the History of One of the Spanish Borderlands.* Edited by Herbert E. Bolton. Berkeley: University of California Press, 1925.

Bartram, William. *The Travels of William Bartram.* Naturalist's Edition. Edited by Francis Harper. 1791; New Haven: Yale University Press, 1958.

Chesney, Alexander. *The Journal of Alexander Chesney, a South Carolina Loyalist in the Revolution and After.* Edited by E. Alfred Jones. Ohio State University Studies, Contributions in History and Political Science, No. 7. N.p.: Ohio State University, 1921.

De Brahm, William Gerard. *De Brahm's Report of the General Survey in the Southern District of North America.* Edited by Louis De Vorsey, Jr. Columbia: University of South Carolina, for the South Carolina Tricentennial Commission, 1971.

Fanning, David. *Col. David Fanning's Narrative of His Exploits and Adventures as a Loyalist of North Carolina in the American Revolution, Supplying Important Omissions in the Copy Published in the United States.* Edited by A. W. Savery. Toronto: Reprint from the Canadian Magazine, 1908.

Forbes, James Grant. *Sketches, Historical and Topographical, of the Floridas; More Particularly of East Florida.* Facsimile reproduction of the 1821 edition. Gainesville: University of Florida Press, 1964.

Johnston, Elizabeth Lichtenstein. *Recollections of a Georgia Loyalist.* Edited by Arthur Wentworth Eaton. New York: M. F. Mansfield and Company, 1901.

Moultrie, William. *Memoirs of the American Revolution, So Far as It Related to the States of North and South Carolina, and Georgia.* Eyewitness Accounts of the American Revolution. 1802; reprint ed., 2 vols. in 1; New York: New York Times and Arno Press, 1968.

Romans, Bernard. *A Concise Natural History of East and West Florida.* 1775; New Orleans: Pelican Publishing Company, 1961.

DOCUMENTS IN PERIODICALS

"Account of the Loss of the Randolph as Given in a Letter from Rawlins Lowndes to Henry Laurens." *South Carolina Historical and Genealogical Magazine,* X (July 1909), 170–73.

Alden, John Richard, ed. "John Stuart Accuses William Bull." *William and Mary Quarterly,* 3d Ser., II (July 1945), 315–20.

Bartram, John. "Diary of a Journey through the Carolinas, Georgia, and Florida from July 1, 1765, to April 10, 1766." Annotated by Francis

Harper. *Transactions of the American Philosophical Society*, XXXIII, Pt. I (1942), i–iv, 1–120.

Bartram, William. "Observations on the Creek and Cherokee Indians, 1789." Edited by E. G. Squier. *Transactions of the American Ethnological Society*, III, Pt. I (1852), 1–81.

Boyd, Mark F., and Latorre, Jose Navarro, eds. "Spanish Interest in British Florida, and in the Progress of the American Revolution. I. Relations with the Spanish Faction of the Creek Indians." *Florida Historical Quarterly*, XXXII (October 1953), 92–130.

Colomb, Pierre. "Memoirs of a Revolutionary Soldier." English translation. *The Collector*, LXIII (1950), 198–201, 223–25, 347–49; LXIV (1951), 2–5.

Cross, Jack L., ed. "Letters of Thomas Pinckney, 1775–80." *South Carolina Historical Magazine*, LVIII (January, April, July, October 1957), 19–33, 67–83, 145–62, 224–42.

Destler, C. M., ed. "An Unpublished Letter of General Lachlan McIntosh." *Georgia Historical Quarterly*, XXIII (December 1939), 394–95.

Grimké, John Faucheraud. "Journal of the Campaign to the Southward, May 9th to July 14th, 1778." *South Carolina Historical and Genealogical Magazine*, XII (April, July, October 1911), 60–69, 118–34, 190–206.

Hamer, Philip M., ed. "Correspondence of Henry Stuart and Alexander Cameron with the Wataugans." *Mississippi Valley Historical Review*, XVII (December 1930), 451–59.

Hawes, Lilla Mills, ed. "The Proceedings and Minutes of the Governor and Council of Georgia, October 4, 1774, through November 7, 1775, and September 6, 1779, through September 20, 1780." *Georgia Historical Quarterly*, XXXIV (September, December 1950), 203–26, 288–312; XXXV (March, June, September 1951), 31–59, 126–51, 196–221.

"Letters of Patrick Carr, Terror to British Loyalists, to Governors John Martin and Lyman Hall, 1782 and 1783." *Georgia Historical Quarterly*, I (December 1917), 337–44.

Lewis, Andrew W., ed. "Henry Muhlenberg's Georgia Correspondence." *Georgia Historical Quarterly*, XLIX (December 1965), 424–54.

"Minutes of the Executive Council, May 7 through October 14, 1777." Transcribed by Margaret Godley. *Georgia Historical Quarterly*, XXXIII (December 1949), 318–30; XXXIV (March, June 1950), 19–35, 106–25.

"Order Book of John Faucheraud Grimké, August 1778 to May 1780." *South Carolina Historical and Genealogical Magazine*, XIII (1912), 42–55, 89–103, 148–55, 205–12; XIV (1913), 44–57, 98–111, 160–70, 219–24; XV (1914), 51–59, 82–90, 124–32, 166–70; XVI (1915), 39–48, 80–85, 123–28, 178–83; XVII (1916), 26–33, 82–86, 116–20, 167–74; XVIII (1917), 78–84, 149–53, 175–79; XIX (1918), 101–4, 181–88.

Padgett, James A., ed. "Commissions, Orders and Instructions Issued to George Johnstone, British Governor of West Florida, 1763–1767." *Louisiana Historical Quarterly*, XXI (October 1938), 1021–68.

"Papers of the First Council of Safety of the Revolutionary Party in South Carolina, June–November 1775." *South Carolina Historical and Genealogical*

Magazine, I (1900), 41–75, 119–35, 183–205, 279–310; II (1901), 3–26, 97–107, 167–93, 259–67; III (1902), 3–15, 69–85, 123–38.

Phillips, U. B., ed. "Some Letters of Joseph Habersham, 1775–1790." *Georgia Historical Quarterly,* X (June 1926), 144–63.

Starr, Raymond, ed. "Letters from John Lewis Gervais to Henry Laurens, 1777–1778." *South Carolina Historical Magazine,* LXVI (January 1965), 15–37.

NEWSPAPERS

Gazette of the State of South Carolina (Charleston).
Georgia Gazette (Savannah).
South Carolina and American General Gazette (Charleston).
South Carolina Gazette (Charleston).
South Carolina Gazette and Country Journal (Charleston).
Virginia Gazette (Williamsburg).

Secondary Works

Abbot, W[illiam] W[right]. *The Royal Governors of Georgia, 1754–1775.* Chapel Hill: University of North Carolina Press for the Institute of Early American History and Culture, 1959.

Alden, John Richard. *John Stuart and the Southern Colonial Frontier: A Study of Indian Relations, War, Trade, and Land Problems in the Southern Wilderness, 1754–1775.* University of Michigan Publications, History and Political Science, Vol. XV. Ann Arbor: University of Michigan Press, 1944.

Bennett, Charles E. *Southernmost Battlefields of the Revolution.* [Bailey's Crossroads, Va.: Blair, Inc., privately published], 1970.

Bonner, James C. *Atlas for Georgia History.* 1969; reprint ed., Fort Worth: Miran Publishers, 1975.

Butler, Lewis [William George], and Hare, Stewart. *The Annals of the King's Royal Rifle Corps.* Vol. I: Lewis [William George] Butler, *The Royal Americans.* London: Smith, Elder and Co., 1913.

Chatelain, Verne E. *The Defenses of Spanish Florida, 1565 to 1763.* Carnegie Institution of Washington Publication 511. Washington, D.C.: Carnegie Institution of Washington, 1941.

Coleman, Kenneth. *The American Revolution in Georgia, 1763–1789.* Athens: University of Georgia Press, 1958.

Corkran, David H. *The Creek Frontier, 1540–1783.* The Civilization of the American Indian Series. Norman: University of Oklahoma Press, 1967.

Cotterill, Robert Spenser. *The Southern Indians: The Story of the Civilized Tribes before Removal.* The Civilization of the American Indian Series, Vol. XXXVIII. Norman: University of Oklahoma Press, 1954.

Cummins, Light Townsend. "Spanish Agents in North America during the Revolution, 1775–1779." Ph.D. dissertation, Tulane University, 1977.

Davis, Harold E. *The Fledgling Province: Social and Cultural Life in Colonial Georgia, 1733–1776.* Chapel Hill: University of North Carolina Press for the Institute of Early American History and Culture, 1976.

De Vorsey, Louis, Jr. *The Indian Boundary in the Southern Colonies, 1763–1775.* Chapel Hill: University of North Carolina Press, 1966.

Doggett, Carita [Corse]. *Dr. Andrew Turnbull and the New Smyrna Colony of Florida.* Jacksonville, Fla.: Drew Press, 1919.

Gold, Robert L. *Borderland Empires in Transition: The Triple-Nation Transfer of Florida.* Carbondale: Southern Illinois University Press, 1969.

Greene, Evarts B., and Harrington, Virginia D. *American Population before the Federal Census of 1790.* New York: Columbia University Press, 1932.

Harper, Francis. "William Bartram and the American Revolution." *Proceedings of the American Philosophical Society,* XCVII, No. 5 (1953), 571–77.

Jenkins, Charles Francis. *Button Gwinnett, Signer of the Declaration of Independence.* 1926; reprint ed., Spartanburg, S.C.: Reprint Company, 1974.

Johnston, Edith Duncan. *The Houstouns of Georgia.* Athens: University of Georgia Press, 1950.

Jones, Charles C., Jr. *The Dead Towns of Georgia.* Vol. IV of *Collections of the Georgia Historical Society.* Savannah: By the Society, 1878.

_____. *History of Georgia.* 2 vols. Boston: Houghton, Mifflin and Company, 1883.

Kurtz, Stephen G., and Hutson, James H., eds. *Essays on the American Revolution.* Chapel Hill and New York: published for the Institute of Early American History and Culture at Williamsburg by the University of North Carolina Press and W. W. Norton and Company, 1973.

M'Call, Hugh. *The History of Georgia, Containing Brief Sketches of the Most Remarkable Events Up to the Present Day (1784).* 2 vols. 1811–16. Reprint ed., 2 vols. in 1. Atlanta: A. B. Caldwell, 1909.

McIlvaine, Paul. *The Dead Towns of Sunbury, Ga., and Dorchester, S.C.* 2d ed. Hendersonville, N.C.: privately published, 1971.

Mowat, Charles Loch. *East Florida as a British Province, 1763–1784.* University of California Publications in History, Vol. XXXII. Berkeley and Los Angeles: University of California Press, 1943.

O'Donnell, James H., III. *Southern Indians in the American Revolution.* Knoxville: University of Tennessee Press, 1973.

Panagopoulos, E[paminodes] P. *New Smyrna: An Eighteenth-Century Greek Odyssey.* Gainesville: University of Florida Press, 1966.

Pate, James Paul. "The Chickamauga: A Forgotten Segment of Indian Resistance on the Southern Frontier." Ph.D. dissertation, Mississippi State University, 1969.

Saye, Albert B. *New View-Points in Georgia History.* Athens: University of Georgia Press, 1943.

Siebert, Wilbur Henry. *Loyalists in East Florida, 1774–1785.* 2 vols. Publications of the Florida Historical Society, No. 9. Deland, Fla.: Florida State Historical Society, 1929.

Sutherland, Stella H. *Population Distribution in Colonial America.* New York: Columbia University Press, 1936.

Swan, Caleb. "Position and State of Manners and Arts in the Creek Nation, in 1791." Henry R. Schoolcraft. *Information Respecting the History, Condition, and Prospects of the Indian Tribes of the United States: Collected and Prepared Under the Direction of the Bureau of Indian Affairs per Act of Congress of March 3rd 1847.* 6 vols. Vol. V. Philadelphia: Lippincott and Co., 1855.

Swanton, John R[eed]. *Early History of the Creek Indians and Their Neighbors.* Smithsonian Institution Bureau of American Ethnology, Bulletin 73. Washington, [D.C.]: U.S. Government Printing Office, 1922.

_____. "Social Organization and Social Usages of the Indians of the Creek Confederacy." *Forty-Second Annual Report of the Bureau of American Ethnology.* Washington, [D.C.]: U.S. Government Printing Office, 1928.

Wright, J. Leitch, Jr. *Florida in the American Revolution.* Sponsored by the American Revolution Bicentennial Commission of Florida. Gainesville: University Presses of Florida, 1975.

Journal Articles

Bennett, John, comp. "A List of Noncommissioned Officers and Private Men of the Second South Carolina Continental Regiment of Foot." *South Carolina Historical and Genealogical Magazine,* XVI (January 1915), 25–33.

"British Regiments in St. Augustine, 1768–1784." *El Escribano,* VII (April 1970), 41–48.

Burnett, Edmund C. "Edward Langworthy in the Continental Congress." *Georgia Historical Quarterly,* XII (September 1928), 211–35.

Chesnutt, David R. "South Carolina's Penetration of Georgia in the 1760's: Henry Laurens as a Case Study." *South Carolina Historical Magazine,* LXXIII (October 1972), 194–208.

Crout, Robert Rhodes. "Pierre-Emmanuel de la Plaigne and Georgia's Quest for French Aid during the War of Independence." *Georgia Historical Quarterly,* LX (Summer 1976), 176–84.

Flippin, Percy Scott. "Royal Government in Georgia, 1752–1776." *Georgia Historical Quarterly,* VIII (1924), 1–37, 81–120, 243–91; IX (1925), 187–245; X (1926), 1–25, 251–76; XII (1928), 316–52; XIII (1929), 128–53.

Green, E. R. R. "Queensborough Township: Scotch-Irish Emigration and the Expansion of Georgia, 1763–1776." *William and Mary Quarterly,* 3d Ser., XVII (April 1960), 183–99.

Hamer, Marguerite Bartlett. "Edmund Gray and His Settlement at New Hanover." *Georgia Historical Quarterly,* XIII (March 1929), 1–12, 52–55.

Hamer, Philip M. "John Stuart's Indian Policy during the Early Months of the American Revolution." *Mississippi Valley Historical Review,* XVII (December 1930), 351–66.

Jackson, Harvey H. "The Battle of the Riceboats: Georgia Joins the Revolution." *Georgia Historical Quarterly,* LXVIII (Summer 1974), 229–43.

Lawrence, Alexander A. "General Robert Howe and the British Capture of Savannah in 1778." *Georgia Historical Quarterly,* XXXVI (December 1952), 302–27.

"The Minis Family." *Georgia Historical Quarterly,* I (March 1917), 45–49.

Mowat, Charles L. "St. Francis Barracks, St. Augustine: A Link with the British Regime." *Florida Historical Quarterly,* XXI (January 1943), 266–80.

Naisawald, L. Van Loan. "Major General Howe's Activities in South Carolina and Georgia, 1776–1779." *Georgia Historical Quarterly,* XXXV (March 1951), 23–30.

O'Donnell, J[ames] H. "Alexander McGillivray: Training for Leadership, 1777–1783." *Georgia Historical Quarterly,* XLIX (June 1965), 172–86.

Olsen, Gary D. "Loyalists and the American Revolution: Thomas Brown and the South Carolina Backcountry, 1775–1776." *South Carolina Historical Magazine,* LXVIII (October 1967), 201–19; LXIX (January 1968), 44–56.

Robertson, Heard. "Georgia's Banishment and Expulsion Act of September 16, 1777." *Georgia Historical Quarterly,* LV (Summer 1971), 274–83.

Rogers, George C., Jr. "The East Florida Society of London, 1766–1767." *Florida Historical Quarterly,* LIV (April 1976), 479–96.

Scott, Ralph C., Jr. "The Quaker Settlement of Wrightsborough, Georgia." *Georgia Historical Quarterly,* LVI (Summer 1972), 210–23.

Siebert, Wilbur H. "Privateering in Florida Waters and Northward during the Revolution." *Florida Historical Quarterly,* XXII (October 1943), 62–73.

Smith, Gordon B. "The Georgia Grenadiers." *Georgia Historical Quarterly,* LXIV (Winter 1980), 405–15.

Wilkins, Barrett. "A View of Savannah on the Eve of the Revolution." *Georgia Historical Quarterly,* LIV (Winter 1970), 577–84.

Williams, Edward G. "The Prevosts of the Royal Americans." *Western Pennsylvania Historical Magazine,* LVI (January 1973), 1–38.

Index

Aaron, George, 40, 121, 157
Aaron, John, 121
Aarons, John, 130
Abeikas, 132
Act for the better ordering and regulating the Militia of this State, 159
Act for the better Security of this State by obliging and making liable Negro Slaves to work on the several Forts Batteries or other public Works within the same, 119
Act for the Expulsion of the Internal Enemies of This State, 117
Act of Confiscation and Banishment, 25
Adams, Samuel: effigy burned in St. Augustine, 54
Admiralty court, 70; at St. Augustine, 128–29; at Charleston, 138
Alabamas, 112
Alachua, 10, 26, 29, 30, 176. *See also* Latchoway
Alexander, Lt., 112
Allen, Capt. Edward, 67
Allen, Lt. Col. Isaac, 166, 167–68
Alligator Creek Bridge, 143; battle of, 144–45
Altamaha River, 1, 2, 4, 8, 9, 10, 28, 35, 39, 40, 55, 62, 63, 65, 66, 68, 76, 77, 80, 87, 94, 113, 128, 130, 131, 134, 139, 141, 142, 155, 165, 173, 174, 181; Georgia detachment on, 37; provision magazine at, 64; desolation near, 82; posts on, 87; Georgia troops cross, 93; cattle south of, 96–97; Georgia scouts on, 122; Americans on, 140; American force crosses, 141; South Carolina militia encamped at, 147; Creek raids on, 155; British enter settlements north of, 161

Amelia Island, 36, 46–49 passim; Georgia troops on, 93–94
Amelia Narrows, 96, 147
Amsterdam, 92
Anastasia Island, 17, 33, 129
Anderson (of Jekyll Island), 48
Anderson, [David], 34
Anderson, Lt. (Georgia Horse), 113, 120
Antigua, 32, 92
Apalachee, 10
Apalachicola, 116, 133
Apalachicola River, 1
Appalachicola, 75
Articles of Association, 14
Articles of Confederation, 154
Armstrong, Gen. John, 24, 62
Armstrong's, 142
Augusta, 2, 10, 43, 56, 73; center of Indian trade, 4; population of, 4; Treaty of (1773), 10; Thomas Brown tarred and feathered at, 14; some loyalist traders move from, 26; Indian conference at, 29, 30; provisions at, 64, 119, 158; East Florida Rangers at, 113, 138–39; British plan to conquer, 159

Bachop, Capt. Adam, 138
Bachop, Master Peter, 44, 55
Bahamas, 25, 89
Baillie, James, 40
Baker, Col. John, 103, 104, 176; on invasion of East Florida, 93–95 passim; at battle of Thomas Creek, 95; resigns, 103; wounded at Bulltown Swamp, 161
Baker, Maj. William, 94, 161
Barber, James, 120
Barefield (East Floridian), 94
Barkley, Capt. Andrew, 23
Barnard, Timothy, 154, 155, 156

Barracks: in St. Augustine, 7, 33; in Georgia, 65, 77, 127; in Savannah (1777), 119, 153; in East Florida, 151
Barry, George, 105
Battle of Sullivan's Island, 170
"Battle of the riceboats," 23, 66
Batton [Ratoon?], 50
Batut, Capt. John, 71
Beard, Cornet Valentine, 66
Beard's Bluff, 68, 76, 77, 79, 80, 87
Beaufort, 47, 66
Beaverdam Creek, 31, 104
Beecher, Lt., 77
Bell (captured by Georgians), 67
Bermuda, 50, 60
Bermuda Island. See Colonel's Island
Berwick, John, 46
Betsy (Capt. Lofthouse), 41, 61
Betsy (Georgia sloop), 31
Bethune (East Floridian), 36
Bethune, John, 38
Big Creek, 94
Big Shoals, 112
Bilbo, Lt., 114
Bishop, Capt. Thomas, 48, 49, 50, 57, 60, 61, 67
Bisset, Robert, 57, 59–60, 107
Black Creek, 43
Black Creek Factor, 94, 155
Blacks. See Slaves
Bloody Point, 55
Blunt, Dr., 141
Bonnell, Maj., 130
Booker, Lt., 114
Bostick, Capt. Chesley, 14, 79, 87
Boston, 12, 23, 29, 67
Boston Committee of Correspondence, Inspection, and Safety, 45–46
Boundaries, of Georgia and the Floridas, 1
Bounties, 25, 63, 64, 101, 136, 153
Bowden's place, 122
Bowen, Capt. Oliver, 64, 139, 145–46
Brewton's Hill, 165
Brim ("emperor" of the Creek Nation), 5
Broad River, 10, 68, 155; Indians attack American scouts on (1777), 113; South Carolina loyalists on, 131
Broughton Island, 66

Brown, John, 140
Brown, Lt. Col. Thomas Alexander, 38, 39, 75, 101, 113, 117, 129, 132, 142, 143, 145, 146, 149, 159, 177, 179, 180; arrives in Georgia, tarred and feathered, 13–14, 171; in Indian country, 28–29; suggests raiding Georgia cattle herds, 35; raises East Florida Rangers, 38, 83; robbed by Cussitas, 75; provincial commission of, 85; at attack on Fort McIntosh, 86–87; stationed on St. Marys, 91; at battle of Thomas Creek, 94–95; Drayton threatens to sue, 106; captures Fort Howe, 130; sends intelligence parties into Georgia and South Carolina, 131; permission to resign commission refused, 136; rations of 1778, 137; sends detachment into Georgia, 138–39; nearly captured, 142–43; at Cabbage Swamp, 143–44; at battle of Alligator Creek Bridge, 144; relationship with Prevost, 150; in battle at Midway Meeting House, 161–62; effective leader of Rangers, 176; gains Indian assistance for British, 178. See also East Florida Rangers
Brown, Capt., 90
Brown, Lt., 113
Brownsboro, 158
Brownson, Nathan, 55
Bryan, Jonathan, 21, 28, 52, 55, 74, 75, 109; Indian land scheme of, 10, 20, 41, 70
Bryan, Langley, 66
Bryan, Marbury, 28
Brune, 100
Brunson, William, 121
Buchanan (loyalist), 28
Bucher, Lt., 44
Bugg, Lt. Jeremiah, 77–78, 79, 80
Bugg, Lt. William, 69
Bull, Col. Stephen, 23, 55
Bulloch, 135
Bulloch, Archibald, 64; president of Georgia provincial Congress, 11, 13; Georgia delegate to Second Continental Congress, 11, 13, 16; elected president and commander in chief of Georgia (1776), 27, 39, 40, 52, 54; pres-

ident of the Georgia Council of Safety, 39; issues proclamation (1776), 65; dictatorship of, 88; death of, 88
Bulltown Swamp, 161
Bunker Hill, battle of, 12
Burel, David, 120
Burke County, 117, 139

Cabbage Swamp: British forces at, 143–44
Cade, Capt., 69, 79, 80
Caine (Indian interpreter), 106
Caldwell, Lt. William, 86–87
Caligies, 156
Camden County, 82, 117
Cameron, Alexander, 21, 114–15
Campbell, Lt. Col. Archibald, 160, 164, 165, 179–80; at battle of Savannah (1778), 165–66; joined by Prevost in Savannah, 168
Campbell, Thomas, 140
Canary Islands, 129
Cannon, Lt., 120
Canoochee River, 68, 121, 122
Cape Fear, 27, 29, 32, 60, 73
Cape Francois, 64, 77
Cape Hatteras, 164
Carlisle Peace Commission (1778), 160
Carney (Georgian), 68
Carney, Arthur, 117
Carolinians at Fort Barrington (Howe), 88
Carpenter, William, 140
Carr, Patrick, 133, 156
Carr's Fort, 104
Casualties, 116, 181; Creek raids on Georgia frontier (1773–74), 10; "battle of the riceboats" at Savannah, 23; skirmish on Beaverdam Creek, 31; Wright's Fort, 44–45; Georgia invasion of East Florida (1776), 62; Satilla River, 67; Indian skirmish with Georgia Rangers, 68; Beard's Bluff, 77–78; Fort McIntosh (1777), 86; South Georgia (1777), 87; Clark's fort, 91; Indian attack on Col. Baker's camp, 93; Amelia Island, 93; Indians and Georgia force under Col. Baker in East Florida, 94; battle of Thomas Creek, 95; *Rebecca*

and *Hawke* battle with rebel brigantine, 96; near Big Shoals, 112; Coweta raids on Georgia, 112; Fort Howe, 113, 130; East Florida Rangers, 113; skirmish between Georgia Light Horse and Cowetas, 132; battle of Alligator Creek Bridge, 144–45; Cussitas, 154; Creek raids on Georgia, 155; Bulltown Swamp, 161; Midway, 162; battle of Savannah (1778), 165–66; Fort Morris, 167
Cathead Creek, 77, 147
Catherwood, Robert, 124
Cattle, 31, 36, 71–72, 157; in Georgia, 3, 35, 46, 53, 70, 77, 82, 84, 88, 130, 131, 163, 181; in East Florida, 35, 46, 79, 145; on Cumberland Island, 44; on sea islands, 63; in Newport and Midway settlements, 161; on Sapelo Island, 167; between Altamaha and St. Marys, removed by Georgians, 96–97; Georgians want to distribute to Indians, 30, 52–53
"Cattle hunters," 35, 38
Cattle-hunting expedition (1777), 85–87
Ceded Lands, 10, 19, 75, 81–82, 104, 128; Thomas Brown invests in, 14; immigration into, 18; Scotch-Irish on, 169; raided by Cowetas, 132; land grants in, 132; Creeks raid, 155
Censorship in Georgia, 16
Chambers, William, 25
Chapman, William, 36
Charleston, 4, 22, 42, 43, 45, 52–56 passim, 62, 67, 74, 88, 128, 129, 134, 135, 164; Stuart flees from, 18; American vessels at, 89; trade with Georgia, 89; Handsome Fellow visits, 109–10; arms from, 119; admiralty court at, 138; British plans to conquer, 159; rumors at, of British invasion, 160, 163–64; General Benjamin Lincoln at, 164; British force off, 164; British fleet defeated at battle of Sullivan's Island, 170
Chatham County, 117; militia, 134, 153
Chattahoochee River, 1, 10
Cherokee, 32, 45, 61, 66, 67
Cherokee Indians, 4, 19, 21, 28, 38, 72–75 passim, 110–11, 114–15; in debt to traders, 9; land cession, treaty of Au-

gusta (1773), 10; hostility toward Creeks, 19; defeat of, 31, 43; requested by Tonyn to attack South Carolina frontier, 91; plight of, 109; warn Creek Indians of American counteroffensive, 155; dispiriting effect of their disaster on southern Indians, 178

Chester, Gov. Peter (West Florida), 100

Chevulky Warrior, 30

Chiaha(s), 74, 75, 155; confer with Stuart and Tonyn, 21; at Lower Creek conference (May 1776), 29; covet Brown's gunpowder, 29; attack Georgia Rangers, 68; guard William McIntosh, 115; promise to assist British, 133

Chickasaw Indians, 4, 115

Choctaw-Creek War, 19, 74

Choctaw Indians, 4, 19, 74, 115, 137

Christ Church Parish: radicals in, 13

Christy, 31

Clair, Joseph, 140

Clarissa, 57–58

Clark (loyalist), 36

Clark, Angus, 38

Clarke, Lt. Arthur, 47

Clarke, Col. Elijah, 144

Clark's [Elijah?] Fort, 91

Clay, Joseph, 22, 103

Clinton, Gen. Sir Henry, 26, 39, 150–52 passim; commander of British troops for southern operations, 23; at Cape Fear, 27, 32; reported by Stuart to want military operations by Indians suspended, 29; directs East Florida governor to raise regiment of mounted infantry and promises to confirm Tonyn's commissions, 38; defeated at Charleston, 42–43; succeeds Howe as commander of His Majesty's army in North America, 148; approves Howe's opinion on command of East Florida Rangers, 148; appoints officers of South Carolina Royalists, 151; on Carlisle peace commission, 160; assembles invasion force at New York, 160

Coates, Capt. James, 94, 105

Cochrane, Jonathan, 64

Cockspur Island, 47, 50, 55, 57, 61; Georgia governor and council escape to, 23;

Georgia slaves desert to British at, 23; cannon and military stores at, 25

Coleman, Thomas, 95

Coleman's: provision magazine at, 158

Colonel's Island, 163

Colson, Capt., 66

Comet, 67

Command: of British troops, British rules of 1757, 82–83, 85; of American troops invading East Florida, 90; of East Florida Rangers and militia, 99, 124

Commissions: sent by Georgia assembly to agents in France, 119

Committee for Indian Affairs chosen by Second Continental Congress, 27

Committee of Correspondence: Georgia assembly appoints, 9

Communication, 15, 33, 61, 72, 84, 93; within East Florida, 35; along St. Johns River, 92; between Minorcans at New Smyrna and rebels, 107

Concord: news of reaches Savannah (May 1775), 12

Confederation of the United States, 81

Congarees: loyalists in, 131

Congress of Augusta (May 1776), 30

Conner, William, 140

Constitutions of Georgia: Rules and Regulations of 1776, 27; first (1777), 81, 88, 100; Georgia first, criticism of, 82

Continental Association, 11, 12, 13, 16, 18

Continental Congress, First: Georgia, the Floridas, Newfoundland, and Nova Scotia not represented, 11

Continental Congress, Second, 63, 64, 113–14, 153–54; Georgia delegates to, 11, 12, 13, 16, 27; removes ban on trade with Georgia, 13; radical sentiment increases in, 16; authorizes one battalion of Continental troops for Georgia and appropriates funds, 18; cuts off trade with Georgia (except St. John's parish), 12; bans trade with East Florida, 12; admits Lyman Hall of Georgia, 12; specifies organization of Continental troops, 24–25; modifies nonexportation association, 25, 27; recommends Continental expedition

against St. Augustine, 25; Secret Committee to handle Indian trade, 27; policy on using Indian warriors, 27–28; Georgia asks aid from, 39; authorizes privateers and opens ports, 40–41; Georgians want funding from for fortifications, 52; augments Continental establishment for Georgia, 53–54; orders Gen. Charles Lee northward, 56, 62; receives Lee's report (1776), 62; aids Georgia, 64, 103, 157; orders North Carolina Continentals northward, 89; recommends arrest of George McIntosh, 90; George McIntosh clears himself before, 100; receives petitions for Gen. Lachlan McIntosh's removal from command, 101; disapproves of Georgia assembly issuing commissions for foreign officers, 102; appoints Joseph Clay as paymaster for Georgia, 103; appoints James Rae as commissary general of purchases for Georgia, 103; appoints John Bohan Giradeau as commissary general of issues for Georgia, 103; considers affairs in Georgia, 104; plans expeditions against Floridas, 104; appoints Peter Taarling as army quartermaster general in Georgia, 119; opinion sought about desertions, 120; resolves that offensive expedition against East Florida should be undertaken, 126; recommends confiscation of property of loyalists, 127; approves plan and authorizes expedition to capture St. Augustine, 157; replaces Gen. Robert Howe with Gen. Benjamin Lincoln as Continental commander of the Southern Department, 157–58; takes precautions against British invasion of south, 160; rejects Lauren's proposal to abandon East Florida campaign, 160
Continental troops: in Georgia, 25, 66, 87; weakened in south, 89; at site of Fort Tonyn, 143. *See also* Georgia Continental troops, North Carolina Continental troops, South Carolina Continental troops, Virginia Continental troops
Convention: constitutional, in Georgia,

81; of Georgia, rejects proposed merger with South Carolina, 81
Cooper, Capt., 161
Corn House: factions in, 132
Correspondence, secret: from East Florida to Georgia and the Carolinas, 17
Counties, replace parishes as units of government in Georgia, 81–82
Court-martial, 140, 153; of Gen. Robert Howe, 166
Courts: in Georgia, 16
Courvozie (East Floridian), 58
Coweta(s), 10, 29, 111, 133, 137, 155; owe debts to George Galphin, 10; confer with Stuart and Tonyn, 21; covet Brown's gunpowder, 29; friendly relations with Galphin, 30; blood feud with Georgia, 30; warriors raid Georgia, 111–12, 113; factions in, 115, 132; guard William McIntosh, 115; on verge of civil war with Cussita, 115; raid Ceded Lands, 132; attack detachment of Georgia Light Horse near Ceded Lands, 132; raiding party from, 137; aid British, 154; war party to aid British raised at, 155
Cowford (on St. Johns River, present Jacksonville), 17, 21, 58, 59, 95; Georgians reach, 94; battery at, 138
Cowford (on Satilla River), 142
Cowkeeper, Chief, 20, 28–29 passim, 30, 177; at St. Augustine, 29; leads warriors to join Graham at St. Marys, 39; leading Indians between St. Marys and St. Augustine, 43; leads warriors between St. Johns and St. Marys rivers, 85; at Fort McIntosh, 86
Creek-Choctaw War, 19, 73, 74
Creek Indians, 4, 19, 21, 28–30, 38, 72–76, 113–16, 137–38, 140, 148, 165, 175–78 passim; numbers of, 4, 19; location of, 4–5, 108, 110; theories of real property, 5, 179; neutrality policy of, 5, 18, 28, 178; trade, 9, 20, 26, 115, 132; land cession, treaty of Augusta (1773), 9–10; factions among, 9–10, 19–20, 74–75, 109–12, 114–16, 132–33, 137, 154–57, 177–78; attack Georgia frontier (winter 1773–74), 10; reject Bryan's

land "lease," 10; hostility toward Cherokees, 19; resent rebel robbery of ammunition, 20; urge resumption of Indian trade, 20; Scots and Englishmen living with, 20; confer with Stuart and Tonyn, 21; refuse to surrender Taitt, 26; conference at Cussita (1776), 28; confer with Whig Indian commissioners, 29, 30, 109, 116; Gen. Charles Lee plans to intimidate, 54; national council of does not sanction proposed attack on rebel whites, 57; Gray flees from, 74; aid British, 76, 108; raid Georgia, 76, 111–13, 116, 154–55, 177; imprisoned by Georgians, 80; requested by Tonyn to raid Georgia, 91; appalled by Cherokees' disaster, 108; Gen. Prevost complains about, 110; food shortage, 110, 137; drunkenness among, 110; Georgia terms for peace with, 114; visit Augusta, 114; council of headmen, 115, 154; confer with Stuart at Pensacola, 116, 132; warned by Cherokees of American counteroffensive, 155; send emissary to Cuba, 156; war party assembles on Ocmulgee to raid Georgia, 156; warriors to go to join British, 160; independence of, 177; reasons for aiding British, 178–79; assimilation of white socioeconomic culture, 179; politics affected by war, 179; war increases disparity of wealth, 179

Cubo line, 69

Cumberland Island, 36, 44, 45, 48, 49, 96, 166; Wrights and slaves camp on, 46; Tonyn proposes fortification on, 153; Fuser at, 166

Cunningham, Lt., 112

Curacao, 91

Curchon, John Baptist, 140

Currency: depreciation of, in Georgia, 103

Cussita(s), 29, 74, 75, 116, 132, 133, 156; confer with Stuart and Tonyn, 21; council at, 28; friendly relations with Galphin, 30; warrior killed by rebel, 30; confer with Galphin, 74–75; factions in, 74–75, 114–15, 116, 156; rob Brown, 75; Daniel McMurphy at, 112; warriors visit Charleston, 114; plunder British

traders, 115; on verge of civil war with Coweta, 115; confer with Stuart, 116, 133; casualties, 154; Fat King of, 155; threaten William McIntosh and loyalists near Pensacola, 155; kill loyalists near Pensacola, 156

Cussita King: confers with Indian commissioners, 109, 157

Cussita King's brother: urged by Tonyn to keep Creeks neutral, 20; robbed of ammunition by Georgia rebels, 20

Daniel, Capt., 138

Daphne, 100

Darien, 77, 97, 113, 121, 135; population of, 4; Highland Scots at, 4, 169; company of Georgia Battalion stationed at, 39; retreating Georgia force at, 96; Georgia force near, 131; hospital at, 141; uninhabited (1778), 152

Dartmouth, William Legge, Earl of, 9, 21, 82–83

Dart River. *See* Broad River

Daufuskie Creek, 55

Davis, Strahan, and Company, 75

Declaratory Act, 7

Defau, Capt., 119

Defence, 67

Defense, 138

Delight, 164–65

de Lisle, Roman, 162

Delk, Samuel, 112. *See also* Dilkes, Samuel

Demere, Major (Raymond ?), 119

Denis's fort, 158

Desertion, 104; from Georgia invasion force in retreat, 96; from Capt. Squire's *Otter,* 105; in Georgia, 119–20, 153; from Georgia Light Horse, 120, 131, 176; of loyalists in Georgia, 131; from Georgia Fourth Battalion, 131, 146; from East Florida Rangers, 138, 150; from American forces invading East Florida, 140–41; British, 164, 172

Dewitt's Corner, Treaty of, 108

Dilkes, Samuel, 112–13

Docherty, Bryan, 43

Dodd, Benjamin, 57

Doffield, Timothy. *See* Duffield, Timothy

Donaldson, James, 120

Dooley, Capt. John, 114

Dooley, Capt. Thomas, 112
Dornself, Sergeant, 166–67
Drayton, 70
Drayton, Stephen, 105
Drayton, William, 41, 71, 107; leaves St. Augustine for England, 42; reinstated as chief justice in East Florida, 42; obstructs war effort in East Florida, 105–07; suspended from office, 124
Drayton, William Henry, 41; commissioner to propose union of South Carolina and Georgia, 81; supports union of South Carolina and Georgia, 104–05
Dreadnought, 146
Drew, Lt., 130
Duel, 145; between Lachlan McIntosh and Button Gwinnett, 100–01; between Robert Howe and Christopher Gadsden, 158
Due West. See Dewitt's Corner
Duffield, Timothy, 120
Duke of Cumberland, 61
Dunmore, John Murray, Lord, 60, 71, 106

Eagan, Stephen. See Egan, Stephen
East Florida, 3, 6, 7, 92; boundaries of, 1; population of, 3, 6, 26; lack of provincial assembly, 6, 41; not represented in First Continental Congress, 11; Council of, 35, 42, 43, 49, 50, 58, 59, 60–61, 113, 124, 135, 152; factions in, 174 [see also Factions, in East Florida]
East Florida Rangers, 46, 69, 70–72 passim, 77, 83–85 passim, 96, 98, 99, 128, 136, 157, 159, 161, 166–68 passim, 175–77; organization of, 38, 83, 99, 129, 150, 151; personnel of, 38, 83, 113, 129, 132, 149–50, 155–56, 176; raid in Georgia (1777), 66, 67, 94, 96, 113, 121–22, 129–31, 138–39, 142, 147–50 passim, 153, 161–62 passim, 177, 181; command of, 83, 85, 99, 124, 128, 136, 148; uniforms of, 83, 144; on cattle-hunting expedition (1777), 84–88 passim; capture Fort McIntosh (1777), 86–87; at St. Marys River, 85, 91, 136, 138; at battle of Thomas Creek, 95, 98; rations for, 99, 137, 150; as model for Georgia "minute men," 101; capture

Fort Frederica, 113, 117; at Fort Tonyn, 129, 142–43, 149; capture Fort Howe, 130; desertion from, 130, 138, 149, 150, 176; at battle of Alligator Creek Bridge, 143–44; Augustine Prevost's opinion of, 149; attrition of, 150, 176; raid South Carolina, 157; in battle at Midway Meeting House, 161–62; at seige of Fort Morris, 167; mounts of, 175–76; success of, 175–76
East Florida Volunteers, 166
Eastmead, Richard, 121
Ebenezer, 158
Eden, William, 160
Effingham County, 117, 130
Egan, Stephen, 48–50 passim, 58
Egan's Landing, 49
Egmont, Lady, 48, 58
Elbert, Col. Samuel, 24, 25, 64, 79, 101–04 passim, 119–23 passim, 126, 158, 161–64 passim; commander of Georgia force invading East Florida (1777), 90–97 passim; complains about armaments, 102; demands assassination of Cameron, Taitt, and McIntosh, 114; dispatches military escort for visiting Indians, 116; opposes loyalists leaving Georgia, 118; commander of all Continental forces in Georgia, 118; tries to improve discipline, 119, 121, 123; orders severe punishment for desertion, 120; tries to trap East Florida Rangers in Georgia, 121–22; on invasion of East Florida (1778), 134–47 passim
Elizabeth, 66
Elliott, Col. John, 130
Ellis, Lt. Alexander, 32, 67, 92, 100, 134–35
Elphinstone, Capt. George Keith, 146, 148, 152, 153
Emistiseguo, Chief, 20, 115, 156
Escochabey, Chief, 10, 20, 30, 111
Esperance, 67

Factions: among Creek Indians, 9–10, 19, 109–16 passim, 132–33, 137, 154–57 passim, 177–78; in Georgia, 12–13, 100, 101, 103, 173–74, 182; polarized by democratic constitution of Georgia,

82; effect on Georgia Horse, 176; in
East Florida, 41–42, 59, 105–08, 124–
25, 136, 182; among Indians, 178
Fanning, David, 131
Fat King (of Cussita), 133, 155, 156
Fee, Thomas. *See* Few, Thomas
Ferguson, Lt. John, 61, 66
Few, Capt. Benjamin, 69, 80
Few, Lt. Ignatius, 79
Few, Thomas, 30
Few, Capt., 95
Figtree, Capt., 66, 70
Fincastle, 60, 61, 106
Fine Bones (of Coweta), 132
Finhalloway Creek, 93
Fitzgerald, Cornelius, 140
Flint River, 133
Florida, 46, 48–49, 51
Florida Keys, 1
Florida Packet, 36
Florida Scouts, 121
Folsom's Fort, 104
Fort Argyle, 122
Fort Barrington, 65, 66, 68, 75, 76, 87,
88, 165. *See also* Fort Howe
Fort Frederica, 25, 113, 117, 134–35
Fort George, 168
Fort Howe, 76–80 passim, 86–89 passim,
96, 97, 102, 113, 120, 133, 134–45 pas-
sim, 165; captured by East Florida
Rangers and Indians, 130–31. *See also*
Fort Barrington
Fort King George, 77
Fort McIntosh, 91, 109; captured by East
Florida Rangers and Indians, 86–88
Fort Matanzas, 17
Fort Morris, 118, 163; seige of, 167
Fort St. Marks, 17, 34, 39, 69, 71, 91, 129,
157; prisoners in, 60–61
Fort Tonyn, 37, 86, 129, 143, 147, 149
Fortune, 146
Fourteenth Regiment, 17, 31, 36, 39, 46,
50, 59, 84, 86, 90, 91, 92
France, 65, 137, 141; Georgia agent in,
102; enters war, 171
Franco-American alliance, 128, 137, 177
Franklin, 45
Frazer, Lt., 93, 95
Frederica, 66, 68, 116–17, 163
Frederica Sound, 141

French, 108; withdraw from Alabama, 5;
serving in Georgia army, 141
French and Indian War, 1, 85, 173
French Protestants: in Georgia, 3
French ships: at Charleston, 114
Friendship, 67
Furlong, Maj. Jonathan, 46
Fusser, Lt. Col. Lewis V., 33, 46, 59, 70,
85–88 passim, 106, 124, 150, 161–66
passim

Gadsden, Christopher, 158
Gage, Gen. Thomas, 7, 21
Gainesville, 10
Galatea, 100, 134–38 passim
Galphin, George, 10, 18, 19, 28, 30, 73–
75 passim, 109–16 passim, 132, 133,
137, 138, 154–57 passim, 177, 178
Galvez, Don Bernardo de, 137
Gamillorn, Christian, 120
"Gaskins," 37
George, 67
Georgia: boundaries of, 1; population of,
3; governor (president) of, 6, 81, 132,
172 [*see also* Bulloch, Archibald; Gwinnett, Button; Houstoun, John; Treutlen, John Adam; Wright, James]; royal
council of, 6, 7, 9; assembly of, 7–12,
96–97, 100–02 passim, 113–14, 117,
119, 126–28 passim, 134, 153, 158, 159;
extralegal meetings in, 11; not represented in First Continental Congress,
11; provincial congress of, 11, 13, 15,
16, 18, 24, 27, 40; St. John's Parish tries
to secede from, 12; Council of Safety
of, 13, 15, 16, 18, 21, 22, 25, 31, 34, 37,
39, 40, 52, 55, 63, 65, 66, 70, 79, 88, 89,
90, 100; parochial committees of, 15,
16, 40; Executive Council of, 104–05,
128, 130, 132, 134, 153–54, 156, 159,
160, 164
Georgia Continental troops, 52, 101, 116,
119–27 passim, 131, 149, 153, 157, 158,
161, 163, 164, 167; desertion from,
104, 119–20, 131, 140–41, 146, 176; on
invasion of East Florida (1778), 134–47;
disappointment to civilians, 171; First
Battalion, 18, 24–25, 37, 39, 55–56, 63–
66 passim, 79, 80, 86–90 passim, 93,
101, 122, 139, 140, 142, 155; Second

Battalion, 64, 87, 90, 93, 101, 102, 104, 114, 122, 139, 140; Third Battalion, 64, 97, 101, 102, 112, 114, 122, 139; Fourth Battalion, 101, 119, 131, 139, 140–41, 146; Horse, 24–25, 37, 45, 46, 52–55 passim, 63–69 passim, 75–80 passim, 87–96 passim, 102, 103, 114, 120, 121, 132; Horse, pay in arrears, 79, 103, 120; Horse, desertions from, 104, 120, 176; Horse, problems of, 175–76; Horse, personnel of, 176
Georgia Gazette, 7
Gerard, Capt., 113
Germain, 135, 138, 146, 164–65
Germain, Lord George, 33–34, 39, 42, 75, 83, 99–100, 110, 123–25 passim, 148–49
Germans: in Georgia, 3, 4, 129; in Sixtieth Regiment, 59, 172; in East Florida, 129
Gickie, Capt., 49
Giradeau, John Bohan, 64, 103, 165
Glazier, Maj. Beamsley, 46, 136, 166
Glynn County, 82, 117
Gordon, Arthur, 107
Goulding, William, 161
Governor Tonyn, 46, 49, 50, 55, 57, 67, 92, 105–06
Graham, Maj. Colin, 17, 36, 38, 46–50 passim, 106, 143, 144, 166–67
"Grahams," 88
Grand, George, 92
Grant, Gov. James, 83
Grant, Lt. William, 31–32, 36–37, 44–51 passim, 58, 105
Graves, Lt. John, 17
Gray (East Floridian), 43
Gray (Georgian), 39–44
Gray, Alexander, 44
Gray, Thomas, 20–21, 28, 74, 76, 101, 130, 140
Great Tallassee, 132, 137, 156
"Greens," 87
Grierson, James, 15
Grimké, John Fauchereaud, 141
Gunpowder, 12, 15, 17, 23, 25, 28–29, 34, 50, 168
Gurard, Capt. *See* Gerard, Capt.
Gwinnett, Button, 24, 27, 54, 63, 66, 81, 88–91 passim, 100–01, 174

Habersham, Col. James, 9, 24, 25, 122, 139, 142
Habersham, Joseph, 142
Halifax, Nova Scotia, 33
Hall, Lyman, 11, 12, 13, 27, 54, 82, 101, 164
Hall, Lt., 83
Hambly, John, 86
Hamilton, Lt. Col. Henry, 110
Hammond, LeRoy, 18
Hancock, 45
Hancock, John: effigy burned in St. Augustine, 54
Handsome Fellow (of the Okfuskees), 75, 109–10, 111, 112, 114, 115
Hardin, Capt., 55–56
Hardwick: population of, 4
Harland, William, 44
Harris, Lt. Col. (Francis ?), 96, 122, 139–40, 142, 145
Hatter, 135
Hawke, 92, 95–96, 100
Haycraft, Capt. Samuel, 92
Heard's Fort, 158
Henderson, Richard, 133
Hessians, 160
Hester's Bluff, 50, 96, 138
Hickory Ground, 114, 115
Hillabies, 113
Hillsborough, Wills Hill, Earl of, 84
Hinchinbrook, 30, 32, 35, 67, 92, 100, 134–35
Hind, 32–33
Hitchita(s), 21, 28, 29, 75, 85, 133, 155, 156
Holmes, David, 20, 73, 109, 154, 155
Holt, Lt., 83
Hornabeque line, 70, 129
Hornet, 89
Hospital: at Wright's fort, 44–45; in Georgia, 65, 127; in St. Augustine, 124; at Darien, 141; at Sunbury, 142; at Sapelo, 142; at St. Catherines, 142
Houstoun, Gov. John, 11, 13, 16, 52, 126, 134, 139–47 passim, 153
Hovenden, Col., 119
Hovendon's Fort, 68
Hover (Georgian), 76
Howard, Christopher, 44
Howe, Adm. Richard Lord, 69, 100

Howe, Brig. Gen. Robert, 53, 54–55, 56, 62, 65, 76, 77, 80, 88, 93, 104, 118, 122–23; urges evacuation of sea islands, 63; estimates defense needs of southern border, 89; defensive policy of, 89, 90, 126, 171–72; orders arrest of Georgia officers who assault peaceful Creeks, 114; on invasion of East Florida, 127–47 passim; attitude toward desertion, 140; proposes another campaign to conquer East Florida, 157; replaced as Continental commander of the Southern Department, 157–58; duel with Christopher Gadsden, 158; in Georgia to oppose British invasion, 158–64 passim; charged with incompetency at Savannah, acquitted with honor by court-martial, 166

Howe, Gen. Sir William, 43, 69, 71, 91, 98, 123, 148; approves sending Indian auxiliaries into enemy territory, 84, 85; instructed to use Indians in war, 110; plans to attack middle colonies, 110; in quarrel between civil and military officials in Floridas, 99, 136, 148

Huger, Gen. Isaac, 53, 164

Hume, James, 66

Hycut, 75, 132, 133

Inatalitchie, Chief, 130

Indian River, 60

Indians, 18, 19, 26, 38–39, 43, 52, 55, 70–76 passim, 84, 106, 110, 111, 116, 128, 137, 140, 159, 169, 170, 173; land cessions of, 2, 8–10, 70, 178–79; land policy of, 4, 5, 6; trade with, 5, 16, 19–21, 26–31 passim, 40, 72, 75, 108–16 passim, 132–33, 156–57, 169, 178–79; traders, 5, 19, 26, 38, 114–15, 116, 132, 133, 154, 156, 179; policy toward, of British, 5–6, 18, 111; policy, of Americans, 6; policy, of Georgians, 31, 113–14; departments of, British, 6; departments of, American, 18–19, 27, 29, 31, 35; political organization of, 19; agents to, confer at Usichee town, 20; agents to, American, 108–09, 111–15 passim; agents to, British, 116 [see also Holmes, David]; as auxiliaries of British, 26, 31, 39, 59, 66–69 passim, 72, 77–78, 80, 84–88 passim, 91–98 passim, 108, 110–13 passim, 116, 117, 120, 123, 130, 137–48 passim, 153, 157, 161, 164, 175, 177–78, 181; as auxiliaries of Americans, 101, 140; presents for, 38–39, 52, 69, 72, 75, 109, 133; Georgians fear, 39; at Mosquito Inlet, 59; superintendent, British, 82, 84; interpreters, 86; towns of, 111; believe France and Spain would repossess Gulf Coast, 137; factions among, 178. See also Holmes, David; Galphin, George; Stuart, John; Taitt, David; and Cherokee, Chickasaw, Choctaw, Creek, and Seminole Indians

Indigo: in Georgia, 3, 16, 30; in East Florida, 3, 71; cargo, 45, 131; cargo from South Carolina shipped to Spain, 129; on Sapelo Island, 166

Inflation: in Georgia, 80, 103; in East Florida, 17

Inland waterway, 4, 26, 45, 47, 71, 93, 118, 119, 134, 136, 147, 161–67 passim

Innes, Col. Alexander, 151

Intolerable Acts, 10–11

Isenpoaphe (Coweta), 111

Jackson, Maj. James, 162

Jamaica, 33, 47, 172

Jameson (alleged rebel spy), 106

Jamieson (American deserter), 47

Jefferson, Lt., 83

Jeffres, Lt., 83

Jekyll Island, 44, 47, 135, 166

Johnson, James, 140

Johnson, Lt., 144–45

Johnston, Andrew, 130

Johnston, James. See Johnson, James

Jollie, Martin, 34, 36

Jordan, Capt., 134–35

Jones, Benjamin, 130

Jones, Charles C. (historian), 162

Jones, Noble Wimberly, 11, 13, 22, 104

Jones, Willie, 19

Joyner, Benjamin, 120

Kebly (East Floridian), 77

Kelly (East Floridian). See Kebly

Kelly (Georgian), 37

Kelsal, Roger, 67

Kennedy (loyalist), 36
King's Rangers, 38. *See also* East Florida Rangers
Kirkland, Moses, 159, 180
Kitching, J., 47, 50
Knox, William, 69, 159

Lady William, 49, 50
Land grants, 2; absentee proprietors of, 2, 70, 18; in Georgia, 2, 8, 102–03, 118, 128, 132; in East Florida, 41, 70, 113, 152
Land office act, Georgia, 118
Lane, Maj. Joseph, 139, 167
Latchoway, 21, 26, 28, 165, 177. *See also* Alachua, Seminole Indians
Laurens, Henry, 40, 101, 103, 104, 157–60 passim
Lawson, Lt. Col. Anthony, 71, 77
Lawson's Fort, 158
Le Conte, William, 65
Lee, 135
Lee, Maj. Gen. Charles, 24, 31, 39, 53, 61–64 passim, 74, 75; urges increase in Continental establishment for Georgia, 53; on expectation to attack East Florida (1776), 54–56; recalled to northern theater, 56; reports to Congress in Philadelphia, 62; urges evacuation of sea islands (1776), 63; opposed to offensive operations, 171–72
Lee, Capt. Thomas, 127
Lexington, 12, 170
Liberty County, 82, 117, 130, 156
Lihalgie, Chief, 130
Lincoln, Gen. Benjamin, 157–58, 164
Lister, James, 140, 141
Little, Lt., 112
Little Cumberland Island, 166
Little Ogeechee River, 121
Little River, 2, 4, 10, 104
Little Tallassee, 108, 110, 111, 115, 133
Lively, 48, 49, 57, 60–67 passim
Livestock, 34, 52, 63. *See also* Cattle
Lofthouse, Capt., 41
Loftin, Lt. James, 55
London, 45, 72
Long Warrior (of Chiaha), 21
Lookout House, 17
Love, Mrs., 122

Loyalists: military potential of, 17; in East Florida, 21, 70, 71, 106, 140, 144, 155, 165; in Georgia, 23, 26, 31, 34, 40, 44, 62, 88, 104, 117–18, 127, 131, 151, 155–56, 158–59, 170–71, 181; in the south, 27, 38, 43, 73, 116, 123, 159, 164, 165, 177, 180; in the Carolinas, 27, 28, 122, 131–33, 151, 159, 160; ordered armed, 84; on Amelia Island, 93–94; as refugees among Indians, 114–15; in West Florida, 155, 156; try to reorient British strategy, 171
Lundie, Archibald, 105–06

M'Call, Hugh (historian): describes battle at Midway, 162
McCay, Daniel, 140
McClendon's plantation, 134
McCredie (loyalist), 45
McFarland [McFarling], Capt., 69, 79, 80
McGillivray, Alexander, 74, 115, 116, 154, 155, 179
McGirth, Col., 66, 138, 143, 162
McGowen, Lt., 95
McGuire, Lt., 77
McIntosh, George, 89–90, 100, 105
McIntosh, Capt. George, 33, 46, 86
McIntosh, Lt. Col. John, 101, 139, 163
McIntosh, Gen. Lachlan, 24, 25, 36, 39, 52, 62–69 passim, 76–80 passim, 86, 87, 96–97, 101–03 passim, 134, 173, 174, 176; leader of conservative factor in Georgia, 82, 174; wounded, 87; brother George arrested, 89–90; as commander of forces invading East Florida (1777), 90, 100; duel with Button Gwinnett, 100–01; reassigned, 101, 103, 118
McIntosh, Lacklan, Jr., 39–40
McIntosh, Roderick, 167, 168
McIntosh, William, 75, 109, 114–15, 133, 137–38, 155
McIntosh, Lt. Col. William, 24, 34, 37, 39, 40, 62–63, 66, 67, 76, 79, 90, 113, 121, 176
Mackay, Mrs., 77
McKenney, Lt., 127
McKenzie (Georgia loyalist), 35
Mackie, Dr. John, 83, 106
McLaurin, Maj. Euan, 83, 151

McLeod, Capt. John, 92
McMurphy, Daniel, 112, 114
McPherson (Indian leader), 155
Mad Dog, Chief, 112, 137
Man, Spencer, 41, 107
Marbury, Lt. Col. Leonard, 24–25, 68–69, 76, 79–80, 120, 131, 176
Maria, 67
Marion, Lt. Col. Francis, 88
Marlborough, 14
Martin (Georgian), 39–40
Martin, John, 45, 47, 135
Mason, John, 140
Matanzas, 136
"Medal" chiefs, 6
Medical supplies, 56, 61, 64, 65, 129, 140
Mercer, Capt. James, 140
Meredith, 92, 100
Middle Indian Department, 27
Middleton, Capt. Charles, S., 77. *See also* Myddleton, Capt.
Midway, 11, 68, 103, 134, 152, 161, 169; population of, 4; robbed, 68; raided by Col. McGirth; battle of, 161–63
Midway River, 32, 118, 163
Mikasuki, 28–29, 57
Mikasukie, King of, 28–29
Militia, 2, 56, 64, 131, 177; reputation of 17; East Florida, 17, 26, 56–57, 70, 92, 99, 107, 124; Georgia, 15, 18, 22, 23, 24, 37, 39, 40, 62, 63, 66, 68, 79, 81, 87, 88, 90, 93, 102, 104, 113, 126, 130, 132, 134, 153, 155, 159, 170; on invasion of East Florida (1778), 139–47 passim; Georgia, at Midway (1778), 161; Georgia, at Fort Morris (1778), 163; at Savannah (1778), 164; South Carolina, 55, 114, 155; on invasion of East Florida, 139–47
Miller ("a Notorious Rebel"), 31
Miller, Capt., 47, 50
Mills, George, 43, 44, 143
Mills, William, 93
Mills's Swamp, 144
Milton, Lt. John, 86–87
Minorcans, 107, 176. *See also* New Smyrna, Smyrna
"Minute men," 37, 101, 128, 153
Mississippi River: as western boundary of Georgia, 1

Mitchell (loyalist), 60
Mobile, 108, 137
Mobs: in Georgia, 11, 15, 170, 171
Moncrief, Capt., 153, 157, 167
Montaigut, Lt. David, 166–67
Montgomery, Sgt., 77
M[oore?], 66
Moore (loyalist), 94
Moore, Gen. James, 62, 89, 104
Moore, Capt. James, 83, 138–39, 162
Moore, Lt. Sam, 121–22
Moore, Capt., 140
Moore's Creek Bridge, 27
Morgan's Fort, 112
Morris, Capt., 118, 119
Morrison, Claudius, 140
Mosquito Inlet, 3, 57, 59, 60, 152, 181
Motte, Col. Isaac, 88
Moultrie, John, 56, 57. *See also* Factions, in East Florida
Moultrie, Col. William, 56, 140–41, 157, 160, 163
Mowbray, John, 22, 57, 58, 80, 92, 95, 100, 106–07, 134–35, 138, 146, 156, 164–65
Muhlenberg, Col. Peter, 55–56
Muller, Lt. John K., 33, 46
Murray, John, Lord Dunmore, 60, 106. *See also* Dunmore
Murray, Capt. Patrick, 46, 85–87 passim, 144, 145, 163, 166–67
Mutiny Act, 7
Myddleton, Capt., 80. *See also* Middleton, Capt. Charles S.

Nancy, 92
Nash, Capt., 144
Nassau Bluff, 144, 163
Nassau River, 26, 95, 143, 144
Naval officers: British, 40–41, 70
Naval stores, 3, 71
Navy Board: of South Carolina, 67
Neaclucluckotico, Chief, 114
Nea Mico, Chief, 114
Neigle, James, 140
Neptune, 31
New Ebenezer, 4
Newfoundland: not represented in First Continental Congress, 11

New Jersey Loyalists (Volunteers), 160, 166, 167–68
New Orleans, 129
New Providence, 25, 89
New Richmond, 14
New Savannah, 158
New Smyrna, 3, 42, 60, 107–13 passim, 124–25, 152. *See also* Smyrna
New York, 43, 48, 50, 57, 60, 61, 71, 92, 129, 138, 159, 160, 164, 172, 179–80
New York Loyalists, 160
Nixon, Thomas, 35, 41
North, Lord, 14
North Carolina Continental troops, 55, 61, 63–64, 66, 89, 160, 164
North Carolina Loyalist Regiment, 132
Northern Indian Department, American, 27
North Newport (now Riceborough) bridge, 161
North River, 58, 129. *See also* St. Marks River
North River (Amelia Island), 49
Nova Scotia: not represented in First Continental Congress, 11
Nuestra Señora del Carmen, 128–29

Ocmulgee River, 30, 156
Oconee, King of, 28–29
Oconee River, 112
Ogeechee Old Town, 109, 111, 114, 154, 155
Ogeechee River, 2, 4, 10, 30, 68, 69, 80, 102, 112, 121–22, 131, 137, 162; provision magazines on, 64; Folsom's Fort on, 104; East Florida Rangers raid settlements along, 113, 122; white trespassers across, 133; rebel fort on, attacked by Creeks, 155; loyalist families on, 155–56
Okchais, 112
O'Keefe, Samuel. *See* O'Kiff, Samuel
Okfuskee(s), 29, 75, 109, 112–16 passim, 132–137 passim, 154, 156
O'Kiff, Samuel, 31
Oklawaha River, 2
Oldis, Capt., 68
"Old Towne," 96
Opeitley Mico, Chief, 109, 115, 116, 137, 155–57 passim

Osborne, Capt. George, 35–36, 40, 46, 50, 55, 57, 66, 92, 105–06, 138
Otassies, 156
Otter, 60, 66, 67, 71, 80, 88, 92, 105, 106, 146, 152

Packet boat, 47, 61
Palmarina plantation, 57, 59
Pannell, Lt. Col., 114, 139
Panton, William, 21, 40, 75
Parker, Adm. Sir Peter, 43, 160, 164
Parker, Maj., 142
Partridge Pond, 121
Patuoy Mico, Chief, 157
Peace of Paris (1763), 2
Penman, James, 41, 70, 106–07, 151
Pensacola, 17, 28, 47, 72–76 passim, 108, 111, 113, 115–16, 132, 137, 148, 155, 157, 165, 172; as center of southern Indian trade, 26, 29; inaccessibility of, 30, 84, 178; threatened by Indians, 75, 133, 137; rumor that Spaniards will take, 137; loyalists near, 155, 156
Perkins, 45
Perryman, Chief, 85–86, 137–38, 179
Perseus, 100, 146, 153
Philadelphia, 11, 16, 56, 62, 67, 89, 104, 109, 157, 172
Philetougi, Chief, 86, 179
Philips, Lt. [Robert?], 83
Phillips's (Captain) Fort, 104
Phillips's (Joel) Fort, 104
Pickering, Capt. Thomas, 67
Picolata, 136
Pike's Bluff, 135
Pinckney, Col. Charles Cotesworth, 139, 140–41, 145
Polly, 92
Pompey, 36, 48, 49, 51
Ponce de Leon Inlet. *See* Mosquito Inlet
Pope, Lt., 120
Population: of Georgia and the Floridas, 3; of East Florida, 3, 6, 16, 17, 26, 176, 182; of Georgia, 3–4, 18, 63, 81–82, 173, 181, 182; of Savannah, 3–4; of Augusta, 4; of Darien, 4; of Hardwick, 4; of New Ebenezer, 4; of Queensborough, 4; of Wrightsborough, 4; of St. David's Parish, 8–9; of St. Mary's Parish, 8–9; of St. Patrick's Parish, 8–9;

of St. Thomas's Parish, 8–9; of Creeks, 19; on Nassau River, 26; on St. Johns River, 26; on St. Marys River, 26; at Smyrna, 26; of St. Augustine, 84, 160–61

Porter, Maj., 139

Porteus (Georgia loyalist), 156

Port Royal, 147

Powell, Joseph, 140

Pray, Capt. Job, 64, 156

Prevost, Gen. Augustine, 33, 35, 36, 38, 46, 49, 58, 61, 70, 82, 84–85, 91–92, 98–99, 110, 115, 117, 124, 130–31, 136, 137, 138, 140, 146, 148–52 passim, 159, 160, 161, 166–68 passim, 179–80; on East Florida Rangers, 38, 98–99, 149, 150, 176; suggests to Tonyn that East Florida join Georgia in neutrality treaty, 59; defensive policy of, 83, 89, 91, 99, 148, 151–52, 171–73, 180; quarrels with Tonyn, 83, 85, 91, 98–99, 124, 128, 129, 136, 148, 150; complains to George Grand about conditions in St. Augustine, 92; complains about ineffectiveness of British Indian allies, 110; forms South Carolina Royalists, 132; leadership qualities of, 172

Prevost, Maj. James Mark, 33, 46, 95, 98, 132, 136, 143–46 passim, 149, 150, 161–63 passim, 179–80

Prisoners, 31, 55, 59, 60–61, 69, 71, 76, 87, 91, 95, 96, 106, 109, 113, 114, 117, 129, 130, 131, 135, 142, 145, 167, 181; exchange of, 90–91, 121, 129, 134, 156, 158

Prizes, 128–29, 135

Proclamation of 1763, 5–6

Proctor, John, 66, 67, 86

Provincial corps: compensation of, 151

Provisions, 32, 34–35, 41, 44, 45, 47, 54, 61, 62, 67, 86, 111, 130, 131, 145, 157; in East Florida, 3, 17, 32, 38–39, 49, 55, 60, 61, 69, 71, 72, 84, 85, 91, 92, 107, 129, 136–37, 142, 145, 146, 148, 150, 160–61, 170, 173, 181; in Georgia, 3, 52, 64, 65, 80, 88, 90, 93, 96, 119, 127, 139, 141, 142, 153–54, 158, 166; British attempt to procure, at Savannah (1776), 22–23; for Indians, 137; lack of, upsets British invasion plans, 180

Pruna, Francisco de, 129

Pryce, William, 93

Puisang, Capt., 120

Pulliam, Capt. John, 31

Pumpkin King, Chief, 21, 130

Purrysburg, 53, 55

Quakers: in Wrightsborough, 4

Quamino Dolly, 165

Queensborough: population of, 4; Irish in, 4

Rae, James, 103

Rae, Robert, 19, 20, 109, 116

Rae, Col., 135, 139

Rain, Niel, 144

Rains, Cornelius, 77

Ramsay, Dr. David (historian), 162

Ranaires' place, 122

Randolph, 89

Ranger, 135–36, 138

Rangers: in Georgia, disbanded (1767), 37–38; in East Florida (1774), 38, 83

Rations, 24, 92, 98, 99, 153. *See also* Provisions

Ratoon. *See* Batton

Raven, 32, 45, 47, 61, 66, 67

Rebecca, 57, 58, 60, 66, 71, 80, 92, 95–96, 100, 134–35, 156

Recruiting: for Georgia troops, 24, 25, 53, 63–64, 76, 88, 101, 112, 141; for British, East Florida troops, 26, 38, 91, 92, 172

Red Shoes, Chief, 137

Refugees, 40, 131, 138; in East Florida, 16, 17, 34–35, 38, 41, 57–58, 69, 70–71, 84, 92, 106, 124, 136, 151, 152, 176, 181–82; among Indians, 84, 114–15; Cherokees among Creeks, 110

Regulator movement: in South Carolina, 128

Reid, Capt. James, 61, 105

Reid, Thomas, 65

Reid's Bluff, 113, 141

Rice, 3, 12, 16, 23, 31, 45, 52, 61, 64, 67, 69, 71, 88, 92, 96, 131, 137, 145, 166, 170. *See also* Provisions, Rations

Rice, John, 120

Riceborough bridge. *See* North Newport bridge

Richmond County, 117
Roberts, Daniel, 65
Roberts, Lt. Col. Daniel, 119, 135, 139
Roberts, Rhuben, 130
Robeson, Lt., 93, 95
Robinson, Lt. Col. Joseph, 151
Robinson, Lt., 120
Rogers (cattleman), 46
Roman(s), Maj., 139, 141
Rook, 48, 49
Ross (East Floridian), 43
Ross, Capt. Alexander Ross, 46, 50
Royal, John, 140
Royal American Regiment. *See* Sixtieth
  Regiment
Royal Artillery, 17, 59, 160, 166, 167
Rules and Regulations of 1776 (Georgia
  temporary constitution), 27
"Russell's plantation," 43
Rutledge, Edmund, 114, 115
Rutledge, John, 129

St. Andrew's Parish, 11–12, 62, 68, 82,
  130
St. Augustine, 3, 4, 15, 17, 26–36 passim,
  40–49 passim, 55, 58, 60, 61, 62, 66, 67,
  71–80 passim, 84, 86, 87, 88, 92, 94, 99,
  100, 106, 107, 108, 110, 113, 116, 118,
  119, 121, 124, 126, 128, 129, 132, 136,
  138, 143, 148, 152, 158, 166, 171, 177,
  178; garrison, 7, 17, 26, 33, 38, 45–46,
  58–59, 91, 92, 146, 159, 172; fort at, 17,
  34; bar, 17; John Stuart arrives in, 18;
  Indians at, 20–21, 29, 85, 116, 155;
  Thomas Gray at, 21; receives gunpowder from Bahamas, 25; American plans
  to conquer, 25, 54, 89, 157; population
  of, 26, 61, 84; barracks in, 33; news
  reaches, of Declaration of Independence, 54; militia district, 57; Prevost
  determined to protect, 91; Prevost reports dismal conditions in, 92; prisoners in, 106, 129, 134; rumor that
  Spaniards will take, 137; Indian assistance for, 137, 148; proposed deporta-
  tion of Georgia loyalist families to,
  155–56; food in, 161, 173, 181; desertion from, 172; strategic value of,
  172–73
St. Augustine Creek, 45

St. Catherines Island, 66; skirmish at, 32;
  hospital at, 142
St. Catherine's Sound, 50
St. Christopher, 58
St. Croix, 91
St. David's Parish, 8, 9, 82
St. Iago, 108
St. James's Parish, 13, 82
St. John, 11, 31, 35–36, 44–51 passim, 58,
  60, 66, 67; moves gunpowder from Ba-
  hamas to East Florida, 25
St. John's Parish, 11, 12, 13, 169; raided,
  68, 129–30, 163; included in Liberty
  County, 82
St. Johns River, 2, 21, 26, 35, 41, 43, 46,
  49, 50, 51, 54, 55, 57, 58, 59, 60, 62, 66,
  68, 72, 85, 92, 93, 95, 99, 131, 136, 146,
  147, 152, 154, 157, 173, 174; popula-
  tion on, 26; militia district, 57; fortification of, 96, 138
"St. Julies," 47
St. Lawrence, 17, 32, 66
St. Marks Fort, 34
St. Marks River, 58, 129. *See also* North
  River
St. Mary's Parish: population of, 8–9; loyalists in, 22; included in Camden
  County, 82
St. Marys River, 2, 8, 9, 17, 21, 22, 26,
  31–39 passim, 43–50 passim, 53–60
  passim, 62, 66, 67, 76, 77, 79, 80, 85,
  86, 91–97 passim, 104, 131, 134, 136,
  142, 145, 147, 154, 163, 173, 175, 176;
  as boundary, 1; Georgia rebels raid loy-
  alist plantations across, 21; population
  on, 26; desolation near, 82; settlement
  on, 152
St. Patrick's Parish: population, 8–9; not
  represented at Georgia provincial congress, 13; included in Glynn County, 82
St. Paul's Parish, 15
St. Simons Island, 68, 113, 117, 163
St. Simons River, 31
St. Simons Sound, 164–65
St. Thomas's Parish: population, 8–9; in-
  cluded in Camden County, 82
St. Vincent, 32, 33, 67
Salters Island, 88
Saluda River: loyalists on, 131
Sampson (loyalist), 60

Sanchez (cattleman), 35

Sapelo Island, 50, 66, 77; hospital at, 142; slaves taken from, 157; British capture, 166–67

Sapelo River, 22, 66, 76–77, 80

Satilla River, 2, 39, 46, 65–68 passim, 76, 77, 86–88 passim, 93–97 passim, 109, 122, 131, 138, 142, 155

Savage, Richard, 140

Savannah, 4, 9, 11, 13, 14, 18, 21, 23, 31, 39, 40, 42, 44, 45, 50, 54, 55, 56, 61, 65, 67, 74, 75, 79, 80, 88, 90, 96, 103, 119, 128, 161, 164, 170, 171; population of, 3–4; Indian conference at (October 1774), 10; revolutionary activities in, 8–15 passim; British ships at, 22–23; American vessels built in, 47; fortifications at, 53; news arrives at, of Declaration of Independence, 54; provision magazine at, 64, 119, 158; Indian prisoners in, 76, 114; Georgia constitutional convention in, 81; East Florida Rangers near, 113, 121–122; Elbert fears riot in, 120; court-martial at, 120; friction in, between military personnel and inhabitants, 121; security measures for, 130; barracks at, 153; fire company for, 153; British plan to conquer, 159; battle of (1778), 165–66; British force from East Florida moves toward, 167; Prevost and Campbell meet at, 168; effect of British conquest on Indians, 178; base for provisioning British army and navy, 180; conquest of, 181; Franco-American seige of (1779), 172, 181

Savannah River, 1, 2, 4, 10, 15, 23, 25, 31, 32, 45, 53, 61, 65, 67, 68, 102, 105, 132, 158, 162, 163, 170

Sawpit Bluff, 93

Scarborough, 23

Schodde [Schoedde], Ens., 138–39, 166–67

Scott, Lt., 130

Scots: in Georgia, 3, 46

Scotch-Irish: in Georgia, 3; in Ceded Lands, 169

Scots, Highland: in Georgia, 3; at Darien, 4, 169

Screven, Col. James, 64, 97, 102, 113, 120, 122; resigns, 139; on East Florida

invasion (1778), 142; at battle of Alligator Creek Bridge, 144; in battle at Midway Meeting House, 161–62; death of, 162

Sebastian Creek, 50, 69

Seeds (Georgian), 141

Seminole Indians, 20, 30, 57, 72, 111; separatist tendencies of, 5, 179; land claim in north Florida, 10; trade with, 26; as British allies, 26, 28–29, 91, 108, 113, 137, 154, 165, 177. *See also* Alachua, Latchoway

Seneca: settlers threaten Upper Creeks, 108

Servants, indentured, 14; in East Florida, 3, 41, 42, 63; at New Smyrna, correspond with rebels, 107; freed at New Smyrna, 107, 113

Settlements: European, location of, 3; English, after 1763, 5; in East Florida, from England, 41; whites beyond treaty lines, 43

Seventy-first Scottish Regiment, 160

Sheftall, Mordecai, 121

Sherards [Creek], 94

Shirreff, C., 33

Silk: production of, 3

Silver Bluff, 75

Sir Basil Keith, 106

Sister's Creek, 50

Six Mile Creek, 145

Sixteenth Regiment, 17, 39, 46, 50, 59, 77, 92; on the St. Marys River, 39–49 passim; unsuitably clothed, 85; on cattle-hunting expedition, 86; at Alligator Creek Bridge, 143–44; invades Georgia, 166–67 passim; detachment at Sapelo Island (1778), 166–67; at seige of Fort Morris, 167

Sixtieth Regiment, 38–39, 46, 50, 59, 84, 139, 166; organization of, 26; recruits for, 26, 84–85, 91–92, 129; unsuitably clothed, 85; problems of, 172; First Battalion, 33; Second Battalion, 32, 33, 86, 136, 143; Third Battalion, 86, 166; Fourth Battalion, 85–86, 143, 166–67

Skidaway Island, 56

Skinner, Alexander, 137, 165, 180

Slaves, 34, 35, 36, 40, 43, 46, 55, 58, 61, 63, 70, 77, 105, 140, 157, 163; in Georgia, 3, 23, 52, 102, 118–19, 153, 181; in

Georgia as seamen, 156; at Midway, 4; of Jermyn Wright, 14, 22, 46–51 passim; on Amelia Island, 47–48, 94; of Egan, 48, 49, 50; in East Florida, 60, 69, 70, 136, 138; on Sapelo Island, 77, 157; on St. Simons Island, 117; at New Smyrna, 152; among Creeks, 179

Smedley, Capt. Samuel, 138

Smith, John, 81

Smith, Capt., 144–45

Smyrna, 17, 26, 57, 58. *See also* New Smyrna

Snodden, John, 44

Sons of Liberty, 7, 12, 14, 15

South Carolina: cuts off trade with Georgia, 12; rejects St. John's Parish's attempt to join, 12; removes ban on trade with Georgia, 13; Committee of Safety of, 15, 16, 18; council of, 16, 53, 54, 56; Navy Board of, 67; decides to annex Georgia, 81; aids Georgia, 88; Georgia buys arms in, 102; loyalists leave, 122

South Carolina Continental troops, 24, 25, 56, 61, 149; on 1778 invasion of East Florida, 139–47 passim; quarrel over command of, 158; at battle of Savannah, 164–65; First Regiment, 54, 55, 139; Second Regiment, 53, 54, 55, 67, 88; Third Regiment (Horse), 54, 55, 64, 69, 76, 80, 86, 88, 89, 93, 139; Fourth Regiment (Artillery), 54, 55, 88, 139; Fifth Regiment, 54, 88; Sixth Regiment, 139

South Carolina Royalists: organization of, 132, 150–51; at Alligator Creek Bridge, 143; desertion from, 145; invade Georgia from East Florida, 166; Dragoons, 144, 145

Southern Indian Department: American, 27. *See also* Galphin, George

Southern Indian Department: British, 72, 73, 148, 154. *See also* Stuart, John

Southern Military Department: changes in command, 24, 62, 157–58

Spain, 5, 35, 108, 129, 137, 171

Sphynx, 45, 47, 61, 66–67, 105

Spitfire, 164–65

Spring Hill causeway, 165

Squire, Capt., 60, 71, 88, 92, 105

Staten Island, 164

Stamp Act, 6–7, 8

Stanhope, Capt. John, 47, 61, 67

Stimpoy, Chief, 130

Stirk, Lt. Col., 139

Strothers, Capt., 162

Stuart, John, 19, 20, 29, 57, 72–76 passim, 82, 108–16 passim, 137, 151, 156, 159, 179; appointed superintendent of the Southern Indian Department, 6; arranges Creek and Cherokee land cession, 9; requests Creek trade be stopped, 10; rejects land "lease" to Bryan, 10; estimates Georgia militia strength, 18; Indian policy of, 18, 74, 84, 111, 177, 178; confers with Indians, 21, 116, 133; intends to supply Creek trade through West Florida, 26; reports from, 27; accused by Whig Indian commissioners of instigating Indian attacks on the frontier, 29; moves to Pensacola, 29–30, 33; criticized by Tonyn, 39, 91, 148, 178; position as Indian superintendent, 84; as military leader, 84, 110, 137, 160, 164, 165; defends David Holmes to Tonyn, 109; Prevost complains about, 110; summarizes difficulties, 110–11; embargoes trade to Creeks, 115; sends agents and traders back into Creek country, 132; denies sending peace talks to Creeks, 137–38; appoints extra officers for Southern Indian Department, 154; fears for Taitt's safety, 155; ineffectiveness as war leader, 178; receives orders to "cooperate" a month after Savannah had fallen, 180

Sugar Act, 6

Sugatspoges, 132, 133

Sullivan's Island: battle of, 43, 56, 114, 157, 170; British fleet disperses from, 45, 170

Sumter, Col. Thomas, 88, 89, 93

Sunbury, 4, 32, 47, 55, 56, 61, 66, 80, 89, 90, 92, 102, 119, 121, 147, 161, 162, 166–69 passim; population of, 4; mob in, 15; fortifications, 37, 50, 53, 118; deaths at (1776), 61; damaged by American soldiers, 62; representation of, 81; provisions at, 119, 158; hospital at, 142; Fuser at, 163; seige of Fort Morris, 167

Sutherland's Bluff, 66
Swaglees, 156

Taarling, Peter, 119
Taitt, David, 20, 21, 28, 29, 57, 72, 73, 75,
    91, 108, 110, 111, 114, 116, 132–33,
    137, 155, 165; expulsion of demanded,
    26, 29, 109; assassination of threat-
    ened, 114, 115, 137; reported taking
    peace talks from Stuart to Creeks, 137–
    38
Tallachie, Chief, 76
Tallapoosas, 115, 132
Tallassee(s), 116, 133, 155, 156
Tallassee King, 137
Tallassee King's son. See Opeitley Mico
Taylor, William, 36, 86
Taylor, Capt. [William?], 106
Telfair, 158
Telfair, Edward, 25, 154
Tenats, 158
Test oath in Georgia (1776), 40
Thomas, Samuel, 73
Thomas Creek: battle of (1777), 95
Thomas's Swamp, 144
Thunderer, 146, 164–65
Timber: in Georgia, 3, 22, 52
Tondee's Tavern, 12, 13
Tonyn, Gov. Patrick, 3, 10, 17, 20, 21, 25,
    26, 28–43 passim, 45–50 passim, 53, 54,
    57–62 passim, 64, 65, 67, 69–75 passim,
    82–85, 88, 90, 91, 92, 95, 98, 99, 100,
    106–11 passim, 123–24, 129, 135–38,
    146, 149–57 passim, 164–65, 172, 173,
    178, 179, 180; invites refugees to East
    Florida, 16; policy of, 39, 83, 91, 128,
    148, 173; and dissident faction, 41–42,
    59, 105–08, 113, 124–25, 174; and East
    Florida militia, 56–57, 92, 136; and East
    Florida Rangers, 83, 148–49, 150, 176–
    77 [see also Brown, Thomas; East Flor-
    ida Rangers; Prevost, Augustine, quar-
    rels with Tonyn]; quarrels with Gen.
    Augustine Prevost, 83, 91, 98–99, 124,
    128, 129, 136, 148; quarrels with Lt.
    Col. Fuser, 106; requests removal of
    Maj. James Mark Prevost, 136; criticizes
    John Stuart, 138, 148, 178; grants lands
    between St. Johns and St. Marys rivers,
    152

Tonyn's Revenge, 135–36, 138
Townshend, Ephraim, 67
Townshend Acts, 7–8
Trade, 3, 11, 12, 13, 16, 22, 25, 31, 81, 89,
    103. See also Indians, trade with
Treaty: of Paris (1763), 1, 2, 5, 8; of
    Augusta (1773), 2, 10; of Picolata
    (1765), 2; of Dewitt's Corner (1777),
    108
Treutlen, Gov. John Adam, 100, 103,
    104–05, 119
Triumvirate, 92, 100
Trout Creek, 57
Trustees Gardens: battery at, 128
Tuckabatchee, 112, 133, 137, 156
Tuckanahathka, Chief. See White, Lt.
Turnbull, Andrew, 59–60, 107
Turnbull, Dr. Andrew, 41–42, 107–08,
    124–25
Turpin, Capt., 57–58, 59
Turtle River, 68
Tybee Island, 61, 88, 131, 164, 165, 180
Tyrrell, Sgt., 140

Union: of Georgia and South Carolina
    proposed, 81, 104–05
Uschitas, 21
Usichee town, 20

Van Braam, Maj., 46
Vergennes, M. de, 92
Virginia, 60, 62, 159; recruits from, in
    Georgia recruiting in, 101
Virginia Continental troops, 55–56, 61;
    Georgia recruits among, 63–64
Volant, 138

Wainwright, Cpl. Thomas, 120
Walker, John, 19
Walsist's camp, 48
Walton, Capt. George, 101
Walton, Col. George, 54, 89, 90, 101, 104,
    146, 164
Walton, John, 154
Ward, Lt., 93
Washington, 135
Washington, Gen. George, 28, 86, 89,
    101, 118
Watauga, 108
Watson, Andrew, 120

Weatherford (Georgian), 14
Weems (East Floridian), 41
Wells (Georgian), 76
Wells, Col. Andrew, 130
Well's Fort, 104
Wereat, John, 22
Westcott, William, 71
West Florida: boundaries of, 1; not represented in First Continental Congress, 11; Congress plans expedition against (1777), 104; Indians threaten loyalists in, 116
West Indies, 6, 22, 26, 31, 45, 60, 64, 65, 71, 75, 84, 89, 129
Wheelock, Anthony, 69
White, Col. John, 119, 141, 144, 158, 161–62
White, Capt., 164–65
White, Lt., Chief, 116, 154
White Skin, Chief, 154
Whittier (Georgian), 68
Wicker, Lt. Benjamin, 46
Wickham, Lt. Benjamin, 33
Wilder, Maj., 128, 153
Wilkes County, 81–82, 117, 155
Wilkinson, Edward, 19
Wilkinson, John, 43
Wilkinson's plantation, 43
Williams (East Floridian), 66, 67
Williams, Nicholas, 120
Williams, Capt. Samson, 83
Williams, Samuel, 38
Williams, William, 68
Williams, Capt. (Georgian), 95
Williams, Dr. (East Floridian), 86
Williams, Lt. (East Florida Ranger), 130

Williamson (South Carolinian), 46
Williamson, Col. Andrew, 139, 142, 146, 147
Willing, James, 129
Will's Friend, Chief, 154
Winfree, Lt., 93–94
Winn, Capt. Richard, 80, 86–87
Wisdall, John, 44
Wissenbach regiment, 160
Woellworth regiment, 160
Wood, Joseph, 101
Woodruff, Capt., 47, 77
Wood's Tavern, 41–42
Wright, Charles, 34, 46–51 passim
Wright, Gov. Sir James, 6–12 passim, 15, 18, 20, 22–23, 25, 37, 170
Wright, Jermyn, 22, 34, 45–51 passim
Wright, Lt. John, 60, 146, 152
Wrightsborough, 4, 158
Wright's Fort, 22, 34, 44–50 passim, 55, 77, 104
Wright's landing, 96, 142
Wulff, Capt., 46
Wyatt, William, 120

Yamassee War, 5, 30
Yonge, Henry, 108
York, Capt. John, 83, 77, 131, 144
Young, Capt. George, 127–28, 135, 141
Young, Thomas, 25
Yuchis, 28, 156

Zubly, David, 18
Zubly, Rev. John J., 13, 16
Zubly's Ferry, 162, 163

ABOUT THE AUTHOR

Martha Condray Searcy teaches history at The University of Alabama in Huntsville. She received her bachelor of science degree from New York University, her master of arts degree from the University of New Orleans, and her doctorate from Tulane University. This is her first book.